BOOKS BY WADE CRAWFORD BARCLAY

THE CHURCH AND A CHRISTIAN SOCIETY
CHALLENGE AND POWER
THE WORLD MISSION OF THE CHRISTIAN RELIGION
THE BIBLE
A BOOK OF WORSHIP
THE WORKER AND HIS BIBLE
  (With Frederick Carl Eiselen)

THE CHURCH AND A CHRISTIAN SOCIETY

A Discussion of Aims,
Content, and Method
of Christian Education

WADE CRAWFORD BARCLAY

THE ABINGDON PRESS

NEW YORK   CINCINNATI   CHICAGO

Copyright, 1939, by
THE ABINGDON PRESS, Inc.

Printed in the United States of America

To

L. B. M.
H. W. B.
G. L. B.
M. E. D. B.
G. B.

Comrades in life's quest, who as children plied me with eager questions; now counselors to whom I turn with insistent interrogations—but still my children.

CONTENTS

CONTENTS

9

CHAPTER II. PROTESTANT HERITAGE IN RELIGIOUS EDUCATION

CHAPTER III. PRESENT COMPELLING OBJECTIVES IN ADULT EDUCATION

CHAPTER IV. CHARACTER AND PERSONAL RELIGIOUS LIVING

CHAPTER V.   CHRISTIANIZING THE WHOLE OF LIFE

A new education required.

CHAPTER VI.   CHRISTIAN EDUCATION THROUGH WORSHIP

The Christian religion and worship.

CHAPTER VII. RELIGIOUS EDUCATION THROUGH SOCIAL PARTICIPATION

CHAPTER XI. EDUCATION THROUGH CREATIVE LEISURE

The changed modern problem.

CONTENTS

CHAPTER XII. LIFE IS THE CURRICULUM

The present adult curriculum.

PREFACE

WITHIN recent years there has been widespread awakening to the fact that wherever life is being lived, education is taking place. Adult education in consequence comes into a place of new importance. It has received relatively little attention in the past as a part of the modern religious education movement. Now, more and more it becomes apparent that all education of children and youth in which society is making hitherto unparalleled investment depends for its permanent significance upon the education of adults. Children and youth are subjected to a continuous conditioning process by the adult world in which they live, and until that world is made to conform more nearly to the ideals which the schools seek to inculcate, most of their formal educational effort will have little lasting effect.

THE CHURCH AND A CHRISTIAN SOCIETY is an outgrowth of years of thought, study, and practical experience in the field of adult Christian education. For five years (1909-1914) the author had administrative and promotional responsibility for the adult work of a denominational educational board. Later, for twelve years (1914-1926) he was related in an editorial capacity to the adult publications of the Methodist Episcopal Church. During this period he wrote two brief books on the organization and administration of religious work with adults, and began to make notes for a manuscript on the aims, content, and method of adult education. Within this latter period he also served (1923-27) as a member of the sub-committee on International Curriculum of the International Council of Religious Education. The group discussions and conferences of this committee helped to clarify thinking, and out of them many suggestions were drawn. The tragic effects of the economic debacle of the decade 1929-38 in the lives of millions of our American people have deepened convictions previously held and have sharpened issues which the author has long been convinced should be resolutely faced by the Church.

In developing the outline of a society worthy to be described as Christian the norm has been found in Jesus. Without argument throughout the book it is assumed that his ideals alike for the personal life and the social relationships of men today, as in the

17

first century, represent the goal toward which we should strive. Our prevailing social order is brought to the test of his personality, life, and teaching.

Although the book sets forth in general terms the outline of a Christian society, it contends that the primary educational task of the Church relates chiefly to its own membership. Until the Church renews its total inner life there is little basis for hope that it can reform the world.

It is impossible for the author to indicate in detail his indebtedness to the many persons upon whom he has drawn in the writing of this volume. Many are indicated in the annotations contained in the "References and Notes." In the somewhat extensive, though far from exhaustive, bibliography, are included only such books as are believed to be significant, most of which have been helpful in the preparation of the manuscript. Special acknowledgment of indebtedness is recorded to the writings of Walter Rauschenbusch, George Albert Coe, and my personal friend of many years, William Clayton Bower of the University of Chicago.

For reviewing the outline and making suggestions on the preliminary draft of several chapters thanks are tendered to Paul H. Vieth of Yale University; for reading and offering valuable suggestions on specific chapters: to William Warren Sweet of the University of Chicago, Chapter II; Gordon L. Barclay of Russell Sage College, Introduction and Chapter IV; Philip H. DuBois of the University of New Mexico, Chapter IV; Gwen Barclay, Chapter XI. For reading the entire manuscript and making detailed criticisms and suggestions I am under special obligation to Lois Barclay Murphy of Sarah Lawrence College.

WADE CRAWFORD BARCLAY.

Evanston, Illinois.

INTRODUCTION: ADULT EDUCATION

INTRODUCTION: ADULT EDUCATION

A NEW focal point of interest today is adult education. Everywhere in educational circles it is a center of attention. Widespread general interest, also, has been awakened. To many people, without question, the term has still a strange and not altogether intelligible sound. Even yet in popular thought, education is something one "gets" during childhood and adolescence; by the time one attains to adulthood he is either "educated" or "uneducated"; whether or not he has made the most of the opportunities afforded by childhood and adolescence his chance for an "education" has gone.

These traditional ideas no longer hold. Almost overnight, education, so long considered a process limited to childhood and youth, has broadened to include adults. Vast numbers of men and women are enlisted in a wide range of formal and informal educational activities. Adult education has attained recognition and standing in the educational world. The capacity of adults to learn has been demonstrated. That both the adult individual and society can be changed in ideology, attitudes, and character by means of education is now a widely accepted conviction. Adult education has attained self-consciousness as an organized movement.

A LONG-TIME GROWTH.—While the term "adult education" did not come into general use in the United States until the decade of the twenties, it represents by no means wholly a recent development. The New England town meeting of the seventeenth century was essentially a form of adult civic education. An outgrowth of the town meeting was the lyceum, first established in Massachusetts in 1826 as a voluntary association of farmers and mechanics "for the purpose of self-culture, community instruction, and mutual discussion of common public interests." Lyceums rapidly increased in number. By 1839 more than three thousand were in operation. The lyceum suggested to Lewis Miller and John H. Vincent the idea of the Chautauqua Literary and Scientific Circle, founded in 1878, which, beginning as a summer institute for the training of Sunday-school teachers, soon incorporated a wide range of political, social, economic, and literary study and discussion. Its activity and influence still continue.

The World War gave immense impetus to effort to remove the incubus of adult illiteracy, and likewise quickened concern for the "Americanization" of immigrants. In 1925 E. L. Thorndike and his associates began extensive research of adult abilities in learning and of adult interests. Results of these studies greatly helped to popularize the idea of adult education. Meanwhile federal programs for the vocational rehabilitation of World War veterans had brought stimulus from a different quarter toward large-scale development of public vocational education programs, and paved the way for co-operation between federal and state governments in behalf of the vocational rehabilitation of disabled civilians.

NEW CONCEPTS OF ADULT EDUCATION.—Just as, using words accurately, one cannot speak of *the* philosophy of education, so one cannot describe *the* objective of adult education. Wide agreement does not exist concerning either objectives, content, or method. Objectives are as variously defined as (1) to broaden adult interests; (2) to increase knowledge and skills of adults in the use of tool subjects; (3) to overcome illiteracy; (4) to promote tolerance and open-mindedness; (5) to develop integrated personality; (6) to contribute to the reconstruction of the social order; (7) to assist adults in the development of a philosophy of life; (8) to give meaning to, and appreciation of, adult experience of life.

Historically, the conception of adult education grew out of conviction of the necessity of ameliorating conditions of underprivilege. In the thought of many, adult education is still predominantly associated with the education of the illiterate, the alien, and the underprivileged. Recently the trend has been toward broadening the conception to include not merely the disadvantaged but, potentially at least, the whole adult population.

Adult education *in fact* is as old as the race. Always adults, as well as children, have learned from experience. Always, also, adults have been subjected to influences and environmental conditions that have resulted in changes in patterns of thought and action. Recent years have brought new and more general recognition that the whole of life is a process of learning, and that, accordingly, education can and should have no ending. Always persons should be discovering new meanings in life, developing new appreciations and new skills, finding new satisfactions, improving personal and social relationships. Education as the process by which all of these are achieved—this is the new emphasis in adult education, virtually a new concept, rapidly gaining currency.

SOCIAL ORIENTATION.—This new emphasis gives adult education a new social orientation and new social significance. Education becomes the means by which not only the minds and characters of persons may be developed but also the means by which society as a whole advances toward more ideal goals.

This new conception, however, recognizes in social conditions an inherent restriction. As a widely influential report some years ago stated: "It becomes impossible to consider adult education apart from those social and industrial conditions which determine to a large degree the educational opportunities, the interests, and the general outlook of men and women."[1] Social conditions, the social order of which men and women at a given time are a part, influence and tend to limit both the content and the character of education.

NEW SENSE OF PUBLIC RESPONSIBILITY.—The growing realization of the social significance of adult education has been accompanied by an increasing sense of public responsibility. The obligation of society to provide opportunity of education for all children long has been generally recognized in the United States, but until recently the provision of educational opportunities for adults, according to their needs, has not been felt as a social obligation. The sense of responsibility first developed in relation to immigrants. The steady stream of immigration—approximately twenty-eight million immigrants were admitted from 1880 to 1925—stimulated the growth of the sense of public responsibility for instruction in the essentials of citizenship, finding expression in a demand for "Americanization." With the World War, several trends were intensified—the narrowing and emotionalizing of the concept "Americanization," the sharpening of race and class distinctions, and increasing interest in overcoming illiteracy. The setting up of quota laws and, later, the tightening of restrictions, with other contributary causes, tended from about 1927 on, to modify these influences. This has been more than counterbalanced by the steadily increasing realization of the significance of adult education.

No longer do school boards and school officials attempt to justify the use for six to eight hours a day only of auditoriums, laboratories, school libraries, shops for vocational training, handicraft rooms, swimming pools, and athletic fields. The realization grows that facilities provided through public taxation should be made available for meeting the needs of all the people regardless of age.

INCREASING DESIRE FOR EDUCATION.—While it is undeniable that immense numbers of adults are unconscious of any sense of need for education and impervious to appeals to make use of opportunities offered, it is equally true that among at least a significant minority the sense of need and desire for education have been increasing. Evidence is found in the fact that in the decade 1924-34 enrollment in some thirty different forms of adult education increased from 14,881,500 to 22,311,000—this in spite of the fact that lowered income necessitated tens of thousands of persons discontinuing high-cost courses—and there has been a continuing increase since the latter date.

Even more significant educationally is the effect of the sense of need upon the process itself. The selection of a course of study under compulsion of a sense of need constitutes a motivation which is a vital factor in learning, too often absent in childhood and adolescence. The homely old adage, "You can lead a horse to water, but you cannot make him drink," has educational implications. The man or woman impelled by changing economic conditions to seek special vocational training; the young parents to whom parenthood has brought a new sense of responsibility—who elect a course in the moral and religious nurture of children; men and women who become conscious of new aesthetic longings and enroll in study groups in appreciation of art, music, and literature, possess in their desire for education a motivation that constitutes an intrinsic factor in all learning.

EXPANDING SCOPE OF ADULT EDUCATION.—Partly cause and partly result of the increasing sense of public responsibility and growing tide of popular interest has been the expanding scope of adult education. Rapidly the scope has widened until in theory at least local, state, and federal agencies acknowledge responsibility to provide opportunity for education of every type that will serve social need, excluding only religious education which is assumed to be the responsibility of the churches. The entrance of the federal government, beginning with 1934, into the field of adult education through subsidies to the states for promotion and administration has been a significant factor in broadening the scope and increasing the amount of adult education.

ADULT EDUCATION MOVEMENT

As an organized movement, adult education in the United States is a recent development. The first formal conference on adult education was held under the auspices of the Carnegie Corporation in 1924. This conference stimulated an interest that resulted in March, 1926, in the formation of an organization—The American Association for Adult Education, with a Council of one hundred, for the promotion of educational opportunities for adults. In the course of ten years (1924-33) the Carnegie Corporation contributed approximately three million dollars for experimentation in adult education and for the promotion and support of adult education activities.

Some thirty-four subdivisions of the field of adult education are represented by organized activity. Among the more important specific types of adult education are:

WORKERS' EDUCATION.—The United States differs from most of the European countries in not having a closely knit, class-conscious workers' education movement. Among the hundreds of thousands of adults enlisted in the numerous types of adult education are to be found a considerable proportion of workingmen and women participating not primarily as workers but as citizens. Stimulated by the success of workers' education in other countries an increasingly well-defined movement has been taking form in America. Workers' education has become a recognized activity of organized labor.[2] In 1921 the Workers Education Bureau was organized, having as its chief objective the promotion of workers' education.

Workers' education in its general connotation means education to meet the needs of industrial workers. Its aim, variously phrased, is well stated in the report of an official committee: "The primary function of present-day labor education is to create an intelligent army of workers conscious of their aims and of the best methods of realizing them. Recognizing that as certain subjects, such as economics, sociology, history, literature, psychology, economic geography, and government are commonly taught, their study tends to supply apology for and to re-enforce the existing economic order, workers' education contends that these subjects should be studied and taught from the viewpoint of labor. But this is not its sole motivation. It aims to broaden horizons, enlarge understanding, and increase social effectiveness." Doubtless the most profound social fact in connection with the movement is its impulse in the direction of a larger and fuller life for workers.

How closely in aim workers' education is allied to religious education is evident from statements of educational theory by its leaders. The secretary of the Workers Education Bureau in an address to the American Federation of Labor Convention (1923) said: "Education is neither information nor training, much less propaganda, . . . but it is an interpretation of life; . . . it is not the exclusive product of the schoolhouse, but is a continuous experience that comes out of and enriches the experience of men's lives, and should be universal and lifelong; . . . it corresponds to the cultural and humanistic aims of the labor movement, and should enable workers to express and direct their organization for the benefit of the whole of society." In another statement the editors of *Workers' Education* say: "Workers' education should strive to create new social values. . . . It should set forth with clarity the nature of modern social institutions on the assumption that no economic institution is permanent and that society is ever changing and modifying them."

PARENT EDUCATION.—The beginnings of parent education in terms of conscious, formal effort under professional leadership may be dated at approximately 1924, although child-study groups and child-welfare organizations were formed as early as 1890. From that time, interest and organized activity steadily increased. In 1924, as a means of co-ordinating the activities of numerous organizations, the National Council of Parent Education was formed. Among the more active of the agencies promoting parent education have been the Child Study Association of America, the American Association of University Women, and the National Congress of Parents and Teachers. Several departments of the federal government have made significant contributions. An immense quantity of literature has been produced by these and such other organizations as the American Library Association, the American Home Economics Association, and the American Social Hygiene Association. Professional leaders have been trained for administrative and teaching positions in the field of parent education and many city school systems have employed directors of parent education. Within ten years following the organization of the National Council, local parent-study groups numbered more than ten thousand, six national periodicals were being circulated, and some organized program maintained in every city and in many towns and rural counties.

In 1931 the International Council of Religious Education inaugurated a year of special emphasis on the Christian home with particular stress on parent education. The Federal Council of Churches co-operated, and both organizations have since effectively promoted parent education. Numerous conferences have been held; articles and books produced; and many study groups organized in local churches. Altogether, the movement has fully justified the characterization made of it by Dorothy Canfield Fisher as "one of the most widespread, enlightened, advanced, thorough, and interesting efforts of American democracy to learn what it needs."[3]

ADULT RELIGIOUS EDUCATION.—Adult education is not a new thing in the life of the Church. Always the Church has been an educational institution. As the historical review of later chapters will show,* during the long centuries before responsibility for and control of education passed from the Church to the State, the Church performed an indispensable service in the education not only of children but also of adults.

Again within recent years the new significance of adult education has begun to take hold on the minds of many leaders of the churches. The churches are taking an increasingly significant part in the general adult education movement. Within denominational boards a place is being made for organized departments of adult religious education with full-time leadership. Practically all denominational boards of education attempt some organized educational work with adults, although by no means all have adult departments as such. It must be admitted, however, that as yet many of the boards conceive of a program of adult religious education as consisting only of adult Bible classes, men's brotherhoods with a more-or-less stereotyped program, and women's missionary societies.

TRAINING ON THE JOB.—Occupational training for adults is carried on by various agencies under many different forms, ranging from elementary to highly technical training. As industrial processes increased in complexity during the early decades of the century, industrial corporations found it to their advantage to provide courses at their own expense, and even on company time, with the aim of increasing the efficiency of the worker on his job. With the

* See Chapter I, pp. 43f., Chapter II, pp. 75f.

rapid increase in more recent years of technological unemployment, together with the difficulty of operating at a profit, much
of this training has been discontinued, although many corporations and individual owners of industrial plants increasingly recognize a responsibility for education for workers of wider practical
and cultural scope.

WIDE VARIETY OF INFORMAL TYPES.—There is a wide variety
of educational activities that do not classify under specific types.
They are promoted by an almost equally wide variety of agencies.
An example is adult education in music and its appreciation. An
increasing number of people are finding satisfaction in active participation in organized chorus and orchestral groups meeting in
schools, community centers, churches, and homes. Interpretative
talks on music over the radio have increased in number and in
popularity.

Although recognition of the extraordinary possibilities of
visual education has grown rapidly, comparatively little has been
done toward the development of educational motion pictures.
Sufficient experimentation has been undertaken, chiefly by universities, to demonstrate assured values, both in elementary and
in adult education, but these yet remain to be realized on any large
scale.

Drama represents still another type of adult education with
which little has been done in comparison with possibilities, although the Little Theater movement has steadily advanced, and
the performance results of the presentation of good plays represent every year a significant educational contribution. Wisconsin
was the first state to develop what may fairly be called a state movement for the development of rural dramatics. As early as 1932,
in twenty-five counties of Wisconsin adult drama tournaments
were held in which local groups participated.

PROPAGANDA.—What is avowedly propaganda may be said in
a sense to be education even though what actually results is mis-
education. Numerous in America are the organizations whose
purposes include the inculcation and spread of propaganda. From
the standpoint of the organization what is propagated is, of course,
"good" propaganda, always "in the interest of the truth and the
enlightenment of the people." An example of the extent to which
such organizations influence public opinion was strikingly shown
in the effects of the work of the Association for the Repeal of the
Eighteenth Amendment.

There are also organizations that may be described as "near-propaganda" bodies, as Chambers of Commerce, the D. A. R., the American Legion, and numerous others whose educational influence in certain respects is of the highest and again at certain times and under certain circumstances becomes "more despicable than the worst of those avowedly organized for propaganda."[4]

EDUCATION FOR PROFIT.—Few, if any, fields of American life have been free from invasion by the private-profit entrepreneur. Adult education is no exception. The increase in recent years of purely private-profit enterprises with the avowed aim of adult education is amazing. The more familiar forms include certain types of subscription-book publication in which sales are effected by the promotion of study courses based on the books, correspondence courses offered by certain private individuals and corporations, and adult education sorority and fraternity organizations.

AGENCIES OF ADULT EDUCATION

No conspectus of adult education in the United States can be even reasonably complete that omits descriptive reference to the more important agencies of promotion and administration.

UNIVERSITY EXTENSION.—An importation from the universities of Oxford and Cambridge in the latter part of the nineteenth century, university extension served an ever-increasing number of adults during the first three decades of the present century. Using a variety of educational techniques including lectures, institutes, conferences, demonstration classes, and correspondence study, by 1930 the number of persons enrolled in credit and non-credit courses is estimated to have reached approximately three hundred thousand. The trend continues to be in the direction of an increasing number of subject-matter fields and an ever-growing enrollment. However, the universities, generously supported and well organized as many of them are, have not yet realized the educational possibilities of university extension. Disproportionate attention has been given to academic credit, resulting in the charge that extension divisions too often are merely "credit mills," with all too little emphasis upon the freer, informal, and more creative forms of adult education.

AGRICULTURAL EXTENSION.—The Smith-Lever law of 1914 brought together into one co-ordinated plan the extension activities of the agricultural colleges, the county governments, and the federal Department of Agriculture with the result that the national agricultural extension system, providing instruction and guidance in "subjects relating to agriculture and home economics" is the largest adult educational organization in the United States. Reaching in one way or another between one third and one half of all farms, and maintaining activities in more than three fourths of all counties, it justifies the characterization "a new leaven in rural life." Project demonstrations are carried on in soil conservation and enrichment, animal husbandry, horticulture, agricultural economics, foods and nutrition, home management, health and sanitation, and various other areas.

PUBLIC HIGH SCHOOLS AND EVENING SCHOOLS.—In spite of the fact that, in some states, it is still illegal to expend public funds for day schools enrolling persons over twenty-one years of age, and that provision for the instruction of adults in evening classes is hampered by legal restrictions, school systems in an increasing number of cases are including within their programs instruction in various subjects intended to meet the needs of adults. By 1937 nineteen states and the District of Columbia had made some financial provision for adult education through the public schools. As the program expands it becomes ever more evident that the interests and needs of adults require a range of method and of subjects as comprehensive as is represented in elementary and secondary education. Schools making provision for adult education are located predominantly in urban centers of twenty-five thousand population or over and for the most part the instruction offered is of three types: (1) a duplication of the day-school program, planned for those who for one or another reason have failed either to complete elementary and high-school courses; (2) technical courses for vocational preparation; (3) classes in English for immigrants.

ADULT EDUCATION UNDER FEDERAL AUSPICES.—Beginning in 1933, the federal government has engaged in adult education on a wide scale. Reports of the Works Progress Administration for a given year supply indication of the scope of the program. In March, 1937, for example, the W.P.A. reported 1,968,260 adult persons enrolled in 136,847 classes, under direction of 35,923 teachers. Under the head of Emergency Conservation Work significant educational activities have been carried on in the C.C.C. camps. In June, 1936, for example, there were 1,835 camp educational advisers, all college graduates, more than one half of whom had majored in education; and 1,841 assistant educational advisers, giving full time to direction and supervision of education. From year to year the specific forms of education under federal administration have been changed, and doubtless will continue to change, but that federal participation in adult education will continue, and probably increase in extent, seems assured.

PUBLIC FORUMS.—Doubtless an outgrowth of the New England town meeting, the public forum, a basically democratic educational agency, gives evidence by its growth in recent years of an increasing interest of adults in the consideration of civic and social problems. Varying widely in form of administrative organization, in programs and in means of support, all public forums represent a common method, the presentation of a subject by some representative speaker, followed by free discussion. Almost always they have a social orientation. Subjects dealt with are such as public welfare, race relations, specific social problems, current economic and political philosophies, municipal government, social security, union labor, world peace, and international relations.

With federal support, since 1936, demonstration centers with community-wide programs have been established in more than twenty states under professionally trained forum leaders assisted by teachers, librarians, and clerical assistants.

Based upon the assumption that the ideology and attitudes of adults can be changed, and developed in the direction of improved social ideals through the sharing of opinion and co-operative group thinking, the forum is undoubtedly a significant educational agency. Its limitation lies in the fact that the program stops short of planned action. It provides no means by which changed convictions can be translated into action.

PRIVATE CORRESPONDENCE SCHOOLS.—A study made in 1924 listed fifty large private correspondence schools and in addition a large number of small enterprises,[5] with a total enrollment of about two million persons. Due to the exorbitantly high fees charged by most of these agencies the enrollment decreased materially in the years following 1929. As an educational method, correspondence study has demonstrated its validity. Possible values have been unrealized in many cases owing to the fact that extravagant advertising claims re-enforced by high-pressure salesmanship have created false hopes in the minds of many persons. Carrying through a correspondence course successfully requires unusual capacity of concentration and sustained effort.

RADIO.—Vast potential, unrealized possibilities of adult education inhere in the radio. The listening audience for years has been of immense size and is steadily increasing. As yet systematic radio education is only in its period of beginnings. Some nation-wide and some local broadcasts have had high educational value. Many more have been of merely indifferent worth, and yet a larger number detrimental to the public welfare. That an instrumentality of almost unlimited educational potentiality should have been for so many years subordinated to the private gain of advertising, much of it specious and false, is nothing less than a national tragedy.

VARIOUS OTHER AGENCIES.—Among a large number of other agencies only a few may be mentioned. The *public library* through its provision of reading rooms and its circulation of books has rendered a steadily increasing service in adult education. By 1937 more than four thousand communities had been provided with public library facilities. Yet, even so, the American Library Association estimated that more than eighty per cent of persons living in rural areas are without access to local public libraries. A beginning has been made in organizing libraries on a county basis.

Women's clubs have enrolled more than three million women in their membership, a large proportion of whom are enlisted in educational programs. *Museums*, art galleries, and allied public institutions provide systematic lectures, guidance for visitors, traveling exhibits, loan collections, and a wide variety of publications.

Farm organizations, particularly the Grange, the Farm Bureau, and the Farmers Union (Farmers' Educational and Co-operative Union of America) have stated educational aims and maintain varied educational activities. Material circulated by the parent organizations to local groups provides suggestions and programs for discussions, debates, plays, open forums, and lectures.

The Cooperative Movement which has grown rapidly in the United States in recent years is committed to continuous adult education through participation and by formal methods.

Special schools, such as folk schools, peoples' institutes, opportunity schools, and schools for social study and research, though they have not as yet commanded either adequate funds or a numerous constituency, represent a real contribution to adult education in their emphases upon the re-creation of individuals, social enlightenment, and cooperative living.

Foreign language organizations, whose membership includes

several million adults, stress education as one of their principal objectives. Some of them systematically maintain lectures, reading circles, and musical and dramatic programs. More informal activities perpetuate customs, folklore, and cultural traditions, some of which are capable of making significant contribution to a cosmopolitan American culture.

AIMS OF ADULT EDUCATION

With adult education of so many types, covering so wide a range of activities, carried on by agencies so largely unrelated, obviously any agreed formulation of aims is impossible. What may be observed as significant is dominant emerging trends of such strength as to make it likely that they will be determinative in future developments.

INTERESTS OF ADULTS.—Modern educational theory holds that account must be taken, in education, of the interests of persons if the educational process is to be of major effectiveness. Persons have significant interests, aptitudes, and powers that do not mature, some not even coming to expression, in childhood or youth. Such interests, for example, as vocational efficiency, knowledge and skill in child care and welfare, and efficient administration of the family budget, require stimulation and direction through adult education.

INCREASE OF VOCATIONAL EFFICIENCY.—Public schools provide pre-employment training in specific lines, a form of training limited by reason of the fact that it precedes responsible functional participation. At least equal social responsibility exists to provide, in terms of the needs of the adult individual and of society, opportunity for increasing vocational efficiency. This responsibility is recognized in the case of physicians, teachers, and social workers; it should also be recognized as regards manual workers and those in other lines of socially useful work.

CULTURAL ENRICHMENT.—Increasingly, attention is being given to the development of the cultural values of life. Aesthetic abilities, appreciation, and production skill in the fine arts, in music, art, literature, and drama, are capable of development in mature persons. Deep-lying desire for fuller personal development, the wish for the satisfaction of intellectual, aesthetic, and spiritual needs, is the motive which impels many men and women to engage in adult education activities. Opportunity for the satisfaction of these desires is a social obligation. Adult education should aim at fullness of life for the individual and for society as a whole.

SOCIAL RECONSTRUCTION.—In many different ways both secondary and adult education are hampered by economic obstacles. Both the content and the quality of education are largely determined by the economic framework of the society within which education is taking place. To improve education it is necessary for the structure and the methods of operation of the social order to be improved.

Also, it is impossible for a man or woman engaged in a desperate struggle for the bare necessities of physical existence to enlist or to be enlisted in wholehearted effort for a richer, fuller life. Hunger, want, destitution, and misery deaden the finer sensibilities and the higher aspirations.

It is not enough for adult education to offer people courses of study for the increase of knowledge and skill. It should be its aim to engage them in the actual tasks of social reconstruction. One of the most needed and most effective forms of adult education is education through re-creative social participation.

IMPORTANCE OF ADULT EDUCATION

It remains in this brief, introductory, summary review of adult education to assess its importance. In the rapidly increasing range of educational activities for adults carried on by an equally rapidly increasing number of agencies, evidence is found of a developing consciousness of importance and need. The reasons are not difficult of discernment.

MAKING THE MOST OF LIFE.—Education is more than the transmission of knowledge and skills from one generation to another. It is a process of making the most of all of life's resources. It relates itself functionally to the whole of experience. It is a means by which growing persons achieve intellectual, social, and moral mastery of their world. It has to do with the whole person's interaction with his total objective world. As such it is co-terminous with life itself. Any limitation of education by the calendar, or by attendance upon formal school programs, is wholly arbitrary. Education goes on, whether consciously or not, independently of formal processes.

Even in the inadequate terms of traditional transmissive education the continuation of formal processes during adult life is necessary. Life in the modern world has become so complicated and complex in its civic, social, and economic aspects that the knowledge, attitudes, and skills necessary for successful living are impossible of mastery within the limited period of childhood and youth. Even the most capable, diligent, and receptive students graduate from high school and college unprepared to grapple with many of the problems presented by the present-day world.

CONSERVING THE VALUES OF CHILDHOOD EDUCATION.—Children and young people are continuously being conditioned by the adult world in the midst of which they live. The subject matter of their education in schools may be all that is to be desired. But even more than by what they are told by their teachers they are influenced by their out-of-school environment. The adult environment to which they are subjected makes them what they become. Even though protected from its influences during childhood and adolescence, when they leave school they quickly become assimilated to its ideology, its attitudes, and its ways of behavior. Education to be of the largest effectiveness must simultaneously educate the child and the adult who by his ideas, attitudes, and conduct makes the world what it is.

IF DEMOCRACY IS TO SURVIVE.—The survival of democracy depends upon the social intelligence of its citizenry. The struggle for survival is on and adult education is destined to be one of the chief factors in determining the outcome.

In the past dependence has been placed on the education of children as the essential means of achieving social reform. Educate the child and the child will make the world what it ought to be, has been the prevailing slogan. But civilization cannot wait for long-range social reform. The world is *now* being remade. The issues of today will determine the long future. Men and women in whose hands these issues are must achieve ability to think clearly, to discern truth, to resist propaganda, to feel deeply, and to act decisively.

IMPORTANCE FOR RELIGION.—The significance for religion of adult education is impossible to overestimate. Education expands to include the whole of life. In the field of opportunity and responsibility of the Church the religious education of adults takes its place side by side with the religious education of children and young people.

The adult education movement testifies to the fact that the

desire for a larger and more abundant life motivates the efforts
of great numbers of adults for education. Significant as the movement is, measured quantitatively, it is far more significant measured in terms of the spirit. It is a movement essentially akin to
religion. It offers the Church a vast new opportunity.

THE CHURCH AND
A CHRISTIAN SOCIETY

A PRAYER FOR THE CHURCH

"O God, we pray for thy Church, which is set today amid the perplexities of a changing order, and face to face with a great new task. . . . We remember with love the nurture she gave to our spiritual life in its infancy, the tasks she set for our growing strength, the influence of the devoted hearts she gathers, the steadfast power for good she has exerted. When we compare her with all other human institutions, we rejoice for there is none like her. But when we judge her by the mind of her Master, we bow in pity and contrition. Oh, baptize her afresh in the life-giving spirit of Jesus! Grant her a new birth, though it be with the travail of repentance and humiliation. Bestow upon her a more imperious responsiveness to duty, a swifter compassion with suffering, and an utter loyalty to the will of God. Put upon her lips the ancient gospel of her Lord. Help her to proclaim boldly the coming of the Kingdom of God and the doom of all that resist it. Fill her with the prophets' scorn of tyranny, and with a Christ-like tenderness for the heavy-laden and down-trodden. Give her faith to espouse the cause of the people, and in their hands that grope after freedom and light to recognize the bleeding hands of the Christ. Bid her cease from seeking her own life, lest she lose it. Make her valiant to give up her life to humanity, that like her crucified Lord she may mount by the path of the cross to a higher glory."
—WALTER RAUSCHENBUSCH.

CHAPTER I

THE CHURCH TODAY

IN no period since the historic beginning of Christianity have there been changes so many, so profound, and so far-reaching in their effect upon human life and upon the institutions of human society as in the present age. Material changes have remade the world in which men live and have reconstituted man's ways of living. Industrial, mechanical, and social changes have brought disruption, disorganization, and chaos to the economic arrangements to which men have been accustomed. Philosophical and theological changes have caused the basic assumptions which in the past have given meaning to human existence, largely determined man's conduct, and immensely contributed to the unity and stability of civilization, to be called into question by many and by many others to be denied validity. These changes, affecting as they do every aspect of living, together constitute a major transition in the life of mankind, one of the great turning points of human history. An epoch in the organized life of humanity is coming to a close; we are standing on the threshold of a new age.

In such a time all social institutions are subject to unwonted strain. It cannot be otherwise with the Church. Can the Church adjust itself to the new world that is in the making? Still more important, what contribution has organized religion to make to the process of change? To what extent will the Church and religion influence society in the choice of the goals toward which it moves, and in determining method of change?

Events of recent decades have roughly shaken thoughtful Christians out of their complacency. The confidence in sure progress that characterized the close of the nineteenth century and the early years of the twentieth now seems naïve. We now know that there is no such thing as inevitable moral and religious advance. What contribution does the Church have within its power to make to civilization?

NEED FOR PERSPECTIVE.—Never was perspective on the life and work of the Church more needed than today. By many, the Church is held in disregard; by some even in contempt. Never a year, seldom even a month passes without attack from a new quarter on the weaknesses, the failures, and the inconsistencies of the Protestant churches. This inevitably has had effect both on public opinion and the estimate of the Church by its own members. Equally extreme is the sentimental laudation of the Church and its influence by some ministers and laymen. There is need of a true perspective on the nature and function of the Church and its possible contribution to the life of society as a whole.

CHURCH MEMBERSHIP, ATTENDANCE, AND GROWTH.—The Protestant churches are gaining in America, at least numerically. The ratio of church membership to population has steadily increased over a long period. It is estimated that at the close of the Colonial period probably less than five per cent of the population was actively affiliated with the churches.[1] During the first fifty years of the national period this proportion was tripled. During the first third of the present century the proportion became approximately ten times as great. By 1926 it was 46.60 per cent; by 1933, 48.34. The number of adult church members (persons thirteen years of age and older) has been increasing at almost exactly the same rate as the population. In 1906, 1916, and 1926, church members thirteen years of age and older were equivalent to 55 per cent of the total population of that age. Since 1926 this percentage has increased, the churches gaining more rapidly than the population. From 1906 to 1926 the total number of local churches and synagogues increased from 210,000 to 232,000. Since the latter year, due to consolidation of local churches and the closing of churches in the open country, increase has practically ceased.

It is frequently asserted that marked decline in church attendance has occurred in recent decades, but evidence of this is lacking. It is probable that there has never been a time since the Colonial period when there was a larger church attendance in proportion to the total population, and this in spite of the fading out of a social compulsion which in the early period was very general. With due allowance for the influence of tradition and habit, may it not be said with some confidence that the extent of church attendance evidences not only prevalence of the sense of spiritual need, but also the feeling of large numbers of people that the churches in some satisfying degree minister to that need?

The past one hundred years has been a period of remarkable geographical expansion in the life of the Church. The growth of the first century, great as it was, is not to be compared in extent to the missionary expansion of the nineteenth and the first quarter of the twentieth centuries touching as it has the whole of the earth's habitable surface. The history of Christian missions in Korea, for example, is comprehended within the lifetime of persons now living, yet there are more Christians in that one small land than in the whole of the Roman Empire at the end of the first Christian century, while India, where William Carey began his work in 1793, has more believers than there were in the whole world after three hundred years of Christianity.

We must do more, however, than consider these surface facts if we are to gain a true perspective on the life and work of the Church, its possible future influence, and possible contribution to the civilization of the future.

THE CHURCH AND SOCIETY

THE CHURCH AND THE CHURCHES.—A distinction is necessary between the Church and the churches. In the New Testament we find the concept of the Church of which Christ is the Head, composed of all those who by a living faith are united to him, whose primary characteristic is that it is "permeated and made organic by the continuing and indwelling presence of a personal God in whose service all its members live and have their being."[2] This invisible Church finds its embodiment in an institution also commonly referred to as "the Church," though what we have is not one organized Church but many churches, of which several claim to be the one true Church.

Nowhere in the world are churches (separate denominations) more numerous than in America. Their number and diversity, in fact, constitute perhaps the most striking characteristic of organized religion in the United States. The religious census lists more than two hundred separate organizations, with a considerable increase in number since the beginning of the present century. Most of these are small, of the entire number only twenty-four denominations reporting more than 200,000 adult members each. The multitude of denominations is a reflection of the individualism of American life and of the heterogeneous origins of the population.

THE CHURCH THROUGH THE CENTURIES.—The Church as a society, a living social organism, is one of the oldest of existing institutions. Civilizations have waxed and waned; political governments have been established, grown to power, weakened and passed into oblivion, yet the Church has lived on. For nearly two thousand years it has endured, meanwhile growing until today its world constituency embraces almost one third of the human race.

The Church is not only one of the largest, it is one of the most basic institutions of human society. In any listing of the forces and institutions that have influenced and molded the life of the race the Church must be taken into account. As a human institution it has shared the limitations and defects incident to human life and character. Its weaknesses and failures when assembled constitute a formidable list. It has embraced some of the worst of evils, and at times has condoned and shielded wickedness in high places. Tension often has characterized its inner life, and ever and anon it has been weakened by internal strife and divisions. Its history has been marked by periods of decline, sometimes so long continued that it has been adjudged to be a spent force, but invariably it has arisen to newness of life and power, reasserting its witness to the truth of God. Always it has been influenced by the spirit of the age, often its moral testimony undermined and its practice conformed to the evils of the times, but in no period of declension has it wholly lost its hold upon those intangible values that constitute its peculiar treasure: the principles, ideals, and standards that represent the aspirations, the faith, and the ethical and spiritual goals of the best of men. In its possession of these the Church always has been, and is, an institution above and beyond the average of human living. Ever it should be borne in mind that above all else it is by these that the Church should be judged; these are the real criteria of evaluation.

THE SOCIAL CONTRIBUTION OF THE CHURCH.—The social achievements of the Church through the centuries constitute an impressive total. Even the record of those most familiar is inspiring. In the beginning of his ministry "Jesus went about all Galilee . . . healing . . . all manner of disease among the people." So also from the first did the Church foster agencies of health and healing, furnishing treatment for disease, founding asylums and hospitals, and providing nursing. It cared for widows and orphans, for the infirm and the crippled, for prisoners and for those overcome by calamities. As Harnack declares, "The new language on the lips of Christians was the language of love. But it was more than a language, it was a thing of power and action."[3] It enforced equal moral standards for men and women, enunciated its own marriage laws, and banned divorce. It refused to recognize the moral validity of the class distinctions that universally prevailed in early society and insisted that in Christ, high and low, rich and poor, free man and slave, alien and citizen, all were one and within its own membership it enforced this equality. Through the centuries it has continued to be the main source of the stream of democratic traditions that have enriched the common life not only of the United States but of other nations of the world.

The Church also has maintained a strong tradition of vital concern for the ethical sources of social reconstruction. From the first it has insisted that personality and the rights of persons are more sacred than the protection of property and the preservation of any social system; that the mere possession of power by individuals or governments cannot justify overriding human rights; and that the maintenance of a stable society depends not upon force, laws, courts, armaments, and armies, but upon character and right attitudes in man.

During the early period of its history, when poverty, extreme privation, and unemployment were widely prevalent in Roman society, the Church established forms of poor relief, aided unemployed men to find work, nurtured the spirit of brotherhood within its own group, and rescued multitudes of persons from despair and frustration to a new life of faith and hope and courage. It literally "put down the mighty from their seats and exalted them of low degree."

When the Roman Empire collapsed and the Teutonic tribes of the north began their slow climb to power, it was the Church that through its teaching set itself against those social and economic principles and practices that had played so large a part in the downfall of the empire. It not only condemned avarice and greed, selfishness and the love of money and power, but expressly condemned the unlimited accumulation of wealth, prohibited the breeding of money from money by interest, outlawed monopoly profit, and enforced the principle of the "fair price" as a just reward for labor cost. While it is true that the Church lost in the long struggle, modified its teaching, and itself succumbed to some of the worst of the evils that it had condemned, and finally saw the tendencies against which it had struggled take new form in the rise of capitalism, through long centuries it waged a brave fight against human exploitation. In modern times the ideals of brotherhood, love, sympathy, and kindness taught by the Church have done much to restrain and modify the rigors and abuses of competitive capitalism.

Among social services of high order must also be recognized the contribution of the Church as the patron of learning. In the collapse of the Roman Empire, when the accumulated wisdom of ages was in danger of being entirely lost, it was the Church that became both the protector and the purveyor of learning in the arts and the sciences, in the languages, in writing, in painting, in government and engineering and agriculture.

At the beginning of the modern era the ruling Church was a despotic and exploitative organization. There were within the Church many persons, clerical and lay, who were true and humble Christians, living honest, pure, austere lives. But as an institution the Church had become rich. It held title to almost one third of the landed wealth of Europe on which rental was paid, besides tithes and innumerable fees collected by civil process. Authority resided in an aristocratic and monarchical hierarchy, whose power was used not only to enrich the institution but also to coerce belief and to enforce conformity by physical constraint. Simony, including numerous forms of graft and corruption, was extensively practiced.

Thus viewing in perspective nineteen centuries of church history it is plainly evident that the record of organized religion is a strange and sad mixture. Its history, a modern protagonist of the Church has declared, is the one really formidable argument against the truth of the Christian religion.[4] Not only has it often made mistakes—this is to be expected of any human institution— it has permitted itself to oppose and obstruct social progress; it has even given its sanction to persecution, war, and slavery. Though many individual churchmen expressed condemnation, and local church bodies issued pronouncements in opposition, no general council or synod of the medieval Church ever officially condemned either serfdom or slavery. In more recent times the Church has accepted the support of privileged individuals and groups, even when it knew that privilege had been purchased at the price of extortion and exploitation; it has elevated minor concerns to a place of supreme importance and treated vital issues as irrelevant; at times and in some quarters it has opposed advances of science and resisted the spread of scientific knowledge.

In spite of compromise with the moral standards of the time, through the influence of the Christian conscience expressing itself through the Church and in other ways, significant social advance has been achieved. For example, consideration for women and children has greatly increased; as also for the aged and the sick, and for the disabled and the handicapped. Numerous far-reaching movements for humanitarian reform, if not directly initiated by the Church, have drawn from it inspiration and support.

It cannot be said that through the centuries the Church in its organized form has operated as an instrument of social change. In general the prevailing tendency has been for the Church to give its sanction, commonly interpreted in terms of divine authority, to those practices approved by the majority or by the powerful as essential to their own welfare and the welfare of society. It has been to a greater extent a conserving than a reconstructive force; and this function of conservation of established ways has operated not alone within society as a whole, but also within its own membership to temper and often obstruct the influence of Christian ideals and teachings in the direction of more ethical practice by individuals and by the organized group. The Church, as such, has seldom acted to effect radical change. Agitation and action in behalf of change have been the work of individuals and minority groups, and not until the change has met with strong social approbation has the Church officially given its stamp of approval.

The social gospel is not new. It was the possession of the early Church. But in the early Church it was predominantly an apocalyptic gospel. Deliverance from the ills from which society suffered was expected to come by direct supernatural intervention and the second coming of Christ. The making of a Christian world through the application of human will, intelligence, and skill to the creative task was not thought of as a responsibility of the Church. During the Middle Ages the Church, as has already been stated, possessed a positive, influential social ethic, but it was in no sense revolutionary. The structure of society, when it had taken form, was taken for granted, as were social classes, slavery, serfdom, and war when these became part of the established order. From time to time radical sects arose to voice the judgment of God upon the structure of society as a whole, and upon institutions and governments, but almost without exception they either looked to supernatural intervention for deliverance or in protest withdrew from the world to live apart as ascetics. Now, however, it is different. A significant change has taken place. Within the churches, especially the churches of America, a growing body of conviction exists that religion is in the world to remake the world; that it is the God-given task of Christians not only to express judgment upon the social order in all of its human and unchristian aspects but to change society; and that all of the knowledge and skill that experience and the sciences have made available are to be utilized, together with the power of religion, to effect the change.

There is much in the record of the Church in America to inspire faith and courage. During the pioneer period in the life of the nation and until recent times organized religion has been a powerful factor in national life. Churches were established everywhere. In fact, zeal for planting local denominational societies was so great that many villages, towns, and small cities were overchurched. The Church operated as a principal stabilizing factor in individual and group life in the face of the hardships and misfortunes of pioneer life, recurring depressions, epidemics of disease, and such cosmic accidents as earthquakes, floods, and droughts. By its rites, ceremonies, and teachings it has sanctified and added to the significance of the universal human experiences —birth, marriage, and death. It has made a contribution to education beyond the possibility of estimate through founding and maintaining secondary schools, colleges, and professional schools for two races. It has advocated hospitals and has established and maintained many hospitals and sanitariums of its own. It has been the chief leader—in some cases almost the sole leader—in crusades against such racial scourges as prostitution, alcoholism, and gambling. It has officially led in the condemnation and renunciation of war. In areas of present-day social conflict such as the defense of civil liberties, the struggle for social justice, the condemnation of the prevailing social order, the advocacy of the rights of labor, the improvement of penal institutions, and the application of psychology and psychiatry to mental disorders, although it has not spoken with a single voice and many of its representatives have been silent in the presence of great evils, the Church has been a strong positive factor of influence. In some of these areas it has been a greater force for social advance than societies established to advocate particular reforms. Some of the most adventurous and strategic social action of recent times has been carried on under direct auspices of churches. Of the actual day-by-day work of social amelioration and service probably not less than four fifths of the total is being done by persons who are members of Christian churches, deriving much of their original impetus and sustaining inspiration from their membership in and the teaching of the Church. It should be emphasized that in the matter of official pronouncements on social issues the statements of church councils in recent years have been far in advance of the social understanding, convictions, and practice of the majority of the membership. This is accounted for by what sociologists call the "social lag." While this situation is much to be regretted, it does offer opportunity for education.

THE CHURCH AN INSTITUTION.—There are different ways of defining what is meant by the "Church," and there is no one definition that is universally accepted. Among Protestants there is no doctrine of the nature of the Church concerning which general agreement prevails.[5] The Church commonly is defined both in theological and in sociological terms, and between these there are wide differences. But a simple fact demanding recognition is that the Church is an institution and as such is subject to certain inevitable institutional limitations.

Life invariably tends to organize itself, to take on an institutional aspect, and in doing so, inevitably becomes fixed, rigid, and unchanging. Institutions in themselves, therefore, are not instruments of progress; they are means by which gains are conserved. Progress is achieved by individuals and groups of individuals, by prophets, reformers, inventors, adventurous spirits, who by virtue of their insights, their moral convictions, their social attitudes, their courage and enthusiasm, determine at whatever personal sacrifice and cost, to accomplish needed changes. That the advance represented by the changes achieved at so great cost may be conserved, they are embodied in structural changes, becoming thereby an integral part of the institution or system, and taking on its rigid, fixed form.

This resistance to change, inherent in the essential nature of institutions, is undoubtedly a hindrance to further progress, but it seems to be the price necessary to be paid as a means of conserving such advance as is made. However, the resistance of the Church to change is positive as well as negative. More than once in the course of the centuries when other institutions have given way before the onslaught of demonic forces, the Church has stood unshaken—the gates of Hell have not prevailed against it. The tribute of Albert Einstein to the Church cannot be gainsaid: "Being a lover of freedom, when the revolution came in Germany, I looked to the universities to defend it, knowing that they had always boasted of their devotion to the cause of truth; but no, the universities immediately were silenced.   Then I looked to the great editors of the newspapers whose flaming editorials in days gone by had proclaimed their love of freedom; but they, like the universities, were silenced in a few short weeks.   Then I looked to the individual writers, who, as literary guides of Germany, had written much and often concerning the place of freedom in modern life; but they too were mute.   Only the Church stood squarely across the path of Hitler's campaign for suppressing truth.   I never had any special interest in the Church before, but now I feel a great affection and admiration because the Church, alone, has had the courage and persistence to stand for intellectual truth and moral freedom."

Many protagonists of the institution, inevitably, are jealous of its existence.   Its interests and concerns must be protected! The Church must be saved!   Times without number during its long history representatives of organized religion have placed the interests of the institution before the needs of humanity.   Even though men suffer from preventable wrongs and injustice in their thought, it must needs be—the institution must be saved!

A further distinction of importance is that between the Church and the sect.   The sect is an exclusive religious fellowship whose standards of faith and conduct are distinct from those of the general community.   Clearly marked differences are plainly discernible between the belief, character, and practices of the members of the sect and those outside the group.   The Church is more inclusive in its membership and tends to be more or less co-extensive with the total community.   No clear line of demarcation is evident between church members and the community at large.   Our American churches with few, if any, exceptions, began as sects.   "One of the basic difficulties of American Christianity," says Reinhold Niebuhr, "lies in the fact that its predominant churches are sects which have become churches and do not know that they have undergone such a change."[6]   Continuation of the church type inevitably means that the Church as a whole is loath to enlist aggressively in efforts to effect basic changes, even though these changes are in the interest of human welfare and are demanded by the spiritual ideals and the ethical principles to which the Church pays homage.   This limitation, which finds abundant illustration in the contemporary life of the churches, is inherent in organized religion in common with the nature of all institutions.

In spite of the continuing increase in number of sects, in the nation as a whole the divisive sectarian spirit has given way to tolerance and disposition toward reunion. Issues, particularly of a doctrinal nature, that a few decades ago would have been bitterly contested are now considered in church conferences, denominational and interdenominational, objectively and tolerantly, without rancor or recrimination. A body of sectarian loyalty of disturbing magnitude persists, its strength drawn from the more unenlightened and older elements of the population, but there is a steady growth in the spirit of unity. The conviction spreads that the religious forces divided into competing and more or less antagonistic groups are no match for the formidable powers that today are in opposition to religion, even as they are incapable of successfully coping with the stupendous task that today's life presents. The recognition steadily deepens that if the Church is to demonstrate its effectiveness as a true fellowship of reconciliation in a world torn by fears, competitive antagonisms, and racial hatreds, it must first heal its own divisions.

THE CHURCH A CONTINUING COMMUNITY.—The significance of the Church in its possible contribution to the life of society is not fully comprehended in a consideration of its institutional aspects. For the Church, as has been pointed out, is something different from, and more than an institution. The Church of the New Testament was above all else a fellowship. It had not yet taken on fixed form as an organization, yet it had reality of existence in the fellowship of its members with God through their faith in, and their devotion to, Christ, and their love for, and fellowship with, one another. One cannot read the letters of Paul without being impressed by the associated life in which the disciples were bound together, constituting them a living "body of Christ," an organism having within itself a vitality, power, and ethical quality which made it unique. Throughout the centuries this associated life, this spiritual fellowship, has endured, a community whose life has been continuous throughout the centuries.

THE CHURCH A UNIVERSAL SOCIETY.—As a continuing community the Church has a universal aspect. In its essential nature it is ecumenical, a universal society possessing in its common Lord a basic bond of unity. It is therefore something more than the church of a local community; it is in itself a world community whose members, found in all of the many and diverse sects and churches, constitute a vastly extended fellowship of people of all races and tongues, representing within themselves many differences of belief and practice but possessing certain common supreme loyalties, ideals, and purposes. It is the one greatest universal society in existence. It is a supra-national fellowship, standing alone as a truly international organism. There are other organizations that embrace peoples of various nations and races, but no other that compares in numbers, expanse, and power of influence with the Church. Its social contribution has been made not merely to one or several but to many nations and races. Its missionary enterprise has been the greatest single human undertaking of modern times.

THE PRESENT ADULT SITUATION IN THE PROTESTANT CHURCHES

To gain a true perspective as regards the Church and its possible contribution to the future, in addition to reviewing the life and work of the Church in history, its nature, and its present importance we shall need to consider the conditions existing within the Church today. Our survey from this point on will necessarily be confined to the Protestant churches. Although representing within themselves a wide range of belief, practice, form of organization and polity, the Protestant churches can be said to represent a certain inclusive identity.

That recent decades have constituted a period of decreasing prestige and influence of the Church in certain areas of the national life will scarcely be denied. The Church is not now the factor of influence and power in society as a whole that it once was.[7] In spite of increased membership, it has ceased to have a controlling influence upon the lives of the majority of the population, both members and nonmembers. To many, as was declared by the Oxford Conference, it "does not seem to have anything to say that is really relevant to the major interests and concerns."[8] No longer does it command the time and effort of its members, particularly of women, that it once did. This is accounted for, in part at least, by the fact that many specific types of social and religious activity formerly carried on by church members as voluntary effort have been taken over by special agencies manned by professional, full-time workers; and by the further fact of woman suffrage with accompanying increase of interest of women in public affairs and political activities. The admission of women in greatly increased numbers to business and professional positions is also a material factor. For a long time the Church was the only institution in which women could find an outlet for group activity. Increasingly, in recent decades, women's clubs, welfare organizations, patriotic societies, and other community activities have made demands upon the interest and time of women and their active participation in the work of the Church has lessened accordingly.

THE CHURCH A CROSS SECTION.—As in the period of beginnings of the Christian Church, the Protestant churches have drawn their adult members from all classes and ranks of society. As a result, within the churches is to be found a cross section of the total population.

The Church includes both the learned and the ignorant. While a large proportion of graduates of the high schools and colleges of the present adult generation are members of the churches, also included within the membership are many who have enjoyed few educational advantages. Among the latter are to be found sincere, earnest, and devoted Christians who possess a high degree of spiritual insight and understanding. Notwithstanding this fact, the churches carry a heavy incubus of ignorance and superstition.[9] In all ages the religious beliefs of the unlearned have contained a considerable element of superstition. This remains true today. Closely allied with ignorance and superstition is prejudice against scientific knowledge. This is not a new phenomenon. It may be doubted whether modern times have witnessed anything to equal the bitterness of popular resentment against Copernicus and Galileo, the latter of whom because of his espousal of the Copernican view that the sun is immovable in the center of the universe was condemned in 1616 by the Congregation of the Index at Rome, and admonished by the Pope not "to hold, teach, or defend" a proposition "expressly contrary to Holy Scripture." But even in recent years attacks have been made in the name of religion on findings of science which in intensity have approached medieval hostility. A generation since, Henry Drummond, remarkable combination of scientist and evangelist, together with other scholars not least of whom was our American saint, Phillips Brooks, convinced many of their contemporaries that religion has everything to gain and nothing to lose through an alliance with thorough scientific investigation. A similar service, it seems, is required for many of the adult men and women of the present generation. So long as the false antithesis between religion and science is suffered to continue in the thinking of any considerable proportion of the adult population, so long will religion be less real and dynamic than is its privilege and obligation to be.

The Church includes within its membership both good and bad. Much popular misconception has arisen from the fact that many think of the Church as a kind of house of refuge of the morally perfect. It was never intended so to be. It could not be that and do its work in the world. "I am come not to call the righteous but sinners to repentance," said Jesus. It is one mark of their success that the churches have within their membership many people who are morally imperfect. The churches have brought them to Christ. He is yet to have his full effect upon them. It is the churches' province to give sight to the blind, to free the captives, to remake broken lives, to build anew the characters of those who have made moral failures, and this is not a work that can be fully accomplished in a day.

And in no small measure the churches are accomplishing their moral purpose in the lives of men and women. They have found men baffled and discouraged in the moral struggle and have created within them hope and courage; they have found men drunk and have enabled them to live sober lives; they have found men polluted and have cleansed and purified their lives. To have kept alive Christian aspiration, faith, and hope in the hearts of millions of common folk in an age when the forces of unbelief, materialism, and moral confusion have swept like devastating winds across the world is an achievement of no slight significance.

The fact that the membership of the churches represents a cross section of the population does, however, have the result of no common religious experience or type of moral character, and of a relatively low *average* level of life. The task of the minister and of the lay leaders and teachers is made an immensely difficult one because so large a proportion of the adult membership possess neither a high ethical standard of personal living nor a foundation of vital religious experience. In how many congregations is it true today that there is little of that strong and abounding faith and hope and love that constitute the radiance of the Christian religion? And of how many churches, both ministerial leadership and membership, must it be said that they represent in moral principles, ethical ideals, and business practice, standards that correspond to the ordinary practice of the market place?

The provincialism that constitutes so marked a characteristic of the population of many American communities has parallel religious connotations. The members of the churches in these communities, with few exceptions, have little contact with, or consciousness of, church-wide, national, and international movements and issues. Their world is bounded by the geographical and social confines of their neighborhood, and however intense their loyalty to the local church they have little or no awareness of belonging to a Christian world community.

SENSE OF MISSION.—As a whole the Church cannot be said to possess a compelling sense of mission in the present-day world. Some assert the existence in the American Church of more realization of responsibility and consciousness of mission than in any preceding period. Possibly this may be true. But it is also true that many evidences are present of confused thinking and of lack of concern regarding the larger purpose and function of the church. Many of the members are more concerned about keeping the church building open and getting the bills paid than they are about making the ideals of Jesus regnant in today's life. Precisely the same conflicts that affect present-day culture as a whole exist within the churches. Concerning these conflicts the members have no unanimous word to offer. They are not even of one mind with regard to the teachings of Jesus. They are agreed in honoring his name, but they are by no means all convinced that his ideals are practical or that the Gospel will work if put to the test of our workaday world. Many, in fact, possess uncertainty concerning the validity of all inner and spiritual values.

The Church is racked with conflicting impulses. It feels under obligation to do something toward the making of a new world, but concrete suggestions are likely to be opposed as "unsafe" or "radical." Many church members appear to be wholly unaware of the tremendous changes taking place in the world and of their significance. They continue to speak and think in traditional terms, using religious methods that were suited to ways of living and types of religious experience now long outgrown, and perpetuating organizational forms and procedures that no longer have vital significance.

MORAL CONVICTION.—Lack of a strong sense of mission on the part of the churches roots in something perhaps even more fundamental. The adult membership of the churches lacks on the whole that strong, clear, positive, moral conviction required to make the

Church a power in the world. Evidence of this is seen in the difficulty of perceiving distinctive differences between the moral standards of church members and members of the community who are non-church members.

The moral canons that have hitherto prevailed in society to which the Church gave its sanction were built up principally from Hebrew, Greek, and Roman traditions, re-enforced and supplemented by the Christian revelation, particularly the writings of Paul. These traditional foundations have been widely called in question and, by many, in part or wholly rejected. As an inevitable consequence the system of morals based on these foundations has suffered the same fate. The present generation is without any generally accepted basis of moral authority. As was declared by the Oxford Conference, "Everywhere the old standards of conduct are decaying because the convictions on which they rested have ceased to be held."[10] Within society at large what J. H. Oldham has aptly described as "an almost complete anarchy of ideas" prevails both as to the principles which should govern personal and social conduct and as to the application of principles to specific situations. There is no inclusive moral standard, either within or without the churches, whose authority for human life and conduct is freely and wholeheartedly acknowledged. While it may be said that the churches for the most part theoretically uphold exact moral canons, it may not be maintained that the majority of the members of the churches feel themselves bound by them.

The very same sins prevalent in the world which threaten the destruction of civilization are to be found within the Church. An economic order motivated by selfish greed for private gain is causing widespread privation, suffering, and destruction of social values, and within the Church are to be found many stanch defenders of the *status quo*. Class divisions separate society into antagonistic groups, and within the Church the privileged are often found drawing apart from the underprivileged. Race prejudice divides people of different color, engendering jealousy and hatred, and within the Church members of different race cannot always meet on a plane of equality. Narrow nationalism arrays nations against nations, and within the world Church Christians share the nationalistic spirit of their respective governments. The Church as no other institution in the world has a conscience on war, but within the Church are to be found many military-minded men and women.

That there are in the churches latent moral resources that may be awakened and mobilized in hours of moral crisis has been demonstrated again and again. But the churches as such are not continuously aggressive against iniquity and unrighteousness in their varied forms. Too often the churches are silent on moral issues when they should be vocal; inactive when they should be aggressive; indifferent when burning passion is demanded. Members of the church in political life profit by, and not infrequently actually participate in corruption in politics; some permit themselves to be aided by the activities of notorious gangsters. Members in high position who are corrupt in practice are suffered to continue as members of the churches. Their patronage is sought by leaders of the churches. By others their acts are condoned and excused, and they are extravagantly praised for the contributions they make as salve for their own guilty consciences.

The righteousness declared by Jesus is not so much a legalistic righteousness, as it is a rich, full, overflowing, abounding life of positive goodness. It is in exemplifying this type of life, rather than in violations of the moral code, that many members of the churches fall short. An immense amount of steadfast devotion, moral heroism, purity and goodness, kindness and sympathy, is to be found in the churches. There are those who declare—and they are probably right—that in the churches the level of moral integrity and devotion to ideals is higher than it has ever been before. Yet there are many church members whose lives are morally colorless and restricted and weak. They exhibit no positive, sacrificial goodness. They manifest attitudes not only lacking in Christian quality, but positively unchristian. They are harsh and ungenerous. They have not that quality and extent of goodness that is required to attract and save the world.

A searching criticism in a widely circulated British report, as applicable doubtless to our American churches as to those of Great Britain, declares that the most serious difficulties actually to be found arise from the fact that the Church is not good enough rather than that men and women are too bad to care about religion. It affirms that men demand of the Church plain evidence of the vital power of the Christianity it professes, asking to see within its membership more sacrifice, more fellowship, more heroism, more brotherhood, more zeal for the uplifting of human life and for the regeneration of the whole social order than they can discover within its borders.

SOCIAL VISION, PHILOSOPHY, AND CONVICTION.—Without doubt, one of the most significant developments within American Protestantism during the last half century, already referred to,* has been what has been called the rediscovery of the "social gospel" and the resulting emphasis upon the social interpretation of the Christian religion. To many ministers and some laymen this emphasis has come as a divine inspiration, bringing with it deepening and revitalization of religious conviction and experience and adding to the significance and power of their ministry. As time has gone on the social interpretation of religion has become more and more inclusive until the conception includes not only justice in economic relationships between man and man but racial problems, international relations, relationships within the family, and education. The influence of social teaching has undoubtedly greatly increased, and the sense of obligation of the Church to Christianize social relations and to aid and guide social change has steadily grown. Something like a general awakening to the unchristian aspects of the economic order has taken place. But it cannot be said that the development of social conviction and concern within the churches has kept pace with the remarkable progress of the social sciences.

With the majority of the adult members of the churches, religion is still thought of in individualistic terms—a personal matter between the soul and God, a thing apart from the rest of life, an inner source of peace and content and rest, a recompense for failure, bringing comfort for the lacks and the sufferings of this life through assurance of endless happiness in another world. The mission of the Church—many would say its only mission—is thought of as saving men with a supernatural salvation. Religion defined in social terms and proclaimed as an active social force, as a means of social redemption, is still unfamiliar to the large majority of comfortable middle-class church members, and to many of those to whom it is familiar it does not strongly appeal. There is a general lack of understanding of the meaning of the Christian gospel for economic organization and practice and of insight into how Christian principles can be correctly applied. A vast amount of kindness and good-natured friendliness exists within the churches, but this exists side by side with an amazing general insensitiveness to the injustice, exploitation, and oppression existing as an integral

* See page 45.

part of the social order, and the desperate human issues involved. The basic problems of the economic order are not understood, and are considered to be outside of the function of religion; a discussion of them does not sound "religious" and action directed toward their solution does not "feel" religious. These attitudes are reflected in the demand that continues to be voiced by laymen that ministers "stick to the gospel" and "preach the simple gospel." It is to be recognized, as was pointed out by the Oxford Conference,[11] that inasmuch as the Church, both national and local, is compelled to maintain an organizational existence, it cannot escape sharing in some measure the features and practices of its environing economic order. But it is also to be recognized that insofar as its officials and members "are sensitive to the spirit of Christ they will be critically aware of that relationship" and sincerely repentant concerning it.

Church membership, it must be regretfully acknowledged, is not a guarantee of conduct to any marked degree above the level of prevailing social ethics in business and industry. In their advance beyond the prevailing antisocial practices, church members today cannot be said to be a "city set on a hill," or even a lighted candle. Often it happens that the employer or the industrial magnate who breaks new ground in applying social principles to business or industry is not a member of the church and does not ground the innovation in religion. Nor can it be said that the Church in recent decades has been an effective force in improving the common life of the people in the disadvantaged areas of America.

The widespread philanthropic and charitable work of the churches is often cited as evidence of social idealism. This should not be glossed over or underestimated. It is of real importance. But, no matter how great in extent, it does not compensate for a lack of social insight and for conviction concerning the inequalities, injustices, and oppressions of the modern social order. So also as regards pronouncements of church councils in resolutions and social creeds, and the growing disposition of ministers to declare themselves in ministerial meetings unequivocally on social issues. These, however significant they may be as indicative of the growth of social conscience within the churches, are, after all, the expression of leaders of the churches rather than the confession of faith and purpose of the rank and file. The majority of church members are not deeply concerned over the prevalence of such concrete social evils as unemployment, child labor, bad housing, stock gambling, and numerous others.

That many evangelical church members are interested contributors to charity and relief is unquestioned. However, palliative measures and gifts in behalf of social amelioration do not take the place of personal devotion and courageous effort directed to fundamental social reconstruction. The brand of Christianity exemplified in the lives of most church members is neither socially redemptive nor re-creative. With some notable exceptions, organized Christianity contents itself "with pouring oil into wounds that desperately call for surgery." So far as vigorous attempts to replace the prevailing social order with a new and righteous order is concerned, the Church as a whole is not even conscious of the task as a religious obligation.

In fact, the Church is one of the chief bulwarks of the present economic order. It is so compromised by reason of the involvement of large numbers of its members and by its own corporate commitments and investments that it is difficult, almost impossible, for it to act. The stake of the Church in the existing order is too great for it to act freely in line with the prophetic conviction of many of its ministers and laymen. As a consequence, churches find themselves patronized by defenders of the economic order as a means of perpetuating the existing system.

Nor is this all. There are areas of Protestantism, both geographical and ecclesiastical, where the preaching and teaching of the social gospel is condemned as heresy and treated as a betrayal of true religion. This attitude is represented by not a few preachers who have a large popular hearing, who are supported in their vigorous opposition by representatives of powerful business and industrial interests. Among others the prevailing attitude is less antagonistic, and tends to take the form of ignoring or even obscuring and distorting the realities of the social situation. Not a few laymen frankly say that they expect religion to be a soothing influence; they wish, when they attend religious services, to be comforted, the sense of strain and tension experienced in business and industry to be lessened.

Consequences of these attitudes involve not only the blinding of many church members to issues of justice and righteousness but actually ally them with obscurantist and reactionary movements. For example, a discouragingly large number of Protestant church members were actively allied with the Ku Klux Klan.

For these conditions our American educational system must share responsibility with the Church. Education and religion together have failed to develop in the mass of the people appreciation of the extent and seriousness of the injustice and inhumanity involved in the social order, and to prepare them to deal with the great social problems of the day in an intelligent, conscientious manner.

RELIGIOUS BELIEFS AND CONVICTION.—Within recent decades historical scholarship and theological thought have profoundly modified the corporate body of religious beliefs of educated ministers.[12] For a large proportion of the better educated lay men and women these changes have undermined the old faith without enabling them to build a new structure of belief. The Church does not possess a common theology. Christian scholars have made in recent years outstanding contributions to theological thought, but these contributions represent no general agreement. A strong trend is evident among both ministers and laymen toward a more positive and authoritative theology, but this only in part makes up for the weakening through many years of traditional theological beliefs upon educated opinion as reflected "in general intellectual periodicals, in scholarly journals . . . in declining relative circulation of religious journals, and in the attitudes reflected in mass circulation magazines."[13]

A large proportion of church members, sometimes estimated to be as high as ninety per cent, hold membership within the religious groups into which they were born. Such beliefs as are held are the result of inheritance, traditions uncritically accepted, rather than having been arrived at through study or experience. The philosophical and scientific implications of their simple creed are realized dimly or not at all. Of the majority it may be said that they believe in God as a power controlling human destiny to whom prayers may be addressed, their conception of him being a confused blending of pre-Christian and of Christian teachings. Beyond this rather vague concept, modified to a greater or less extent by a traditional anthropomorphism, they have few theological convictions. Generalization by no means applies to all, for there is usually a wide range of belief even within particular congregations.[14]

To many, Christ is as dim and unreal as God the Father. They do not clearly distinguish between God and Christ, and use the terms almost interchangably. Their faith is not intimately personal; God is not thought of as imminent in all life, a present help at all times, so much as a mighty Being living afar, apart from the world, who breaks into the existing order from without at times of crisis or in answer to the call of extremity. Yet in almost every church, however small, there are those who live day by day consciously aware of God as their ever-present friend and helper, to whom religious faith is of all things most real.

Despite the fact that the open Bible is the corner stone of Protestantism, few of the members of the churches possess any thorough or deep knowledge of the Bible. By many it is held in a kind of sentimental regard, but there are few who read it regularly and fewer still who study it systematically.

From these generalizations it becomes clear that the sharp differentiation between belief and unbelief in Christianity of a few generations ago has faded out. No longer are people sharply classified as "believers" or "agnostics," or "infidels." As an outstanding Christian leader recently declared: "The traditional Christian ideas have ceased to have any living meaning. It is not so much that men disbelieve in Christianity—as that they feel it to be entirely irrelevant to their actual experience of life."

For the majority of church members the conflict between science and religion which so deeply disturbed the Church in the second half of the nineteenth century no longer exists. Adjustments in beliefs required by assured results of science have been made. But this does not hold true for all, notably the fundamentalists, who insist both upon maintaining traditional theological interpretations and in taking the offensive against certain aspects of modern knowledge which they hold to be antagonistic to religion. The five "fundamental" dogmas upon which they are most insistent are the virgin birth of Jesus, his physical resurrection, the inerrancy of the Bible, the substitutionary theory of the atonement, and the imminent physical second coming of Christ. There is a high degree of correlation between fundamentalism and depreciation of and antagonism to the social gospel and this correlation is in part the explanation of the vigorous support of fundamentalism by not a few prominent representatives of powerful business and industrial interests. In certain geographical areas the generally prevailing attitude, largely influenced by fundamentalist preaching and teaching, is strongly antagonistic to social religion. The social gospel is anathema, a dangerous heresy, representing "a betrayal of true Christianity." In many sections of the country the membership of local churches is divided between "liberals" and "fundamentalists."

SECULARISM.—Throughout the whole of Western civilization, it is contended by many whose judgment cannot be ignored, there is in progress a slow disintegration of the spirit of culture, a fading of high vision, and the substitution of outer expansion for inner cultivation and growth—a concomitant, and in all probability a result of the predominating secularization of life and thought. The spirit of the age is secular and the Church has been infected with the prevailing secularism. Instead of the Church having succeeded in Christianizing life, the prevailing culture has secularized the Church. Evidence is seen not only in the characteristics already described but also in the tendency of churches to lay disproportionate stress upon the material aspects of organized religion—increase in size, improvement in organization, the building of larger, more magnificent church plants, and the creation of endowments. Too often these are accepted as substitutes for more vital and dynamic expression of religion. Success, too frequently, is measured in materialistic terms. Sharing the urge for bigness, borrowing the slogans of the promoter, and the methods of competitive business, churches allow themselves to appeal to the identical motives that attract customers and enlist members for clubs and other secular organizations. In extreme cases some even bid for attendance by offers of entertainment and novel attractions, and sensational stunts. What wonder, under such conditions, that persons are found uniting with the church merely to gain social prestige, and contributing to its support from no higher motive than in paying their club dues.

More significant as an evidence of the secularization of the Church is its involvement in the dominant social order, entanglement in the forms, customs, and practices of an economic system that in many particulars is unchristian. Having given hostages to the system through the investment of endowments in bonds and stocks, the giving of mortgages, and the competition of its publishing houses with commercial publishers, it not only finds its institutional prestige and fortune bound up with the perpetuation of the system, but its practice conditioned by prevailing practices.

Jesus charged his disciples, being in the world, to be not "of the world," but the Church today is so involved in the secular economic order that its institutional life is to a very large extent "of" that order. It has so identified itself with secular society that it has lost its power effectively to challenge it.

INSTITUTIONALISM.—There is no warrant in the New Testament for thinking of the Church as an organized society as an end in itself. Few, indeed, are the temptations that can come to the Church more subtle and spiritually devastating than that of regarding itself as an end, rather than as a means to great human, social, spiritual ends. Yet this is precisely the temptation to which many leaders and lay members of the churches have succumbed. Protestantism is honeycombed with a deadly institutionalism.

The interest of officials ofttimes seems to be centered in the machinery of organization. The members of local churches in typical instances are absorbed in the details of organizational activities, exhibiting an immense amount of busy-ness and withal a commendable, good-natured friendliness, but almost wholly lacking in sensitiveness to and concern with the desperate issues of today's life.

With many men and women, membership in the Church is a supreme interest but to an almost exclusive degree loyalty is concentrated on the local church. With some the institutional consciousness is so extreme that instead of church membership constituting a means of integrating religion with and making it a controlling influence in the whole of life, preoccupation with petty concerns of the local church separates them from the main currents of life in the community and the world at large. With a few this preoccupation takes the form of a superior air, a better-than-thou spirit. Such persons are separatists who have come apart from the world, indifferent to its oppressions, its sufferings, and its woes. They are the scribes and Pharisees of our time; they tithe mint and anise and cummin and omit the weightier matters of the law and the gospel. Jesus declared true religion to have no greater foe than a narrow, intolerant, legalistic ecclesiasticism, and there is no reason to believe that his judgment would be different today concerning religionists who exhibit a like spirit. Churches whose members are unchristian cannot Christianize their neighbors, much less our civilization.

A concomitant of the institutional spirit is the denominationalism that characterizes some church groups and many local churches. The denomination, particularly in the case of many of the smaller sects, has sought to maintain certain characteristics that tend to separate it from other religious groups. This separatism holds the group apart and prevents its members both from grasping the problems of society as a whole and from making any creative contribution toward social reconstruction. Even in the case of denominations that have lost the distinguishing marks that characterized them in the beginning, the tendency to think of themselves, each as a self-sufficient unit, has persisted, causing them to be relatively unconcerned with the problems of society. In this is to be found a prime factor of explanation of the provincialism mentioned earlier in this chapter as characteristic of numerous areas of American life. This aspect of the life of the churches reveals a strange contrast to the universal love and spirit of brotherhood for which the Church historically has stood for two thousand years.

LACK OF INTEREST AND INACTIVITY.—Apparently, the members of the churches, both men and women, have less interest both in the Church and in religion than was formerly the case although no dependent criteria are available. Decline of interest is seemingly evident both among the more highly educated part of the population, the business and professional classes, and among the workers, both industrial workers and farmers. Not only indifference, but criticism of and antagonism to, the Church has increased to a marked extent.

A few people do the work of the churches. A few members constitute the official boards and important committees. A few bear the entire burden of necessary administrative responsibility. A somewhat larger number are enlisted as church-school officers and teachers and as leaders of affiliated societies, guilds, and clubs. The very large proportion of men and women engage in no church activity whatsoever unless irregular attendance upon the public services of the church may be considered an activity. Many men are incessantly, tirelessly active in secular pursuits. Many others are wearing out body and soul in unrewarding toil in the attempt to make a living for their families. Some are exhaustingly busy in getting rich. But of all these, only a few are active in making the churches a power in the world.

There are few church members who contribute in any sacrificial measure to maintain the Church and its program. The members of one of the largest of the denominations contributed in a recent year an average of three fourths of one cent per week for the Church's foreign-missionary enterprise. Probably not more than one third of the members of the average church make any contribution whatsoever to the work of the church outside of its local maintenance.

The Church is sometimes criticized by business men for tying up huge capital in plants that stand idle for five days out of seven, a criticism accentuated by the increased investments in recent years in costly structures. However serious this fact of nonuse may seem to materially-minded men, from the standpoint of religion there is a far more serious lack—the failure to enlist the time and energies of capable men and women in activities within the churches and in creative activities within their respective vocations in behalf of the Kingdom of God. The average church member, as a church member, feels little or no responsibility as a part of the obligation of church membership, either for unselfish remedial service in ministry to human need or in constructive effort toward the reconstruction of the present social order into the Kingdom of God.

A partial explanation of the prevailing inactivity of the majority of church members, in contrast to the pure devotion and the sacrificial effort of a few, is to be found in the fact that the Church has no definite, comprehensive program requiring of its members socially creative service.

CLASS CONSCIOUSNESS.—No one can deny that within the churches there are brought together more diverse and varied and cosmopolitan groups of people than are to be found in any other fellowship. "In Christ," said the apostle, "there is neither Jew nor Greek, barbarian, Scythian, bond nor free." That is the Christian ideal, and there are many local churches in whose inclusive fellowship the ideal is gloriously realized. The membership of many a local church represents almost a perfect cross section of the community of which it is a part.

While this is true, it is also true that increasingly in recent decades the membership of the churches has tended to be made up predominantly of the well to do, the well-fed and well-clad, the respectable and respected people of the better-class communities. More and more the churches have been becoming middle-class institutions.

A distressingly large proportion of the population are compelled to live below the level of adequate maintenance. The majority of the low-income masses, particularly the wage earners, are not included within the membership of the churches. The Roman Catholic Church ministers to a larger proportion of them than do the Protestant churches. The leaders of the local churches, with few exceptions, do not belong to this stratum, and many of them are not concerned that the Church shall extend its membership to include these underprivileged people.

An associated fact, partly a consequence of the foregoing conditions, is that the middle-class members of the churches are becoming increasingly class conscious. Much the same pride of place and power and wealth is to be seen in the attitudes of people within the churches that are so much in evidence without. "The Church is saturated with the philosophy and ideals of the dominant class" is a judgment adopted after long discussion by a recent inter-denominational student conference; and from another group comes the declaration, "The class distinctions of this world are carried over with little alleviation into the fellowship of believers." These judgments are based upon observable conditions. Class consciousness has rapidly increased in recent decades, particularly within the ranks of industrial workers, a fact frequently deplored by religious leaders. Equally significant, and even more to be deplored, though not so frequently acknowledged, is the fact that Christians of the comfortable middle classes are actuated by class interest quite as much and in many cases even more than are industrial wage-earners. And this class-interest domination, as the Oxford Conference emphasized, is accompanied by "the assumption that the interests of the middle classes are identical with the interests of the community, . . . an illusion which unconsciously blinds many of the most sincere Christians and makes them unfair and self-righteous in their attitude toward those classes which at present are the chief sufferers from the economic order."[15]

THE EDUCATIONAL TASK OF THE CHURCH TODAY

The conditions existing within the Church affecting its membership, which we have attempted briefly to describe, broadly define the educational task of the Church today. Concerning existing conditions differences of opinion exist. Local churches vary so widely in spirit, in program, and in experience, character, and attitudes of their personnel, that any degree of generalization concerning the life of the Church as a whole is certain to seem to some inaccurate and unjust. *But all agree that conditions are not as they ought to be.* The Church of today is very far from being the dynamic, effective instrument for personal and social righteousness that it might be. If organized religion is to be a dominating force in the remaking of civilization, at least three things are necessary: (1) The Church must sufficiently free itself from the control of contemporary secular culture to re-establish its prophetic function as a critic of the secular order; (2) it must engage its adult members, with all the ability and earnestness it can command, in a restudy and reformulation of its own function, its objectives, its methods, its materials, and its program; and (3) it must prepare its adult members to carry forward its program with greater intelligence, skill, enthusiasm, and power than they now possess.

CONCEPTION OF FUNCTION.—The Church's conception of its purpose in the modern world is confused. Protestantism emerged from the Reformation with clear and definite convictions of its function. Today it confronts a changed world uncertain and hesitant concerning its mission. Though there are many notable exceptions, in considerable part it is attempting in a new world of science, technology, machines, new economic conditions, new international and intercultural relations, and changed philosophical and theological outlook, to carry on with concepts, ideas, and methods belonging to a past that for many of its people no longer exists. Moreover, this already changed world is continuing to change, now more rapidly and in more far-reaching ways than ever before. If the Church is to serve the present age, it must rethink its mission and come again to clear and compelling conviction of its function.

Religion is an essential part of man's nature and the central conceptions of the Christian gospel are ultimate. Its principles, ideals, and spiritual dynamic will continue in the future as in the past, to inspire, influence, and empower men, but if the Church is to have its full part in determining the shape of things to come, it dare not be hesitant or vacillating as to its function, its objectives, its method, and its program.

As the Oxford Conference declared, "Let the Church *be* the Church." Let it stand on its own foundation. Let it insist, at whatever cost, on its independence. Let it acknowledge its one Lord only, resolutely refusing to bow to any other sovereign power. Let it free itself from whatever subservience it now owes to other masters, whether nationalism, capitalism, or humanism. Let the Church know its purpose as a *Church,* distinct from all other institutions, powers, and agencies, and to that purpose be true.

MAGNITUDE OF THE EDUCATIONAL TASK.—The Church has

done more, is doing more today for popular religious education than any other institution or agency, reaching more people with a moral and religious message than any other institution. Yet it is very far from measuring up either to its opportunity or its responsibility. It is not clearly conscious of its educational mission. It fails in the person of many, doubtless of a majority, of its leaders and of its pastors to interpret its function in educational terms. Large numbers of its ministers are themselves uneducated men. In spite of these limitations it is believed by many to be the greatest single educational influence in modern life.

In recent decades there has been no more outstanding feature of church activity than the development of religious education as a distinct movement. With increasing conviction and assurance the churches have turned their attention to it as the chief means by which they hope to achieve their objectives in the lives of their members and in society as a whole. The shift in emphasis and method involved, together with the provision of facilities and equipment required, is the most remarkable phenomenon in present-day Protestantism. The fact that the churches have been able to make so radical a change, even considering the fact that the thought and practice of thousands of local societies have been but slightly affected, is a significant testimony to their virility.

While there has been a remarkable turning to religious education, and while confidence in the educational method has been extending and deepening, it cannot be said that unanimity exists in intelligent, deliberate choice of, and reliance upon, religious education. It has not had an undue amount of official encouragement! It is to be questioned whether any one of the denominations in America as yet can be said to have a comprehensive and complete program of religious education for all age-groups from beginners to adults, *officially approved and promoted by the Church as a whole.* Confronted as it is today with an educational task of the first magnitude as regards its own membership, an important question for the Church is whether it will wholeheartedly adopt religious education and as a chosen instrument make full use of it as a means of achieving its objectives. The urgency of the times demands that this question shall be faced and answered.

In the growth of the religious education movement, *adult education* presents a case of retarded development. It has by no means kept pace with elementary religious education. In the elementary field there has been a degree of intelligent interest in objectives, method, and materials; a concentration of effort; a development of skill; and an improvement of organization and administration, not paralleled in the adult area.

The total situation confronting religion today stresses the necessity of new emphasis upon adult education. Conditions, which we shall later describe, that threaten the very life of civilization owe their continuance to the lack of insight, conviction, courage, purpose, and dynamic will of the adult generation. For lack of understanding and sympathetic cooperation on the part of adults much of the effort of the Church with its children and its youth goes for naught. The conditioning they receive in the home and in other contacts with adults frustrates most of what the Church attempts in the social education of the young. Forces operating in community and national life in the direction of social progress are retarded by the social illiteracy, the apathy, the prejudice, and the active opposition of many adult members of the Church. In a day of rapid social change the Church has an obligation to society that it cannot possibly meet unless it gives itself with new earnestness and new purpose to the Christian education of its adult members.

More is involved than choice of religious education as a means, or instrument. Even more important is the clear and definite determination of the ends for which the instrument is to be used. There are many today, active in the work of the churches, who exhibit a kind of blind adherence to the use of religious education in the program of the Church without any clear recognition of the ends to be achieved. Throughout this book our discussion is concerned with the objectives, method, and materials of adult Christian education. At this juncture we emphasize the point, later to be more fully developed, that Christian education concerns itself with the entire life of the individual and of the community, conceived as a unified whole. The purpose is nothing less than the transformation of the complete life of society so that all its resources and activities—material, economic, political, educational—shall be directed to the development and welfare of persons. In Christian education at its best, effort for the achievement of this purpose concerns itself with the intellect, with the will, and with the emotional life; with the increase of knowledge, with conduct and action, and with the appreciations, the affections, the aspirations, the ambitions, and the loyalties. It supplies information, quickens insight, develops intelligence and capacity for mature judgment. It provides motives, guides ambitions, and influences achievement. It appeals to the sense of obligation and responsibility, awakening conscience, stimulating both self-respect and regard for others, and creates character both in the individual and in the group, the Christian man and the Christian society.

A PROGRAM OF ACTION.—Conceived in these terms, adult education involves a program of action. In this conception, in fact, education and action may be said to be inseparable. Without action—we do not mean merely physical motion, but action in its comprehensive sense—there can be no socially effective education.

Not only does sound educational philosophy require a program of action. The Christian religion insists on the same requirement. Christian faith is essentially a principle of action. If religion is again to come alive in the experience of men in full realization of its historic prophetic function, it must become the determinative principle in the lives of those whose conduct and activities constitute the business, commerce, industry, and politics of today's world. The traditional program of the Church, apart from activities in behalf of its own maintenance as an organization, has been chiefly a process of verbalizing in terms of ideas and ideals. The time has come when the teaching and preaching of abstract ideas and ideals must be translated into action.

In its application to the traditional church program, this is a revolutionary conception. In what in recent years has passed for adult religious education the Church has taken over the prevailing ideas and paraphernalia of general education, associating the term with a school situation, with formal courses, classes, and lectures, a conception re-enforced by a psychology of adult learning which treats education as a process limited chiefly to the acquiring of information, subject matter, and sensory motor skills.[16] While in any type of education these are doubtless important, in Christian adult education they comprehend only a small part of the comprehensive whole. An adequate conception involves a social philosophy of education which conceives the process to be one not merely of increasing information and knowledge but changing social attitudes, individual and collective behavior, and the reconstruction of the social order in terms of a truly Christian pattern. Not but what adult classes, discussion groups, and lecture courses will continue to be required. More rather than fewer of these probably will be needed, but they must needs have a different motivation and constitute merely one element rather than the whole program. The sphere of adult religious education will be thought of not merely as a group-meeting on Sunday morning, but as the community life as a whole, and wherever individuals or groups are engaged in purposive activity in the direction of a better world there, it will be recognized, Christian adult education is taking place.

The immense difficulty involved in the changing of collective behavior and the transformation of institutions deeply rooted in the past should not be underestimated. One element of difficulty is lack of knowledge of the process of such change—how and in response to what influences change takes place, and what procedures and types of activity may be most effectively used. Tested principles and methods are for the most part lacking. A second element of difficulty is the resistance to change on the part of individuals and groups whose privilege and vested interest either are threatened or are believed to be threatened, together with the influences and forces, large-scale propaganda and various forms of pressure, that they are able to invoke. A third element is made up of the difficulties inherent in adult human nature. J. H. Oldham, in a remarkable summary in which he acknowledges indebtedness to John C. Bennett, has described these difficulties.[17] He calls attention to such factors as these: the small-scale minds possessed by many adults as revealed by limited knowledge, lack of imagination, and restricted interests; the prejudices, highly emotionalized loyalties, and emotional maladjustments from which a large proportion of men and women suffer; egotism, personal pride, and moral weakness which are the common lot of many; immersion in a particular task, highly specialized, which is demanding upon time and energy; and, not least of all, the effects of age, especially in frequent instances of hardening of the mind, and such conditions as excessive fatigue, lack of physical fitness, and long-continued ill health.

So great is the difficulty there are those who contend that the Church is helpless to accomplish any significant change in transforming the social order in the direction of the Kingdom of God.[18] Such a contention is a counsel of despair. Resources human and divine, we are constrained to believe, are available for moral, religious, and social progress, even in such a period of crisis as that which has now overtaken humanity.

REBIRTH OF THE PROPHETIC SPIRIT.—That advance may be achieved it is imperative that religion in the Church shall come alive in fresh contact with Reality, a rebirth such as has taken place in every great creative epoch of twenty centuries of the life of the Church. Neither complaint concerning conditions, nor any manner of retreat, will avail anything. Equally vain is certain to be all effort to recapture the vital experience of the past through recital of triumphs of long ago and the celebration of anniversaries. Nothing, in truth, will avail unless religion shall be able to break through the crust of convention, formality, and indifference to fresh, immediate contact with the living God.

What is required is rebirth of the prophetic spirit in the Church. A prerequisite is repentance for corporate sin. The Church has stultified itself by becoming involved to the extent that it has in a social order that is sinful and unchristian. This must come to be clearly recognized, not merely by a few but by many and the recognition must be accompanied by sincere repentance. It must accept the prophetic conception of religion and achieve the conviction and confidence that in prophetic religion it has as its unique possession the instrumentality by which it can reconstitute itself and fulfill its mission in recreating the society of which it is a part. In doing this it will look inward upon itself and will look out upon the total life of society with the eyes of Christ. It will achieve a new and penetrating insight into the real nature of the motives and the inner workings of the existing social order. It will no longer be content with sentimental hopes, pious but vague prayers, and abstract statements of general Christian principles. It will fearlessly pronounce judgment on those aspects of personal and collective life that are contrary to the teaching of all high religion.

Doing this will mean setting itself against many who are beneficiaries of the present order and calling down upon its own head persecution such as always in the past both from without and from within has been the lot of prophets when they have dared to attack vested interest. It will involve a frank and courageous facing of alternatives: whether it is prepared to lose its life in order to gain life. The doing of these things will constitute what the Church longs for—a "revival"; not in an other-worldly or superficially emotional sense but in a revitalizing of the spirit and life of the Church that will make it again the instrument of the power of God.

The Christian religion clearly points the way to a new order of life. Following the way indicated by the Christian gospel requires that both individuals and society shall change their ways. If they do not, our democratic civilization is doomed. Democracy cannot long continue under conditions such as have prevailed in recent years.

AN EVER-PRESENT TASK.—Stimulus to faith and hope and courage may be found in the history of the early Church. Many of the deficiencies and needs described as characterizing the churches of today were present in the churches of the first century. "For you see your calling, brethren, how that not many wise men after the flesh, not many mighty, not many noble, are called." Thus wrote Paul to the church at Corinth. And that general condition doubtless was fairly characteristic of the Church at large. Many of the members were grossly ignorant of spiritual truth; some held narrow and what today seem grotesque religious ideas; some had moral and ethical standards that were far below the Christian level; others were material-minded and unsocial in their attitudes; not a few were more spiritually dead than alive. Yet with all these limitations and shortcomings under God the Church rendered a service to the world of the first century beyond all estimate. Its possible service to the twentieth century is likewise beyond estimate.

CHAPTER II

PROTESTANT HERITAGE IN RELIGIOUS EDUCATION

THE Protestant churches have a significant historical background as regards religious education. All that is done or attempted today is conditioned by what was thought and done in the yesterdays. A church no more than an individual can cut itself off from its past. The governing ideas and practices of today root in social, economic, intellectual, and religious backgrounds. Without some knowledge of the earlier and later history of the Protestant faith it is impossible to understand the currents and countercurrents in the present-day life of the churches. Whether theory or method, the newest candidate for favor, while it may seem suddenly to make its appearance full-grown, has a long history. Like a spring emerging in a pool at the foot of a hill upon which one comes suddenly in his journey—although it may appear to boil up from the ground immediately below, one well knows that the living water comes from far off hidden sources.

Although by no means the original source of many of the most significant influences and trends within the evangelical churches, the Protestant Reformation does represent both a dividing point between the medieval and the modern world, and a period of beginnings, and for our purpose offers a convenient starting point.

THE PROTESTANT REFORMATION

So complex a movement was the Protestant Reformation that it does not lend itself to simple analysis. In any brief statement such as this is compelled to be there is danger of making it seem far more simple than it really was. The break with existing systems which it represents was quite as much political and economic as religious. The era was one of widespread and profound dissatisfaction and unrest. Essentially moral and religious in character, the prevailing discontent was also social, economic, and political. A new age was in process of coming to birth. Traditional beliefs, customs, and institutions which had served their day had become outworn and decayed, but they nevertheless retained suffi-

73

cient life to possess power of resistance, and the effort to do away with them involved long and bitter struggle.

THE PRIMARY CONTRIBUTION OF LUTHER.—Martin Luther (1483-1546) was neither the earliest of the reformers nor the most radical. He had two forerunners, both named John—Wyclif in England and Hus in Bohemia—who prepared the way for him. Erasmus, the humanist, also shared the work of preparation. But for numerous reasons, chief of which perhaps was his commanding personality, Martin Luther was the central figure of the Reformation. He was not a great theologian, and he accomplished no thorough work in the reformation of theology, but in the realm of practical life he made large contribution to the construction of the modern world.

Of Luther's ideas, fundamental and most modern was his principle of Christian liberty.[1] The thought was not original with him. He caught up and gave effective expression to an idea basic in the spirit of the dawning age, a desire and purpose widely existent—escape from the binding restrictions of authority—an effectiveness owing to the fact that he interpreted the idea in spiritual terms and the purpose as deeply and essentially religious. The Middle Ages had not only brought the individual into bondage to institutions, in religion into bondage to the Church, but had taught that the individual has no existence apart from institutions. Apart from the Church the individual possessed no significance, no worth, no goodness, and without the Church no hope of salvation. Once for all Luther broke these bonds. In his great declaration, "The just shall live by faith," Luther re-established the principle of the freedom and independence of the individual, the dignity and worth of the common man. There is a goodness apart from that which inheres in the institution; the individual man as man has worth, and significance, and standing in God's sight; he has direct access to God, and he can live without the institution.

A correlative principle, likewise asserted by Luther, is that inasmuch as the individual has the privilege and right of direct access to God, he is answerable to his own conscience, and possesses the right of judgment of the institution. Institutions must answer at the bar of individual conscience, enlightened by God, for their teachings, their rules, and their practices. Institutions, even as men, become corrupt and sinful, and they must answer to the judgment of men for their inertia, their corruption, and their sins. It is a part of the right of men to reform, even to remake, and if necessary to do away with institutions, no matter how hoary with age or how sacred they may claim to be, and to build others in their place.

Two other closely related principles Luther asserted. Not merely the priesthood, but all callings are sacred and may be made the means of serving God, even those regarded as most secular and most humble. Thus a long step was taken in bridging the gulf between the clergy and the laity. A cobbler or a merchant, dependent solely upon his faith in God and devotion to his will, may be as holy and serve as real a place in the Kingdom, as the priest or clergyman. Religion is not a matter of the priest only, it is a matter of all the people.

THE REVIVAL OF LEARNING.—In all that he did for education and for religious education Luther shared in the life and times of which he was a part. The Reformation cannot be disassociated from the Renaissance, one of the most amazing periods of intellectual awakening, educational progress, and social revolt and change, in human history. Although the Church through long centuries had cherished the hope of sufficient learning for the masses so that all might be able to comprehend the fundamental doctrines which it taught, nevertheless the agencies and means of education were lacking. But about 1425 the printing press was invented. Soon the Bible was translated into the vernaculars of the common people throughout Europe, and hundreds of thousands of copies were circulated. In 1453 Constantinople was captured by the Turks, an event which compelled the migration of Greek scholars to Italy, where their activity awakened a new interest in the classics. In Germany alone nine great universities were founded in the brief period between 1456 and 1506. The new interest in learning caused elementary schools to spring up everywhere. Colleges in the interest of the better education of the clergy were founded at several universities, among others Christ Church College at Oxford. Marking the transition from the medieval to the modern age, the period was one in which shackles which for centuries had bound the human mind were broken and a new freedom for man was made possible. Renaissance culture, however, stopped short of the development of a socially progressive theory and practice in education.

The implications of Luther's principles of Christian liberty and the right of individual judgment demanded the education of all the people, noble and common, rich and poor, a fact which

Luther was quick to see. By personal influence, by popular agitation, by writing, he promoted education. He sought to awaken the minds and the hearts of the common people by translating first the Greek New Testament and, later, the entire Bible. He wrote many tracts and letters, and published many addresses, both distinctly religious and pedagogical. Whatever his subject, references to the importance of education and to method were almost certain to be made. He was concerned for the education both of children and of adult men and women, and published two catechisms, one for children and one for adults. Luther's passion for education was shared by other Protestant reformers, and in their writings one gets at least a foreglimpse of the later emphasis upon the social purpose of education.

REVIVAL OF MORAL AND SPIRITUAL LIFE.—The Protestant Reformation involved an intellectual awakening, but in its nature was more than an educational movement. In the south of Europe the nature of the new birth was aesthetic, but in the north among the Teutonic peoples, where religion had more of moral quality in its makeup, it was strongly ethical. Although the generalization is subject to particular exceptions, for the most part it is true that the mediaeval centuries had been a long-continued period of spiritual barrenness. Over all the western world a spiritual drought had prevailed and the springs of inspiration and life had wellnigh failed. In the Reformation the drought was broken and the life of the spirit was revived. Whatever else may be said of Luther, he was pre-eminently a religious man, and his greatest influence was in the field of religious life and experience. In him the spiritual history of Paul and of Augustine was repeated. In his experience of the free grace of God through an act of personal faith in Christ is to be found the central fact of the Reformation. Nor was Luther's experience an isolated one. The floodgates of divine grace had once again been opened, and there were many others, not a few of whom remained within the Roman Catholic Church, who experienced personal salvation through union with God achieved by meditation, prayer, and faith without the mediation of priest or ecclesiastical rite.

In addition to its positive expression as a moral and religious revival the Reformation had a negative aspect in its active protest against the corruption and moral abuses of Rome.

SOCIAL AND ECONOMIC ASPECTS.—An accompaniment of the revival of learning was a profound and widespread discontent with the existing social order. So closely interwoven were the two that it is impossible to separate between them or to distinguish between cause and effect. Feudalism was breaking up, aided by geographical expansion and new inventions and discoveries, and by deep-seated conviction which had been gradually developing over a long period that existing systems both religious and social needed to be made over. The outcome was the transition from the feudal order to the commercial and industrial system commonly known as capitalism. The moral defense of the new capitalism, elaborated by Adam Smith and his successors, took as its basis the thesis that "the pecuniary self-interest of each individual if given free play, would lead to the optimum satisfaction of human wants." Free play for self-interest (*laissez faire*) was provided through such concepts and institutions as the profit motive, individual initiative, competition, private property, and private enterprise.

There were two strains in Catholic medievalism in its relation to the world's life. One is represented by the monastic ideal, the conception that the more completely one is detached from the world's life, the interests and concerns of the present evil world, the more truly Christian he is. This made of religion an ascetic, other-worldly affair, an effort to escape from the world, leaving it to its inevitable fate rather than attempting to make it over into the Kingdom of God. In contrast with this was the hope of the establishment of theocracy, the rule of God on earth, toward which no inconsiderable effort, both in teaching and in the enforcement of discipline, was made. Illustrations are to be seen in the attempts of the Church to limit feudal warfare through establishing the Truce of God, and in thoroughgoing efforts to determine fair wages, just prices (the fixed price), and right conditions of labor. The lust for unlimited gain was immoral and usury (rent or interest for the use of money) forbidden. The loaning of money was not a commercial transaction entered upon for gain, but an act of succor, a friendly means of aiding a person in distress. A moderate rate of interest was not a serious moral offense, but exorbitant interest was disreputable.

With vast, new commercial possibilities presented by the opening up of the new world, stimulated by the new emphasis upon individualism, an ethical struggle began between the old morality and the new capitalism. As R. H. Tawney clearly shows in his *Religion and the Rise of Capitalism*, this struggle centered in the doctrine of the fixed price and of usury (interest). Both new sources of supply and new markets appeared with vastly widened opportunities for buying and selling, and a correspondingly wider demand for money for use in commercial enterprises. The fixed price was subjected to new strain, and interest as friendly aid became rent and commercial capital. In this is to be seen the historical beginnings, in their modern form, of the profit motive and the method of competition.[2] The exact relationship between Protestantism and capitalism is not clear. Whatever it may have been, the fact is undeniable that Protestantism fostered a social idealism which found expression in a variety of general patterns of an ideal society, recorded in a considerable body of utopian literature. Perhaps most influential was John Valentine Andreae's *Christianopolis*, published in 1619.

NEW BIRTH OF INDIVIDUALISM.—Another element in the many-sided protest of the Reformation was revolt against the excessive solidarity of the Roman Church, in which the individual in his own right had almost no place. His salvation was guaranteed by virtue of his inclusion in a divine corporation, whose privileges he shared and by whose sacraments his spiritual life was nourished. As the Renaissance represented a turning from the search after the universal to the encouragement of individual genius in scholarship, art, and literature, so Luther asserted the supremacy in religion of the inner life of the individual. The consequent rebirth of individualism was to have profound social and religious results.

FROM AUTHORITY TO AUTHORITY.—A prominent element in Luther's teaching, as has already been noted, was his emphasis upon Christian liberty. In this also he caught up in himself and his message the spirit of his age. Inner revolt against the tyranny of the ecclesiastical system, demand for freedom of thought and escape from the trammels of traditional authority, were widespread. In his declaration of Christian liberty, a principle fundamental in his thinking, declared in such statements as: Through his faith in Christ the believer becomes a "most free lord of all and subject to no one," Luther was the spokesman of the deeper spirit of the Reformation. Luther's appeal was essentially from the Church as the seat of authority to an inner experience. Following his act of faith in throwing himself wholly upon the free grace of God in Jesus Christ he acknowledged no need for any external authority whatsoever. His own conscience enlightened by the Spirit of God was his guide and he needed no other. Subsequent events, however, compelled him to recede from this position. In the intense and long-continued controversy with his Catholic opponents he was constrained to bolster his arguments more and more by appeals to the Scriptures. Faced with the decrees of councils and of popes he turned to the Bible, appealing from the Church as authority to the authority of the Scriptures. This was natural and, doubtless, inevitable. He himself had come into his experience of spiritual freedom through a study of the Bible, particularly the Epistles of Paul, and he was thus able of his own experience to testify to the lifegiving power of the Word. Moreover, its authority was generally recognized. The claims of the Church to supreme authority, however loudly asserted, had not dispelled confidence in the Bible as divinely inspired.

Prominent in the teaching of Luther was a distinction between the word of God and the Bible. The word of God, he held, was contained in the Bible but not all of the Bible was the word of God. Plain-spoken and numerous were his assertions to this effect. It is the gospel, he maintained, that gives the Scriptures their pre-eminent value. The New Testament as a whole is superior to the Old, and the Gospel of John and some other parts of the New Testament superior to the remainder. To him the Epistle of James was an "epistle of straw" and the apocalypse of very little value whatsoever. Unfortunately, this distinction was not made by some other leaders of the Reformation and the older conception of a dead level of inspiration throughout the entire Bible displaced it. As a consequence a net result of the Reformation was to elevate the Scriptures to a height they had never before occupied and to substitute for *the authority of the Church the authority of the Bible*. The absolute Church, by a gradual process, was replaced by the absolute Book. The freedom of the individual conscience, as a basic contention of the Reformation, was obscured, and an external authority—the authority of an infallible Book instead of that of an infallible Church—was imposed as means of control of belief and conduct. This transfer of the seat of authority, while it had vital values, had also the unfortunate result of hindering emphasis upon the possibilities and need of men's realizing their vital experience of God in human relationships.

In our analysis of the Protestant Reformation should have been included, had space permitted, consideration of the significant influence of other great leaders of the period, particularly Melanchthon, Zwingli, and Calvin, each of whom made distinctive contributions, leaving permanent impress upon that composite known as Protestantism.   Of the English reformation it must suffice to say that independent religious thinking in England during the period was comparatively limited.   Great figures there were, some of them men of power, but they chiefly concerned themselves with matters of government, church organization, and worship. None of them greatly influenced Protestant teaching.

RELIGIOUS EDUCATION FOLLOWING THE REFORMATION

One thing in common shared by all the great religious leaders of the Reformation period was their recognition of education as the chief instrument for achieving their ends.   Even in such brief reference as has been made to the main currents of the life and thought of the time may be found the clue to the system of religious education developed by Protestantism following the Reformation.

THE BIBLE THE CENTER OF PROTESTANT EDUCATION.—In the medieval Church universal standards of doctrine and conduct were provided.   No need for study on the part of the individual believer was recognized; implicit obedience and unquestioning acceptance of what was handed down to him were the requirements. The meaning of life, essential beliefs, and patterns of conduct, fully and authoritatively revealed in ancient times, were held in the custody of the Church whose sole responsibility it was to pass on the completed, unchanging deposit of faith and knowledge. All this the Reformation changed.   The Holy Bible, not holy Church, now constituted the depository of divine revelation, and to it every seeker for God and the truth had free access.   Not only so; it was his responsibility to study the divine Word for himself.   The eternal verities contained therein were self-authenticating; only contact with them was needed to produce conviction of their truth.   Obviously, so great a change could not but have immense influence upon education, realization of its importance, desire for it, and influence upon its content and method.

There could be no other result in the religious schools growing out of the Reformation movement than that the Bible, its study and its interpretation, should be made central.   The classical languages were given a prominent place in higher education, since they were necessary for the study of the Scriptures and the interpretation of the early church Fathers in the original tongues. Emphasis upon training for the practical duties of life both in the home and in secular occupations was given a prominent place, but throughout the schools the study and teaching of the Bible was made the pre-eminent objective.

DOCTRINAL INSTRUCTION EMPHASIZED.—A cardinal purpose of the Reformation, the Reformers contended, was to restore sound doctrine, corrupted by the teaching of the Church. To purge religious teaching of all error and re-establish the true faith was a supreme duty. Out of this purpose came the tendency to view the Bible as a doctrinal code. As such it must have, if the teachings of the Church were to be refuted, absolute infallibility. In response to this necessity the dogma of an infallible Bible, the literal Word of God, dictated in every phrase, word, and letter, infallible not only in religion and morals but likewise in history, geology, astronomy, and every other field, was developed. The effect of this development was twofold—to obscure the idea of the Bible as a book of life, a transcript of experience, and to make of it a depository of authoritative doctrine, and, second, to establish the proof-text method of persuasion and teaching.

Zwingli, the great Swiss reformer, a contemporary of Luther, differed from him in his central emphasis. For him the Bible had its significance not chiefly, as Luther declared, in its proclamation of the free grace and love of God in Christ, but as a revelation of the divine will by which it becomes for all men the authoritative code for the regulation of human life and conduct. For Zwingli religion consisted primarily in doing the will of God as revealed in the Bible. The first division in the ranks of Protestantism came in a break between Luther and Zwingli on doctrinal grounds. Melanchthon and, more especially, Calvin carried forward the distinctive emphasis of Zwingli, formulating, systematizing, and supplementing the doctrinal teachings of both Luther and Zwingli. Melanchthon's idea of the church was that of a school for the teaching of sound doctrine. As a result of the influence of these men, with that of others less prominent, the teaching of doctrine in time became elevated to a place of equal importance with that of the Bible itself, so that three hundred years later John Henry Newman could declare, "From the age of fifteen, dogma has been the fundamental principle of my religion. I know no other religion, and cannot enter into the idea of any other religion."

The Geneva Bible (1553-1558) the first English Bible to have

Roman type, and verse divisions, which passed through one hundred and forty editions, contained numerous explanatory notes and doctrinal arguments which strongly influenced religious thought. It was the authoritative textbook of the Puritan movement, and was widely used among the early settlers of New England.

By the middle of the seventeenth century there had developed within Protestantism a system of doctrine so rigid as almost to extinguish the spark of vital religion. The Formula of Concord, first formally adopted in 1580, came to be considered, particularly in Germany, the final and perfect canon of Christian doctrine. Religion came to be regarded as consisting of little more than acceptance of doctrinal formulas in literal statement. Sermons throughout the Christian world were intensely doctrinal in content. Controversial pamphlets were widely circulated. Catechisms, both for children and adults, became the textbooks of religious instruction, and ability to recite the catechism the *sine qua non* of church membership.[3]

DEVELOPMENT OF SECTARIANISM.—Freedom of conscience and the setting up of rigid dogmas derived from an infallible Book worked at cross purposes. Doctrinal differences were the inevitable result. The authority of the Pope, exercised through an infallible Church, held discordant elements together in one institution.[4] The authority of the Bible operating through the interpretations of individuals, each claiming full freedom of conscience, stimulated the formation of sectarian groups. The precedent of schism once established as between Protestantism and Rome, divisions within Protestantism were easy. As a result, within a generation Protestantism was divided into numerous sects, each basing its separate existence upon some difference of doctrine regarded as essential. Political and economic theories and conditions in many cases were also influential, and questions of organization and government likewise were made matters of controversy. The principal groups were the Lutherans, the Calvinists, and the Anglicans, though the Zwinglians, the Socinians, and the Anabaptists were important divisions, each in turn with numerous subdivisions. Each group had its own creed, in most cases minutely elaborated, claiming for itself all the authority of the Scriptures. Melanchthon's view of the supreme duty of the Church came generally to prevail, and as a consequence during the latter half of the sixteenth and the whole of the seventeenth century the doctrinal emphasis predominated in religious education. So intense was the spirit of controversy that education in both higher and lower schools came to define its aim in terms of teaching the tenets of a particular sect. In time doctrinal emphases crystallized into institutions, resulting in our modern denominations. Most, though not all of them, were originally organized around certain specific doctrinal emphases which to the founders seemed of pre-eminent importance. In their development each was influenced by the political forms and economic ideas and conditions prevailing within its environment.

There were both gains and losses in this process of the growth of sects within Protestantism. The conflict of sects prevented the principle of freedom from being stifled. No one church developed sufficient prestige and power to exercise absolutist control such as Rome had long maintained. There were other influences, as we shall see, affecting the growth of liberty in the modern world, but the multiplicity of divisions within Protestantism, re-enforcing the principle of freedom of conscience, gave it opportunity of continuing life and room within which to breathe and grow. Over against this gain is to be set the fact that a major defect and a serious weakness of divided Protestantism resulted from concern with doctrinal controversies. Interest and attention were so centered upon dogma and petty differences of theological belief and practice that basic social and economic evils affecting religious and moral life and character were lost sight of. Through neglect the churches lost their opportunity in part to determine and largely to mold the forces shaping the life of society, and their public influence in more recent times has steadily declined.

DEVELOPMENT OF THE CAPITALISTIC ETHIC.—We have seen how the Protestant emphasis upon the individual fostered the early development of the profit economy.[5] The need remains of pointing out how later developments aided the growth of the capitalistic ethic.

Whatever the initial relationship may have been, it is undeniable that Protestantism early came to the support of the rapidly developing economic system. The new order based upon credit and interest as rent, with private profit as its actuating motive and competition as its method, gradually overcame the ethical stigma attached to usury by religion, and banished by neglect the ethical emphasis upon a fixed price. Invoking the medieval principle of the divine sanction of the natural order, Protestantism took its stand within the new system, pronounced the blessing of God upon it, and prepared to utilize its fruits for its own advantage. The ground was laid for the fiction which now curses society—the dogma of capitalism as a feature of a natural order to which sanctity attaches by virtue of its existing by the will and approval of God. A new constellation of Christian virtues gradually arose. Labor was invested with new dignity. Self-support, industry, and thrift became prime duties to God. The making of money and the accumulation of wealth became highly laudable. The "calling" of the Christian came to be interpreted as his work, or trade, or business, the purpose for which he existed, the means by which he is to glorify God. The extent of pecuniary gain came to be regarded as the measure of success. The pursuit of riches, once feared as the deadly enemy of religious life, even came to be regarded as the ally of religion. Diligence, frugality, and other qualities required for success in the economic struggle became the foundation for Christian living, the elements of Christian character. The Church, particularly the Church of England, took upon itself as a duty the indoctrination of the masses with the ideas of obedience, submission, and even subservience to the rich and the wellborn as Christian virtues. Under these circumstances it is not strange that Protestantism became predominantly the religion of the trading and the business classes.

The picture is not wholly consistent. Protestantism, without doubt, by its individualism fostered the growth of *laissez faire* capitalism. But Protestantism also had a strongly subjective element. Luther repudiated that conception of the Christian life which held the more completely one detached himself from the interests and concerns of this present world the more Christian he thereby became. But at the same time he conceived of salvation almost wholly in terms of the inner life, a subjective experience unconnected with social relationships.[6] This idea tended to restrict religion and to encourage the view that Christian principles and ideals are apart from the social relations of mankind, unconcerned with them, and suffer contamination and debasement by being mixed with secular affairs. From this tendency came that neglect and "absence of the sense of responsibility for the social order which has from the beginning maimed and distorted Protestant Christianity."[7] From the same source came the justification of the modern capitalist in his oft-reiterated charge, when in the name of religion unethical and antisocial practices are condemned, that religion has nothing to do with and should be kept uncontaminated by business and politics.

The distinctive emphases pointed out in the preceding paragraphs are reflected in the corporate life and teaching of denominations. The Calvinistic and Puritan churches, living at peace with capitalism, attempting only to curb its excesses, have tended to place their emphasis in religious education upon the moral virtues which the system has extolled. German Protestantism and the Lutheran churches have interpreted religion and religious practice predominantly in terms of a mystical quietism "while the nationalistic state and the capitalistic system have been allowed to develop in the arrogant consciousness of freedom from all ethical and religious restraint."[8]

Nor was eighteenth-century Methodism deeply concerned with broad ethical and social interests. In accord with the Moravian emphasis, salvation was conceived primarily in terms of a subjective experience, from which right social relations were expected to develop as a matter of course. Although John Wesley and other Methodist leaders imposed upon themselves a discipline which in its rigor reflected an austere social conscience, and although they were deeply concerned about the plight of the poor, apparently they were more impressed by the vices and irreligion of the poverty-stricken multitudes than by the social oppression and injustice responsible for the conditions which contributed to their evil ways. Drunkenness, swearing, Sabbath-breaking and the sins of the flesh were roundly condemned by the early Methodist preachers, and their fervent evangelism was the means of converting vast numbers to newness of life; but one searches in vain for any clear recognition of the social effects of the pagan industrialism of Wesley's day or for indictment of the selfishness, greed, and injustice which condemned the victims of the factory system to lives of grinding poverty lived in hovels while the owners built their palaces and swollen fortunes upon the miseries of the poor.[9]

That dynamic forces for social reform were generated in the Evangelical Revival is a fact amply attested by history. Not only did the movement give rise to determined effort, as the historian John Richard Green has said, "to remedy the guilt, the ignorance, the physical suffering, the social degradation of the profligate and the poor"; it also inspired movements of social reform whose fruition in legislation are only now being realized. But the evangelicals stopped short of attaining a philosophy of the social order which controverted the basic principles and the motivation of the rapidly developing *laissez faire* economy.

The net result of this long development, thus hastily sketched, was a Protestant ethic which accepted the economic order built upon the ruins of feudalism as something "given"; a fixed part of the created universe, to whose evils it was necessary to be resigned. True, Wesley roundly condemned the slave trade, and later, certain vigorous reform movements that characterized the early nineteenth century were led chiefly by evangelicals, but for the most part Protestant religion taught that one should be content with his lot, ordained of God, suffering hardship as a discipline which develops the graces of resignation, patience, meekness, and inner strength. Thus, once again, in modern times as under the rule of Rome, in Constantinople, and in medieval Europe, organized Christianity permitted itself to be "used by the dominant culture as the sanctifier of the secular system,"[10] an order essentially pagan and unchristian.

RELIGION AS EXPERIENCE.—While Melanchthon, Zwingli, and Calvin did not lose Luther's conception of religion as vital and experimental, the net effect of their influence was to bring into prominence the conception that religion is belief; the gospel, a system of truths intellectually apprehended. The church, they contended, is composed "of those who hold pure doctrine and agree to it."[11] But the conception of religion as personal experience was to find other exponents. Some of these appeared before the end of the sixteenth century, and many others in the seventeenth, eighteenth, and nineteenth centuries.

To infer that Luther's vital experience of religion and his gospel of the free, forgiving love of God in Christ were unknown in the medieval Church is a mistake. Both long before and in the decades following Luther there were many plain people who by inner experience knew and rejoiced in Paul's secret of the life hid with Christ in God. But in general by the close of the Thirty Years' War religion in Protestant Germany had suffered serious decline. Emphasis upon formal orthodoxy, the rigidity and barrenness of the doctrinal formulas, the absorption of leaders of the churches in doctrinal controversy had again brought on a period of spiritual sterility. That religion again came alive was due in no small measure to Philip Jacob Spener (1633-1705). As a substitute for doctrinal controversy, which he decried as sinful, he exalted the life of simple trust and piety, the devotional study of the Bible and prayer, and the exemplification of the spirit of Christianity in mutual love and service. The all-important thing he held to be the transformation of character through vital union with Christ. By vitalizing faith, giving prominence to the will and the emotions rather than the intellect, and centering emphasis upon religious experience, pietism, as it came to be known, became a dominant force in German religious life and was immensely influential in religious education, particularly elementary education, as well as in the field of social service.

While in Germany Spener was exercising his vitalizing influence, in England George Fox was insisting that religion is not primarily concerned with creeds and institutions but is an experience of God within the soul—a spirit, an inner light, which from its center within flows outward. From the time of George Fox, the Quakers, though never a numerous folk, through their quiet influence have imparted to personal and social life a beauty, a sanctity, and a peace out of all proportion to the size of their movement.

From German pietism a line of direct connection may be traced through the Moravians to the Evangelical Revival of the eighteenth century in which John Wesley (1703-1791) was the most conspicuous and influential leader. If religion in seventeenth-century Europe was in need of inner renewal, that of eighteenth-century England was in even worse plight. According to competent testimony the depth of apathy and moral degradation to which organized religion had sunk beggars imagination. But a leader was in preparation who through a work of evangelism extending over fifty years was to transform the religious life of England.

The similarity between the turning point in Luther's religious life and that of John Wesley is striking. Both had for years lived lives of exceptional piety and devoutness. Both had long sought in vain for inner peace. Both came into an experience of the saving grace of God through a simple act of faith in Christ. In both instances this experience was the beginning of an extraordinary career. Wesley's emphasis upon personal experience as the heart of religion not only vitalized the religious life of England; his insistence upon love and service to others as the badge of the sincerity of Christian profession introduced a new era of humanitarian feeling and practical social service, and effectively put an end to the formalism and barren rationalism of the religious education of the eighteenth century.

The Evangelical Revival in England was paralleled by the great awakening—the Colonial awakening and the great revival in the newer regions, of America. In the New World, as in Great

Britain, immorality and irreligion had become widely prevalent. A barren intellectualism and a growing formalism characterized the life of the churches. Church membership was at such a low ebb that not more than one person in twenty, it has been estimated, was enrolled as a member of any church. Jonathan Edwards (1703-1758), a man of great intellectual power, became the leader of a revival which, beginning in New England, did not stop until there was hardly a town or village or backwoods community anywhere but had felt some spiritual quickening.

RESULTANT PROTESTANT AIM.—As the result of the historical development thus briefly traced in outline there came into existence within early Protestantism a fourfold aim destined to control the religious education of the Protestant churches for three hundred years. In some denominations, and in some local churches of all denominations, this fourfold aim is still the controlling factor. In summary form this aim may be thus stated:

To teach:

    (1) the Bible, as the authoritative Word (truth) of God;

    (2) the Christian doctrine, the truth of the Bible in systematized form;

    (3) The distinctive doctrinal emphases of a particular denomination;

    (4) religion as a personal inner experience of the saving grace of God through faith in Jesus Christ.

The separate streams of influence from which this composite aim came have never become completely merged. Groups, and individuals within groups, tend to magnify some one element at the expense of the others. The fourth element is likely to be held as something separate and apart from the other three. Out of such separation springs the oft-asked question, "Can religion be taught?" If religion be considered to be a direct and immediate seizure of the person by God, apart from the normal processes of the mind, it cannot be thought of as mediated by study and teaching of the Bible and Christian doctrine.

Statements by ministers and lay leaders in church schools, of their objectives as teachers, afford abundant substantiation of the aim of religious teaching as stated. A few of many quotations recently gathered may be given. A young woman, teacher of a young women's class: "To me religious education means the knowledge I obtain from studying the Bible and other religious literature. My purpose is to instruct my class in the Bible teachings and apply them to life." An elderly layman, teacher of a class of men: "My aim as a teacher is to present the Bible as authority for what we should believe and for everyday living. My objective is to combat evil and to promote righteousness." Young minister, college and seminary graduate, teacher of men's class: "Adults must be taught the content of the Christian faith. The historical facts of our faith and the teachings of the Bible must be taught. In addition, religious education involves living—living like Christ. Christian attitudes must be developed and unchristian attitudes reformed."

MODIFYING INFLUENCES IN MODERN TIMES

The traditional aim of religious education has been profoundly modified by influences that have entered into the making of the modern world.

From the period of the Reformation education under State and private auspices, apart from the churches, has developed rapidly. General education (somewhat inaptly termed secular education in contradistinction to religious, or church, education) came into being and began to gather to itself educational interest and effort. Developmental changes in general education have likewise influenced both aim and content of religious education. At the same time it must be said that the Christian religion has exercised a profound influence upon the development of modern general education. Indeed, it is not too much to say that the Christian religion has been the fountain from which have flowed most of the streams which have vitalized and enriched modern education. The ideal of universal education, for example, with its resulting demand for the founding and extension of free schools, was integral to the Christian gospel. With the separation of Church and State, secular schools grew apace; progress in secular education outstripped religious education, and, particularly during the past one hundred years, religious education has received from secular education contributions which have influenced it both in theory and in method. The interdependence of these two, secular and religious education, has been overlooked by many religious leaders.

The Reformation leaders all were citizens of the medieval world of thought. Of modern philosophy, science, history, and politics they knew little, and by them they were influenced not at all.   To them Christianity was wholly a supernatural religion. They believed in the depravity and helplessness of human nature and that men could be saved only by a miraculous salvation.   The effect of these two sets of facts was to make the Protestant Reformation essentially medieval in its spirit and interest.   But a new era had dawned.   The world was being remade, and the influences and forces which were accomplishing the remaking were bound to make themselves felt within Christianity.

NATURALISM, AND ITS ALLIES.—Among the more or less distinct movements that have had a basic part in the making of the modern world there are three which have much in common—humanism, naturalism, and rationalism.   Each has a long history.

Humanism as a movement of thought definitely emerging in the fifteenth century was a revolt against intellectual and ecclesiastical authority in behalf of centering interest in men, their affairs and their welfare, as opposed to abstract thought and the supernatural.   It gave itself to the rediscovery and study of the ancient classics.   Its historical expression is known as the Renaissance.   It has had a direct relation with every phase of modern thought and life—intellectual, scientific, and social.   In humanism, with its reaction against a sterile, rigid intellectualism, and its appeal to the emotions, natural impulses, and social fellowship of human nature, the humanity of men experienced a new birth.

From the earliest times a tendency has been manifested by men to ignore all law save that of their own unbridled instincts and impulses, to exalt the natural and the material, to identify the highest values with primitive nature, and to give rein without restraint to their passions and unregulated desires.   This tendency, identified as naturalism, may be more or less clearly traced as a distinct movement through a long course, paralleling humanism. In its effect upon education it became strongly influential in the eighteenth century as a rebellion against what it declared to be the ignorance and superstition of religious thought, the hypocrisy in morals, and the despotism and tyranny of Church and State. The movement found its most effective exponent in Rousseau (1712-1778), through whose influence was caused perhaps the most thoroughgoing revolution in thought and practice ever experienced by education.   Lawless, wayward, sensual, irresponsible, filled with contradictions, Rousseau at forty became possessed with an idea that "was to revolutionize the social structure of his adopted country . . . modify profoundly that of many others; [and] . . .

applied to education . . . to create a new epoch. . . . Human happiness and human welfare are the natural rights of every individual, not the special possession of a favored class; legitimate social organization and education exist but to bring about the realization of . . . [these ends]."[12] Against the contention of both education and religion that human nature is essentially bad, the purpose of education and religious training to eradicate original nature with all of its impulses and desires, Rousseau held that human nature unmodified by culture is innately good; whatever is natural is right; education is a development from within not an imposition from without; an expansion of natural powers not the acquisition of information; life itself, not a preparation for a future life. Education is to be received from nature, from men, and from things through fearless and intimate contact with animals, plants, and physical forces of all kinds. The key to effective educational method is the discovery and stimulus of interest. Education begins in infancy and continues throughout life. Rousseau's influence was not an unmixed good, but it developed a new faith in man, infused a new spirit in society, and re-established a basis for religion in man's nature.

Rationalism, in common with humanism and naturalism, emphasized the good of man, not the glory of God, as the highest end of life. The essentials of progress, it held, are freedom of thought, liberty of conscience, and recognition of the sufficiency of reason for the conduct of life. It undertook to destroy the absolutism over thought and the tyranny over action exercised by institutions, especially the Church. Oppressed by religious intolerance, bigotry, and sectarian strife, those rationalists who did not turn against all religion sought to substitute for rigid theologies and elaborate rituals Christ's simple gospel of love for God and man, and the spirit of universal good will as a common principle of conduct.

MODERN SCIENCE.—The Renaissance stood for two great discoveries—the rediscovery of the meaning and worth of this present world and the rediscovery of the dignity and worth of human nature. Out of the new interest in nature grew modern science. Francis Bacon (1561-1626), whose whole interest centered in the phenomena, forces, and processes of nature was the forerunner of the scientists. The scientific spirit began to be embodied in the universities in the sixteenth century, and before the end of that century the natural sciences began to appear in the program of university studies.   Astronomy was first listed in the program of Harvard in 1642.   The development of the natural sciences produced three results of profound significance and influence upon all education: the building up of vast bodies of new and exact knowledge; the gradual development of a new attitude toward the facts of life (the scientific attitude); and the gradual elaboration of a new method (the scientific method).

The scientific method found early exemplification in the labors of Copernicus (1473-1543), who was excommunicated by the Church; Galileo, Kepler, and Newton.   Through these devoted apostles of science and many who followed after them, the process of observation, analysis, experimentation in verification, and accurate recording of verified findings, became a definite, recognized method.

In the area of religion science forced a re-examination of reasons for all religious beliefs and of the processes by which they had been arrived at.   For the attitude of passive trust in authority and unquestioning faith in its dogmas science substituted the spirit of critical inquiry.   The historic creeds, the institutions of religion, and finally the Bible itself were subjected to the most thoroughgoing, exact, and critical examination, analysis, and evaluation of which the human mind is capable.   Not only the scientific attitude, but the scientific method also, after justifying themselves in the laboratories of the natural sciences have found more and more welcome entrance into the area of religious education.

Another offspring of science, one which has placed "the whole educational enterprise in a new perspective," is the developmental view of life.   The science of biology gave birth to the theory of evolution as a hypothesis in explanation of the origin and development of life.   Geology offered verification in opening to all the record of organic changes written in the fossil remains embedded in the rocks, and the parallel record of successive changes in the earth's structure.   Thus a revolutionary force, the idea of progress, was introduced into all education.   The Middle Ages believed implicitly in a static universe—as things are, so have they always been, and so will they always continue.   The world is in a sad and deplorable plight, and it will never be any better.   Only in heaven will ideal conditions be realized.   To be impatient with conditions of evil and suffering, or to revolt against them, is to exhibit lack of trust in God.   From progress in the realm of nature to the idea of progress in human relations is an easy transition which soon began

to be made. Moreover, scientific investigation revealed that man
had gradually risen from a state of primitive animalism to a higher
level of culture, from ignorance and barbarism to enlightenment
and a civilized state. Offering rude shock to traditional religious
dogmas, the developmental theory was stubbornly resisted by an
influential element of official Christianity. But from its earliest
promulgation there were not lacking prophetic souls who discerned in the new scientific view a new hope. If man is so largely
formed by his environment, let the forces of religion undertake to
remake environment. Gradually hope developed into conviction
that the reconstruction of society in accord with the ethical ideals
of religion is both possible and imperative.

The application in education of the idea of development owes
much to Rousseau, Pestalozzi, and Froebel. For Pestalozzi, as for
Rousseau, education is the unfolding of the natural powers with
this addition, that his theory is undergirded by a deeply religious
view of nature and of human nature. Pestalozzi emphasized that
the "inner indestructible impulse toward development" is im-
planted by the Creator for religious ends. A similar view was held
by Froebel who, in his turn, added an emphasis upon expression,
especially through play, as a means of more complete development.

What these leaders did for education and for religious education was for the latter, much later, immensely aided and supplemented by the theologian Horace Bushnell, who in 1847 wrote
his epoch-making book *Christian Nurture,* by means of which the
implications of Jesus' teaching concerning the child and child
nature were brought with compelling power to the attention of
the Church. Previously popular theological thought had included
no adequate theoretical basis for religious education as development. Thanks to Bushnell, and others who followed after him,
such a basis now exists.

The brevity of our treatment permits only a word on the
modifying influence of psychology on education. Such brief mention at this point of our discussion is partially justified by the fact
that its influence pertains more to educational method than to
aim and content. A basic contribution is its insistence that education is a development, an organic growth, a natural process of
unfolding of the capacities of human nature, an emphasis closely
akin to those of natural science which we have just considered.
Largely due to the influence of psychology is the concept of education as the natural, progressive, harmonious development of all

the powers and capacities—physical, mental, and moral—of the individual. From psychology thus comes a wholesome corrective to a too materialistic conception of progress, re-enforcing the contention of religion—the insistence that for the cure of degradation something more than the improvement of material conditions, important as this is, is necessary. If men are to be lifted to a higher level of living, their intellectual and moral poverty and depravity must be cured, and for this cure education and religion both are necessary.

EDUCATION AS DISCIPLINE, KNOWLEDGE AND INSTRUCTION.—The Protestant Reformation re-enforced by other influences and agencies, some of which we have reviewed, effectively undermined authority and discipline, the twin forces which had ruled the human spirit for a thousand years. But these age-old forces refused to give way. The new influences were compelled to make their way against stubborn resistance, and to this resistance both religion and education contributed.

The content of the traditional education, subjected to fierce attack from the new quarters, was defended both by Protestants and Catholics as valuable for discipline. The formulation of a philosophy of education that would justify the authoritarian and disciplinary content and method was undertaken by John Locke (1632-1704). He reverted to the conception that original nature must be thwarted at every point, all natural desires denied. The best education, he insisted, is that which trains, and disciplines, and fortifies the mind. The materials of education should be selected on the basis of their value in forming the mind, disciplining the desires, and bringing all the elements of the nature under control. This theory of education as discipline, the training of the intellect, teaching to think, was destined to dominate education until the beginning of the twentieth century. The disciplinary conception of education received support from religious leaders, who held on to the conception of human nature as evil, whose impulses and desires required discipline.

Closely allied to the disciplinary conception is that of education as instruction, a process of imparting knowledge. The gaining of knowledge is, of course, the oldest of all conceptions of education, as old as the beginnings of human life on the earth—did not the first man look upon the tree of knowledge as good, its fruit something to be desired? The formulation of the theory in modern times owes much to Johann Friedrich Herbart (1776-

1841), who rejected entirely the faculty psychology on which the disciplinary conception was chiefly based. The mind is to be formed, declared Herbart, through the proper presentation of subject matter. Thus subject matter, systematized bodies of knowledge, became central in the educational process, and educational method the pattern by which the knowledge may be most effectively presented.

Herbart's emphasis was grist for the mill of science, which exists for the sake of acquiring knowledge. Its tendency has been to identify education with instruction. As a result the knowledge aim in all education has had immense re-enforcement during the past three quarters of a century from the scientific movement. The natural sciences have not only added tremendously to the store of human knowledge; they have accentuated the importance of acquiring knowledge both for its own sake and as a means of increasing one's powers of achievement.

Throughout the nineteenth century in general education the primary emphasis was placed upon subject matter. In fact, this conception still may be said to hold the field, although since the turn of the century its rule has been strenuously contended. Education popularly even yet is identified with instruction; its aim the impartation of knowledge. In religious education the conception re-enforces the traditional objective of teaching the Bible and religious doctrines. The effect of the conception, whether in general education or in religious education, is to put education under bondage to tradition, re-enforce the authoritarian emphasis, and develop uncritical acquiescence in the *status quo*.[13]

FREEDOM AND DEMOCRACY.—Luther's principle of Christian liberty, though stifled in the heavy air of a later period and bound with the graveclothes of authority and tradition, refused to die. In the free air and wide open spaces of a new continent it was to find the breath of life and an environment in which it could live and grow. It gave form and strength to the American experiment in popular government, even as earlier it had nourished the aspiration for political freedom of the German princes, the Ironsides of Cromwell, and the ideals that came to partial expression in the French Revolution. Freedom, asserted the Declaration of Independence, is the natural right, the inalienable inheritance of every man.

The ideas of freedom and democracy out of which our American institutions grew, although primarily concerned with the individual, also possessed social content. Not only the individual, but all individuals have right to equal opportunity and freedom of personal choice and action. The conviction prevailed that free, unhampered personal initiative and action contributed not only to individual development and success, but also to social welfare and progress. During the early American centuries this conviction was substantiated by prevailing conditions, and apparently by outcomes. The wide expanse of unoccupied soil and unlimited natural resources, together with the scattered population, made the economic struggle not a battle between individuals but a contest with natural forces. Victory in the struggle was not merely individual success; it had social significance in that it helped to meet social needs and contributed to community welfare.

The educational implications of the concepts of freedom and democracy very slowly came to be realized. Some, in fact, never have come to popular acceptance. Not until the aggressive missionary labors of Horace Mann (1796-1859) in behalf of free schools *for* all the people controlled *by* all the people did the principle of universal education win general acceptance. Only much more recently has the conception won wide acceptance that the end of education is not merely the gaining of information and attainment of skills but a free personality with fully developed powers at home in its world. Only within recent decades have widespread efforts been made in the schools to apply such principles as these: determine procedures and choose subject matter on the basis of interest and needs for growth; provide conditions favorable for spontaneous unfolding and development instead of imposing ready-made ideas and rules; persons learn by doing, there is no impression without expression; utilize, do not repress, curiosity and imagination and natural impulses to play and to create.

Practice in education lags from two to three decades behind theory. As the nineteenth century drew to its close, the aim of education most generally accepted among educators devoted to the ideals of freedom and democracy was individualistic; the complete and harmonious development of all the powers of the individual, physical, intellectual, moral. About the turn of the century evidence of a significant change began to appear. Latent social implications, long neglected, began to be developed. This requires us again to retrace our steps, that we may take note of certain other significant movements.

THE INDUSTRIAL REVOLUTION.—Beginning about 1750 a revolution began which in its direct immediate effects upon personal and social life dwarfed all the influences of religion and philosophy, science and politics. Throughout the entire Western world within a few short decades the industrial revolution changed the ways of life of tens of millions of human beings. It tremendously accentuated and intensified the drive for profit and concentrated it upon manufacturing with its accompanying exploitation of human beings. By destruction of the handcrafts and the crowding out of cottage industries it changed both the habitat and the mode of living of multitudes. Vast populations were quickly shifted from rural communities, where they had lived in comparative isolation, in close contact with nature and the soil, to crowded, miserable, ugly, unsanitary factory settlements.[14] The burden of human suffering involved in the change was colossal, but this physical element was relatively insignificant in comparison with the deeper effects upon the moral, mental, and spiritual life of vast numbers of persons. In many ways the task of religious education was made more complex and difficult.

Under the Roman rule the majority of the population were slaves. When the empire was broken up the institution of slavery was destroyed. But freedom was not achieved and the masses, as serfs, continued to live under the dominance of the lords. Throughout the Middle Ages the slave mentality continued, the vassals thinking of themselves as inferior to their masters who asserted themselves as superior. With the Renaissance and the Reformation, serfdom was compelled to give way, and under the influence of ideas and forces some of which we have described the emancipation of humanity appeared to be drawing near. But again before physical, intellectual, and spiritual freedom was fully achieved the coming of the industrial age reforged the chains and serfdom was replaced by wage-slavery, a condition involving not only serious material disabilities but also the perpetuation of slave mentality and a subject class. Thus the evil intellectual and spiritual inheritance of slavery was continued.[15]

BIRTH AND GROWTH OF THE SOCIAL SCIENCES.—Within the life and thought of the eighteenth century partly as a result of the earlier emphasis of humanism upon the worth of man, there were deep and strong influences inculcating human sympathy, kindness, and cooperation. The evangelicals, although they stressed other-worldly ideas and ideals, also placed much emphasis upon the Christian requirement of love and service of one's fellow men.

A new era of humanitarianism was begun and the ground was laid for the modern social movement.

It was extremely fortunate that this development preceded the industrial revolution, since it made more easily possible a realization of the glaring inconsistency between the inhumanity of the factory system with its accompanying commercial exploitation and the ideals of the gospel. When conditions were at their worst in England Charles Kingsley, F. D. Maurice, Thomas Hughes, and others reasserted with earnestness and power and applied to contemporary conditions, the great social teachings of the prophets and Jesus. The influence of their emphasis upon a social interpretation of the gospel and on the obligation of social service ever since has been increasingly felt, even more in America than in England.

From another quarter came an influence of a different kind. F. D. Maurice and other Christian socialists were convinced that the ruling class could be so impressed with their social duty and responsibility and so imbued with the principles of equality and cooperation that they would voluntarily relinquish privilege and power and remake the private profit system in terms of social justice and of equal rights and privileges; but in Germany Karl Marx re-enforced his basic doctrine of economic determinism by the thesis that the holders of privilege would never voluntarily relinquish power; that if a new order is ever to be established it must come by the exercise of force by the working class.[16] His philosophy and teachings have been profoundly influential and chiefly instrumental in the development of the class struggle.

Just as the new, profound interest in nature of the age of the Renaissance gave birth to modern science, the new, deep interest in human life resulted in the emergence of the social sciences. The term "sociology" was first used about 1830. It was not until after the middle of the nineteenth century that the social sciences (sociology; politics; political economy) made an acknowledged place for themselves in the program of studies of the colleges. From that time on the social concept of education has been increasingly influential. To this fact is very largely due the widening social vision and the deepening social conviction within religious education.

Traditionally, education has been thought of as the process of the development of the individual. This view has been re-enforced by psychology, which has tended to center attention upon the development of the mind and has conceived method as school-room procedure. Sociology, in contrast, conceives education primarily as the process of developing the community and society as a whole. It centers attention upon social needs, social activities and relationships, and social structure. Education, from the point of view of social science, is concerned with the individual, not with the individual in isolation, but with the individual in his relationships with other individuals, with the individual as a member of society; and with the group. There are no isolated individuals complete in themselves. Personality is a social product. The educated man is the man who is prepared to live his life as an intelligent and effective member of society. The virtuous man is the man whose relationships with other men exhibit the qualities of justice, righteousness, and truthfulness.

From defining the aim of education in terms of the individual, more and more from the beginning of the twentieth century the tendency among educators has been to stress social aims and to take account of social forces and factors. The preparation of persons to participate creatively in the reconstruction of a constantly changing society has received increasing attention. In increasing measure the school itself has been viewed as a form of community life in which pupils learn through participation, and both teaching method and discipline have been redefined in the light of this conception.

HISTORICAL METHOD IN BIBLE STUDY.—During the centuries since the Protestant Reformation significant changes have taken place in conceptions of the Bible and in methods regarded as valid in its interpretation and teaching. These changes have registered far-reaching effect upon religious education.

Although Luther differentiated between various books of the Bible as to religious value and authoritativeness, the popular conception coming down from medieval times was that one level of inspiration prevailed throughout the entire Bible. The net effect of the Reformation was to fasten upon the Protestant churches the dogma of infallibility of the Bible as a whole and the method of literal interpretation. The truth of any statement whatsoever could be established or disproved by the citation of a miscellaneous assortment of proof-texts from books of the Old and New Testaments.

In 1680 a French priest, Simon, called attention to parallel accounts of the Creation in Genesis and to the further fact that in Genesis various events are described in different words.   He asserted that these facts suggest different authors whose writings Moses had pieced together.   This was the beginning of the long process of the modern criticism of the Bible, a process participated in by many French, German, British, and American scholars.   As a result it became evident that much which had been believed and taught as authoritative truth contained an admixture of the transient and hypothetical, and that certain traditional doctrines had elements that could be traced to non-Hebrew and non-Christian origins.   The emphasis has shifted from the teaching of the Bible predominantly as doctrine, to a search for and teaching of the historical facts.   Increasingly the Old Testament has come to be regarded as a record of the spiritual history of the Hebrew people, and the Bible as a whole as a book of life, a transcript of moral and religious experience, of unique and transcendent value.

NEW EMPHASIS UPON THE KINGDOM OF GOD.—Both the growth of the social conception of education, with its emphasis upon the great society, and the historical study of the Bible, contributed to an emphasis upon the concept of the Kingdom of God as a pattern of society to be realized upon the earth.

A prominent element in the Reformation was an insistence upon the initiative and the sovereignty of God, an emphasis which was expressed in strongest terms by Calvin.   This reaffirmation of God's sovereignty carried with it the renewal of faith in the establishment of the Kingdom of God, not, however, as something to be realized by man's effort but, rather, the reign of God which having been established from eternity needed only to be recognized and obeyed.

In the Great Awakening and the succeeding period of widespread revival this Reformation emphasis again became prominent.   The preachers of the revival movement fervently exhorted men and women to seek entrance to the Kingdom, by which they meant submission to the rule of God in their lives.   Closely allied to this emphasis was that of the reign of Christ, as King, upon the earth.   So prominent a part of their preaching did this come to be that the hope and expectation of the millennial reign became predominant in the thought of multitudes of church members.

From about 1890 attention began to be directed to the fact that the Kingdom of God, as a ruling concept in the thought and teaching of Jesus, may be interpreted as meaning the will of God applied to and expressed in the total life of man, the development of a social order that in its motive, its human relationships and activities, and its institutions is an expression of the principles and ideals of the gospel. This awakening has had significant effects upon religious education; the Church is conceived less as an end in itself, and more as a means of bringing in the Kingdom of God; the individualism of Protestantism with its primary concern for the saving of the soul has been modified by a growing concern for a truly Christian social order and for the preparation of persons for creative participation in the reconstruction of society.

RELIGIOUS EDUCATION MOVEMENT.—As a result of certain of the influences described above, particularly the growing emphasis within organized religion upon education and educational method; the development of psychology and within the general field the emergence of educational psychology, the psychology of religion, and scientific child study, there came into existence at the beginning of the present century what is known in a specific sense as "religious education" and "the religious-education movement." Ministers and lay teachers within the churches began to re-examine objectives, materials, and methods in the light of the new knowledge of human nature, especially child interests and needs, of the laws of learning, and of social objectives. Graded lessons began to appear; the Religious Education Association was organized; and courses in religious education began to be offered in theological seminaries and in denominational colleges.

OUR COMPLEX HERITAGE

As a result of the historical process, which we have traced in bare outline, conceptions of the aims of adult religious education vary widely within the Protestant churches.[17] No one of our existing denominations can be said to present in its educational program a clear-cut, generally understood, and accepted aim. Within the teaching procedures of each of the larger Protestant bodies a variety of aims more or less contradictory will be found to be represented.

CONTRASTING EMPHASES.—Protestant religious adult education is a conglomerate. Within the whole, however, it is possible to distinguish two more or less distinct strains, or lines of emphasis, broadly representing streams of influence that have come down through the Christian centuries. These may be distinguished in outline as follows:

1. Religion, from the standpoint of content, is thought of primarily as formulated belief, a systematized body of doctrine.

a. The Bible, consisting of revealed truth, is the fountain head of religious teaching.

b. Faith is belief, the acceptance on divine authority of the truth contained in the Bible and in creeds based on the Bible.

2. Religion, from the standpoint of objective, is the supernatural salvation of the individual.

3. The Church is a divinely founded institution; authoritative in its form, structure, sacraments, and doctrines.

4. Education is instruction: education of the child, preparation for adult life; education of the adult, preparation for heaven.

Learning is a storage process by which the individual stores up facts, knowledge, and skills for future use.

5. Religious education is an intellectualistic process; instruction in the Bible, Christian doctrine, and other important subjects.

6. Training is a process of indoctrination; from the standpoint of the teacher, instruction; from the standpoint of the pupil, memorization and drill.

7. Method is a formal procedure

---

1. Religion, from the standpoint of content, is thought of primarily as experience, a way of living, a life of fellowship.

a. The Bible, containing a record of the development of the Hebrew and Christian religions, is essentially a transcript of religious experience.

b. Faith is personal response—will and action in accord with the experience of God of the individual and the race.

2. Religion, from the standpoint of objective, is life in fellowship with God and men expressing itself in love and service; the building of the Christian social order.

3. The Church is a fellowship, a voluntary association of persons seeking to aid one another in living the life of Christian faith and service.

4. Education is the living of life on ever higher levels, the continuous reconstructing of experience in terms of higher values.

Learning is the interpretation and enrichment of experience.

5. Religious education is the continuous reconstituting of experience in terms of the ideals and values of the Christian religion.

6. Training is activity; from the standpoint of the teacher, guided activity in the light of experience; from the standpoint of the pupil, creative activity in the light of experience.

7. Method is all procedures by

consisting of well-defined steps—the five formal steps of Herbart.

8. The objective of religious education is a religiously educated person—one who is inculcated with authoritative doctrines and imbued with the sanctity of established religious institutions.

which the learner enriches and reconstitutes his experience; from the standpoint of the teacher, it is a procedure of guidance.

8. The objective of religious education is the fully developed and enriched person living the more abundant life; and the development of a social order which makes possible the abundant life for all.

These contrasting emphases, it is to be noted, are not at all points mutually exclusive. At some points they overlap and are interwoven. Current religious education at its best embodies in its aim vital elements of both strains and avoids the exaggerations sometimes found in association with each.

AIMS IN PARTICULAR SITUATIONS.—The aims dominating actual practice in particular situations present a confused blending of traditional theological and educational objectives, modified more or less by customs and other social forces influential in the making of the modern world. Ideas move slowly, and vast numbers of men and women, among them many teachers and leaders of the churches, still live and think in the age of the medieval reformers. Outgrown survivals of pre-Reformation doctrine exist side by side with more or less superficial, unthinking adaptations of the latest developments in educational theory and practice.

Conversion.—The evangelical churches make much of conversion: men are lost because of sin and are saved by an inner regenerative act of God "which takes place between God and the soul alone, through the mediation of Christ who is the soul's personal Saviour." The relation of religious education to man's part in this spiritual transaction is only vaguely defined in the thought of many adult leaders and teachers. Commonly, conversion is regarded either as starting point or goal (depending upon the religious status of particular persons) of the process.

Instruction.—By many the aim of Christian education is conceived to be instruction in the Bible and religious doctrine. Underlying this conception of aim are usually the beliefs, uncritically held, that the Bible is a storehouse of religious truth, divinely revealed, essential to salvation; that the Christian religion consists primarily of a body of authoritative doctrine to be accepted, learned, and believed; and that salvation on the human side involves in part a process of learning preparing for conversion and, following conversion, in developing Christian experience and character. In connection with the latter phase moral precepts are to be inculcated. The teacher's part in the process is sometimes described as educational evangelism, although this term has never won general acceptance.

The chief dependence of the evangelical churches for the conversion of men and women, however, at least since the period of the evangelical revival, has not been upon instruction but upon successive waves of revivalism. Nor has the aim of instruction been considered sufficiently important to lead to comprehensive plans. Dependence for religious instruction has been placed almost wholly upon the International Uniform Lessons, a system involving the study from week to week of more or less unrelated, fragmentary blocks of Scripture material, a thoroughly unsatisfactory plan from the standpoint of offering an intelligent understanding of the growth, structure, and content of the Bible, and leaving wholly untouched great areas of knowledge of much worth for Christian experience.*

Growth in Christian character.—By some adult teachers and leaders Christian education is conceived primarily as a process of stimulating and guiding growth in Christian character.† Character more often than not is conceived in individualistic terms as a status to be attained. In this the assumption is likely to be implicit that the righteous religious man will as a matter of course bring about a just social order.

A few adult teachers have been intrigued by the compartmental conception of character as consisting of traits which may be separately distinguished and likewise separately developed. The aim in a particular lesson or block of lessons may be the inculcation of "honesty"; in another "justice"; in yet another "cheerfulness."

Development of personality.—Increasingly in recent years the conception of development of Christian personality has become influential as the aim of religious education. By a Christian personality is meant a completely unified and dynamic self—one who possesses clear ethical insights, profound loyalties, thorough moral integrity, deep human sympathies, fine appreciations, strong spiritual perceptions of life's meaning, and a controlling purpose to live in accord with the principles and ideals of Jesus as reveal-

---

* See page 279.
† See pp. 128f., 253f.

ing the will of God for man. Predominantly the development of personality is thought of in individualistic terms, although increasing emphasis is being laid upon the importance of developing the kind of society conducive to the growth and maintenance of Christian personality.

Loyal, effective church membership.—Permeating all of the preceding objectives is the institutional aim, the purpose of developing loyalty to and active, effective service in and through the Church. Too often the Church is conceived as an end in itself rather than a means for the reconstruction of the community, the nation, and the world.

UNSATISFACTORY OUTCOMES.—By common agreement the outcomes of the traditional aims of adult religious education are far from satisfactory. The assumption has generally prevailed that by listening to the preaching of the Bible and of Christian doctrine, by studying the Bible in the church school and believing the doctrines, people would become high-type Christians and would build a Christian society. The actual result is that described in the preceding chapter. Some have become saints. They constitute the salt of the earth. Many have not become in any real sense Christians at all, that is, persons who exemplify in personality, conduct, and in social relations the spirit, attitudes, and ideals of Jesus.

Granted that many included within the constituency and membership of the churches have been very irregular attendants upon the preaching services and many more never attended the church school at all, yet it must be admitted that our educational processes have been comparatively ineffective. What more could be expected considering the fact that in many of our churches the teaching has not advanced very far beyond an ideology centered in the theological thinking of the sixteenth and seventeenth centuries, and the ethical teaching bears the unmistakable imprint of an economic system essentially pagan in motive and predominant method?

There is yet to be undertaken in any thoroughgoing educational way the task of creating churches, and a Church, whose membership is wholeheartedly and intelligently committed to the realization in personal and social life of those ideals of freedom, human equality, social justice, cooperation, moral integrity, love, and service of others in vital fellowship with God, which constitute the warp and woof of the Christian religion.

CHAPTER III

PRESENT COMPELLING OBJECTIVES IN ADULT EDUCATION

THE objectives of Christian education have undergone profound change within modern times and demand for change persists. In this is one of the best evidences that Christianity is a living religion. Religion is alive in a universe in which change is inherent.

Insight into human nature, what it is, how persons learn, how character is formed, the influences and forces affecting physical, mental, and spiritual growth, has grown, particularly within the present century. Conceptions of human relationships and of social responsibilities and duties have changed. All such changes affect men's ways of thinking of life and the goal of life, and this in turn affects the aims of Christian education, both of children and of adults. So long as the Christian religion continues to be vital and creative the objectives of Christian education may be expected to be subject to modification and restatement.

As the discussion of the preceding chapter has shown, it is impossible to state *the* aim of religious education of the Protestant churches, for there is no clearly conceived, universally accepted aim dominating their thought and controlling their practice. The prevailing objective, particularly as regards the religious education of adults, is chiefly a collection of odds and ends, principally hangovers from the culture of bygone ages. Meanwhile, within a century, quantitative and qualitative changes have taken place affecting methods and conditions of living, and the habits, occupations, interests, and sense of values of men and women, greater than have occurred within a similar period of time since human history began.

SOME INESCAPABLE NEW FACTORS

Certain of the factors of which Christian education must take account are unchanged from age to age. The nature and power, and the necessity of control, of basic physical drives, such as hunger and sex, do not change. The primacy and the supreme worth, and the importance of sustaining and ripening the most real values of life—faith, hope, and love—remain constant through the ages. Unaltered by time also is the necessity of development of poise and morale in meeting with courage and enduring with patience inevitable vicissitudes of life—the death of loved ones, the strain and suffering of incurable disease, the ingratitude and betrayal of trust of friends, the failure of enterprises in which time and much of life's energies have been invested—experiences which constitute the common lot. Nothing that we may say concerning new factors detracts in the least from the requirement of taking account of these fundamental things. With these and yet other unchanging factors acknowledged it remains true that we in America are living in a new world of resources, powers, and achievements.

NEW KNOWLEDGE.—The advance in human knowledge during the past one hundred years has been unprecedented. The growth of the natural and applied sciences, and accompanying developments, have made available a body of usable knowledge of such extent, together with tools and techniques of such potency, that in various realms what formerly was beyond man's power is now possible. We now know, for example, that our world of human relationships is a flexible, modifiable world. Forms of social organization are not determined by necessity. They are not fixed in rigid molds. They have not been ordered in unchangeable form by God. They are the result of material and social forces that themselves change and are changeable. There is therefore nothing sacred about them. However it may have been in previous ages we can now have the kind of society we want.[1] Only the insight and purpose to make a new world are necessary in order that we may have a social order that will serve the needs and highest interests of men.

Evidence that this kind of social order is possible is found in significant progress already made. For over a long period there has been noteworthy advance. Chattel slavery has been abolished. Recognition of the rights of women has been gained. Child labor has been mitigated. Increased social protection has been extended to the aged, and to crippled and otherwise incapacitated persons. Social service in the form of collective ownership and control of the means of meeting basic needs has been gradually expanding over a long period. What good will and social concern, re-enforced by new knowledge, have achieved in the past can be achieved in the years ahead at accelerated rate because of vastly increased knowledge.

RESOURCES FOR ABUNDANT LIVING.—A century ago, for lack of resources, the processes of production were unable to keep pace with the needs of a rapidly increasing population and an expanding culture. This is no longer true. Mastery over the processes of natural and material production has so advanced that now for the first time in human history abundant food, adequate shelter, assured security, and other essentials of health, comfort, and welfare are entirely possible for all people. Conditions have wholly changed. No longer is it rigidly limited resources to which economics of distribution must be adjusted, but, instead, a superabundance of resources. If ways can be found of equitably distributing the foods and the services now available through the application of the new knowledge to agriculture, mining, manufacturing, processing, and engineering, a civilization far surpassing in its ministry to the physical, cultural, and spiritual needs of men anything that the world has hitherto known is possible of achievement.

America, in particular, with its superabundance of natural wealth, its extraordinary equipment of industrial machinery, and its unparalleled personnel of highly trained engineers, technicians, educators, and professional and skilled workers, possess all the resources needed for abundant living for all its people. There are no necessary physical reasons why children or aged persons, or men and women of good will and industrious habits, should suffer from hunger or cold or for any of the necessaries of life.[2] Poverty and the physical deprivations which for ages have restricted and hampered the physical, moral, and spiritual welfare of mankind, from now on are inexcusable and sinful.

AN OUTMODED ECONOMIC SYSTEM.—Despite well-nigh unlimited possibilities the prevailing economic system[3] is neither producing in accord with its capacity nor supplying the people with the things that they need. For physical and moral welfare the people require decent homes in which to live, food and clothing sufficient for nutrition and health, and the opportunities and instruments for education, culture, and recreation. All of these requirements, under the present economic order, are denied to a large proportion of the people. Both as a system of production and as an agency of distribution the prevailing economic system has ceased to function efficiently. Its breakdown in recent decades has driven multitudes of the population of the United States into destitution, dependency, and despair. The number has been variously estimated at different times from twenty to thirty million people.

Forced unemployment on a vast scale has been created. Over a period of thirty-seven years, preceding the great depression beginning in the latter part of the third decade of the twentieth century, the lowest average percentage of unemployment in any one year in manufacturing, transportation, mining, and construction was six per cent. From this low, unemployment spread, affecting all trades and professions, and increased, until at the depth of the depression of 1929-36 between fourteen and sixteen million wage-earners were unemployed. The more than twenty-one million young adults between 18 and 26 make up approximately one sixth of our total population. In 1938 it was estimated that six million of them were unemployed. Between 1929 and 1938 approximately eleven million persons attained the status of adulthood, of whom at least half had not found steady jobs.

As these facts indicate, the system operates in such a way as to cause excessive extremes of wealth and poverty. In 1929, for example, thirty-six thousand families with the largest income received approximately the same income as the eleven million families with the lowest income. During the depression the income of the lower level declined to such an extent as to throw more than twenty million persons, one in five of the total population, on relief. The decline was accompanied by an extent of fear, anxiety, despair, and physical suffering far beyond possibility of computation. Even after conditions had materially improved, during 1935-36 fourteen per cent of the 29,400,300 families in the population had an annual income of less than $500; forty-two per cent an income of less than $1,000; and sixty-five per cent less than $1,500.[4]

These ills are not limited to oft-recurring periods of depression. Chronic insecurity affects business and industry under the competitive system. Involuntary bankruptcy is a specter constantly haunting the small business man. For many years more than one third of the people have been living under subnormal housing conditions, and about one tenth under conditions that constitute an acute menace to health, morals, and family life. It has been reliably estimated that fifty-nine per cent of all families, even in the most prosperous years, have suffered from inadequate feeding, deprived of fruits, vegetables, and meats required for a balanced diet, making up only in part for the deficiency by the consumption of cheaper starches and sugars.

In addition to forced unemployment, gross inequalities in income and wealth, chronic insecurity, persistence of bitter and degrading poverty finding expression in inadequate diet, subnormal housing, and undermined health, other conditions more or less directly related to the failure of the economic system to function efficiently include (1) waste of natural resources; (2) the prostitution of science to private profit in business enterprise, including the deliberate sabotage or suppression of large numbers of scientific inventions that if used would improve service and reduce costs to consumers;[5] (3) the rapid and excessive increase of corporate debt; (4) deliberate destruction of goods for which desperate need exists; (5) growth in number of violations of fiduciary trust; (6) the spread of banditry and racketeering; (7) accelerating rate of panics, crises, and depressions with accompanying loss of private property, including vast numbers of homes; and (8) increase of nervous disorders and neuroses due to fear and the sense of insecurity.[6]

Even during the long-continued period of rapidly growing population and constantly expanding home and foreign markets capitalistic industrialism was responsible for conditions which presented insuperable obstacles to adult education, such as excessive hours of labor; heavy and exhaustive work; for many laborers night shifts; a steadily increasing amount of monotonous work as machine processes displaced hand labor; and irregular hours (the shift system).

With population in the Western world approaching a stable level, no new frontiers remaining, and world markets contracting, the profit economy reached a stalemate. *Laissez faire* as an emotionalized concept having become for many a kind of economic religion, is zealously maintained as a theory but repudiated in practice by industrialists and other leaders of business. When the economic storm, generated by the principles to which they adhere, breaks, as it has again and again in recent decades, they themselves are the first to run to cover and to invoke the protection of government.

Under the domination of the profit economy society has been led to the verge of complete collapse. It has created prosperity for the few, and destitution or near destitution for vast masses of the population. The chief reason lies in the fact that it lacks ability to provide the mass-consumer-purchasing-power necessary to keep its production facilities in operation. The earnings of the workers are not sufficient to buy back the things they have made, and must have if they are to live. Its fatal incapacity, as has been indicated above, is evidenced by the vast reserve army of unemployed that it compels; by its requirement of enforced scarcity in order to maintain itself; and by its irresistible drive toward all-destroying international wars.

WEAKENED MORAL SANCTIONS.—A corollary of economic breakdown which probably exhibits causal relationship is the evidence of moral decline among the people of the nation. As long ago as 1912 Rudolph Eucken declared, "The moral solidarity of mankind is dissolved." There is reason to believe that the process of disintegration has steadily advanced during the intervening decades, that what has been occurring is nothing less than the crumbling of the greater part of the Hebrew-Christian moral tradition that has at once constituted the most ancient element and the major content of the moral heritage of Western civilization.

It is certain that on a wide scale the people of America have become indifferent to any form of restraint; that there has been a serious decline in the sense of moral responsibility, and a revolt against conventional codes of conduct; that promiscuity and lack of restraint in sex have greatly increased; that the prohibitions against adultery, theft, and lying embedded in the ancient Mosaic decalogue and embodied in the penal statutes of almost all modern States are constantly disobeyed; and that commercial bribery and the cruder forms of "racketeering" have become nationwide. The taking of "emoluments" and "perquisites" by purchasing agents and officials of commercial and industrial corporations, and, even more commonly, by political officeholders is justified by the assertion, "Everybody does it." The extent of increase of crime cannot be accurately gauged because of lack of accurate statistics. What is known is that its annual cost is computed in terms of billions of dollars.

The breakdown of the economic system has involved government in national policies so inconsistent and basically immoral that the recognition of these qualities has undoubtedly had repercussions in private conduct. The inherent immorality of the private-profit system, a characteristic which we shall later emphasize, is not new. But in its inability to function a new feature has emerged, namely, the phenomenon of millions of people being undernourished, many of them starving, while fruit in vast quantities is permitted to rot and the acreage of grain is deliberately delimited: the government actually rewarding farmers for decreasing the production of commodities for the lack of which millions of its people are physically and morally degenerating.

Some of these things are, more than anything else, symptoms. That which lies deeper needs also to be discerned. The element of sinfulness in the human heart, difficult to eradicate, is a thing that recent decades have tended to overlook. It requires re-emphasis. Another is the fact that religion, during long ages of scarcity and the rule of tyranny, insisting that man can live nobly and exemplify in his character the highest virtues in spite of privation, destitution, and crushing poverty, exalted as chief virtues such attitudes as submission, resignation, patience in suffering, humility, and courage in facing the inevitable. But what becomes of these virtues in an age of abundance, when production constantly tends to outrun consumption, when privation and destitution are no longer inevitable? Do they really continue to be virtues? May they not in effect become evils, tending to make of religion a soporific? In the new world, created by scientific knowledge and technological and engineering skill, is it not encumbent upon religion to create new moral ideals and new virtues, or at least adapt its traditional teachings to the new conditions? People today know that many of the old virtues in their traditional interpretation have lost significance and vitality. They do not know what should take their place.

MALADJUSTED AND DISORDERED PERSONALITIES.—In every age Christianity has had to deal with men and women exhibiting defects and disorders of personality. The victims of habits that have undermined morale and destroyed character have offered a continual challenge to the power of the gospel. In addition, modern conditions have brought new problems.

Many of the effects of modern economic and industrial conditions are devastating in their influence upon personality. Some of these influences are so subtle as not to be generally recognized. The growth of factories into immense concerns employing hundreds and even thousands of workers, the subdivisions and specialization of processes, the constantly increasing use of mechanical power, the growth of impersonal corporative control with accompanying widening separation between the worker and the employer, all have tended to stifle initiative and to deaden vital interest of the worker in his work.   Before the rise of modern industrialism the craftsman possessed a pride in his skill and a joy and satisfaction in his handiwork that were significant assets in the development of character.   These same processes, subordinating human beings to the position of mere "hands," "cogs in a vast industrial machine," with their labor regarded as a commodity to be bought and sold, have in countless cases outraged and degraded human personality.   These victims of modern industrialism constitute a new challenge to the Christian religion.

The insecurity that in many areas of living characterizes the behavior of the profit economy is productive of a degree of anxiety and fear that not only threatens physical health but seriously drains nervous resources.   Practically all problems of human adjustment are thereby intensified.   Normal relations between parents and children, husbands and wives, employees and employers, are seriously disturbed.   Many young adults are overwhelmed by a sense of frustration and what they feel to be the uselessness of conscientious effort and faithful endeavor.   The lack of common honesty in ordinary transactions, the increase in delinquencies of many kinds, and the vast prevalence of crime are phenomena that evidence in many instances a process of personality disintegration. The present adult generation probably has experienced more disintegration of personality than any preceding generation.   In millions of men and women personality has been and is continuing to be thwarted, depressed, crippled, and distorted.

GROWING CLASS CONSCIOUSNESS WITH INCREASING TENSION.— In the early period of American history the spirit of friendly cooperation widely prevailed.   The founding fathers exalted democratic ideals of liberty and equality and looked forward to a time when a common culture and the higher values of life would be shared by all the people.   Today these ideals are far from being universally held.   Fostered by economic inequality and inequitable distribution, a divisive class consciousness has been developing for many decades, until today the population is sharply divided into conflicting classes, with class distinctions, class exclusiveness, superiority and inferiority complexes widely prevalent.

Ownership and control are increasingly concentrated in the hands of the few, who by their possession of economic power become the real rulers of the nation.   This gives to the economic order, as the Christian conscience of Christendom, expressing itself through the Oxford Conference, declared, resemblance to a tyranny where rulers are not accountable for their actions to any superior authority representing the community over whom power is exercised.[7]

An increasing number of the American people, particularly within the ranks of labor, are accepting the philosophy of class struggle, some in full realization of its implications, the dogma of class war being increasingly embodied in the constitutions of labor organizations, while conflict bearing many of the marks of civil war steadily increases.[8]

Both class conflict and the concept of class are a denial of Christian principles, and their increasing prevalence, not to say their very existence, constitute a challenge to the Christian religion.

NATIONALISM AND THE TOTALITARIAN STATE.—From the early period of American history conflicting concepts of the nation have existed side by side: one viewing mankind as a family of nations, each with its separate identity as the United States of the American union but all possessing common interests, needs, and mutually helpful relationships; the other regarding the nations as wholly independent, unrelated, antagonistic, with opposing interests, each bent wholly upon gaining its own ends irrespective of the rights of other nations. Although in the earlier period the former concept widely prevailed, and the development in modern times of industry, technology, transportation, and communication has contributed toward the growth of internationalism and a new world civilization, the popular trend has been in the direction of sharpening and strengthening the second of the two views.

For a hundred years and more the functions of the State gradually have been expanding. In numerous aspects this development has been of immense social value. The recognition of responsibility for public education and for public health, for example, has represented greatly significant social progress. So also with various other lines of development. But this development has contributed to a tendency that has gained impetus and re-enforcement from other quarters, the tendency to assert dominance over the whole life of the individual and of the community.

The dominant drive of the profit-motivated economy has been in the direction of extreme nationalism. State measures have been developed designed to increase exports and to decrease imports. Associating themselves together in pressure groups industrialists, manufacturers, and commercial overlords have utilized the State as a means of enforcing their joint wills, making of government a means of increasing and guaranteeing their private profit.

Increasingly the State tends to assert sovereignty in an absolute sense. It tends to hold that its authority is inherent in itself and that it is answerable for its acts to no other or higher authority. The corollary of the assertion by the State of absolute sovereignty is the claim to the supreme loyalty of its citizens. In the majority opinion of the Supreme Court in the Macintosh case duty to God was made subordinate to duty to the State. Here is a basis for the assertion of a totalitarianism comparable to that of the German State under Hitler.[9]

The totalitarian State, a phenomenon which has emerged in various forms in different parts of the world since the Great War, is a creature whose nature and claims it is of the utmost importance for every person clearly and fully to comprehend.

The totalitarian State, of whatever type, declares its authority to be supreme, the source and the verification of all lesser authorities: the State is the Supreme Being. It asserts complete dominance over the individual in the totality of his being. It disallows individual freedom and liberty. It denies and disallows the authority of religion, of culture, of education, of parents and the family. While it is concerned for the general welfare—for education, morals, and social well-being—its fundamentally secular nature is revealed by its predominating concern for finance, commerce, and industry. It tends to give property rights precedence over human rights. The organized government, as such, is not itself the real governing power; it is the front, back of which powerful, dominating economic interests exercise control. The State has its own philosophy of life, which it asserts to be the one true philosophy, and which it imposes on all of its citizens. It uses all of the instruments within its power —education, propaganda, example, and coercion—to produce this particular type of person. It acknowledges but one purpose and end for the individual: man exists for the State, to serve the purposes of the State and to lose himself in the State.

In the United States, with our traditions of religious liberty and our inheritance of political democracy, we have fondly cherished the hope that our liberties are secure. But recent decades have brought disturbing conditions. The same tendencies that have culminated in totalitarian rule in nations of the old world have appeared in varying degree within our own nation. Times without number civil liberties have been violated, often without recourse on the part of the victims. Civil courts, particularly municipal courts, have become in specific instances courts of injustice and misrule. Powerful corporations have used ruthless force and violence, and their example has provoked the use of force by individuals and groups whose rights have been infringed. Pressures of various sorts have compelled the enactment of discriminatory legislation. Teachers have suffered the imposition of loyalty oaths. Censorship of teaching and textbooks has been exercised by privileged groups using the agency of law and government. Pastors have been intimidated and the freedom of the pulpit has been infringed by individual laymen and official boards. Increasingly, influence has been used to bring the teaching of schools and churches into conformity with the will and the purposes of economic privilege exerting itself through government.

By virtue of its essential character the relations of the totalitarian State to other nations are determined by economic self-interest. The characteristic expression of its sovereignty is in terms of economic imperialism expressing itself in attempted control of raw materials, struggle for exclusive markets, and execution of favored trade agreements, backed up by armies and navies.

WAR, THE GREAT DESTROYER.—War is not new. Always from the beginning of recorded time tribes and nations have engaged in warfare. World history often has been so written as almost to appear a constant succession of wars. But war on an international scale, waged with instruments of destruction and death so powerful as not merely to kill combatants but capable of wiping out civilian populations wholesale and turning great and populous cities, with their huge business structures, their colleges and universities, their hospitals and asylums, their museums and art galleries housing the priceless treasures of many generations, into wildernesses where not one stone remains upon another and with no semblance of life—war of this description is a new phenomenon in human history.

Modern war not only destroys human life on an unprecedented scale, it is destructive of all values that civilization holds dear. Truth, right, justice, love, sympathy, cooperation, all spiritual values that give meaning and worth to human existence are ruthlessly trampled under foot. The worst sins and vices that men know are invoked as virtues, a procedure that yields through succeeding decades a deplorable harvest of hate, lust, revenge, cynicism, prejudice, dependence upon force, and scorn of tolerance, justice, and right. Nor is this the full measure of the tragic aftermath of war. Its lawlessness lives on to deny the value of personality, to make mockery of statutes and of moral and social ideals, to foment class warfare, to spread disease, and to express its disregard of human values in crimes of all descriptions. Successive generations are burdened with war debts, reparations, and payments for its incredible waste and destruction. So devastating is modern war on an international scale that its continuation threatens the very existence of civilization.

War does not merely happen. It is not a natural catastrophe like an earthquake or a tidal wave. It has well understood causes, easily discernible. It is the corollary of economic nationalism. The profit economy fosters industries whose continuance depends upon a war market. The munitions industry, for example, stimulates jealousy and rivalry between nations, manufactures war scares, and by every possible means promotes the increase of armies and navies that themselves in turn constitute an incitement to war. The profit economy, moreover, is dependent for its continued existence upon access to sources of raw materials, and to markets for its manufactured products. To gain privileged access to these sources and to exercise dominance over limited markets it uses political government as its tool. To build up markets it loans capital and, again, uses government to protect its property holdings and to guarantee and collect its loans. These processes, complicated in various ways, provoke rivalries and conflicts between nationalist States that lead to war. Predatory economic imperialism, the outgrowth of economic life motivated by greed and strife for private profit for individuals and for great corporate aggregations of individuals, backed up by the armies and navies of governments, inevitably results in war. Herein is to be seen the basic cause of war in a period of human history when continued resort to war means the suicide of civilization.

These are some of the inescapable new factors of the current situation. With others, equally significant, whose discussion is forbidden by limitations of space, they combine to constitute a condition so critical as to demand that all the resources of the Christian religion and of its institutions shall be brought to bear if civilization is to be saved.

Moved by irresistible forces, society is in a process of transition as marked and as significant as that from the feudalism of the Middle Ages to the capitalist economy of the past four hundred years. The old order, characterized by individualism in economic practice, in ethical teaching, and in religious experience, has broken down and is unable longer to function.   Its characteristic expressions linger on, undergirded by the authority of tradition, blatantly asserting their validity, tragically unaware that life and creative power has gone from them.   If the Church in the new day is to prove itself a dependable agency of instruction, guidance, and leadership in the great task of reconstruction, it must come to a clear understanding and wholehearted acceptance of the objectives that should govern the educational process.

PRINCIPLES THAT DETERMINE THE NEW OBJECTIVES

This new situation, some of the chief factors of which we have all too briefly presented, is one with which religion cannot live at peace.   Inherent in the Christian religion are certain great central verities which with their implications determine the objectives of Christian education for times like these and basic motives for maintaining the struggle for a better world.

THE JUSTICE AND RIGHTEOUSNESS OF GOD.—For Jesus, God was the great central fact of the universe and of life.   Everything depends upon him, and derives its meaning and worth from him, his character, his purpose for the universe, and his will for men.

The God of Jesus upon whom everything depends—the Christian God—is a God of justice and righteousness, whose predominating characteristic is ethical love, an active outflowing good will. He is the Father of all men, not merely of a privileged few, infinitely concerned for the personal welfare of all his children, with whom he desires to maintain intimate, solicitous, sustaining, personal relationships.   He is a living God, the cosmic power that is working at the heart of the universe and throughout the whole process of nature, creatively related to the human struggle, to the end of perfecting humanity and the creation of a universal society, working as Jesus said from the beginning even until now, manifesting himself in the struggles of men for personal and social righteousness and for the development of a society of love and justice, the Kingdom of God.

The nature of God and his attitude toward all men are such that relationship with him in the most real and complete sense can be established and maintained by the individual only by just and right relationships with fellow men.   To do the will of God is to associate oneself with God in his creative process, working courageously and sacrificially for a higher and better order of life for the individual and for society as a whole; in other words, to exemplify the same outflowing love as constitutes his nature. The God of love, he asks and expects of his children an answering love, a love that is not mere pious sentiment but an active outreach of the entire personality toward him.

The nature and character of the Christian God determines the character of a religion entitled to be regarded as Christian. It cannot be merely a corpus transmitted by the past to the present generation, a sacred deposit to be revered and declared without change. It is living, dynamic, evolving, creative. It transcends the culture of which it is necessarily a part, approving that in it which is good and true and just but reviling all that is evil, false, and unjust, and challenging these elements in the name of the God whom it exalts and whom it calls upon men to worship and serve.

THE PRIMACY OF PERSONALITY.—The world, according to the Christian view, is above all else a world of persons. The material world is not an end in itself; it exists for persons. Material things have value, but their value is not intrinsic; they are of value for the use of persons. Of all valuable capital possessed by society, the incomparably most valuable is people. That which is of supreme worth is the human person. For men—all men—every man, woman, and child in the world, God's redemptive purpose plans fullness of life.

All institutions, systems, orders of society, whether political, economic, or social, are of worth only as they contribute to the development of personality. They exist for the purpose of serving persons, not the privileged few but all persons. To the extent that they do this they are to be cherished and perpetuated. To the extent that they fail to do this they are to be changed and if necessary done away with.

The supreme worth of persons rests upon the evaluation placed upon them by God and upon the fact, recognized by Jesus, that deep in the nature of all men there is that which responds to the good, the true, and the beautiful, and the further fact that human nature as such is capable of unlimited moral development. Jesus knew what is in men. He recognized clearly how selfish, greedy, and utterly alienated from God men may become, but he never despaired of human nature or of any man.

Not in an abstract sense, but because of their relation to persons and to personality, the Christian religion is primarily concerned with such new factors as are described in the preceding pages. Human values are involved, and to the Christian religion human values are of supreme worth. Not institutions but persons are of first concern. Institutions are made for man and not man for institutions.

Happily, this principle is one that is embedded in our national tradition of government and society. Government, our national tradition holds, is organized in behalf of the highest welfare of the governed, individually and collectively, the interests not of the few but of all, paramount to all other considerations. Since personality is supreme and since every person is of moral worth and dignity in himself, "no man, woman, or child can be exploited by another without doing violence to the essential spirit of American democracy and liberty."[10]

INTERACTION OF THE INDIVIDUAL AND SOCIETY.—Life cannot be lived in a vacuum. All persons necessarily live in a world of persons. It is in this world of persons that personality is developed and character is achieved. An integrated personality cannot be developed apart from the social group. No person can separate himself from, or make himself impervious to, the influences constantly playing upon his total self—his inner life and his practice—from the society of which he is a part.

Modern Protestantism, as we have seen in the preceding chapter, has tended to assume that personal experience can be separated from the social milieu, produced and perpetuated as a something isolated and apart. As an outcome of this concept of religious experience, and the attempt to beget it in individuals, the artificiality, unreality, and barrenness of much that passes for religion has resulted.

A similar false assumption has characterized much recent religious education, both of children and adults, the assumption that effective Christian education can take place apart from a recognition of the effect upon personality and character of the motives, forces, and practices dominating economic and social life. The assumption that adult Christian education is concerned solely with the creation, maintaining, and enrichment of a detached religious experience which justifies itself by purely subjective evaluation is destined to give way to a recognition more in accord with the known facts concerning how personality and character are actually determined. It is not enough to beget a religious experience satisfying to the individual on the assumption that the "converted" or "religious" man will make society what it ought to be. The twofold fact is that the individual makes society what it is and society makes the individual what he is. The individual no more deter-mines the character of society than society determines the character of the individual. There is constant interaction in influence of the one upon the other. The social and economic environment molds personality, and within personality are found the motives and dynamic forces that change and improve society. It cannot be truly said that the one is primary and the other secondary; neither can it be said that either is first in point of time. Often one hears: the *first* task of religious education is to make the individual Chris-tian. But it is impossible to make the individual fully Christian in an unchristian environment. The first task of religious educa-tion, and the last, is to make both the individual and society Chris-tian, and to work upon both simultaneously, realizing that neither can be Christianized in the fullest sense without the Christianiza-tion of the other.

SERVICE AND COOPERATION.—Another principle inherent in the Christian religion is the duty of service. Love of the Father and fellowship with him involves—indeed, is dependent upon—love of men as brothers, a love that is not mere sentiment but that expresses itself in a dedication of life to the service of men. Prac-tically, this means that so far as it is open to men and women to choose their occupation in life they shall do it on grounds of serv-ice; that they shall regard their occupation as their Christian call-ing, not primarily as a means of making money but as a way of serving God and men.

As never before the social forces, influences, and powers which control, dominate, and determine our human world, shaping both the character of individuals and of society, are now known. This is a part of the new knowledge possessed by this generation. Men of earlier generations could only vision what ought to be and cherish the faith that what ought to be some day could be and would be. Today there is available for use the knowledge and technical skill necessary to realize the vision of the prophetic souls of former generations, actually to bring into existence a society in which brotherhood is a reality, in which service and cooperation replace competition, and in which exploitation and class privi-leges are done away. Such a society involves a democratically owned and controlled social economy, a planned and a planning economy, which shall continually adjust economic effort to meas-ured needs, both cultural and material.

Under the profit economy, the need of the people for goods and services is not the measure of production. Instead, production is artificially limited by profit. Not production for use in terms of need but production for private gain in terms of profit is the law of individualism. It has been estimated that in 1929, a year of maximum production in the United States, goods and services worth ninety-three billion dollars were created, but that goods and services worth an additional forty-two billion dollars capable of being produced by existing resources, equipment and man-power were not created.[11] By 1932 the process of artificial limitation had been intensified to such an extent that less than half the goods and services capable of being created were produced, with need increasing to the point of widespread destitution, misery, and suffering. The economic masters, under the rule of the profit economy, sabotaged the creation of potential plenty while year after year idle workers multiplied, machines and equipment rusted, hunger and despair spread like a contagion.

Meanwhile in the United States, as in other countries, these conditions and accompanying developments are convincing increasing numbers of people that on moral and religious grounds the age of individualism and *laissez faire* must pass, and that a new age of cooperation must be created. Resources and primary means of production and distribution must be cooperatively owned and controlled. There are various forms of social ownership: government ownership and operation as in the case of the mail service; public ownership as in the case of the rapidly increasing number of publicly owned and operated utilities in local communities; and democratic ownership and operation as in the case of the fast-growing number of consumers cooperatives.

A current fallacy holds that social ownership and control means the doing away with all private property, a notion often exploded but tenacious in its hold upon the popular mind. On the contrary, it means much wider extension of private property than now prevails.[12]

The central ideals of the Christian religion—love, brotherhood, service, good will, and justice—for their realization in our day require implementation by social ownership and control. Otherwise in the light of knowledge now possessed these ideals will increasingly become hollow mockery, the mention of which will evoke from the multitudes only shouts of angry derision.

CONTRIBUTION OF RELIGION.—Predominantly, as the preceding chapter in its review of the history of Protestantism has shown, the Christian religion in its Protestant form has concerned itself with the individual. The aims of Christian education have been predominantly individualistic. Christian evangelism became, and in the thinking of a large proportion of pastors and laymen still continues to be, for the most part the rescue of individuals from the guilt and power of sin, begetting in them an inner peace and establishing them as individuals in the way of personal righteousness, a process set in a theological framework consisting chiefly of the dogmas of depravity, guilt, regeneration, individual forgiveness, and redemption out of the present evil world. In this lies the explanation of the fact that by and large Protestantism has allowed an essentially pagan social system to go unchallenged. It has not been deeply concerned with the redemption of the world. It has been preoccupied with the ideology of the inner life. It has been occupying itself with the conversion of individuals while all the time the unchristian environment by which these same persons have been surrounded and the pagan practices in which they have involuntarily and voluntarily engaged as members of an unchristian society continued to affect personality and character. In recent decades the evangelistic process has very largely ceased to function for the twofold reason that the old ideology has lost its hold upon the minds of the younger generation of adults, and there is general recognition that the process is ineffective. After centuries of this individualistic emphasis, the social system which is neither more nor less than the economic creed and practice of persons, many of whom are members in good standing of the churches, presents the same inequalities, injustices, brutalities and greed that have characterized it from the beginning, with only slight mitigation. And men are coming to realize the explanation: the motives and practices of the economic order debase men's characters, degrade their personalities, and damn their souls more rapidly and more surely than individualistic evangelism can save them.

Religion has a contribution both to the individual and to society. The Christian gospel offers grace and power for the regeneration of the individual and for the regeneration of society, and it must be brought to bear simultaneously and equally upon both. Humanity both in its personal and in its collective life must be saved.

This is not to say that there are two gospels, a personal gospel and a social gospel, but that the gospel is one, with both a personal and a social reference.   Once and for all the illusory, misleading distinction between the individual and the social gospel, between personal sin and social sin, between individual salvation and social salvation, should be done away.[13]

Let there be no misunderstanding.   There is no substitute for personal righteousness.   No plea is here being made for a substitute for the moral regeneration of individuals.   No program of mere social reform or social reconstruction apart from the grace and power of God in the lives of men can possibly be sufficient.   It is sometimes assumed that the social ills today present in society are wholly due, not to any moral defects in individuals but entirely to economic and political institutions.   No such assumption, we trust has been made clear, underlies our discussion.   All persons need to have the full power of the Christian religion continuously brought to bear upon their lives.

But this alone is insufficient.   A purely personal gospel applied to the inner life of individuals apart from the society of which they are a part is not enough, and no amount of pious or sentimental manipulation of theological, religious terminology can hide its ineffectiveness.   It is not "either" the one "or" the other; it is a matter of the synthesis of the one "and" the other.

It is now a matter of knowledge, scientifically attested, that personal experience is socially conditioned, that the person cannot be separated from the social medium of which he is a part, that personality and character are constantly being influenced, developed, and modified by the responses made by persons to social situations.   Although this is beyond dispute, the fact has not yet been taken sufficiently into account either in religion as such, or in the program of the Church.

FUNCTION OF THE CHURCH.—The Church is primarily a religious fellowship.   But it is also an instrument by which and through which religion is brought to bear upon individual and corporate life.   Committed to the building of the Kingdom of God on the earth the Church is under compulsion to face the implications of the gospel both for the individual and for society.   The gospel as the power of God must at one and the same time be brought to bear upon the individual for his salvation and upon the social order for its regeneration.   The problems of society today are of unparalleled seriousness, but a chance still remains of their solution without widespread violence and without democratic institutions suffering destruction.   The situation offers the Church an unprecedented opportunity and places upon it a unique, urgent, and fateful responsibility.

In the light of the present situation, the primary requirement is that the Church shall repent and get a new mind: repent of its self-centeredness, its institutionalism, its moral impotency, its lack of social intelligence and social concern; achieve a new mind in terms of the radical nature of the Christian gospel and its ability and purpose to create a society patterned in accord with the mind of Christ. This involves nothing less than Christianizing its own membership, thereby attaining self-consistency as a Church of Christ, so that no longer it can be said to its shame that there is little or no difference between the Church and the world.

A second necessary element in this contribution is attaining a more widely diffused and higher degree of social intelligence. A knowledge of the social forces at work in present society, of the factors conditioning the lives of men, women, and children, of how these forces exert themselves and how their effects are exhibited, is readily available. Also within easy reach is first-hand acquaintance with the actual facts concerning unemployment, working conditions, hours and wages, housing conditions, loss of homes and property, and a wide range of other significant information. The mere surface facts are not enough. The social intelligence of Christians should penetrate beneath these facts to the discernment of how and where the economic institutions of our time in their inner nature are infected with evil.

A third element is insight into the consequences, the physical, moral, and spiritual results of existing conditions. Religion should beget such insight, enabling the Christian man and woman to see more clearly and feel more deeply these consequences than can anyone else. If pastors and lay workers are faithful in their ministry, they have unlimited opportunity of seeing what present economic conditions are doing to character and personality and to both individual and family morals. What Christian insight reveals as to consequences of the economic situation should be given publicity, emphasized in preaching and in teaching, and published abroad.

A fourth necessary element is a wider diffusion of a deep sense of social responsibility, including a deeper realization of obligation for making the ideals and principles of the Christian religion controlling throughout the social order, in all of the institutions and agencies and practices of society in all of its operations. This involves the creation of a new public conscience—keen, dynamic, and compelling.

There are other elements in the mission of the Church that will be emphasized in subsequent chapters of this book. Here, we are saying, are certain elementary requirements, which if fulfilled will enable the Church to make a contribution peculiarly its own.

PRESENT COMPELLING OBJECTIVES

In the light of new, inescapable factors in the present situation, and the determining principles that have been stated, compelling objectives of adult Christian education clearly emerge.

CHRISTIAN PERSONS.—The Christian religion began in new and unique experience of God. It is this which first of all and beyond all else gives to the Gospels their religious distinction. They present a life-size portrait of a new type of person, One who was himself so unique, so full of grace and truth, as to compel his disciples to acknowledge him as incomparably more than themselves, their Master and Lord. What seems to have impressed them above all else, shaping their conviction concerning him and compelling their recognition of him as more than man, was his consciousness of God and the character of his relationships with men. Always present in all he said and did, penetrating his every word and deed, imparting to both a tone and power different from anything they heard or saw in other men, was his experience of God. He told them about God, but, more, he brought them into the presence of God; he talked to them about God as a loving Father, but, more, he led them into an experience of God as Father.

To beget in men and women an experience of God that has the reality, and that presents marks of verification such as his contemporaries saw in the life of Jesus, is a primary objective of Christian education today. A consciousness of God's presence and power, sincere, realistic, and genuine, together with a sharing of God's creative purpose for his world and an exemplification of God's righteousness and justice in character and conduct, nothing less will match the requirements of an age such as this. Every century of the Christian era supplies some examples of persons who have had an experience of God answering to this description. They are to be found today in all walks of life, men and women whose lives reveal a quality, a depth, a dynamic that sets them apart from their fellows.   They may or may not be brilliant in intellect or distinguished in achievement, but in the character of such men there is that which compels others to say of them, "They are men of God."

Experience of God is not to be narrowly interpreted.   It may properly be understood to include all experiences of life in which persons become aware of spiritual realities—the realization of human freedom and responsibility; of the beauty and music of the created universe; of the deep, awe-inspiring mystery of life; of the sacrificial, redemptive quality of love.   Of every such experience it may truly be said, God is there.   But there is a distinctively Christian experience, which including any or all of these, involves also a consciousness of the nearness and the helping presence of God, and an assurance of dependable response to those attitudes and efforts that are in accord with his will and purpose.   In religious experience of this quality new and deeper resources than are otherwise known become available, God is indwelling Spirit, and the life and power of the creative God are liberated and set free in the soul of man.

The attainment of the experience of God cannot be reduced to exact formula.   To no fact does the spiritual experience of the race testify more clearly than to this.   Communion and fellowship with God are mediated to different individuals in different ways. Perhaps in no aspect of total human experience do individual differences become more controlling than in man's approach to God.   It is the task of religious education to discover and utilize all available means.   Of all that are known, worship in its various forms is one of the most dependable.   Christian education, accordingly, places much stress upon worship.   There are many to whom the approach to God by way of thought and study seems most rewarding.   Christian education, therefore, emphasizes their importance as means of leading persons to a knowledge of God. Experience of God is mediated through fellowship with Jesus. His word to his disciples, "If ye had known me, ye would have known my Father also: from henceforth ye know him, and have seen him," has been verified by multitudes of men of every generation since his life on earth.   For Christians Jesus is the way, the truth, and the life.   Friendship with Jesus is of worth on its own account; it is also the way of fellowship with God.   Through understanding and appreciation of the life, personality, and teaching of Jesus, persons come to know God and enter into fellowship with him. For these reasons Christian education gives a central place to the development of this understanding and appreciation.

Increasingly, in modern times, persons are finding God through the service of their fellow men. As the will and purpose of God for human society become more and more clear, in purposeful participation in efforts for the creation and maintenance of such a society, men and women come into consciousness of fellowship with God. To give oneself sacrificially to continuing efforts to reconstitute human relations on the basis of good will, justice, and cooperation constitutes for many persons the surest way of experiencing reality in the divine fellowship. For increasing numbers of persons God is to be found where his people are: among the oppressed, the downtrodden, the dispossessed, the suffering, he is there bearing his eternal cross. To undertake their cause and labor for their deliverance is to enter into fellowship with him.

The compelling need for social sensitiveness and for social reconstruction in our times emphasizes the importance of stressing the development of the experience of God in terms of human relationships. Basic to the development of vital experience of God throughout the Church is a more general understanding on the part of men and women of the religious significance of social relationships, that as human relationships are continuously revalued and reconstituted on the basis of love, good will, justice, and cooperation the experience of God becomes real and vital. Only as the purpose of the reconstruction of society as a Christian society, and the creative attitude, become controlling in their lives will it become possible for the men and women of the churches to enter most fully into fellowship with God, the central, creative power of the universe working continuously for the perfecting of the whole creation.

The objective of Christian education is growing Christian persons. Much emphasis in recent years has been placed upon "character education." In the voluminous literature that has been produced the term "character" is used with a variety of meanings. In saying that Christian character is the objective of religious education we are using the term in a vital, dynamic sense, not in a static sense. Character is not to be regarded as at any time finished, or completed, or once for all achieved. It is to be thought of, rather, in a vital, dynamic, creative sense. The person of Christian character is one who in specific situations habitually acts in harmony with the moral and spiritual principles and ideals enunciated and exemplified in the example and teaching of Jesus. Personality, of which character is the expression, likewise is not something fixed or static but is the self in the process of becoming, the potential self that is constantly influencing and being influenced by the elements of the ongoing stream of experience and by the social and material environment of which it is a part.

A person of genuinely Christian character is one whose total self is constantly undergoing reconstruction as with deepening insights, increasing clearness of understanding, and strengthening convictions the personality becomes more and more fully integrated, embodying those ideals and values represented by the Christian gospel. Such growth by virtue of its very nature cannot be purely individualistic; it is a shared and sharing process, growing persons participating with other growing persons in a society that as a whole is similarly undergoing reconstruction in terms of the ever fuller realization of Christian values.[14]

Growth in personality and character defined in these terms requires that love and service shall be made central in life as the determining motives of all conduct. That Jesus made love and service basic in the Christian life no intelligent student of the Gospels is likely to dispute. But the words have been so enveloped in a mist of vague sentiment that their meaning for living has been very largely lost. Meaning may be clarified through contrast. The antithesis of the service motive is the profit motive. Dominated by the desire for private gain, for material acquisition, persons subordinate human values to material values, men to things. By so doing the profit motive degrades everything that it touches, whether commerce, industry, recreation, art, or religion. The service motive, subordinating material acquisition and material values to personality, is creative of spiritual values. It substitutes the making of men, the development of personality and character, as an end, for the acquisition of material wealth, of private fortune. There is no way in which the competitive struggle for money and property and financial power can be spiritualized or humanized. So long as its driving motive is the increase of material resources the outcome will be brutalized men. When the purpose becomes predominantly one of creating human values in terms of personality and character, the activity, whatever it may be, becomes life-giving. Adult education must make these truths clear. It must teach that the individual can only experience growth in a Christian sense as his activities contribute to the welfare and growth of others, and that contributing one's utmost to the common good is far more satisfying and personally rewarding than engaging in the competitive struggle for private gain.

The objective of Christian education, accordingly, becomes that of developing men and women of creative attitude toward the whole of life, persons who, coming constantly to fuller self-realization, are growing in disposition and ability to contribute constructively to a Christian social order.   The Christian's whole attitude toward life, if he is true to Christian ideals, is creative. His consuming desire, to share creatively in the development of a better society, makes him willing to follow out the implications of love.   To him love is not merely a sentimental ideal; it is a purpose, of which to find practical ways and means of implementing is his duty as a Christian.   It involves responsibility for promoting changes in an unchristian society even to the extent of enduring personal hardship and loss for the sake of the Christian ideal.

Christian education, thus conceived, is far more than a process of imparting abstract ideas, or the increase of knowledge and of skills by which the individual may be enabled to make adjustment to the conditions and circumstances of life.   It is nothing less than the development of persons capable of creative participation in life for whom the service of their fellow men and contribution to the common welfare are the dominating motives.   Men and women of this sort are the world's greatest need, indispensable to the realization of the divine purpose of the Kingdom of God.   Almost invariably when the ideal of a cooperative commonwealth is presented, the question is asked, "Where will you get the kind of persons required to make such a social order work?"   The question betrays a consciousness, as Rauschenbusch long ago pointed out, that the present order is not producing the type of personality and character needed to equip any social order resting on a really ethical basis.   A social order whose actuating motive is private profit has so overdeveloped the selfish side of man's nature that many are incapable of unselfish devotion to the common good.

The development of Christian persons in the fullest sense of that term, let it be said by way of summary, is a compelling Christian objective of our times: men and women capable of wide, creative participation in the activities of life, able to judge clearly, to act confidently and vigorously, and to share joyously and helpfully in the cooperative exchanges of a shared life; persons who are active, not merely passive and inert, motivated by the purpose of service, not by greed for selfish gain or by unguided impulses; who are not opinionated or dogmatic but open-minded and adaptable, possessing inquiring minds, eager to learn but at the same time reverent and devout, earnestly desirous of knowing and doing the will of God.[15]

An objective akin to this was the root idea of the Danish folk schools, schools for young adults, that succeeded in rebuilding the civilization of Denmark, completely changing both its economic base and its spiritual outlook within a half century. The idea of the founder was that these schools should, before and beyond all else, concern themselves with awakening the sense of freedom, of responsibility, and of individual initiative in men and women, their aim above everything else being the development of free personalities.

A CHRISTIAN SOCIETY.—A unique concept given to the world and the Church by Jesus is that of the Kingdom of God, the Beloved Society, within which men live in fellowship with God as Father and with all men as brothers. The implications of Jesus' teaching of the Kingdom have not in the past been fully understood by the Church. Within recent years its meaning, with all its exclusiveness and its profound individual and social reference, has been dawning anew upon the minds of prophetic spirits. It is a concept whose implications are so far-reaching and so revolutionary both as to personal living and the social order that the interpretation of the teaching to the Church becomes an educational task of the first magnitude whose fulfillment requires the lifetime of a generation. This rediscovery of the original gospel, with its synthesis of the individual and social elements in religion, is so significant that it constitutes nothing less than a compelling mandate to the Church as regards its teaching function in relation to its own membership.

The Church is called upon to translate Jesus' concept of the Kingdom into terms of today's life, to lead its members to understand what it means both in personal living and in collective life, and what these meanings demand in social, economic, and political reconstruction. The Christian conscience is already aware that the present social order disregards, and even denies, many of the principles and ideals of Jesus' teaching. The convictions already held by a few of the more clear-sighted of the members of the Church need to be made the common possession of all, together with a conviction of the changes necessary in the social order, that it may be brought into harmony with Christian principles.

A Christian society is a democratic society. The term "Kingdom," with its associations of monarchial rule, of autocracy, and of disregard of individual rights, does not convey to the modern mind meanings that are basic in the Christian conception. "Democracy of God" comes much more nearly expressing the full content. Jesus' teaching of the brotherhood of men involves as an implication the ideal of a democratic organization of society.

By the founders of the American republic democracy was conceived both as a form of government and as a moral imperative, combining in itself political institutions and a social ideal, a way of life involving all human relationships, the family, the local community, industry and commerce, and the State. The ideal, as the founding fathers strongly emphasized, involves the recognition of the intrinsic significance of personality, and of the dignity and worth of all human life. All persons have an equal right to life, liberty, and the pursuit of happiness. Any institution, system, or practice that denies this right, that uses persons as means for the mere pleasure or profit of others, is undemocratic and therefore un-American. From the Colonial era to the present, leaders of the American people have continued to think of their country as designed for and as offering the opportunity of the realization of the ethical ideals of democracy. Through the entire life of the nation in successive historical documents, in expanding social institutions, and in many of the ordinary relationships of life they have given expression to their hope and their faith.

The Reformation, as the preceding chapter has pointed out, revitalized the democratic principle by making the universal priesthood of believers a distinctive emphasis. But the full implications of this emphasis were not recognized, and this, together with the substitution of the absolute Book for the earlier absolutism of the Church, prevented their realization. It has remained for the Protestantism of the twentieth century to complete the Reformation by insisting the Christian religion requires that the freedom and worth of personality shall have opportunity of full and complete expression in all relationships and in the very ways and means of life itself.

The Christian ideal of a democratic society far transcends existing democratic forms and institutions. A society expressing the ideal in truth and reality would be a society of the people, by the people, and for the people, offering equality of opportunity for all persons of whatever profession, occupation, or race; with special concern for the weak, those less highly endowed by nature, and the unfortunate; with all forms of privilege done away; with adequate material rewards for every kind of socially useful work, without class or social distinctions, a society in which the moral, cultural, and economic interests of the masses of the people are paramount, and in which the powers of government are impartially devoted to the cultivation, refinement, and enrichment of the common life. That present-day society comes far short of the realization of such an ideal must be patent to all. The form of political democracy is observed through elections in which each qualified citizen has a vote, but the dominant influence in control of the State is not the people as a whole but the few whose possession of a disproportionate share of the property, the credit, and the industries of the nation gives them economic power. Thus society possesses the form of democracy without its substance, for there is no such thing as democratic reality without both political and economic democracy.

Within the prevailing social order autocracy, not democracy, still reigns. In business, industry, and commerce the autocratic principle controls. Every separate concern is essentially an autocracy; in many cases a limited autocracy, benevolent and paternalistic, but nevertheless an autocracy, in which the vast majority, the workers, possess no property rights in the instruments of their labor, no voice in the management of the factories, shops, or stores in which they work, no jurisdiction over the output of their hands, no real control over their standards of living. They are not in any true sense free persons; they are wage-slaves. The major part of the choice, control, and determination of a large proportion of the vital factors in the lives of these masses is in the hands of a comparatively small group of persons, economic royalists, numbering not more than three to five per cent of the population. Such conditions represent neither a democratic nor a Christian society; instead, they are the antithesis of both.

From its period of beginnings in the Middle Ages the profit-motivated economy around which capitalistic society has been organized in modern times has been challenged by the Christian conscience. There has never been a period in its history when it has not come under the condemnation of prophets of religion. In recent decades the basis of condemnation has steadily become more and more clear and prophetic judgment ever more severe, as was evidenced by the declaration of the Oxford Conference that sin enters into and infects the structure of the social order, and there must be combated.

The profit economy is condemned by the Christian conscience in three basic particulars: *its central motive, its dominant method, and its chief end*.[16] Its *motive* is in its nature intrinsically selfish and productive of greed. It is the antithesis of cooperation and of the service motive. The fact that many persons involved in the system are unselfish in individual purpose and habit is no disproof of the essential motivation of the system. The predominant *method* of the profit economy is competitive, creating a society in which competitive struggle, a kind of perpetual warfare, is universal. The *end* of the profit economy is the making of money, the acquisition of property, the gaining of power through the control of wealth and property rights. In both motive and end the profit economy is an acquisitive society. The fact that many persons who within an acquisitive society amass wealth are philanthropic in character and dispense gifts lavishly is in no sense a disproof of the intrinsic evil of the profit economy as such.

A Christian society is dominated by respect and reverence for personality. The Christian religion, as has been stated, is primarily concerned with persons and attaches supreme worth to persons. It becomes, therefore, a prime objective of adult religious education to create respect and reverence for personality.

Respect and reverence for personality in their social expression demand that laws, customs, and institutions give persons and personal rights priority over money and property and over property rights. Our present social order falls far short of doing this. In many particulars it shows superior respect for property, and too often it reveres property at the expense of persons. History bears witness to the fact that in its period of early development in the rise of the factory system in England it impoverished and degraded vast numbers of the population. Only the strength of the democratic principle and the power of the Christian conscience finding expression in steadily growing restrictive legislation has prevented equal devastation in this country. As it stands the record is black with examples of violation of rights of personality. Great corporations have kept their employees on a less than decent wage while they have amassed immense fortunes for their owners. American capitalism boasts of higher wage payments than prevail in any other country, yet the notorious fact is that for decade after decade in the age of the most rapid and extensive industrial development the world has ever known some millions of workers have not been paid a wage sufficient to maintain themselves and their families at normal physical efficiency. Of numerous other sins against persons the mention of two, for our present purpose, must suffice. Government records readily accessible bear evidence of immense extent of adulteration of food products injurious to health and to the manufacture in violation of law of a long list of proprietary medicines containing habit-forming drugs. Perhaps most serious of all, because inherent in the very nature of the competitive economic system as a requirement for its self-perpetuation, is the necessity of a reserve army of unemployed and the maintenance of enforced scarcity, conditions destructive of personality on an immense scale.

Respect and reverence for personality generate the motive and purpose of service in contrast to the motive of private gain. They replace the desire to acquire things by the desire to contribute to the welfare of humanity. In defense of the profit motive it is often claimed that it has produced the most efficient system for the production of goods and the creation of wealth that the world has ever seen. The fact is that the private profit economy in its rise happened to be contemporary with the development of science. The profit motive was thus enabled to make use of applied science for its own ends. Much if not all that it has apparently achieved, the application of power to production, the speeding up of the processes of production, the perfecting of the processes and the improvement of the products, is justly to be credited to science, not to the profit motive. Greed for private gain, it may be shown, instead of improving and refining its instruments and products tends to debase everything it touches; instead of generating energy and strength and contributing to health and efficiency it is productive of decay and disintegration. The more completely a society becomes acquisitive in motive the more unhealthy and weak it becomes in its inner life.

A Christian society is a fraternal, brotherly society, without antagonistic class divisions, based upon the motive of service. The Beloved Society envisioned by Jesus is a human brotherhood. To reconstruct the existing social order in ways that make brotherhood a reality is, again, a basic objective of Christian adult education.

Our present society is essentially a two-class system. No amount of insistence that our nation is a democracy can disguise the fact that the prevailing economic order divides men into two groups with conflicting interests, the employers and the employed, the rulers and the ruled, the masters and the servants.   There is a strong tendency and disposition against recognition of the fact. Many deprecate any mention of class consciousness, as though refusal to recognize its presence is tantamount to doing away with it.   But the fact is, as Sombart and other economists clearly recognized long ago, that division of men into two distinct social classes is of the very essence of the profit economy: "the capitalist class which owns the necessary material factors of production—the machinery, the factories, the raw material; on the other side the class of free wageworkers, who own the personal factor of production, their working ability, and nothing else . . . what differentiates the capitalist system from all other methods of production is the fact that these two essential factors are represented by two distinct social classes."

Out of this basic maladjustment arise the unrest, the protest, the resistance that sporadically develop into force and violence, and a whole swarm of moral evils of serious nature.   Fundamentally related to the spirit of resistance is the consciousness of living in "the land of the free" but deprived of the substance of freedom, not being treated as free men and as of equal worth; the consciousness of always being under pressure, often compelled to labor too fast, too long, and under conditions detrimental to health and physical welfare; and the realization of being exploited, not receiving the proportion of the proceeds of industry that justly belongs to the personal factor.

Basically, these are moral considerations, and being moral are of concern to religion.   From its beginning the Christian religion has condemned class divisions, and has passed judgment upon all exploitation of persons in the interest of material gain.   The Church cannot be consistent with its historical teaching and do other than express condemnation upon a system that divides men into antagonistic economic classes, a situation which with its inevitable resulting conditions denies human brotherhood and sets at naught the central ideals of Christianity.   The Christian goal is a classless society, not merely a democratic political organization of society, but a democratic economic and social organization as well, that does away with class divisions and accords to every individual the degree of freedom and recognition of worth that is his right as a person.

The achievement of this goal is almost if not quite as essential in behalf of the exploiter as the exploited. Both groups suffer in character and personality from participation in an unbrotherly, exploitative social order. If the exploited suffer from privation and the effects of the kind of environment that low income creates, the exploiters suffer not always consciously but none the less really from the subtle effects upon character wrought by the heavier burden of communal guilt. The personalities of all need the positive help toward complete self-realization that comes from the consciousness of participation in a society that as a whole is moving forward toward the ever-fuller control of its relations and functions by Christian motives and ideals.

To be fraternal and brotherly it is necessary for the motive of private gain and the method of competition to be replaced by the motive of service and the method of cooperation. So long as commerce and industry are organized and operated primarily not for the service of the community but for financial gain of the owners of the instruments of production and distribution, the class structure of society will be perpetuated, class conflict will continue, and the moral fiber of the social order will be subject to the destructive influence of a motive and practice essentially unchristian.

There is no valid excuse for the conditions that now exist. The adult generation of today possesses the technical knowledge, the skill, and the necessary instruments to create a fraternal, classless, equitable, cooperative society. There is lacking only the will, the purpose, the faith, the self-discipline to make real what religious and social idealism have visioned and what science, technical progress, and experience have brought within our grasp. And these requisites it is the function of religion to create. The reconstruction of the social order thus becomes a compelling objective of adult Christian education, the creation of a society in which living the Christian life is possible to all persons. Or, to use the terminology of Jesus, "the kingdoms of this world," in today's life the kingdoms of the political state, of economics, of commerce and industry, of education and literature and art, must be made the Kingdom of God, the order of brotherhood, love, and service.[17] This is the redemptive, re-creative mission of Christ in which the Church of today is called to share.

The strategic point of beginning is the adult membership of the Church. Far removed as the Church may be from realistic acceptance and consistent practice of the Christian ethic it is nevertheless more sensitive to the iniquities of the social order and more responsive to the appeal of love and justice than any other group. The gradual growth within the Church of a social conscience and the steady development of social conviction and purpose constitute the Church an institution whose influence can be brought powerfully to bear. As content and form of education of the young are determined by the adult men and women who are their teachers, and as the young are constantly subject to the influence of the ideals and practices of their parents, the possibilities of social change through education of children are easily overestimated. Moreover, any process of change initiated by the young can be blocked and nullified by parents, teachers, and employers.

Is the goal of a Christian society possible of achievement? Little merit attaches to holding before the religious forces of the nation as a compelling objective that which is unattainable. Without doubt the reconstruction of society in terms of the principles and ideals of Jesus is a tremendous undertaking, too big and too difficult to be fully accomplished within any one generation. The idea that society as the outcome of any process of social change, quickly carried through, can be made fully Christian is a naïve, utopian illusion. A society corresponding to Jesus' description can only be achieved through a long, hard, and painful process of progressive change. Social intelligence, insight, sympathy, and the will to engage in cooperative activities must be gradually developed. A supporting climate of opinion must be built to sustain essential changes.

To some the way of force always seems a short cut to a desired end. Apparently, an increasing number of earnest persons are coming to believe that the only way and the quick way to a just, humane, and equitable society is that of violent revolution. That social righteousness can be suddenly established in the nation by force is just as naïve and utopian an idea as that it can be quickly attained by education. The minority who own the bulk of the wealth and who are the holders of economic power possess effective means of exercising political control and very largely also control the police and military power. Resort to violence on the part of a minority would inevitably result in counter violence directed by those who hold and control the surplus wealth, the surplus food, the military equipment, and the power of coercion to determine the outcome of the struggle. No other country, least of all Russia, offers a parallel to the situation that prevails in the United States.

THE FAMILY AND THE CHURCH EFFECTIVE SOCIAL UNITS.—Jesus' concept of the Kingdom of God, the Beloved Society, is that of the family of God. The prototype is the Christian family. There can be little hope of the realization of the Kingdom of God on earth apart from making the family groups, of which human society as a whole is constituted, units that exemplify in their character and practice the ideals for which the Kingdom stands. This being true, an objective of adult religious education becomes that of understanding the place of the family in the social order, developing in the members of the family the disposition and ability to make the home contribute to the creative social process, and exemplifying those attitudes and engaging in those practices that in themselves constitute a truly Christian society. No individual member of the family, neither the father nor the mother and certainly not the children, even when they have become young adults, is exempt from the influence of the group as a whole upon religious and social attitudes. The life of the family, therefore, is to be judged not by its contribution to the material comfort of the individual members but by the extent to which it becomes in truth a democracy of God, an exemplification of the good society, and through its members an influence toward the remaking of society as a whole.

The Church likewise is a social unit of primary significance. It has today, as was said at an earlier point in this chapter, a unique opportunity and responsibility, a responsibility that can be met only as local churches exemplify in their fellowship what a genuine Christian society can and ought to be. The objectives of Christian education include that of developing in the adult members an understanding of the social function of the Church, a purpose to make the local church as a social group contribute creatively to the building of a Christian society, the while within itself it exemplifies the spirit, the attitudes, and the type of group action that the Christian ideal envisages in society as a whole when it shall have become in a true sense the Kingdom of God.

If in the early centuries there was supreme need for an institution gathering to itself the influence and power of a multitude of separate individuals, exemplifying in corporate life the meaning of the gospel of love and brotherhood, and standing as a witness to the highest moral and spiritual values against the might of pagan economic and political power, so also in this latest century. Again the stage is set for the old conflict between Christ and Caesar, between unalienable spiritual rights of men and the Great Beast, this time not in one national area only but in many parts of the world.

With conditions as they are what chance has the lone individual? And what chance have those unalienable rights for which modern men have learned most to care—the rights to life, liberty, and the pursuit of happiness; freedom of speech, spiritual liberty, freedom of conscience and of belief? Standing alone the individual is helpless against entrenched power. And not only is the individual imperiled, the civilization built upon these rights likewise is in danger of being destroyed. Under conditions existing today the Church as the advocate and the guardian of the spiritual rights of the individual and of the group takes on a new and unique importance. Without the Church, a reborn, revitalized, immensely strengthened Church, inspired and emboldened to challenge and stand against the power of the State, the individual Christian and the Christian society both are imperiled. Other than the Church there is no institution dedicated to the defense of the unalienable rights of man, devoted specifically to the preservation and the realization of those rights and ideals that represent the most precious heritage of humanity.

CHAPTER IV

CHARACTER AND PERSONAL RELIGIOUS LIVING

ONE who reads the New Testament with any degree of discrimination is impressed with the profound concern for the individual which characterized early Christianity. The Gospels, so far as they are a record of the activities of Jesus, portray him as occupied for a large proportion of his time with individuals, dealing with them in a wide variety of ways in meeting their personal needs. In the light of early Christian practice, and of Jesus' emphasis upon the supreme value of human personality, the Church cannot do other than make the individual the object of primary interest and effort. Repeatedly the discussion of preceding chapters has emphasized the twofold objective of Christian education—Christian persons in a Christian society.

PREVALENCE OF PERSONALITY DISORDERS.—Christian concern for the individual cannot but be deepened today by conditions prevailing in our present-day world. Even within the churches there are multitudes of maladjusted, unsocial, and selfish persons. Of these many are the victims of more or less serious personality disorders. This statement is substantiated by the analysis presented in the first chapter of this book, but even that left much evidence untouched. A more detailed presentation would add many particulars. Among a vast number of cases it would cite those of men and women with mental conflicts, oppressed with irrational fears, borne down with disappointments, worries, and grief, enfeebled by repressions which sap their energies, thwarted by a paralyzing sense of inferiority, enslaved by habits against which they feel themselves helpless, many of them hiding behind a false exterior of pretense and show but inwardly unhappy and miserable, living year after year close to the breaking point and ever exclaiming to themselves, with Paul, "Who shall deliver me from the body of this death?"

There are many, be it said with satisfaction, to whom none of these characterizations apply—men and women who engage in their daily tasks in the home, in the community, and in business and professional life with a calm, serene, even triumphant spirit,

141

exemplifying an exalted level of character and a high degree of mental and spiritual health. Of these a considerable proportion are persons for the most part engaged in ordinary labor, the menial humdrum tasks that must be performed if the daily round of life is to go on, uttering no word of complaint, exhibiting neither bitterness nor self-pity, meeting the tragedies of life as they come with poise and calm endurance, overcoming fear, loneliness, and physical pain with what seem to be inexhaustible inner resources of courage, faith, hope, and joy. How can their number be increased? How can unity be introduced into lives that are divided? How can harmony and wholeness be made to prevail where now it does not exist? How can the individual who is the victim of the chaotic disordered world in which he lives be brought to mental health, emotional balance, and consistent Christian living? Christian education confronts few if any more important questions than how individual persons may be more effectively aided in the achievement of personal character and triumphant Christian living.

There can be no doubt that human society is moving into an era in which greatly increased attention will be given to the collective aspects of life. This is a development carrying immense promise for social progress, but it may be seen out of perspective. There is no possibility of health in the social organism as a whole apart from health in its individual members. Without Christian persons it is impossible to build a Christian world. The remaking of the social order is a task so complicated and difficult, involving such qualities and gifts of personality, so much of courage, patience, meekness, love, and selflessness that every person of insight, in humility, is compelled to ask: "Who is sufficient for these things?" He who would contribute to the saving of society must himself be saved.

MANY PERPLEXING PROBLEMS INVOLVED.—When religion was oblivious of sociology and of psychology, having regard to saving persons but thinking of them as "souls" with little or no realization that personality and character are conditioned by physical well-being and by social relations, the development of character and personality appeared to be a relatively simple matter and to offer little difficulty. There are still many religionists, including not a few leaders of the churches, who talk and act as if there were really no problems involved. They are blind leaders of the blind.

Any process of adult religious education that is to be in

measurable degree successful must be based on an accurate scientific knowledge of the individual. Nor has any program of social reconstruction even a slight chance of success that fails to take into consideration the individual units of which society is composed. Among the services rendered by modern psychology not least is its having made clear the immense difficulty of the social problem because of the infinite complexity of human motives, drives, interests, and passions.

Speaking of the development of personality in growing children, a psychologist of recognized standing says, "The closer our observation, . . . the more difficult, the more puzzling, the problem of telling how personalities grow."[1] If this is true of children, it is equally true that the problems involved in the changing in adult men and women of attitudes and loyalties; the creation of new insights and enthusiasms; the breaking of old habits, replacing them with new; the conquest of fear, anxieties, and griefs; the resolving of inner conflicts; the replacing of social obtuseness and lack of social obligation by social sensitivity, social insight, and sense of social responsibility, bring psychologists and religious leaders alike face to face with many perplexing problems.

ORGANIC BASES OF MOTIVE AND CONDUCT

Any serious approach to these problems requires that some attention shall be given to the organic bases of motive and conduct.

THE PHYSICAL BASIS.—A human person is not a disembodied spirit; he is a physical organism—a physical organism of animal ancestry with innate physical needs. So long as he continues to live in his body it is impossible for him to separate himself from his animal inheritance. Scientific study of the various forms of life, higher and lower, has convinced scientists that certain directing tendencies, trends, urges, drives, are properties of all living matter, and that these are so basic that without them the organism could not survive. When we ask, as we are bound again and again to ask, "Why do persons act as they do?" the answer to a considerable extent is to be found in the way in which the human body is organized. All persons are physical beings with specific organismic needs and corresponding urges that insistently clamor for fulfillment. The origin of many though not all of these urges or drives is chemical. "They relate to the need of the body for certain substances, or to the activity of the body in response to substances secreted by the glands."[2]   Not only activities but alertness and differences in disposition and temperament, and even continuing interests and desires, are strongly influenced, possibly even controlled by the chemical balance of the body.   It is known, for example, that an overactive thyroid gland not only affects the rate of physical growth but also the rate of operation of certain bodily functions; that an overactive adrenal gland not only speeds up heart action but creates excitement and nervous tension; that a certain disorder of the pituitary gland not only results in physical sluggishness but actual loss of initiative and creativity.   Other than chemical factors also are significant.   From the fact that most of the higher animals spend much time in exploration and in play it is inferred that some urges are the outgrowth of brain activities neither chemical in their origin nor closely related to the vital organs.

To take into account the physical and chemical factors in bodily activities is not at all to discount or to overlook the more distinctively human moral and spiritual elements.   It is only common sense to recognize that conduct, behavior, disposition, and habits depend not only upon purposes but also upon bodily and environmental conditions.   There is a direct relationship between bodily health and moral character.   No man or woman who is continuously fagged physically can attain to his highest and best morally and spiritually.   Overlong hours of labor under unwholesome physical conditions, lack of sunshine and fresh air, an atmosphere impregnated with dust or chemical impurities, the tension of muscles and nerves caused by the "line" and the "speed-up"—these and other conditions which prevail in many factories and mills, and even in some offices, create irritability, discouragement, loss of initiative and ambition, morbidity, and undermine moral and spiritual ideals.   Undernourishment and fatigue create a demand for artificial stimulants.   There is a direct causal relationship between sordid environment, with its accompaniment of poorly nourished bodies, and immorality and crime.

In any problem case, whether the chief difficulty seems to be mental or moral, the religious leader will do well to begin his diagnosis, enlisting competent aid, with an inquiry into organic physical conditions—the functioning of the glands, of the digestive process, of the condition of the nervous system, proceeding to a study of psychological and social factors.

THE INTELLECTUAL BASIS.—Human beings have qualities in

common with other animals, but the human person is distinguished by the power of self-direction, of formulating and choosing ends of action, of reflective thought and discrimination between ends, and of the organization and reconstruction of social institutions which conserve his chosen ends. While some animals—dogs, for example—are capable of discriminations in certain situations superior to those of persons, in a vast number of instances situations to which human beings make response are structured in a more complex and involved manner than those to which the lower animals respond; objects and events possess for human beings much more past and future reference; and their immediate behavior is subject to modification or inhibition in relation to abstract ideals.

One measure of intellectual maturity is the ability to inhibit thoughtless, impulsive actions and to respond with discriminating judgment. As childhood and early youth pass, the growing person normally grows in ability to discern meanings and values and to discriminate. Knowledge and skills increase, and social relations take on new significance. As a mature adult he wants things not merely because of a biological urge but as a person of discrimination, possessed of self-control, capable of weighing values and outcomes. He definitely prefers and chooses.

How the brain acts in resolving conflicts between impulses, desires, and critical judgment is not understood. What actually takes place in terms of process, or method of the brain's functioning, in the development of ability to hold physical stimuli and the expression of feeling in check until ends can be considered and alternative outcomes evaluated is not known. It is known that there are what may be called levels of reaction, of which at least three are clearly differentiated. The first, or lowest, is that of automatic physical reactions, below the level of conscious choice, examples of which are the flow of saliva in response to the stimulus of food, the jerking of the knee in response to a light blow, and the winking of the eye, the response being made by some part of the body influenced by total bodily conditions such as emotional tension and fatigue, but not co-ordinated with a total bodily response. The second is that in which actions, some of which may involve complex forms of response, are performed more or less mechanically, with various degrees of partial consciousness and volition. The third is highly conscious and purposeful. The higher powers of the mind are called into operation; response is inhibited while alternatives are weighed, outcomes are foreseen and evaluated, and decision deliberately made. Adult education involves development, on this higher level, of the power of reflective thought.

One of the baffling problems confronting adult education arises from the number of persons in our society who are of low intellectual level. We shall discuss this problem at a later point,* here merely referring to the fact that it involves serious difficulty in the development of moral character. The person whose intellect is of such low type that his reactions are predominantly upon the merely automatic level, and who lacks capacity to develop beyond this level, can scarcely be said to possess moral character in any proper sense of the term. His conduct is neither moral nor immoral; it is nonmoral. From such persons neither exalted conduct nor social creativity can be expected.

THE EMOTIONAL BASIS.—On our emotional organization as much or more than on anything else, most psychologists would probably agree, our character depends. One reason why this is true is that we feel more than we think. Yet, despite all the psychological study devoted to the subject and the extensive scientific laboratory experimentation of recent decades, the emotions remain the most obscure part of our lives as adults.[3] It seems impossible for any such list of distinct, identifiable emotions to be made, as was formerly common. No one seems to be able to catalogue them exactly or to describe them adequately. Justification probably exists for the assertion that there are as many kinds and varieties of emotions as there are distinctive behavior situations, and one emotion is as unique and primary and fundamental as another.[4]

Much of the significance of the emotions for education lies in the fact that it is emotionalized knowledge and attitudes that lead to action. Unsupported ideas won't work. Knowledge is doubtless of worth on its own account, but it is doubtful whether on its own account it is of ethical or religious value. The man who knows most is often far from being either a good man, not to say the best of men, or a religious man. Christian education is concerned, not merely with what knowledge is gained, or what attitudes are developed, but more with the degree to which the knowledge and attitudes are endued with emotion. There are many current situations concerning which the facts are generally known, and indisputable—for example, unemployment; but because of the

---

* See page 277.

emotionalized attitudes that have been developed around the facts, there are wide differences in men's minds concerning the significance of the facts, the issues involved, and what is to be done about them.

So basically characteristic of human nature are certain emotions that they compel special attention. Of these the most demoralizing and devastating in present-day life is fear, the more so because of the way in which it has been accentuated by certain characteristics of the social order on which emphasis already has been laid in our discussion. Originally, animal fear served a highly useful purpose, and in many situations today fear operates to aid the individual. But in many more cases, particularly in some of its more subtle forms, fear is detrimental both to character and to personality. This is owing partly to the fact that fear produces certain chemical changes in the bodily organism that, while they assist in combat or flight, are deterrents to clear reason, the weighing of alternatives, and the making of moral judgments. A further reason is that in man fear attaches not only to actual, present experience but associates itself with imaginative situations.

Common among adults are fears, not so much of persons or of events, as of ideas, attitudes, programs, courses of action, and possible consequences. The average adult is timid about unaccustomed ways of doing things, fearful of new opinions, suspicious of proposed changes, afraid to oppose custom or tradition. When he is confronted with a new idea, he tends to shrink from it with dread because of fear of possible consequences to himself. Closely associated with this is the fear of losing caste or prestige with immediate associates, making the person unduly sensitive to the opinions and pressure of the business, professional, or social group with which he is associated. Almost universally present in our competitive social order is the fear of not possessing enough to insure security for oneself and for his family, and fear of losing what one possesses. As the result of economic insecurity, multitudes of persons in recent decades have become the victims of a fear of life itself—it seems fraught with such consequences of danger and of suffering, so chaotic and uncertain, that both men and women become not only fundamentally unhappy but obsessed with dread at the thought of going on trying to live.

Akin to fear is loneliness. It seems a strange anomaly, with increase of population and the crowding together of people in great cities, that human loneliness should have increased, but such seems unmistakably to have been the fact. The more complex society has become, the more the individual has seemed to be conscious of his alone-ness. The competitive, profit-motivated economic order, instead of binding people together in a sense of unitary, collective fellowship, inevitably separates and divides, setting the individual over against his fellow, and contributing to his inner sense of loneliness. The rapidly increasing rate of divorce in recent decades challenges exploration as to whether the growing inability to find in marriage the intimate companionship that it was by nature intended to provide is not also a by-product of the competitive social order that admittedly conditions all aspects of living.

It would be a serious mistake to permit the impression that the net effect of the emotions upon life is necessarily negative. To do so would be counter to fact. There are positive, life-giving, and life-enriching emotions. Life offers the chance, if its possibilities are realized, of abounding joy and happiness. If fear, anger, and disgust involve a negative-feeling tone in many of life's experiences, love, joy, courage, and contentment not only contribute to the happiness of living but actually add content to the meaning and worth of life.

A UNITARY BASIS.—An implication of our discussion to this point is that the intellectual and the emotional bases of motive and conduct cannot be sharply separated. As a functioning organism, man cannot be divided into separate parts. Any action has both mental and emotional elements so closely associated that they cannot be clearly differentiated.

Character and personality are developed through moral decisions expressed in action. The "will to do" has both an intellectual and an emotional reference. The will is not a separate faculty of mind, with ready-stored reserves of energy waiting to be tapped. An act of will, involving moral judgment of approval or disapproval, testifies to a set of the mind organized in a drive toward the regulation of chosen ends to the cumulative force of which emotion has made its distinctive contribution.[5]

So also with ideals. Character of the highest type is that in which conduct is controlled by an ideal which provides power to act independently of the approval or disapproval of one's associates. Human nature has the capacity to rise above crippling limitations —besetting sins of selfishness, greed, and lust; inner fears and inhibitions; the economic behavior imposed by a pagan order, and the customs which it dictates. Ideals, ideas made dynamic through feeling, are instruments by which that capacity may be realized.[6]

Required for the development of full-rounded personality is balance between rational and emotional elements. Information and ideas are not enough; knowledge and ideas need to be interfused with emotion until they are expressed, becoming determinative factors in conduct. Neither are emotion and feeling sufficient in themselves; they must be rooted in authentic knowledge.

Attitudes are influential in determining conduct. From early life, as knowledge grows, attitudes are formed, finding expression in likes and dislikes, favor and disfavor, appreciations and distastes. Every attitude has in it some content of both thought and feeling. Basically, an attitude may be said to be a way of thinking to which emotion has attached. Attitude always has a content of feeling. The thought, or knowledge, basis of attitude may have in it a marked emotional element of prejudice, hatred, or scorn. An example is racial attitude in which these elements are so frequently present that "race attitude," "race prejudice," and "race hatred" have become all but synonymous. Conversely, the thought basis of attitude may be strongly interfused by reverence, awe, gratitude, and trust. Many scholars are disposed to think of religion as an attitude toward the universe, by which is meant a response or reaction to the universe that includes thought, feeling, and will, and which in its Christian form is social, reverent, trustful, and active.[7]

Belief, likewise, to be dynamic, requires both intellectual and emotional content. Belief, to be sure, is distinct from knowledge. In Christian faith, the mind ventures beyond the limits of acquired knowledge; it takes that which is known as its point of departure, but it projects itself beyond the known into the realm of the unknown. But if it is only cold, unfeeling belief it has little power. Only when belief is interfused with the emotions of awe, reverence, and love does it become, as faith, a powerful factor in character and conduct.

DYNAMIC FACTORS IN HUMAN CONDUCT

We have reviewed the physical, intellectual, and emotional bases of motive and conduct, but our brief examination has not yet supplied an adequate answer to the question as to why people act as they do. It should be recognized that involved in any satisfactory answer to this question are problems that tax the scientific

acumen of the most learned of men.   While some things are fairly
clear there yet remains much that is unknown concerning the main-
springs of action.   In pursuing this problem, let us in the light
of the organic bases already described seek to discover other dynamic factors in human conduct, at the same time making more
explicit some things implicit in the preceding discussion.

BASIC DRIVES.—All organisms as stated above possess as basic
constituents certain directing tendencies, trends, urges, without
which they could not exist.   These, biologists declare, are properties possessed by all living matter in common.   Concerning the
existence of these basic drives in human nature all psychologists
are in agreement.   "The human mind has certain innate or inherited tendencies which are the essential springs or motive powers
of all thought or action whether individual or collective, and are
the bases from which the character and will of individuals and of
nations are gradually developed. . . ."[8]

While the fact of innate tendencies as a part of biological inheritance is unquestioned, psychologists no longer attempt to catalog a list of instincts for the reason that it has proven impossible
to agree upon their number or exact description.   Even the term
itself has fallen into disrepute.   Evidence is lacking of an inborn
tendency of a particular pattern such as would justify, for example,
a statement that "wars always will continue because man is a fighting animal, born with an instinct for conflict."

If we cannot speak of specific instincts, what can be said with
certainty?   Lying back of the actions that make up the daily lives
of men and women lie more or less definite drives of a compelling
sort.   All behavior basically is an effort to find expression for, and
to satisfy, these tendencies, urges, and biological hungers.   Among
the latter, appearing in human beings, as in all other mammals,
are food hunger and sex.

Any scientific attempt to discover explanation of the upsurge
of the depressed classes throughout the world today must take account of the power of the hunger urge in human nature.   Again
and again in human history food hunger has given birth to the
spirit of revolution among normally peaceful populations.   Starving people who engage in mob violence are not to be adjudged
basically criminal.   They are driven to violence by forces as natural
and inevitable "as those that cause tempests to sweep out of the
skies."   Undernourishment and hunger in our own land of plenty
are responsible for no small part of the sum total, not only of

physical suffering, but also of the anxiety, emotional instability, and moral degradation of recent decades.

An equally fundamental impulse is that of sex, also named by psychologists a tissue hunger. More or less directly the sex urge contributes to almost every interest and activity of men and women. Misconceptions, false ideas, and prejudices concerning sex, together with sex excesses, are the cause of an immense amount of unhappiness in married life, and underlie many of the divorces granted by the courts.

In present-day society the thirst for good opinion and prestige, and the will to power, seem to be nearly as powerful, and with some people more powerful than the biological urges. Together with the "vanity" motive, these seem almost universal.

Probably closely allied is the impulse to dominate or control others, the urge to achieve success and to rule. These several drives are fundamentally egoistic, involving the urge to express or serve the self, although in individual cases often there is a more or less marked admixture of altruism, regard for the interests of others, and desire to serve.

Persons tend to act in ways that furnish expression for and satisfaction of basic hungers and urges. When the tendency or urge for expression and satisfaction becomes so compelling as to induce action, it becomes the motive of conduct. Often, observing a particular act we ask, What is the man's motive? by which we mean, What is the basic drive finding expression in his act? The analysis of conduct is, however, by no means so simple as such a statement seems to imply. Back of most specific acts is not merely a single motive but complexes of motives to which various basic drives have contributed, modified by environment, custom, experience, habit, and moral judgment. Nevertheless it remains true that those motivations strongest and most persistently operative in day-by-day conduct are intimately related to the unceasing demands of those basic drives that we have mentioned. The urge for food, for satisfaction of the senses, for good opinion and prestige, for avoidance of what is disagreeable—these and other fundamental desires are the conscious and partly unrealized compulsions that keep persons on the move—striving, toiling, exploring, adventuring, experimenting, overcoming handicaps and obstacles.

This well-attested fact is of the utmost significance for the development of character and personality. Much has been written in recent years concerning ways and means of character building.

We are on surer ground if we concern ourselves with developing, organizing, and unifying motives. Stable, dependable character is a by-product of integrated motives and sense of values. The integration of motives is achieved by choice, and development of devotion and loyalty to a hierarchy of values, including a supreme object or cause. Let the building of the Kingdom of God become the supreme object of a man's hope and desire, let him become convinced that by his effort he can make significant contribution to its building, and all of the basic urges of his nature are sublimated and controlled to the one great end. In terms of integration of personality the result is much the same whatever object is made supreme. At the height of his career the notorious gangster Capone is said to have been a thoroughly integrated personality.

The egoistic impulses, all of which are subject to direction in behalf of worthy ends, are not only often misdirected but in many cases assume abnormal forms. Failing to find satisfaction in real achievement, the person finds compensation in some one of numerous ways of fictional satisfaction, chiefly emotional, which becomes a substitute for achievement. Examples are the numerous fraternal orders whose members bedeck themselves with gaudy uniforms and march down the streets with immense satisfaction to themselves, "acting out their infantile fantasy of military heroism." In their social effects these are comparatively harmless, but when the same egoistic impulse and craving for distinction leads men to adopt the sinister garb of the night-rider, the terrorizer, and the lyncher, though they rationalize their conduct in terms of executing swift justice, acting for the good of the community, or wielding "the scourge of God," they become a social menace of high degree. The by-products of such misdirection of egoistic impulses include not only harmful, even criminal acts, but also the development of prejudices, intolerances, warped judgment, and complacencies that stifle social effort.

Religion itself is not free from the charge of contributing to compensatory conduct and belief. The chief example is the way the idea of "heaven" has found expression in the hymns, preaching, and beliefs of many orthodox Christians. Nurtured by a sense of their futility and helplessness in their social and economic conditions, the idea has too often been made the justification for lack of interest and effort in behalf of social reconstruction.

DEFINITION AND CAUSE OF NEUROSES.—Physicians and psychologists call attention to the steadily increasing number of neurotics among men and women, persons who are the victims of neuroses of one type or another. These terms are not easy to define with exactness. Neurotics are persons who, not all having characteristics in common, in one way or another are socially maladjusted. As a rule, though not always, they are victims of functional physical disorders, of excessive fears, phobias, and depressions. All neuroses possess, as a common factor, abnormal anxieties and defenses that have been built up against these anxieties, together with conflicting tendencies for which compromise solutions are sought and practiced. The concern of adult education with neuroses lies in their deformation of character. It may even be said that character deformation is the one constant factor in all neuroses.

Freud was one of the first of the psychologists to emphasize the biological and physiological causes of neuroses. He insisted that practically all neurotic conditions root in such causes, giving chief emphasis to sex. Psychologists are now increasingly emphasizing that while neuroses are generated from biological roots, their prime causes are to be found in specific cultural conditions under which the prevailing economic order compels persons to live. The typical neurotic personality of today, competent psychologists maintain, is a result of competitive pressures which characterize our economic order.[9]

The profit economy is based upon the principle of individual rivalry. Competition as it exists in present-day society is not a natural human phenomenon, but artificial, stimulated by given cultural conditions. Fear and anxiety of many different forms are its products. The fear of failure is more or less constant as the actual numerical chances of failure are much greater than of succeeding. Ever present also is actual or potential hostile tension between competitors. Failure entails the frustration of real or fancied needs and diminished self-esteem. Altogether, these and similar conditions not only provide fertile ground for the development of neuroses but actually cause their development. Fears increase abnormally, grandiose ideas are substituted for attainable goals, and the individual not only feels himself to be but actually becomes inferior to what he might otherwise be.

EFFECTS OF ENVIRONMENT.—What has been said has clearly shown that environment is one of the dynamic factors in human conduct. While this is an unquestioned fact, it is not possible to sharply separate those factors which are the direct outgrowth of environment and those which grow out of biological inheritance. From the day of birth the two interact, each affecting the other.

It is an indisputable scientific fact that for great numbers of people overcoming the effects and limitations of a particular environment is impossible. Religionists render a disservice to social progress when they insist that if a man will "open his heart to divine grace," or "lay hold on the resources of God," he can surmount any obstacle imposed by his environment. It is unquestioned that through the power of religion millions of people from the first century to the twentieth have overcome poverty, suffering, crime, the influence of dissolute associates, and other untoward effects of environment, but it is equally true that other millions have found it impossible, with all the help that religion has offered, to transcend such physical and social limitations, not primarily because the power of religion is insufficient but because their environment has so conditioned them that it has been impossible for them to realize what religion might do for them or to open their minds and hearts to the influence of religion.

So long as unnecessary poverty and destitution are permitted to continue: men, women, and children suffered to be housed in dark, damp, and insanitary dwellings in impoverished and crime-infested areas, subjected to the influences of gambling and liquor joints, melodramatic movies, the illicit drug traffic, houses of prostitution, corrupt politics and courts of law, and merciless, exploitative landlords, environment will effectively bar religion from the exercise of its regenerative power upon the lives of any considerable proportion of the victims. Such an environment damns persons far more rapidly and more surely than religion is able to save them.

POSITIVE BASES OF SOCIAL CONDUCT.—Moral conduct, we have repeatedly emphasized, is social conduct. Christian character is a way of living motivated by love, sympathy, good will, and cooperation. For such character and conduct positive bases exist in human nature.

That human beings have fundamental social needs everyone agrees. Many psychologists hold also that there are within man's nature inherent tendencies in the direction of social qualities and social conduct. For some reason the negative aspect of basic impulses and drives has received more emphasis in scientific literature than has the positive aspect. But positive bases exist and it is a part of the task of Christian education to recognize the fact and to build upon them.

We have referred to the fundamentally egoistic drives within human nature. If these drives are recognized as finding expression in jealousy, competitive struggle, and fighting, it should also be recognized that they are expressed in sympathizing, aiding, protecting, and loving. These latter forms of expression, though they have received less scientific emphasis, are quite as basic and natural as the former.[10]

By nature man is a social being. He seeks and enjoys the society of his fellows, and he tends to be vaguely uncomfortable and uneasy when he is alone. As most of the higher animals and many of the lower forms are gregarious, congregating in herds, so people form clubs, associations, and groups of many different kinds. Both in work and in play this tendency manifests itself. Competitive struggle is no more natural and necessary than is mutual aid. In fact, in certain senses, at least, it is less so. The desire for association and for approval is certainly more deeply rooted and more nearly universal than the impulse to strive with and contend against others. Struggle, in nature, is not so much a struggle between individuals or even conflict between species as it is a struggle against unfavorable factors of environment in the course of which cooperation between individuals often occurs. Competitive struggle prevails only when natural or artificial restrictions impose limitations upon food supply or the satisfaction of other natural desires.

Sympathy, feeling with and for others, is a primitive and natural response. A common illustration, of which all have frequently seen examples, is the spread of fear finding expression in flight in flocks of fowl and birds and in animal herds. "Sympathy of this crude kind is the cement that binds animal societies together, renders the actions of all members of a group harmonious, and allows them to reap some of the prime advantages of social life in spite of a lack of intelligence."[11]

It is reasonable to believe that in human nature the depth and spread of this primitive impulse is increased, taking a wider variety of forms, such as the sharing of joys and satisfactions, and experiencing distress and suffering when others suffer. At least, there are sufficient grounds for holding that the impulse of sympathy supplies a reasonably universal and dependable basis for cooperation, whereas there is no parallel basis for competitive struggle.

Neither in cooperation nor in competitive struggle are techniques of response to particular situations hereditary. They are acquired. It is necessary for the techniques and the situations in which they are used both to be learned, and the patterns of both are supplied by the culture in which persons live. Our economic order sets the pattern of competitive struggle. Men engage in selfish, destructive competition not because of an instinctive impulse, but because the social order of which they are a part, with its competitive practices, teaches them to see the interests and efforts of others as antagonistic to their own, and insists that they can succeed only as they outwit and overcome others. To attain success it becomes necessary for them to inhibit their natural impulses of fellow feeling and sympathy, and to do this they must blind themselves to the fact that those against whom they compete and those whom they oppress by low wages and hard conditions of toil are human beings like themselves. They persuade themselves that they are "dagoes," "greasers," "lazy louts," shiftless, improvident, and incompetent. It is significant that the wage oppression, brutalities, and injustices of corporate management to a considerable extent vary in direct ratio to the distance by which the directors and stockholders are removed from the scene of operations, making impossible close, intimate, personal acquaintanceship.

Other positive bases of social conduct are found in human nature. Closely allied to sympathy is the natural impulse to help weaker persons, a tendency which, although it exhibits wide individual differences, is to some extent reasonably universal. It can at least be said that in all normal human beings the capacity inheres to be motivated by concern for the well-being of others. Another tendency of social significance is the desire to build, to make something, which finding expression in the child's urge to build a playhouse of blocks may in the grown man or woman be made a contributing motive to the building of a new and better social order.

The net effect of the foregoing is that there exists in original nature adequate basis for moral goodness defined in terms of social conduct. Within man's nature are to be found inherent tendencies which under cultivation and guidance constitute dependable materials for truly Christian character.

CONSCIENCE AND THE POWER TO LIVE BY IDEALS.—In our discussion of the dynamic factors in human conduct we have yet to list that power which more clearly and definitely than any other sets man apart from the animals as a higher order. Man is a moral being. There is within him the potentiality of inner authority, the sense of "ought"; and he possesses the capacity of development of this inner sense of moral obligation to a point where it becomes the dominant factor in the determination of conduct. Confronted by specific issues the individual finds hindrance to what he believes to be the right interposed both from within and without, and likewise re-enforcement both from without and from within. The decision in a particular case may come quickly and easily, or the conflict may be severe and prolonged; but in either case, if this inner moral potentiality has been developed, it is finally determined more than by anything else by the inner authority of conscience.

The attainment of adulthood, as has already been said, is less a matter of age reckoned by years, or of physical maturity, than it is of development of discriminating judgment, by which we mean judgment that includes ethical insight and moral discernment, and the power to live by ideals. The fully mature person is the man or woman who has reached that stage of moral development where he is no longer governed by constraint but regulates his life from within in obedience to the dictates of his own conscience.

In that development much more is involved than increase of knowledge. Growth in appreciation of social values and in social sensitivity is included, and likewise of the will to do as well as one knows and of acting in accord with the impulse of feeling with others. Social intelligence and sympathy, important as they are, in themselves are not enough. It is not uncommon to find persons who are keenly aware of the significance of certain social situations and extremely sympathetic in the sense of feeling deeply, who nevertheless are utterly selfish and do not turn a hand in the direction of relieving distress or changing causal conditions.

The development of ability of discrimination and of evaluation in ethical terms, and of power to choose the greater good at the cost of a lesser or a mere whim or sensual gratification, does not come as a free gift of the passing years, much less as a result of blind yielding to physical urges and emotional impulses, but must be achieved by conscious effort and as a by-product of struggle, conflict, and problem solving.

Nor can ideals be imposed from without. They must grow from within. Many costly failures have resulted from attempts to clamp down moral and social reforms upon people by legislation. Such attempts are bound to fail. No moral reform or social advance is either real or permanent unless it proceeds from within, finding expression in law or in institutional form as the response of individuals and of groups to ideals which have been developed. To aid in this development is one of the chief functions of Christian education.

THE RÔLE OF HABIT.—It is a great gain for character if the mind may be brought to a decision once for all to do no act that injures or degrades the personality of a fellow being. Such a decision contributes toward the integration of tendencies into a general pattern. Since one's habits are largely specific to particular situations, such a general decision, however, to be of major significance, must be followed by corresponding practice in a wide variety of situations.

Physiologically, habit is a conditioned response. By frequent successful repetition an initial response is developed into a pattern or set of tendencies so fixed in form that on the recurrence of like situations identical responses tend, without reflection, and even against one's will, to express themselves. Habit, therefore, inheres in the tendency for any process to be more readily repeated by virtue of previous occurrence, and in proportion to the number and frequency of previous successful repetitions. This so-called law of use or frequency is, however, subject to certain coincident conditions such as degree of satisfaction associated with completion of the process, and existence of a conscious purpose to achieve the result.

In adult life by far the greater part of all action and conduct is determined by habit. Every adult has built up through the years an immense number of action patterns which have become habit systems. Overstreet lists[12] *bodily habits,* which may include frequent or infrequent bathing, washing the hands and face, brushing the teeth, using cosmetics, rapid eating, gum-chewing, and many others; *work habits,* such as accuracy, diligence, thoroughness, or slovenliness; *play habits,* fair play, cheerful losing, particular forms of play and recreation; *consumer habits,* keeping a budget, paying cash, running up accounts, living beyond one's means; *moral habits,* truthfulness, deceptions, lying, sexual excesses, gluttonous eating, intemperate drinking, use of narcotic drugs; and *emotional habits,* sympathy, irritability, joyousness, moodiness. Thought will suggest numerous additions. A person is what he is in character and personality by virtue of the aggregate of his habit systems. Generalization regarding habits under any such list of categories needs, however, to be guarded by the principle, already mentioned, that all habits are very largely specific to situations. A man may be consistently kind and sympathetic in relations with his own children and utterly indifferent to the welfare of children living "across the tracks" on the other side of town.

It is plainly evident that if Christian education is effectively to aid men and women in the achievement of high-type character and personality it must give attention both to the formation and the re-forming of habits. Not infrequently what appears to be a serious personality defect may be nothing more than the lack of a right habit which the individual by counsel may be aided to form. It is of first importance, therefore, for Christian education to give attention to the formation of desirable habits. The improvement of character involves the substitution of more desirable goals and satisfactions, with corresponding activities, for those less desirable. Even so, religion insists that power is available by which evil habits may be overcome.

Without doubt, there are various types of habits which in time become so inwrought into patterns of action that no possibility remains of breaking them; they have become so ingrained that they cannot be broken. Nevertheless, religion has to its credit through the centuries an innumerable list of victories over destructive habits—drunkards reclaimed, panderers and prostitutes restored to virtue, and drug addicts cured. Unfortunately, religion has tended to center its power almost exclusively on the self-destructive habits of individuals to the neglect of social habits equally destructive. The warfare of the churches against the liquor traffic during an earlier period is an exception that merely confirms the rule.

Study of the basis of a particular habit suggests a necessary approach to re-formation. In every case the basis is found in response to a situation associated with a biological or physiological stimulus. Success in breaking the habit depends upon breaking the association. This may be most successfully done by separation from the situation that provides the association, or by replacing the particular type of association by another that is equally satisfying or pleasurable. The Salvation Army well knows that the permanent reform of the drunkard depends upon re-enforcing his personal decision by keeping him away from the saloon, from the sight and taste and smell of liquor, and by providing new friends and associates whose company he enjoys.

RECALCITRANT HUMAN NATURE.—It is clear that the existence in human nature of such positive bases for moral character as have been emphasized does not imply that man inherently is wholly good. Negative bases also exist, such, for example, as the impulse to defend oneself first and to advance oneself at the expense of others. In every man something of the brute remains. Whether one looks without, observing the conduct of individuals and of society, or within in self-examination, he finds abundant evidence of this fact. Other than human goodness, there is no more universal fact affecting human life than that of moral evil. Where is the adult who, if he is honest with himself, is not compelled to confess with the apostle, "The evil which I would not, that I do"? In these ancient words we hear the perennial cry of the baffled spirit. The higher one's aspiration, the stronger his purpose, the deeper his ethical insights, the keener his realization of his own shortcoming. The "lusts of the flesh," the "pride of life," and the "deceitfulness of riches," are as real obstacles to purity, humility, and exaltation of character as ever they were. As with the individual, so also with corporate life. No social system, however ideal its principles and its program, will be free from moral defects in practice so long as evil persists in human hearts.

The fact, stated in theological terminology, is that man is a mixture of original evil and original goodness; stated in the terminology of psychology, his personality is pulled by opposing impulses. Sin implies moral responsibility. The impulse to evil becomes sin when the person has knowledge of a moral standard which is violated; a realization that the action in intention or results violates the standard; and when he has capacity and freedom to obey the standard.[13] While it is a serious mistake for religionists to assume, as has so commonly been done in the past, that all personal and social maladjustments root in sin in the individual and are to be cured by individual repentance and conversion, it is equally mistaken to ignore the fact, as is frequently done today, that many maladjustments, both individual and social, are the direct outcome of an evil will in the individual for which repentance and conversion constitute the only effective cure.

FACTORS IN CONFLICT.—Thus is brought before us the eternal conflict between good and evil in human nature, if not in the majority of persons a strife so sharply drawn between flesh and spirit as was depicted by Paul and Augustine, nevertheless a conflict the results of which are reflected both in the inner life of the individual and in overt conduct.

Not infrequently one tendency is in conflict with another.

The acquisitive desire, for example, with the self-giving purpose. At other times native tendencies clash with social habits which restrict or inhibit them. To bring about a harmonious, consistent, and dependable organization of conflicting factors is a difficult undertaking, one in which the aid of religion is indispensable. Without harmonization the person becomes a slave of impulse. Failing to achieve integration, many an adult is a bundle of inner contradictions, driven now in one direction, now in another, taking refuge from the lashings of conscience by one or another form of rationalization of his courses of action.

COMPLICATIONS IN ACHIEVING INTEGRATION

The nature and outcomes of complicating factors peculiarly characteristic of present-day life are of such importance as to require further analysis.

COMPLEX NATURE OF EXPERIENCE.—Human experience always has been complex, but present-day experience has a degree of complexity all its own. To the modern man or woman life presents manifold situations. For a particular individual group situations may include, for example, the family, the church, a social club, a university club, the chamber of commerce, the American Legion, a board of directors, and several others to each of which he is called upon to make more or less distinctive adjustments, and in which the several rôles may be not only inconsistent but to a considerable degree conflicting. To attempt to make even a partially complete catalogue of specific adjustments involved in the different rôles assumed by the average man would make a long and varied list. In making adjustment to the several groups he is compelled frequently to compromise some of his ideals or self-approved standards; or if he adheres rigidly to his ideals, he is uncomfortable in his group adjustments and the associations are unsatisfying. Often, ideals being conceived in static terms whereas group associations offer variety and stimulation, what happens is that he lets his ideals go and conforms to the pattern of the particular group he is with at the time.

In an individual case either of several types of effect may result. The conflict of group practices and customs with his own standards may stimulate reflective thinking, critical examination of group behavior, and deliberate choice of nonconformity, resulting in independence, freedom of conduct, and something of creative contribution to group standards. More frequently the individual tends to assume the different rôles more or less unconsciously, without any clear realization of the inconsistencies involved. He becomes, not a conscious hypocrite, but nevertheless an unintegrated person.

CONFLICTS IN CONTEMPORARY CULTURE.—The existence of such disparate groups as have been mentioned reflects the fact that contemporary culture as a whole is characterized by serious inner conflicts that have a direct effect upon the individual.

Inherent in our culture are Christian traditions teaching kindness, humility, self-abnegation, nonviolence, and cooperation. Within the same culture another strain emphasizes the goal of individual success with self-assertion, aggressiveness, ambition, and competitive zeal as necessary components. Society asserts that the individual is free, independent, and unhampered, with unlimited material rewards within his reach if he is ambitious, energetic, and efficient. At the same time it subjects the large majority of its members to limitations and restrictions that thwart the ambitions it has inspired. Again, our culture exalts the individual and personal worth, theoretically placing a high value upon life and character, but at the same time cherishing an economic system which exalts property rights above the rights of personality and gives profit priority over human need, resulting in widespread unemployment with anywhere from one in ten to one in five of the total population in deprivation and want. Then, declaring that people must not be allowed to starve in the midst of potential plenty, the destitute millions are given "relief" at public expense on a basis somewhat above a starvation level. This obvious conflict is further complicated by the fact that although the Church and other social and educational institutions espouse the principles of justice, freedom, and brotherhood, they are dependent for maintenance upon income from the securities and the beneficiaries of the profit-centered economic order, and thereby committed to defense of the *status quo*. Obviously, the difficulty of persons achieving integration is immensely increased by their sharing the life of a social order that is a house divided against itself.

PERSONALITY DISORDERS.—Various types of personality disorders on the one hand result from such inner and outer conflicts as have been described, and on the other make the achievement of personal integration extremely difficult if not impossible.

Among the sources of personality disorganization are antagonism or struggle between motives; between conflicting impulses; between motives or impulses and ideals; between motives or impulses and custom or public opinion; and between individual capacity and group expectation. These inner conflicts often give rise to fears, hates, jealousies, inferiority complexes, and various types of emotional disturbance. They tend to influence the individual to seek compensation in some form of unreality; in bluffing, fantasy, or daydreaming; they disturb the mental balance, undermine physical health, and if unresolved and permitted to develop, may result in complete personal disorganization.

A basic method of psychotherapy in attempting treatment involves discovering and utilizing ways in which conflicting motives or impulses can be harmonized by bringing them into line with a goal which satisfies them all.

CONTRIBUTION OF RELIGION TO CHARACTER AND PERSONALITY

Our discussion has emphasized the necessity, if integrated, dependable character and personality are to be achieved, of the physical, intellectual, and emotional forces within human nature being co-ordinated and unified, so that they can work together. Implicit in this discussion has been recognition of the contribution of religion to this end. The form and extent of religion's contribution, especially the contribution of the Christian religion, requires more explicit statement.

PERSONS CAN BE SAVED.—A starting point is the assurance the Christian religion supplies that persons can be saved. The gospel is good news to the lost. Its word of hope is "whosoever." It refuses to limit God's power.

Psychology has not tended to be optimistic about the possibility of changing adult personalities in fundamental ways. It has emphasized the importance, even the necessity, if high-type personality is to be achieved, of beginning with the child. It has stressed the fact that adult habits, attitudes, opinions, and beliefs are fixed and for the most part permanent. But recent years have brought a change. Educational thought, and to a considerable extent psychology itself, has re-enforced the confidence of religion in the possibility of re-forming wrong trends, of purifying and regenerating motives, of co-ordinating impulses, of resolving conflicts, and of inspiring and developing new dynamics for living.

The saving help of religion, moreover, is not limited to those of high-grade intellectual ability. The limitation of moral development attributed to men and women of low-grade intellect* does not place them beyond the pale of religious help. Indeed, one of the greatly significant services of religion is what it is able to do, and is constantly doing, for persons of comparatively limited intellect.

A UNIVERSAL ASPECT OF EXPERIENCE.—A second basic consideration is the universal character of religious experience. Everywhere and throughout historic time men have been religious. Scientists today see in religion an irreducible aspect of experience.

It cannot be said, however, that within human nature there is an identifiable impulse or urge that can be separately labeled, along with other basic drives, as *the* religious urge.[14] Nor do distinctive religious reflexes exist, or emotions that are peculiar to religious experience.

The universal character of religion is seen again in this, that it is a quality, an attitude, a value which tends to attach to every and all experience of life. This same general characteristic of religion is to be seen in the fact that its nature and function cannot be defined exclusively either in terms of the intellect (religious beliefs), the emotions (religious feeling), or the will (doing or conduct), but are inclusive of all. The contribution of religion is to the total, unitary life of men.

A GOAL, A CAUSE, AND A PERSON.—The Christian religion is unique in that which it offers. In historical Christianity religion holds before men a supreme goal, eternal life in fellowship with God; presenting for men's allegiance and loyalty a supreme cause, the Kingdom of God on earth; and a supreme Person, Jesus Christ, as the object of love, reverence, and service.

There is no other goal of life comparable to that of social living —in fellowship with the Father of our spirits and with our fellow men, sharing in the life of God, and cooperating in human relations with the divine will and purpose. The appeal is to the highest aspiration of which the human heart is capable.

In cooperating with God in effort for the realization of the Kingdom of God on earth one discovers a cause greater than his own individual interests which calls for the full measure of loyalty and devotion. In its appeal to the imagination, its capacity of awaken-

---

* See page 146.

ing emotion, and of evoking wholehearted effort what other cause is comparable to this?

As abstract ideas, or even as programs of action, causes have limited power to inspire, to evoke enthusiasm and devotion, and to stimulate nobility of conduct. But the Christian religion offers a cause embodied in a Person who in his personality and character concretely represents all for which the Kingdom stands; it demands complete and unreserved commitment to him as Leader, Friend, and Saviour, and in so doing captures the imagination, stirs the emotions, and stimulates effort.

The man or woman who responds with his whole heart to the appeal of the Christian religion becomes an integrated person whose life takes on wholeness, unity, harmony, consistency of character, and strength and beauty of personality.

POWER FOR LIVING.—Religion opens a way of access of the individual soul to God, and in this contact with God is found a unique means of purifying the inner springs of motive and feeling. "From within," Jesus declared, "the designs of evil come." As the spirit, the motive, and the purpose of the individual are subjected to the cleansing, renewing influence of the divine spirit new orientation, new direction, and necessary dynamics come into life.

It is not to minimize the importance or the possible influence of environment upon the individual to say that no amount of change of environment will affect the character or personality of the man who lacks the inner resources to benefit by the change. Moreover, in innumerable instances overborne, frustrated men and women, baffled by their environment, by the power of religion have been lifted out of their confusion, saved from final defeat, and enabled to live victorious lives in the face of what had seemed insuperable obstacles.

The Christian gospel also provides deliverance for persons defeated in their struggle against sins. It provides a means of appropriating the saving grace of God. One who opens his mind and heart to God and surrenders his evil will finds a power coming into his life that he recognizes as more than his own. He finds himself experiencing a power to resist the temptation by which he has been overborne, and realizing new assurance, strength, and stability.

Specific cases of moral breakdown offer laboratory opportunities for re-education of which advantage should be taken.

CONVERSION.—In the literature of religion the word "conversion" has been commonly used as a kind of blanket term covering a wide range of religious experiences.   One writer of the psychology of religion distinguishes six distinct senses in which he has found the word used.[15]   This lack of discrimination, accuracy, and agreement in terminology has contributed to widespread confusion of thought.   Notwithstanding this fact there can be no doubt of the reality of a type of adult religious experience involving change of purpose, attitudes, ideals, and conduct, or of the large part that the conversion experience has had in the moral and religious aspects of both adolescent and adult life.

Adult conversion today is a much less frequent phenomenon in the evangelical churches than it was a few decades ago.   Certain reasons are not difficult to discern.   (1) The religious education movement has popularized the conception of normal religious experience as a gradual growth.   Children are recognized as having a religious life in their own right, to be continuously fostered. Large numbers of children, a constantly increasing number, are received into church membership.   Consequently, certain of the most significant conditions formerly lying back of adult conversion no longer exist.   (2) Certain types of conversion were to a considerable extent superinduced by prevalent theological teaching and preaching: a lost state due to sin, "original" sin (a sharing in the sin of Adam), and present sin, both presented in an abstract sense.[16]   There is much less of this teaching and preaching than formerly; consequently, fewer conversions.   (3) A reaction has taken place against some of the methods more or less common in revivals, and against the mass psychology frequently employed, by reason of which the results achieved were often not only superficial and lacking in reality, but were followed by "backslidings" and revulsions of feeling as a consequence of which the last state of the converts was worse than the first.   Some revivalists were more interested in working up intensity of feeling than in deliberate decision based upon consideration of all the factors involved, and there has been a wholesome reaction against emotional excesses.

The fact remains that conversion is both a needed and a possible experience for many adults.   There are many men and women, in the earlier lives of the most of whom religion has been a negligible factor, whose emotional and volitional makeup is such that if the Christian religion is ever to become a power in their lives, contributing in any large way to the remaking and development of personality, it must needs be by way of conversion in the sense of a radical change, a right about face, the choice of a new center of integration, and the development of new loyalties and utterly different attitudes. Such a conversion may be either sudden or gradual, although it is to be noted that even in the case of many of those whom William James termed the "twice-born," in whose lives a complete reversal of direction took place, the sudden change was preceded by a long conflict between conflicting motives and loyalties.

SPIRITUAL ILLUMINATION.—There is another type of experience which may perhaps be most fittingly described as spiritual illumination. It is to be doubted whether there may be said to be a typical form, but there are many examples, varying in particulars. A noteworthy instance is that which occurred in the life of Horace Bushnell, a man who has profoundly influenced the religious life and thought of America, and which made him a new man, or, as one has said, "the same man with a heavenly investiture." "On an early morning in February [1848]," reads his biography, "his wife awoke, to hear that the light they had waited for, more than they that watch for the morning, had risen indeed. She asked, 'What have you seen?' He replied, 'The gospel.' It came to him at last, after all his thought and study, not as something reasoned out, but as an inspiration, a revelation from the mind of God himself." Concerning this experience Bushnell himself said: "I seemed to pass a boundary. I had never been very legal in my Christian life, but now I passed from those partial seeings, glimpses, and doubts, into a clearer knowledge of God and into his inspirations, which I have never wholly lost. The change was into faith—a sense of the freeness of God and the ease of approach to him."

What is to be said of such an experience other than it is one whose reality, and value for the enrichment of life, is beyond all estimate? And how many adults there are who are in need of just such spiritual illumination!

RELIGION IN EMOTIONAL CRISES.—To any person life is likely to bring emotional crises of one sort or another, and not infrequently such an experience holds within itself possibility of significant contribution to the development of personality. A deep experience of love or of joy, of bereavement or of renunciation may be a highly educative force. In such an experience a vital truth never before clearly realized, or a significant conviction previously lightly held, may take hold upon life in a dynamic way. New insights may be gained and wide areas of life previously obscure may be illuminated as by a flood of light.[17]   Biography supplies many authentic examples of experiences of this kind.

EDUCATION THROUGH SUFFERING.—Just as the cross, according to the teaching of the Christian religion, is more than an incident in the life of a man, nothing less than a transcript of a deep and continuing self-giving of God for the redemption of man, so pain and suffering carry within themselves redemptive significance and possibility.

"The most educative experience in my life has been intense suffering," writes a woman of noble character.   There are many whose testimony is to the same effect.   It is for comfort in sorrow and suffering that many men and women are led to turn to God. Perhaps religious influences to which they were responsive were strong in their lives as children but in adult years they allowed themselves to become careless and indifferent.   Then sorrow or suffering came and they turned for consolation to religion.   Without doubt, this is a primary service of suffering: it directs the thoughts and desires of people toward God.   "In my sorrow," cried the psalmist, "my heart turned unto God," and innumerable others since his time have echoed his words.

But this is not all.   Observation and experience alike testify to the spiritual discipline of suffering.   It has the capacity to deepen, refine, and purify the springs of life.   It may develop the finer qualities and attitudes of character.   Patience, kindness, sympathy, and love are often its fruits.   Not always is this true.   The invalid is often petulant, fretful, and complaining; full of self-pity, evil forebodings, hypersensitive.   These things frequently are the concomitants of physical weakness and do not reflect the real effect of suffering upon the spirit, but in many cases suffering fails to produce desirable fruits.

The Christian conception of God—his goodness, his Fatherliness, his love—is dependent upon the view of human life and experience as discipline.   If there is no disciplinary value in the hard experiences of life; if pain and sorrow, disease and suffering, are not designed of God to be educative, if they do not actually refine and purify the human spirit, how is it possible to believe in the goodness and the love of God?   We live in a world of inevitable and abounding suffering, and if it may not be made to have influence or effect in the developing and perfecting of personality, we have slight basis for confidence in the benevolent purpose of the Supreme Being.

SOCIAL ASPIRATION AND EFFORT.—Again, if in all sincerity we believe that at the heart of the universe there is a power evermore striving for righteousness and justice, can we believe other than that through persistent effort to discover and through struggle to establish the conditions of a better world men come into fellowship with God? There can be no doubt that for a rapidly increasing number of socially sensitive persons religious forms and observances that are oblivious of or that gloss over the oppressions, injustices, and life-destroying factors of the prevailing economic system are morally offensive. Certainly for these and doubtless for many others personal participation in the struggle to bring society more nearly into conformity with the Kingdom of God is the most effective means of establishing contact with God. As men, misjudged and maligned, strive against great odds, enduring opprobrium, for the regeneration of the social and world order, they find coming into their lives a new assurance, a deepening sense of the sacredness of life, and a consciousness that they are sustained by a Power that is omnipotent and eternal and that finally shall prevail.

A GROWING RELIGIOUS EXPERIENCE.—The fact that religion relates itself to the whole of life requires, if religious experience is to continue to be vital, that the area of its application shall not be limited. Decision to live the Christian life most often is made in terms of a specific moral issue and in response to the decision fellowship with God is experienced. But if the experience of fellowship is to continue to be real, other areas of living must be brought into accord with the purpose and will of God. Either religion is a growing, expanding experience or it tends to lose its vitality and become sterile. In the refusal of so many church members to apply the ideals of their religion to business, industry, and the ordinary economic activities of everyday living is to be found sufficient explanation for the powerlessness and sterility so widely prevailing in the churches.

PERSONAL AND SOCIAL INTEGRATION INTERDEPENDENT.—In all that has been said the fact is not overlooked that personal and social integration are interdependent. Personality disorders within and without the churches are matched by chaotic conditions in society at large. Description of these conditions in preceding chapters has fallen far short of doing justice to the actual situations existing in many areas of our national life.

The individual human being is never disassociated from other human beings. Neither character nor personality can be achieved in isolation. The process of interaction is basic in all life. It has both a psychological and a biological foundation. Deprived of the possibility of sharing of life through association with other persons, the human infant could not possibly become a person in any full sense of the word. The sharing of the thoughts, the ideas, the folkways, the ideals, the loyalties, the very life of the group is a condition of the achievement of personality. Difficult under the most favorable conditions, the achievement of integration of personality becomes immensely more difficult in a chaotic and disordered world. The conclusion is inevitable that personal integration and social integration must go forward together. The two are inseparable. Neither can be achieved on the highest level without the other.

CHAPTER V

CHRISTIANIZING THE WHOLE OF LIFE

THAT the whole of life personal and social shall be made Christian is demanded by the conditions and needs of the new day. Nothing less than this will assure that the modern world can be saved from catastrophe. Christianizing life in all of its relationships, individual and social, is the new task of adult education.

The goal is fully developed Christians, men and women of strong, rich, fully developed personalities, who in personal and in group life are living in fellowship with a righteous God, to the working out of whose purpose in society they have dedicated their lives. A social order is required that values personality above property, so organized in its corporate life that the rights of persons are respected, and growth in character is not only possible but is stimulated by the social order itself. The demand of the times, in other words, is for Christian persons who validate their character as Christians by the kind of society they constitute in their social relationships.

ACHIEVING CHRISTIAN PERSONALITY

The type of personality to which the term "Christian" can fittingly be applied has been described at some length in the two preceding chapters. Personality of this type does not merely happen. If it is to be achieved in any large number of cases, the technique of achievement must be understood. What are some of the most important elements of successful technique?

EXPERIENCE OF CHRISTIAN LIVING.—Christian personality might almost be said to be a by-product of Christian living. Growth, as long ago Jesus declared, does not take place by sheer act of will. Persons grow as the conditions of growth are observed. As love, good will, cooperation, and the purpose to serve are made regulative in all of the intimate contacts of daily living involving human relationships, Christian personality is developed. In other words, Christian personality is achieved through a process of purposive growth.*

_____
* See page 246.

A continuous process of critical evaluation and reconstruction of experience is involved. What is the loving thing to do in this particular situation? What is the just course of action? How can cooperation be put into effect? These are the questions that one must insistently ask. In a period when a new social order is coming to birth there are few dependable patterns of action. There are no molds that can be trustingly followed. New patterns and molds must be created. Continually, therefore, the man or woman set on achieving Christian personality seeks critically to analyze his experience to discover not merely its surface aspects but its constituent elements, its very inwardness; to determine possible outcomes in the light of the highest ideals; and to reconstitute his practice in the interest of the enrichment of his own personality and the service of others.

A new technique this may seem to be in the face of traditional prescriptions for religious growth, but not new in the light of the process by which the first Christians became men enabled to go forth to turn their world upside down. Study anew the process by which a group of simple Galilean peasants became spiritually illuminated, intellectually awakened, morally energized, and socially motivated, in the company and under the guidance of Jesus, and one finds a first-century example of the very process described, in an age in many respects strikingly like our own.

Christian living is living in right relationships with men and in fellowship with God. It involves sharing the purpose of God. When our wills are in accord with the will of the Father, when we participate with him in his eternal task of creating a just, loving, and cooperative human society we most truly enter into fellowship with him. God does not live apart from men in solitary grandeur. He is within human society working even until now, striving, persuading, entreating, achieving. To engage with him in the building of a Christlike world, intelligently and with determined purpose to make his will our own, is to enter into an experience of divine fellowship which has reality.

This declaration is not a plea for mere activism. Christian living is not merely a program of action. The Kingdom of God is both an inner experience and a social achievement; both objective and subjective. For the individual it does not exist in separation from himself; only as it comes into existence in his own heart and mind does it for him become a reality.

A UNITARY EXPERIENCE.—The conditions of living of many as

involuntary participants in a pagan social order make unity of experience impossible: one cannot serve God and Mammon. Business men are exhorted to put religion into their business, but one cannot put the religion of Jesus into business that is essentially antisocial in its nature: oil and water do not mix. The realization that our economic and industrial life is so largely pagan in motivation and practice robs religious experience of much of its sense of reality, its vitality, and power. If one's vocation, and work within his vocation, are to contribute to the achievement of Christian personality it is necessary that the vocation itself shall be essentially Christian; that is, that it shall be essentially fraternal, brotherly, serviceable in its very nature, so one may truly feel in his business or professional relations that in carrying on his daily activities he is serving his fellow men and in so doing is serving God. It is only in serving human society that one in any real sense serves God. All talk, therefore, of serving God while one is engaged in vocational activities inherently selfish and antisocial is mere sham, a form of self-deception or of hypocrisy that undermines personality and tends to its disintegration.

A SENSITIZED ETHICAL CONSCIENCE.—A third requirement in achieving Christian personality is a conscience sensitized to the ethical issues involved in Christian social living. Widely prevalent in our present society, both within and without the churches, is a tendency on the part of many who possess more or less acquaintance with social facts and conditions to rationalize unethical practices. There are various familiar ways of doing this, one of the most common, for example, being that of excusing one's own unethical practice by the plea of making contributions to community chests, to churches, and to educational institutions. The Christian attitude requires clear recognition of participation, and frank acknowledgment of personal implication and responsibility. Wherein one willfully closes his eyes to unsocial conditions and practices, openly or tacitly refuses to acknowledge his own involvement in them, and rationalizes his conduct by saying either publicly or to himself, "All this has nothing to do with my religion; I contribute generously to the church and to charitable causes," he is showing himself to be less than Christian.

PARTICIPATION IN SOCIAL RECONSTRUCTION.—Growth in Christian character and personality involves participation in achieving the objectives visioned as necessary for a truly Christian world. No amount of sentimental, unfocalized good will can possibly avail for the reconstruction of the social order. It is not enough merely to give verbal assent to the objectives as desirable ends. "Why call ye me, Lord, Lord, and do not the things which I say?" The ineffectiveness in personality growth of much religious education lies at this point. Generalized ideals, abstract goals, are emphasized and high tribute is paid to them, but no specific attempt is made toward their realization. It is necessary to press beyond the mere visualization of objectives to decision as to means for their realization and, further, to the actual utilization of the means. This involves nothing less than wholehearted dedication of one's effort to the rebuilding of society as the Christian's lifework, each addressing himself to the task of reconstruction within the sphere of his daily occupation. In this way, whatever the Christian man's occupation may be, within it he will be engaged in its reconstruction, changing its motivation, reshaping its standards, reforming its practice.[1]

In some quarters, even among Christian leaders, disposition exists to stop short of deciding upon and putting to use specific methods. Practically everyone is willing to agree as to the desirability of Christian goals in a general, unfocalized sense. It is when specific methods and measures are proposed and adopted that disagreement and antagonism develop. Because of this difference of judgment and opposition, often among equally sincere persons, many draw back from determination upon and use of specific steps.[2] To adopt this course is to fail at precisely the point of greatest significance. To profess adherence to general goals and yet do nothing toward their attainment is not merely futile; it is, again, a kind of self-deception, a species of hypocrisy. Abstract principles and ideals are, of course, essential but they become intrinsically meaningful and dynamic only as they are made concrete in action.

MASTERY OF LIFE SITUATIONS.—General principles and ideals are translated into concrete actions in specific situations. The specific situation is the matrix in which the principle or the ideal as the object of desire and of purpose is transformed into character. The mastery of life situations, therefore, becomes the means of achieving Christian personality.

Technique of mastering situations will be discussed at a later point in this book.* Here it is perhaps sufficient to emphasize the

* See pp. 312ff.

importance of developing competent judgment as an element in achieving Christian personality.   Many of the problems faced by Christians today in the decay and disintegration of an out-moded social order are distinctly new.   Old formulas no longer apply.   A dynamic, creative attitude toward life is required if ade-quate solutions of new problems are to be found, an attitude that is expressive not of a sense of obligation to conform to traditional patterns but of a sense of responsibility to make a creative contribu-tion to the building of a better world.

PHYSICAL, ECONOMIC, AND SOCIAL DISCIPLINE.—Strong and rich personality cannot be achieved without personal discipline.   It is not something that comes by withdrawing from besetting problems, difficulties, and struggles, but by participation in life, acknowledg-ing its imperfections, accepting its limitations, but continually striving to overcome.   Unity, poise, and power come as the result of following a consistent, established way of living.

A primary requirement is keeping the body fit.   Attention to regular bodily habits is necessary.   Diet must be intelligently regu-lated.   Hard work, physical and mental, is beneficial, but there must also be relaxation and recreation.*

Strict moral discipline in all economic activities is necessary. Prevailing standards of ethics in the most common activities of everyday living must be subjected to the test of Christian ideals, buying and selling in all ordinary functions as consumers and producers, all relationships as employers and employees, all savings and investments.   The fact that evil has entered into the structure of the prevailing economic order and is a part of the warp and woof of the social fabric must be recognized.   One cannot with-draw from all participation in prevalent economic practices if he is to continue to live in this present world, but he can bring to bear upon them a Christian conscience and subject his own activi-ties to strict discipline.   So also as regards all social relationships.[3]

DISCIPLINE IN MEDITATION AND PRAYER.—For several decades there has been not only growing neglect but also positive reaction against long-practiced techniques of Christian living such as private prayer, directed meditation, and family worship.   During a period when in certain other areas of life there has been an increasing emphasis upon method and technique, systematic methods of nurture of the spiritual life have become almost taboo.   One after

---

* See pp. 342ff.

another, observances which former generations regarded as sacred have been all but discarded. If not for all, for many persons the result has been serious. Instead of unity, poise, and power, uncertainty, superficiality, confusion, and in many cases, moral weakness, characterize the inner life.

The value which the Christian religion places upon personality means that each person has a definite place and work in God's world. Successful living depends upon discovering the place one is fitted to fill and giving oneself to it with persistent energy, courage, and determination. Meditation and prayer aid in the discovery. A brief period of time daily for clarifying one's thought of his vocation and of the immediate tasks which it presents, and for cultivating the attitudes which religion requires, contribute to the unity and poise of the inner life and unlock hidden reserves of power.

Everyone has need for perspective on his own purposes and activities, viewing them from a vantage point removed from the distractions and confusions of the everyday whirl of things. Neither obsession with the details of immediate experience in dealing with a situation nor objective detachment from it are conducive to the most sound judgment. But both together are.

What method of meditation and prayer shall be followed by a particular person may not be prescribed. That which one finds most rewarding, to another may not prove to be so. Some will be helped most by listening in silence to the inner voice after the manner of the Society of Friends; others by systematic use of a selected ritual; yet others by the faithful observance of a daily period of extempore prayer; and yet others by wholly different methods.

Emphasis is not upon the virtue of a particular method, but upon the value of *method* systematically used. Especially in times such as these, when the foundations of the established order are crumbling, and outer conditions are turbulent and chaotic, it is necessary for the inner life to be systematically nurtured and well disciplined.

The authenticated values of meditation and prayer are many. Ethical insight is clarified and deepened, poise is cultivated, life purpose is strengthened, energy is increased, and courage is achieved to carry on in the face of whatever difficulties the day may bring. Dare any man venture to undertake the reformation of society without the faithful use of demonstrated means of reconstruction and purifying of his own inner life and conduct?

PRACTICE OF UNIVERSAL BROTHERHOOD.—The Christian man is a citizen of the world. Acknowledging allegiance to the nation whose government grants to him the right of suffrage, he is also bound by a higher allegiance to the Kingdom that knows no boundaries of nation or race. One of the strange anomalies of our age is the fact that at the very time nationalism is expressing itself in the most extreme and rigid forms a world culture, for the first time in human history, is in process of development. While racial prejudices and antagonisms are rampant and barriers of racial exclusiveness abound throughout the world, at the same time interrelations between people of different nations and races have never been so full or free. The interchange of racial cultures goes on apace, the channels of intercommunication are multiplied, and the ultimate possibility of a world democracy draws constantly nearer. To be a Christian at all one must be a world Christian. The practice of universal brotherhood becomes necessary to the development of Christian personality.

ACHIEVING A CHRISTIAN SOCIETY

A person cannot live his life apart from the community at large. The act of living inevitably involves participating in the common activities of society. The individual and society are so interrelated that the achievement of Christian personality in any complete sense is impossible in an unchristian society.

We have described the general characteristics of a Christian society.* It will be generally agreed, we believe, that a social order to be worthy of the name Christian must be democratic, brotherly, and without conflicting class distinctions. What does this general description require in terms of specific characteristics?

What the precise form of an attainable ideal society should be, who is prepared to say? Certainly, we shall not undertake within a few pages to present a detailed picture. Nevertheless some particulars seem reasonably clear.

PHYSICAL BASIS OF THE GOOD LIFE FOR ALL PERSONS.—The natural resources of the earth are a divine gift to mankind. Faith in a righteous and just God, the Father of mankind, involves as an inherent element the conviction that God intended these resources not for a privileged few, but to be conserved and used for the benefit of all. We have come into an age of the world when science, indus-

_____
* See pp. 131ff.

try, and technological skill have made possible the utilization of these resources in such a way as to provide the physical basis of the good life for all people. No longer is there need for any man, woman, or child to suffer from hunger, cold, or poverty. Food, clothing, and housing can readily be made available in adequate supply for everyone, as also an individual income or social provision adequate for all other material elements of a satisfying life. Sufficient energy resources, production facilities, technological skill, social intelligence, and professional personnel are now available to make possible a high standard of living for the total population. This is certainly true of the American nation, and with artificial barriers restricting international exchange removed, probably true of the whole world. Only selfishness, greed for individual privilege and power, and social inertia involving resistance to change,[4] stand in the way. To be Christian, society must overcome or remove these hindrances and make available the minima of the good life for all people.

There is, of course, truth in the contention often advanced that poverty is a relative matter and that in any society, due to deficiencies of character and of native endowment, poverty will be present in some degree. But what we are now discussing is the unnecessary deprivation of the physical necessities of the good life, the abolition of which depends on the form of organization of economic life rather than on factors of character and ability. Under conditions now existing such deprivation becomes a moral issue since the persistence of crippling poverty is a matter for which individuals, who hold economic power, and society, are responsible.

A FREE SOCIETY.—Freedom is a necessary condition of a Christian social order. The principle was asserted by Paul in unequivocal terms: "Where the spirit of the Lord is, there is liberty." His word has been verified by the history of succeeding centuries. A passion for freedom and an insistence upon individual liberty have characterized Christian people of every age since the beginning of Christianity. The Church in the Middle Ages ceased to be the defender of the spiritual liberty of the individual, but the central emphasis of Protestantism upon freedom of individual conscience and the sacredness of the individual person as a free moral agent, in interpretation of faith and obligation, renewed the original Christian demand for the maximum personal liberty consistent with the equal liberty of all other individuals. Unfortunately, it cannot be asserted that the churches that grew out of the Reformation possess a consistent record, either in the promotion of spiritual and civil liberties or in their defense in the modern world.

A significant factor in the settlement of the North American continent and in the establishment of government was the demand for liberty—freedom of religious conscience, freedom of speech, freedom of assembly and petition.   Granted that the demand for liberty stopped short of a broad tolerance and that some of the colonies exhibited an unwillingness to grant to others the liberty they demanded for themselves, even in some instances excluding minorities and denying civil and religious rights to those whom they regarded as heretics, it remains true that this heritage played a significant part in doing away with chattel slavery.   Conscientious people found it impossible to reconcile slavery with the inalienable right of every human being to liberty.

In the meantime with the rise and development of the industrial order a new type of slavery, economic serfdom of industrial workers, and, more recently, of corporation employees, has come into existence.   The degree of regimentation and the wage bondage of many industrial workers in recent decades has exceeded the deprivation of liberty of many chattel slaves of an earlier period. As long ago as 1912 a government commission, on the basis of extensive study of industrial conditions, declared: "These investigations have shown that under the best possible conditions, and granting the most excellent motives on the part of employers, freedom does not exist either politically, industrially, or socially, and that the fiber of manhood will inevitably be destroyed by the continuance of the existing situation."[5]

So widely possessed as to be almost universal in America is a sentimental regard for freedom as an inalienable part of our national heritage.   But freedom must be given a new content. The old *laissez-faire,* every man for himself, concept of freedom must be revised.   Freedom must be conceived in what are at one and the same time economic and thoroughly Christian terms.   Toward this end progress is being made.

Gradually the Christian conscience has shaped the conviction that economic freedom is essential to human liberty.   It is clearly recognized by many today that without economic independence political and religious liberty becomes null and void, a mere hollow sham without substance or reality.   The man or the woman —of whom there are millions in America—who has become a mere tool, subject to the will and economic caprice of another, spending and being spent for the other man's profit, is robbed of his freedom and suffers the degradation of his personality. Together with political and religious liberty, economic freedom is a necessary condition of a Christianized social order.[6]

First steps toward breaking the force of wage bondage are found in insistence upon the right of workers to organize and form group associations capable of dealing as economic equals with their employers, and the associated right of bargaining collectively with employers through representatives of labor's own choice. These initial steps, now almost universally approved by the Christian conscience, should be supplemented by recognition of the necessity of, and provision for, production for use in place of production for private profit.

A JUST SOCIETY.—To be Christian, a free society must also be just. This is a clear implication from the nature of God. A just God requires justice in human relationships. The maintenance of institutions and practice involving deep-seated or flagrant injustice is a denial of faith.

Testimony to the basic quality of justice is found in the fact that most of the great mass upheavals in human history have rooted in a deep sense of injustice and in persistent determination to resist at whatever cost.

Widespread and continuing difference in the economic level of large groups of people in an age when resources for abundant living for all are available bears indisputable testimony to injustice in economic arrangements. Individual differences in ability, initiative, and industry account for considerable differences in material circumstances of individuals, but differences in group or class levels cannot be accounted for on this basis. These differences find their explanation in the exploitation of one class by the other, an exploitation that not only robs great numbers of people of their rights but destroys human solidarity, makes true fraternity impossible, and prevents realization of fullness of personality on the part of the members of the exploited class. Exploitation is based upon privilege, such forms of privilege, for example, as disproportionate power of corporate wealth, the private ownership and monopoly control of mineral wealth (coal, oil, aluminum, etc.), of water power, of transportation and means of communication, and of heavy industries.

Not only in its inequality and class exploitation is our prevailing social order unjust. The poor are commonly regarded as of inferior moral worth.   They are more subject to arrest and to cruel and inhuman treatment than are the rich.   Access to the courts, because of court fees and costs of counsel, is for them difficult—often practically impossible.   The same things are true of cultural and racial minorities—immigrants, the Indians, and Negroes.   Flagrant denial of justice to Negroes has been long continued and in some parts of the country is believed to be steadily increasing.   Members of minority groups other than racial also are often denied the full protection of the courts, particularly political nonconformists and advocates of fundamental social change.

If a Christian society is to be achieved, ways must be found of doing away with the numerous forms of injustice which now so widely prevail.

A COOPERATIVE SOCIETY.—The Christian principle of the brotherhood of man finds its concrete application in a cooperative society in contrast to the profit economy dominated by the method of competition.

Competition makes a direct and powerful appeal to selfishness and greed and stimulates jealousy and ill will.   It is not good sportsmanship; it permits the unscrupulous and the greedy to set the pace that others must follow, and, since it always involves insecurity, stimulates uncertainty and fear.   Although free competition is assumed as basic by *laissez-faire* capitalism it has proven itself so destructive that corporations in recent decades almost universally have undertaken to work out pacts and agreements among themselves restraining and limiting competition, thus testifying to its destructive character.   Moreover, within their organizations they are earnest in their promotion of cooperation.   Indeed, it is increasingly being said that the greatest strength of capitalism is to be found in the degree of cooperation that it possesses.

It is contended by some that the assumption of possibility of development of a truly cooperative society is pure utopianism; that no method of organization or gradual refinement of culture will materially affect for the better the deep-lying strain of selfishness embedded in human nature; that in the nature of the human case even man's altruism and idealism are so infected with self-interest that they "easily become subterfuges of the will to power and of self-assertion."   Granted that the subjugation, not to say the elimination of self-interest always has tested the power of religion, it is also true as we elsewhere emphasize* that impulses of sympathy and

---

* See p. 155.

of mutual aid and cooperation are likewise deeply inwrought in human nature. The issue of social advance largely depends upon what set of native drives our social structure encourages and cultivates.

If it be true, as it is, that self-interest is native to human nature, it is equally true that selfishness is a product of a competitive, individualistic civilization. A chief problem of our culture, therefore, becomes one of developing a social order that stimulates and provides the means of strengthening and developing mutuality and the cooperative impulses, at the same time conserving the positive values of individualism through providing possibility of individual initiative and development.

Organized cooperation has made remarkable progress in recent decades.[7] It has progressed sufficiently to have proven not only its practicability but its economic efficiency. There is no longer excuse for the assertion that cooperation is a beautiful ideal that will not work. There is far more justification for the claim that, under modern technological conditions and power production, cooperation is the only economic system that will work. At any rate, it is so indispensable to the development of moral character in persons and to peace in society that the Christian conscience must insist on the elimination of the profit economy and the substitution in its place of a cooperative society.

WITH PROPERTY RIGHTS FOR ALL.—The possession of private property, within reasonable limits and without transgressing upon the rights and privileges of others, increases the sense of personal responsibility and the sense of security and therefore contributes to moral character. In a truly Christian society property will be more widely diffused and more generally held than at present. A situation such as has prevailed in recent years in which many millions of people own no share whatever in the productive capital of the nation, vast numbers of them dispossessed of their homes and farms, leaving them with insufficient furniture, clothing, and food for comfort and bodily nourishment, presents a condition abhorrent to religion.

The much-vaunted ownership of shares in immense corporations by workers and by the general public in a very large proportion of cases resolves itself into the holding of mere certificates of ownership, in many cases the holding by many individuals of a very few such certificates, which carry with them no means of effective control: the small management group within the corporation has usurped ownership functions. It may fairly be questioned whether possession of certificates of ownership without a corresponding measure of control constitutes ownership in any real sense.

Before the rise of modern industrialism under the aegis of the profit economy the worker owned the tools of production with which he performed his labor. Though his output was small what he produced he owned. The workman in modern industry owns nothing. The machinery he operates is owned by the corporation for whom he works. The modern system has immensely increased the output of the workman but has eliminated his ownership.

There are at least two ways by which property rights and property holding by all can be increased. One way is the wide extension of public ownership and control. The community of persons possesses property rights not only in the property to which its individual members hold title but also in the property which it holds in common as a community. Of the latter the most common examples at present are the parks, waterworks, libraries, schools, and playgrounds. The property rights and holdings of the people as a whole should be further increased by the speedy socialization of property in which private ownership by establishing virtual monopoly has become immoral. A second way is by wide extension and development of the several types of producers' and consumers' cooperatives.[8] Cooperatives offer a peaceful democratic means by which the masses may gradually regain the property that has been filched from them by economic overlords and greedy corporations.

WITH APPROXIMATE EQUALITY.—The North American nation in its founding was dedicated to the proposition that all men are created free and equal. To the Christian still more fundamental is the fact that his religion asserts and insists upon the equality of all souls before God. There is no lack of reason, therefore, for the Christian conscience to demand equal rights, equal opportunities, and equal privileges for all as marks of a Christian society.

In these days of vast inequalities and enormous special privileges possessed by the few one hears with increasing frequency the loud declaration that men are not in fact born equal and that any claim to equality is visionary. Equal in native capacity and in acquired abilities, by no means; a kind of inequality that in any society will probably in some measure be reflected in inequality of possessions. But all men are equal in the fact that all are persons, endowed by their Creator with personality and the intrinsic rights and privileges that are inherent in its possession. The maintenance of these rights and privileges, including approximately equal opportunities, and the abolition of special privilege, a Christian society will not only demand but find means of enforcing.

PROVIDING EDUCATIONAL OPPORTUNITY.—Among the rights common to all persons is that to the cultivation of native abilities through education. Society has made notable progress in the growth of provision for institutional education, particularly of children and youth. But what has been done is scarcely more than a beginning. Facilities for the free education of all, both youth and adults, through making available the cultural resources of mankind to millions who heretofore have had no access to them should be provided as a necessary element in the service of society to the individual.

For well-rounded personal development leisure is necessary. Persons whose occupational activities consume their entire time other than the hours required for sleep cannot take advantage of cultural opportunities. Regulation of hours of labor by law is necessary. Provision also is required for recreational facilities offering possibilities to all for the creative release of energy during leisure time.

UTILIZING ART, SCIENCE, AND TECHNOLOGY FOR THE COMMON WELFARE.—Time was when labor and industry essentially were the means by which men made possible the type of living that represented their conception of the good life. In Athens, for example, labor, industry, and wealth were utilized for the public welfare. Temples and theaters representing the triumph of art were built for the culture and enjoyment of the citizens.

In modern times science has made phenomenal advance in numerous ways, including power production. Engineering knowledge and technological skill have progressed to a degree hitherto undreamed of. To what purpose? The triumphs of modern science and technology have been used to enrich privileged individuals. They have been prostituted to private exploitation to the end of profit. Our communities, as communities, are generally poor; in many cases the communities in which there has been the greatest concentration of industrial production and from which a few individuals have extracted the greatest wealth, the poorest of all.

A Christian society will change all this. It will recognize that science and technology exist for the support of life on the higher levels.   It will undertake to make industry again the means by which humanity as a whole provides for itself a life of beauty, dignity, and culture.   It will design a production system in which the quantity of goods produced is determined by the consumption needs of all the people instead of permitting quantity of production to be determined by the desire of the few for profits.   In other words, the Christian conscience will insist that science and technology shall serve the needs of mankind; that production shall be for use, not merely for material gain; and will not tolerate their irrational, immoral perversion in the interest of selfish greed for power and profit.

A PLANNED AND PLANNING SOCIETY.—We have said to be Christian a social order must be democratic, brotherly, and without conflicting classes.   More specifically, that it must provide the physical basis of the good life for all; that it must be a free and just society, cooperative, with property rights for all, affording approximate equality, providing educational opportunity, and utilizing art, science, and technology for the common welfare.   To thinking people it must be clear that a society answering this description must be a planned and planning society.   These gains will not come merely by chance or by individual caprice.

Social planning involves a considerable degree of social ownership but not necessarily to a degree that excludes private ownership.   As already stated, private property is essential, in widest possible distribution, for development of responsibility and other character values.   But some things are so basic in their relationship to the utilization of natural resources by science and technology for the common welfare that a Christian society cannot be content with futile attempts to regulate their private ownership and control.   Included are: (1) sources of power such as water, coal, oil, gas, and electricity; (2) transportation and communication systems; (3) instruments of banking and credit; (4) such production plants of necessary commodities as developing experience may prove to be required.   Social ownership of this degree will make possible the utilization of good will, intelligence, knowledge, skill and technical processes in adjusting production to measured needs, both material and cultural.   It will generate and give free play to the motive of service.   It will reduce privilege and the possibility of exploitation to a minimum.   It will eliminate starvation and body-and-soul destroying deprivation.   It will vastly increase the possibility of an integrated, emotionally adjusted life for all. Finally, it will give meaning and reality to Christian brotherhood.

Can a planned and planning society at the same time be a democratic society? First, let it be clearly and definitely understood that by a planned and planning society is not meant overhead planning by government of the economic life of the nation. There is prevalent a type of collectivist thinking which contends for overhead planning in terms of highly centralized government within which an economically supreme general staff, with dictatorial powers, governs the technical operation of all major sources of raw material and supply.[9] This would be the antithesis of democracy.

Is it possible to plan efficiently, and to enforce the plans agreed upon, through the use of democratic instrumentalities? Or, does planned production for use inevitably mean the totalitarian State? Is not the lust for power as deep-seated and as subject to selfish abuse as the greed for profit and wealth? Will not the planners who, if planning is to be effective, must possess some degree of coercion, inevitably become the dictator?

Herein, undoubtedly, is one of the central, basic issues of our times. To these questions no one can return a dogmatic answer, for the past offers no guidance growing out of experience.

Technological knowledge and skill are available for democratic use. If the schools and the churches are utilized with anything approaching maximum possibility, there is reason for faith that the present adult generation can be educated to act intelligently, effectively, and democratically in planning for and providing the things society needs and should have.

CHRISTIANIZING ALL AREAS OF LIFE

Our discussion concerns Christianizing the whole of life. Life as it is lived today is exceedingly complex. The wide variety of experience embraced within adult living presents such extent and diversity as seemingly to defy analysis.* Any attempt at analysis reveals the fact that experiences are located in many different areas more or less clearly distinguished. Much that has just been said has concerned the economic area of life. Another important area involves the parental relationship. Still another, one's relationships and activities as a citizen. If life as a whole is to be Christianized, education must deal, not merely with one or

---

* Further discussion of analysis of functions and relationships will be found in Chapter XII.

with a few, but with all of the varied relationships and activities of living.

TRANSFORMING ALL AREAS AND ACTIVITIES OF LIVING.—In daily life and conduct many persons are Christian in certain relationships and areas and very unchristian in others. Many apply Christian principles to some one particular area of living and fail utterly to apply them to others. It is not at all uncommon to find church members who within the relationships of the family are kind, loving, generous, self-sacrificing, and forgiving, but in their relationships with their employees are selfish, ungenerous, and unduly exacting; and with their competitors in business are greedy, crafty, and drivers of cheap bargains. Many who are sympathetic and kind as neighbors are uncharitable and selfish in the principles which they contend should apply in international relations.

The possible service of Christian education in Christianizing the whole of life has been hindered in the past by the general, unfocalized sense in which religion has been construed in popular thought. It has been assumed by many in the evangelical churches that a person is either a Christian or not a Christian, either "saved" or "unsaved," whereas a person may be Christian in certain attitudes and decidedly unchristian in others. Probably most of the men and women who become Christians in later youth or in adult life make their decisions around some specific moral question. Some specific unchristian act or habit becomes the "hot spot" in consciousness. They determine by the help of God to quit the act or practice. In religious terminology they repent and are converted. That is, they begin to live a Christian life in some specific area of experience. That is the natural and normal way for a Christian life to begin, but it is a tragedy if the process stops with that. It is the business of religious education, beginning with the limited area within which a change has been made, to increase the spread of Christian principles until the whole of life is Christianized.

TRANSFORMING GROUP STANDARDS.—It is necessary for adult education to concern itself not only with individual living but with group practice. Group standards and practices are compellingly influential upon the individuals of the group. Many of them are so insidious and powerful that persons are influenced in spite of themselves. It is only the occasional man or woman who is able to withstand the coercive influence of the group. Methods and techniques are required that aim at group reeducation.

CHANGING THE STRUCTURE OF THE SOCIAL ORDER.—It should be realized that the achievement of a Christian society possessing the characteristics described involves structural changes in the economic order. Mere changes in the attitudes of owners and managers of industries will not suffice. For directors of a corporation to become more kind and benevolent is desirable, but it does not change the nature of the profit system by whose motive and method in the last analysis their actions are governed: an evil tree cannot bring forth good fruit. What has indisputably proven itself to be an inhuman social order must be changed and in its place must be established "a more humane order which will create a true hierarchy of values, put money in the service of production, production in the service of humanity, and humanity itself in the service of an ideal which gives meaning to life."[10]

It is possible for basic structural changes to be made gradually and by peaceful means. It is a part of the responsibility of Christian education to teach that this can be done, how it can be done, and to guide the process of change.

Structural change in the economic order is seldom, if ever, effected by political means. When an election has been won at the polls, if the new administration should make an attempt to take over profitable industries, the owners in all probability would resist, and as the holders of wealth and power they would be in a position to resist successfully. Futile governmental attempts by law, operating through political instrumentalities, to control, modify, and reform corporate industry afford abundant illustration of what would take place.

So also with an attempt to effect structural change through a revolutionary uprising of the proletariat. Such an attempt in all probability would result in the establishment of Fascist rule with the holders of economic power using the military forces on a national scale to re-enforce and permanently strengthen their control. Force begets force. Violence, used in behalf of whatever objectives, can only lead to discord and to further violence.

Convinced that the profit economy is unjust, undemocratic, and unchristian, beginning in local communities to build cooperatively owned and controlled units of production and distribution, thus developing economic power, at the same time encouraging trade union organization and using political action, the people can gradually and peacefully effect the structural change necessary in the economic order. It will not be easy. A long and doubtless in many instances a painful struggle will be involved. The process of gradually regaining basic economic power by and for the people, the power that inheres in ownership and control of the basic means of production and distribution, is bound to be resisted. But with clear vision, social intelligence, skill, and determination it can be done.

CHRISTIAN LIVING AN ADVENTURE.—In a day when Christian principles require that profound social change shall be made, earnest Christian living takes the character of an adventure. Beyond elemental convictions that the prevailing order is basically unchristian and that particular changes in its character are required, it is not always entirely clear what is the Christian thing to do in specific situations. There are honest differences of opinion as to what constitutes Christian practice. Men and women of equal intelligence and conscientiousness differ as to what are the implications of particular Christian principles in terms of concrete actions. Within various areas of living there is today both opportunity and need for adventure and creativity.

THE PROCESS: RECONSTRUCTION OF EXPERIENCE

The primary objective of adult education, we have reiterated, is new persons in a new world. Stated from the viewpoint of persons as learners, achieving Christian personality and a Christian society. A central problem, therefore, as has already been emphasized, concerns the process by which Christian personality and a Christian society are to be achieved.

CHRISTIAN RELIGIOUS EDUCATION.—Persons realize themselves through their experience. Life is made up of a constant succession of experiences to which responses are being made, simple or complex, in thinking, in feeling, in acting, in various combinations. Christian personality is achieved when the responses of which living consists may be said to have a thoroughly Christian quality.

From the standpoint of the adult leader and teacher Christian religious education is a process of lifting all the experiences of living to a Christian level, of guiding persons in responding to all the situations of life in Christian ways, and thus aiding them in achieving Christian personality. Since persons are constantly responding in many cases to identical or similar situations, religious education becomes a process of altering responses, of making them more and ever more fully Christian, or of reconstructing experience in the light of a growing understanding and appreciation of Christian principles and ideals.

Achieving a Christian society involves the reconstruction of an immense number of concrete situations which make up the total life of a complex social order. The process required is that of the understanding, mastery, control, and change of actual group-life situations.

RESPONSIBILITY OF ADULT RELIGIOUS EDUCATION.—The religion of Jesus with its ideal of perfection of persons in love and in brotherhood constitutes a challenge to our present-day world. We know that a process of reconstruction involving radical, basic changes in personal living and in the structure of the social order can go on, and in the face of a continuing crisis must go on. That it shall go on it is necessary that more and more men and women, as individuals and as groups, shall be enlisted in the actual task of reconstruction of the concrete, day-by-day situations that they face in daily living. This is the responsibility of adult religious education. It is called upon to relate itself to the experiences of men and women in day-by-day living in every area of experience. Its task is continually so to bring concrete experiences into consciousness that they will be reflected upon, to aid in interpreting them in the light of their relation to God, and to assist in bringing them under control in terms of the ideals and principles of the Christian religion.

The objective is not only becoming Christian in an ever-increasing number of the areas of life but, equally, becoming more and more Christian in each of them. The man or woman who has determined to live as a Christian in his home, in his economic relations, and as a citizen has only made a beginning. Jesus insisted that the disciple should advance beyond the standard commonly accepted by the religion of his day. "Ye have heard that it was said, . . . but I say." In each of the particulars that he mentioned Jesus called for an advance over the practice of the most religious people of the time.

Conceived in these terms the religious education of adults is never finished, since life is forever changing, not always expanding, perhaps, but shifting—presenting new and different experiences growing out of the changing relations and functions of daily living.

SOME EDUCATIONAL PRINCIPLES

Measured against the needs and objectives that have been described, the limitations and shortcomings of what has passed for adult religious education in the churches become profoundly disturbing.   Clearly, traditional religious education has not and cannot meet the demands of such times as these.

An element in the ineffectiveness of much that has borne the name of religious education is that it has been merely the repetition of familiar doctrinal platitudes that bear no relation to the problems and difficulties and burdens of everyday living.   Some of these bear the label of religion because at some time in the remote past they were a part of the religious experience of living beings. The currents of everyday living long since cut new channels, leaving this "doctrine" as so much driftwood high and dry on the hills of long ago, utterly unrelated to the everyday problems and needs of men and women of the present age.

APPLYING RELIGION TO LIFE.—Religion is so integrally a part of the processes of living, of the very warp and woof of today's life, that when it is treated as something separate and unrelated, it tends to lose those very qualities by virtue of which it maintains its integrity as religion.[11]   So also with religious education.   It is the business, therefore, of religious education to establish and maintain contact with the whole of life.

Prevailing practice in religious teaching wholly neglects many areas of daily living.   Asked what he is trying to accomplish in teaching his adult class, a teacher is likely to reply, "I am teaching the Bible," or "I am trying to lead the members of the class to become Christians," or some variation of either or both answers. If the question is pressed in terms of specific objectives, or of areas of living, how much awareness is discovered of the concrete life situations within the experiences of members of the group wherein lie the real issues of Christian living?   So far as the teaching concerns actual problems of daily life and conduct are not these confined to very limited areas, with other large areas of life seldom or never touched in definite, positive terms?   Similarly, a careful check-up of the content of most of the "lesson helps" used in the adult classes of the churches would show predominant attention given to a few limited areas of living with other equally important areas almost entirely overlooked.

Especially neglected has been the economic area.   The religion of Jesus has seldom been applied in concrete terms to the motives and the practices of the profit economy.   The clear implications of Jesus' teaching concerning the nature and character of God, brotherhood, love, and service have not been so enforced as to make plain the unchristian character of the motivation and practice dominating our prevailing industrial and economic system. The criteria that our religion supplies have not in the past been so clearly and definitely made the possession of the members of the churches that they have had the conviction and understanding necessary for intelligently evaluating the social order of which they are a part.   Religious education cannot escape condemnation for failure in making plain to religiously earnest men and women the essentially unchristian nature, and effect on character, of the dominant forces working within our economic life.   Such virtues and traits as can be inculcated within the framework of a profit-motivated, competitive society, without coming sharply into conflict with its prevailing practices, have been concretely emphasized. But others, even more central and basic in Christian ethics, which in concrete application would sharply challenge the *status quo,* have been commonly presented only as unfocalized ideals, not effectively taught.   As a result the moral thinking of church members has been superficial and in large measure unreal; it has strained at gnats and swallowed camels; it has not sensed those immoralities in the structure of economic society whose outcome has been the excessive enrichment of the few and the exploitation of the many together with the moral degradation of both.

It is necessary for teachers of adults to realize these things. They should be aware that there are areas of experience in the lives of men and women to which the principles and ideals of the gospel are not being applied, and that it is their responsibility to see that the Christian religion enters these areas of living as a factor of control.   They should feel a corresponding responsibility for planning leading-on influences and activities as means of introducing the men and women whom they teach to situations in new and unfamiliar areas of experience.   Particularly should they feel under obligation to uncover in realistic terms situations in the economic area and to present in good temper but forcefully the causes operating to produce unchristian conditions.   As adult leaders it may be possible for them to create or organize situations which call for new and unfamiliar adjustments.

In the opposition which the churches so frequently encounter in attempts to make the Christian religion a factor of control in business, industry, and politics they are reaping the fruit of the practice of confining religious teaching so largely to the area of specialized religious activities. The current objections, coming not infrequently from laymen who are church members, to religion "forsaking its proper sphere," "interfering with business," "mixing in politics," "trailing the banner of religion in the mire of politics," and so forth, are not so much a testimony to the sinfulness of human nature as to the shortsighted and deplorable limitation of religious teaching to restricted areas of living.

RELIGIOUS EDUCATION NOT CONFINED TO FORMAL PROCESSES.— An obvious implication to be drawn from our discussion to this point is that for once and all we should cease thinking of adult religious education as restricted to the church or to any formal agency. For most people probably far more religious education is gained apart from the formal processes of teaching than as the direct result of them.

To this fact there is abundant testimony. Evidence may be cited from answers to the question: What has been the most educative influence in your life, to broaden, deepen, and enrich it? "My experience as a pastor in helping people who have come to me in sorrow and distress has meant more in the development of my religious life than any other one thing." "My experience in teaching, especially as a Y. M. C. A. secretary, has done more to broaden my conceptions and deepen my life than any other influence." "Motherhood has been the most influential factor in the development of my religious life. I have had constantly to modify my thinking and to grow to meet the demands for religion in my children." "Hard knocks have done more to educate me than anything else, disappointments of various kinds in my friends, and failures in business. These things have done more to develop my religious life than anything else." This is life. Thousands of similar testimonies might easily be assembled. Many outstanding examples might also be given, one of the most notable of which is that of Lincoln. His education and religious education were gained not through the organized agencies of education and of religion, but through constant and persistent utilization of the educative values of experience. In this way he achieved a faith in God so profound and controlling that he was able to say: "I have so many evidences of his direction, so many instances when I have been controlled by some other power than my own will, that I cannot doubt that this power comes from above. I frequently see my way clear to a decision when I am conscious that I have not sufficient facts upon which to found it. . . . I am satisfied that when the Almighty wants me to do or not to do a particular thing, he finds a way of letting me know it."

Perhaps there is no mistaken idea more prevalent among adult teachers and leaders than just that of identifying religious education exclusively with those organized agencies consciously engaged in attempting to educate adults religiously. In part the error is due to confusion of the formal means of education, called into existence by society to facilitate and direct the educational process, with the process itself. Agencies are external to the individual. A church school is an agency called into existence to further the educational process and to give it conscious direction, but it is not itself the process. The educative process goes on outside of and independently of schools and all other organized agencies of education. An important problem, therefore, becomes one of introducing control in Christian terms as far as possible into all the experiences of life.

FUNCTION OF THE LEADER IN ADULT EDUCATION.—It becomes clear from what has just been said that there are two principal aspects of method in adult education, method from the standpoint of the experiences (the learner), and method from the standpoint of the leader or teacher. From the standpoint of the learner, whether an individual or a group, method is control of and means of reconstituting experience. From the standpoint of the leader or teacher, method of adult religious education is predominantly a matter of guidance, assisting the learner in various ways in mastering situations and in reconstituting experience.

In traditional procedure in adult religious education the part of the teacher has been conceived to be that of an instructor, the presentation of selected "lesson materials," with the assumption that they would thereby be impressed upon the minds of the members of the group and eventually work out into life. It has been a process of transmission.[12] Thoughtful leaders have long been oppressed by the uncomfortable realization that very little of what they have said in presenting even the most carefully prepared "lessons" has actually transferred into changed life and conduct.

In the educational search for more effective procedures it has become evident that what persons react to is not "lessons," or sermons, or to any materials as such, but to concrete life situations.

A step in the direction of recognition of this principle has been the emphasis in past years upon "the point of contact" in teaching. Adult teachers and leaders who have been concerned with life, conduct, and character have placed much stress upon points of contact. In more recent years it has become clear that a "point of contact" with a life situation is not enough. The life situation itself is the thing to be dealt with, together with its control and ways of its reconstruction.

The function of the leader and teacher in accord with this conception becomes pre-eminently that of the interpreter and guide. He is no longer merely the "lecturer," the "instructor," or, indeed, any kind of oracle who speaks with the voice and from the platform of authority. He is a friend and comrade, a fellow seeker after the way of life, who to the extent that he has a broader and richer experience becomes an interpreter and guide in responding to situations in such ways as will enrich and reconstitute experience.

In a transition period such as the present, involving basic changes that cut across traditional ways of thinking and acting, undermine long existing institutions, destroy party loyalties, and require the development of new social processes, special qualities of leadership are required. Vigorous resistance, misrepresentation, and recrimination are certain to be expressed. In some quarters resort to force by legal and illegal means will be in evidence. To serve their generation in such times as these Christian adult leaders must possess a high degree of tact and skill, good nature and patience, courage and determination to carry on in the fact of opposition, and faith that in the end justice and righteousness will prevail.

BASIS OF GROUPING.— Emphasis upon the fact that religious education is not confined to church or school does not imply that formal processes are unimportant. They are both important and necessary. A discussion of principle and method, therefore, requires consideration of basis of grouping for the formal process of adult religious education. What kinds of groupings are likely to be most effective?

If groups are to be enlisted, *as groups,* in social reconstruction, it is necessary for them to be so constituted that, possessing some degree of cohesiveness, they shall be capable of acting together.[13] Many of the adult groups of our churches possess this quality only in superficial measure; others have a high degree of cohesiveness.

Friendship, if genuine, supplies the necessary element of cohesion. A group bound together by the bonds of real friendship is certain to be capable of significant group action. Special interest likewise supplies the needed cohesive element. The special interest may be any one of numerous kinds. It may be an interest in studying the Bible to discover its message on a specific subject, or an interest in parent education, or in dramatics. Again, common occupation furnishes a degree of cohesion of which account should be taken. There is special need, also, as has been stated, for the various occupational groups to study what contribution each can make to the achievement of a more Christian social order. Engineers, lawyers, physicians, merchants, as well as teachers and ministers, are under obligation to discover the form of reconstruction required in their respective occupations and professions in developing a social order motivated by service rather than struggle for private profit.

CHAPTER VI

CHRISTIAN EDUCATION THROUGH WORSHIP

WORSHIP, it is often declared, is *the* religious experience. Not infrequently today religion and worship are used as synonymous or almost synonymous terms. Not that worship includes the whole of religion, but that without worship a person is not religious.

Worship is an outgrowth of a sense of need for God. It is an expression of desire for fellowship with the inner Reality of the universe. Forms of worship are many and various, ranging from such primitive mechanical forms as the use of the prayer wheel to the practice of the presence of God in the ordinary tasks of day-by-day living in the consciousness of thereby fulfilling the will of God.

THE CHRISTIAN RELIGION AND WORSHIP.—Christianity is the outgrowth of a religion of which worship was the most prominent single feature. While Jesus apparently attached little importance to the perpetuation of the institutions and forms of Jewish worship, both in practice and in teaching he grounded religion in fellowship with the Heavenly Father and in prayer. The early Christian Church within a few decades discarded the whole elaborate paraphernalia of Jewish worship—temple, sacrifice, and offering—but the practice of worship remained as the heart of religion. "They all with one accord continued steadfastly in prayer," we may confidently believe, reflects both the example and the conviction of the apostolic Church. Historically, therefore, worship is basic and central in the Christian religion.

How is worship related to the realization of the compelling objectives stated in preceding chapters of our discussion: to develop Christian persons; to build a Christian society; and to engage men and women in the sharing of God's creative purpose for his world? What contribution is within the power of worship to make to the achievement of Christian personality? What is the part of worship in achieving a Christian society? When does worship become a sharing of God's creative purpose?

To answer these questions requires consideration of the nature of worship, of its educational as well as its emotional values, and of the possible contribution of educational method to worship.

197

NATURE OF WORSHIP

Like religion itself, worship defies analysis and complete definition, but we may be helped in our understanding of it by viewing its several aspects.

EMOTIONAL ASPECTS OF WORSHIP.—While the worship experience may not be analyzed into constituent parts, it is undoubtedly true that the emotional aspect of worship is fundamental. It is sometimes said that worship is the emotional aspect of a complete experience which is religion.

In one of his novels, H. G. Wells makes a distinction significant at this point. In a passage of the book which describes the hero's discovery of God the writer says, "Hitherto, God had been for him a thing of the intelligence. Now he realized that God was with him." "This transition," says William Adams Brown, "from thought to experience, from theory to appreciation, is where worship begins. That is why worship is the greatest thing in the world. It brings us into the way of personal appropriation. . . . We find God in worship."[1] And this act of finding, this personal appropriation, is not so much an intellectual awakening, an apprehension, as it is an emotional response.

Worship is awareness and appreciation of transcendent Reality; it is a feeling of God's presence, the immediate sense of God. It is something other and more than knowledge. In worship faith, hope, and love come to fruition in an experience of God.

Protestantism, by and large, has made the mistake of resting religion too predominantly upon ideas and knowledge. Man is not primarily intellectual; more than in his ideas he lives in his imagination and in his feelings. In worship these aspects of his life find expression.

It is to be recognized, of course, that everywhere and always knowledge is power. But the power which knowledge gives is by no means always used to beneficent ends. In accounting for war, that supreme tragedy of modern times, one element of explanation is to be found in the fact that cultivation of love, good will, and feeling for others, and the understanding of human emotional needs has not kept pace with scientific knowledge and the sense of power that knowledge gives. It may be said that religious education has not concerned itself with knowledge *per se,* but only with what it has believed to be religiously fruitful knowledge. Even so, it remains true that no knowledge, not even knowledge that is potentially fruitful religiously, carries within itself the assurance that it will be fruitfully used. As a matter of common observation very much religious fact information laboriously acquired is carried in the minds of many people as unused baggage, never applied to any socially beneficent or religious ends. Learning in itself is not sufficient either to make men religious or to direct their conduct in socially desirable directions. The most learned men, not infrequently, are the most self-centered and selfish, and even the man steeped in religious lore has been known to become a moral bankrupt and an enemy to society. Knowledge, if it is to be redemptive in the life of the individual or of society, requires the motivation that comes through the worship of a loving, self-giving, righteous God.

Granted the importance of knowledge, it is quite as necessary for the principles and ideals of the gospel to be deeply felt, and thus made dynamic in life, if they are to become effective, as it is for them to be taught. Too generally it has been assumed that it is only necessary for them to be proclaimed, overlooking the fact that their mere proclamation in preaching and teaching leaves them suspended in midair. A prime need of the hour is for the Church to incorporate into its worship those social ideals which constitute the objectives of the Kingdom of God, thus making them live emotionally in the experience of worshipers, the services of worship becoming acts of dedication to these goals.

At an earlier point in our discussion we emphasized the emotional basis of motive and conduct. We need also to realize that there is a way of learning other than that of scientific analysis, explanation, and reasoning. We learn through the growth of appreciation, through the recognition of worth. As we observe, listen, and contemplate with wonder and awe the good, the true, and the beautiful, these enter into and become a part of us. It is thus, perhaps more than in any other way, that we develop a taste for and an attitude toward poetry and music, painting and good literature. That which we appreciate and admire, we come to desire. That which we admire and desire influences and shapes conduct and character. We are both inwardly transformed, and our conduct in no small measure determined by that to which we lift up our hearts. In this the significance of worship is to be seen in relation both to the development of personality and to the building of a Christian society.

INTELLECTUAL ASPECTS OF WORSHIP.—Emotion is not the whole

of worship. Worship has an intellectual as well as an emotional aspect. Belief in God is a necessary condition of genuine worship of God. One cannot worship a God in whom he disbelieves.

The common practice in religious education of separation between worship and instruction is not in accord with sound psychology. All instruction should be interfused with the spirit of worship, and all corporate worship should have in it an element of instruction. Worship as predominantly emotional expression is vitalized and its influence made more enduring if it contains the elements of interpretation of its meaning and of its social application.

VOLITIONAL ASPECTS OF WORSHIP.—At its best worship often springs naturally out of some worthful activity, which in turn it enriches. Worship is too closely allied to feeling to be arbitrarily willed. It is the experience of exaltation that arises unbidden from worthy endeavor; it is the emotional glow that illumines stern effort; it is the spirit of devotion that reaches out for the aid of a higher Power in consecration to one's task; it is the adoration of the Supreme Worker that one feels as he contemplates his own work.

In this characteristic of worship is to be found an explanation of the artificiality and barrenness of many so-called "worship services." By ordering a specific time and place they attempt to command that which refuses to be commanded.

AN INTEGRATED EXPERIENCE.—The implication from the preceding discussion is that worship, to be worship in the truest sense, requires integration with the total experience of the person. It is not to be thought of as something separate from and unrelated to life as a whole, but as intimately bound up with the whole of experience. Experience enriched by intelligence, appreciation, and purpose is the matrix out of which the most real and fruitful worship should be expected to emerge. Any attempt to impose worship apart from any one of these factors may only be expected to produce a barren, unfruitful experience lacking in really vital significance.

Christian education increasingly concerns itself with the development of personality as a whole. It has regard to man's capacity and need for knowledge, but it also has regard to his capacity and need for love and faith and righteous conduct. It interests itself in instruction but interests itself also, and quite as much, in the cultivation of religious feeling, the development of spiritual warmth, and of all those feeling attitudes such as reverence, trust, loyalty, and gratitude, which lie so near the heart of the Christian religion. It is concerned quite as much with the fruits of the Spirit in loving service of others as with knowledge; it addresses itself not more to the intellect than to the affections, the loyalties, the devotions, and the aspirations.

This is to say that the emotional and volitional aspects of life bulk quite as large in the process of religious education as does the intellectual. In popular thought even yet, unfortunately, religious education is concerned almost entirely with the intellect. This misconception accounts for much popular indifference to religious education, even suspicion and opposition. Religion, some are wont to declare with the lack of discrimination so common in the use of the words, is of the "heart," not of the "head"; of the "spirit," not of the "mind"; it is a matter of love, devotion, loyalty, enthusiasm, earnestness, and righteousness, and these come not through instruction. This insistence is very largely correct. The mistake, so far as there is one, is in a faulty psychology which divorces the "heart" from the "head," and in the identification of religious education with instruction.

That type of religious education which concerns itself wholly with talk, whether wordy argument, question asking and answering, sermonizing or lecturing, has convincingly proven its ineffectiveness. No longer can it be relied upon as the exclusive nor even the chief method of Christian education. Without belittling the function of knowledge in religion, dependence is today being increasingly placed upon worship and service as means of realizing both the individual and social objectives of religious education.

CONSTITUENT ELEMENTS OF WORSHIP

From consideration of the nature of worship let us proceed to its content.

PRAYER.—If, as has been stated, worship is central in the Christian religion, it should also be said that prayer is the central element of worship. Prayer is of the very nature of worship. All true prayer is worship, and all worship is of the spirit and essence of prayer.

Prayer is something more and other than mere verbal expression; it is religious adjustment. Christian prayer is adjustment to the God of the Christian religion. It springs from aspiration, the outreach of the human spirit toward the higher and the better;

the soul's sincere desire for the good, the true, and the beautiful. The act of prayer involves the concentration of desire and of attention upon God, surrender to what is believed to be his will, becoming conscious of his presence and power, and response to his leading.[2]

As with individual worship, so also with group worship: prayer is central in any genuine service of worship. No part of the service is more important than that which follows the injunction, "Let us pray." When the minister prays, do the members of the congregation also pray? If they do not, can it be said that the service is truly a service of worship? This problem of making corporate worship vital we discuss later in this chapter.

SONG.—For ages music and song have been recognized as carrying unique appeal to the emotions. There is no more effective way of creating the atmosphere and spirit of worship than by the singing of meaningful hymns. Most effective, provided the congregation as a whole really sings, is congregational singing. If the selections are actually hymns of worship and their rendition sincerely worshipful, choir singing and, better still, chorus singing are also helpful.

But song does more than create the atmosphere of worship; in religious song at its best singing becomes an important element in the act of worship. It is an essential part in a complete experience of worship.

Singing has a positive socializing effect. It is a significant fact that most great social movements have gained strength and solidarity from group singing. In no other way may a company of individuals be so quickly and at the same time so fully unified as a worshiping group, becoming one in aspiration and feeling. The mere physical act of singing provides release. Tensions are eased, inhibitions are broken down, barriers are melted away, and a sense of fellowship and of common purpose is developed.

BIBLE READING.—Both in individual and corporate practice the reading of the Bible and of well-selected poetry and expressions of aspiration and challenge from great religious and social thinkers other than Biblical holds an assured place as an element in worship. In reading the Bible we are lifted above the limitations and restrictions by which we are hedged about and become sharers in that larger experience which is in a unique way the spiritual heritage of the race. Or, as another has expressed it, we come up from the ravines and underbrush of daily life and stand on a summit, our vision sweeping the breadth and depth and height of the hills and valleys where the feet of many generations of men have trod.[3]

As with the reading of the Scripture, so also with responses in which the congregation joins as with a single voice in expression of its aspiration, its desire, or its purpose of worship, its gratitude or its praise; these, as well as the confession of its faith in a creed which the members sincerely believe, are aids to worship and, at least at times, acts of worship. The recitation in unison often is a help to the individual in the unrealized confirmation it gives his own faith.

EDUCATIONAL VALUES OF WORSHIP

Since we have defined worship as an experience of fellowship with God, to convey the suggestion that it is to be evaluated in terms of utilitarian standards would be wholly to miss the mark. The experience of fellowship with God, to the extent that it has the quality of reality, is like friendship and love, an end in itself. It is to be valued for its own sake. In and for itself it is one of the highest values of life. While worship is a means, to interpret it only in terms of its effects is to disregard a primary significance.

In many ways worship may contribute to the growth of personality and of a Christian society. Of special significance are these:

Association of Persons.—Soul is kindled by soul. To teach religion, Carlyle declared, it is first necessary to find a man who has religion. Fellowship of persons with religious persons in worship stimulates and nurtures religious personality.

There is much of religion that can and must be taught. There are other elements of religion, elements that lie very near the heart of the Christian religion, that are awakened rather than taught. They may be said to be taught in that they are in part at least communicated, but the communication is not so much by word as by attitude, demeanor, and atmosphere. Times without number through worship persons have had experiences of illumination, enrichment, uplift, and strengthening.

Association with others in worship also has a humanizing influence. Man is a social being. Seldom is he fully satisfied by the individual expression of his deep inner longings and aspirations. Association with others is naturally sought. In corporate worship, worshipers are conscious of the presence of other worshipers. This consciousness lifts the worshiper out of the individual and solitary into the social and universal and assists him to open his mind and heart to other socializing influences. By participation with others in worship permeated with reality feeling is deepened, sympathy is enriched and widened, and the sense of unity with the group is strengthened. The aspirations, faith, purpose, and spiritual realizations collectively represented become available for the life of each. Social forces are at work. New values are created and new powers are released.

FELLOWSHIP WITH GOD.—Corporate worship is more than the association of persons as a worshiping group. Real worship—social worship and individual worship—involves entering into fellowship with the Supreme Person. "Men pray and will continue to pray to the end of time," said William James, "because they are seeking and finding the Great Companion."

This contact with a power within and yet beyond oneself is what the devout worshiper means when he says that through worship he comes to "know" God. It is more than attaining to an idea about God. Worship is not primarily an exercise of the mind about God; it is an awakening of the mind to a consciousness of God. It is the realization of a Presence felt within, a discovery of inner depths, a kind of spiritual subsoil of life, untouched by ordinary thoughts, feeling, and conduct. The figure is one suggested by Rufus S. Jones, who insists that the roots of our real life lie in this spiritual subsoil of innermost being. Genuine worship, he says, liberates the energies of this deeper region. "It opens the avenues of the interior life and lets the spiritual currents from beyond us flow in and circulate about the roots of our being."[4] It is this, establishing contact with the hidden power within and beyond oneself, that more than anything else keeps religion alive and fresh and strong.

There have been many who have sought to discredit the experience of fellowship with God. For some it is enough to label it as mysticism, and to say that it has often been associated with abnormal and even with perverted forms of experience. To this the Christian replies that it cannot be so easily discredited; that if many have been sadly mistaken in their interpretation of their experience, multitudes of others, and among them many of the bravest, most enlightened, and most noble of men have testified that not only have they attained "a knowledge of God," "communion with God," "possession of the Spirit of God," but that in the experience has come to them the inspiration, the courage, and the strength for whatever of worthy achievement has been theirs. By the testimony of many witnesses both learned and unlearned, highly cultured and illiterate, of every race and age, fellowship with God is brought within the realm of the empirical just as truly as the phenomena of the material with which natural science deals.

Men greatly need, and never more than today, a sustaining, inspiring sense of the presence of God within their own souls and within society. Most men, even today, believe in God, if belief be defined in terms of a kind of loose intellectual affirmation. They believe in God much as they believe in the sun as the center of the solar system. Their belief has little influence over their lives. Worship gives reality in consciousness to the intellectual affirmation that there is a God.

If religious education is actually to be education in religion, if it is actually to result in the development of religious persons, it must do just this, it must make God more real to people, open their minds to God as a living Presence, bringing them into contact with him as ultimate reality, so that they partake of the strength of the Infinite. "I can do all things," said Paul, "through Christ who strengtheneth me."

This is a principle which for some reason many religious teachers tend to overlook. They are forever tending to think and act as though religious education consists primarily and chiefly in telling people about God, whereas the greater business of religious education is to make God real to people, to bring God into their lives, making him real in consciousness, and to help them appropriate the divine Presence and power in their lives. Certainly, one of the most effective means of accomplishing this is worship. One may go on indefinitely telling about God, even though the instruction be ever so wise and ever so skillful, and the hearers continue as far removed from God as in the beginning. Not so with worship. Engage people in genuine worship and God becomes a present, dynamic reality in the life. For worship is just this: communion with God, and a so-called worship service that does not lead the participants into communion with God is not worship.

IDEAS ARE CLARIFIED.—At its best worship stimulates thinking and deepens religious and social conviction. Not infrequently earnest worshipers testify that intellectual inspiration and new ideas come to them in worship. It may be claiming too much to say that worship directly imparts new ideas, but without question it does clear the way for the entrance of new ideas, impart perspective, and quicken intellectual insight and discernment.

Vital worship carries a challenge to look at life and its relations not merely from the viewpoint of one's individual interests or from the viewpoint of his immediate social group, but from the viewpoint of the exalted, eternal Being whom he worships. When one in reality worships the God revealed by Jesus, he places himself, his social relationships, and his world, in a receptive attitude toward a God of love and good will, supremely pure and righteous, and in response there comes to him perspective and insight, intellectual and moral quickening.

It is essential that this potential value of worship shall actually be realized if the evaluation of worship by the Church is to be maintained. Unless the current movement for the re-emphasis of worship results in increase in social insight and social concern, and a deepening of religious conviction, it is certain to be discredited by the forces in our present-day world that are making for social reconstruction.

FEELING ATTITUDES ARE DEVELOPED.—Through all the centuries, inner peace, joy, and content have come to those who worship. In every troubled era, even in the midst of hard and bitter circumstances, through quiet meditation and prayer men and women have found means by which life has been kept sweet and hopeful and triumphant. Sometimes, as we shall emphasize later, worship has bred submission to conditions that should have been rebelled against. Fully as often, under conditions impossible of change by the victims of circumstance, it has given strength to bear trials and burdens.

Worship relaxes tension. It resolves contradictions. Things often are seen more nearly in their proper perspective. When no new emotion is created, choice is made between competing emotions, so that energy is exerted without conflict.

Worship of God as revealed by the prophets and by Jesus aids in creating, developing, and perpetuating feeling attitudes that constitute an essential element in Christian living. Good will, sympathy, friendliness, brotherliness, kindness, love—these basic attitudes fundamental to the building of a Christian social order are born and nurtured in the worship of the Christian God.

APPRECIATION IS ENHANCED.—There exists within Protestant religion what B. E. Meland has labeled its "unaesthetic and unappreciative side."[5] Without doubt Protestant stress upon the moral, the active, and the utilitarian aspects and ends of religion carried with it a lack of emphasis upon the aesthetic, a defect which recent years have done much to remedy. To the extent that the service of worship gives expression to the beautiful and the true in music and poetry, painting and architecture, in conduct and character, appreciation is enhanced and the whole life is thereby enriched.

The way of enhanced appreciation is a way of learning. The fallacy that all learning consists of acquiring information and knowledge, exploration and reflective reasoning, is all too widely prevalent. As persons bring open receptive hearts to the service of worship they experience a growing recognition of value which in itself is learning.

MORAL DYNAMIC IS CREATED.—One of the chief problems of social reconstruction is that of discovering possible sources of the enormous human energy required, and of releasing the energy available in the lives of men and women who already possess social intelligence and social conviction but are held back from creative effort by fear, anxiety, timidity, and worry concerning possible consequences. Worship, socially motivated, offers possibility of such discovery and release.

Many, it must be admitted, who are deeply concerned for necessary social reconstruction see no value in worship. It may be that worship seldom has immediate, direct result in social effort but, even so, it may be of supreme social significance. How often men and women experience disappointment and a feeling of exhaustion as a result of their disillusionments and sense of frustration in social effort. What they need more than anything else is renewal of faith and hope and courage, a realization of alliance with a Power greater than themselves. Fellowship with God in worship is not merely the quickening of emotions and the enhancement of appreciation. Far more deeply it involves a sense of life and help received from a higher Power, a re-enforcement and strengthening of the moral and religious motives, purposes, and ideals—of all, in fact, that enters into spiritual morale.

Worship offers possibility of generating the morale needed for persistence and determination in the long, stubborn struggle for social change. As John C. Bennett has said, if the Church fails through its worship to make this contribution, it might perhaps as well leave the rest of its social strategy to other agencies. Many men and women have a truer apprehension of Christian social relationships and of principles of Christian living than are reflected in their daily conduct. What they most need is the will to do as well as they know. Dynamic rather than knowledge is the greater need. The ethical principles and ideals of the Christian religion are comparatively few and simple of statement. Prolonged study is not required for their apprehension. To discern their application in specific situations is not always by any means easy, but the greater lack is moral dynamic for their application. In this, again, the central importance of worship becomes apparent.

In Christian worship the worshiper seeks to know the divine will and to make that will his own. He seeks the identification of his will with the divine: "Not my will but thine be done." He goes from his worship with the intent of ordering his purposes and activities around the supreme purpose which he believes to be the will of God. The unification of the self around an integrating center, we have emphasized, is the secret of consistent, strong character. A chief difficulty with many men and women is a divided self. They are both generous and selfish, kind and cruel, pure and sensual. In the case of many, their souls are battlefields, and they are never certain which self will prevail in the conflict. Effective procedure in the formation of character does not concern itself so much with the cultivation of specific qualities and attitudes such as honesty, unselfishness, and courage, as with the unifying of the self in devotion to a supreme purpose, a supreme cause, a Supreme Person, a unification which may be achieved, perhaps more effectively than in any other way, through worship.

Our discussion has sought to emphasize that just as the Christian religion relates itself to the whole person, so worship is significant in relation to the development of the total personality. Any emphasis in religious education that tends to place exclusive or even predominant stress upon any one aspect of experience is to be deplored. The outreach of the entire self toward God in worship, the attempt in thought and feeling and will to enter into relationship with the Most High; the experience of fellowship with One beyond oneself, immeasurably greater than oneself, and yet akin to oneself, is certainly quite as important as acquiring knowledge and ideas, and engaging in outward activities.

DEFICIENT WORSHIP

We have discussed worship in terms of its ideal values. But candor compels the admission that many of the worship services of our churches, and doubtless much individual worship, carry a minimum of these values. Undoubtedly many persons engage in worship without experiencing any of the values mentioned.

THE GOD WHO IS WORSHIPED.—The value of worship in achieving Christian personality and a Christian society depends very largely upon the kind of God worshiped. Always a concept of the God who is worshiped exists in the mind of the worshiper. Worship does not take place in an intellectual vacuum. Entering upon the act of worship no worshiper takes with him a *tabula rasa* as his mental furniture. Always in greater or less measure the worshiper's concept of God is a reflection of experience. In a monarchical society the prevailing idea of God is that of a supreme monarch. As the social order changes the concept of God is revised. Both cause and effect are at work. Prophetic insights as to the nature of God effect changes in society. Other influences also are at work. As changes occur, from their changed social experience the multitude gains a changed view of the nature and will of God.

The concept of God dominating much present-day worship is a composit. There are vestigial remains of an Oriental monarch, mingled with ideas of a loving Father, and with other ideas representing an infiltration from capitalist society. For the social values of worship to be realized it is necessary that the God of the prophets, the God and Father of our Lord Jesus Christ shall be worshiped.

FLIGHT FROM REALITY.—The tendency of mysticism is to make worship a flight from the realities of present-day society, a retreat from the real world in which men suffer from pain, oppression, and injustice to a dream world of fantasy. It involves the fallacy of shutting out the main issues of life in order "to be with God," as though God dwells apart in some solitary place, out of relation to the social process in which are caught up the lives and activities of mankind.

Here, again, the concept of God is involved. God, whom Christians believe to be personal, is at the same time the creative process continuously at work in the world. The whole creation which "groaneth and travaileth in pain together until now" is the creation within which the purpose and power of a Creator is constantly at work. The finding of God in worship is not the result of going off on a tangent from the issues of today's life, hoping to meet with God out yonder at the end of a byroad or in a "beautiful isle of somewhere," but, rather, in the midst of life's struggles and pains putting ourselves in such attitudes and relationships that what is Divine within the world is revealed to us.

The vitalizing and enrichment of worship cannot be accomplished by a retreat, of whatever nature.[6]   It, rather, depends upon our identification of ourselves with the purpose and will of God; losing ourselves in a social struggle so profoundly meaningful that in it we come into contact with the creative God.   In a time of profound social change such as the present the fate of keeping alive the experience of God in worship depends upon carrying forward the movement for the larger realization of human values.   As men and women are led purposefully to engage in the reconstruction of the social order they find God.

WORSHIP AS COMPENSATION.—The type of worship that involves a withdrawal experience tends to make the rapture of worship an end in itself—the purpose of worship, to enjoy God.   Or, as Soares has said, "the substitution of a certain luxury of emotion for the organization of life."[7]   The result is that the concept of "spiritual" takes on an esoteric meaning and is robbed of its social content.

Without question the worship of many adults is compensatory. Denied, because of conditions under which they live, the satisfactions which human nature normally and rightfully craves, they find compensation by utilizing worship as a means of making real the satisfactions promised by religion in a future world.   Relaxation from strain and conflict, inner quietness and peace, the renewal of faith and hope—these are legitimate compensations of worship, greatly needed in a troubled world.   But when the forms and the experience of worship are such as to dull and deaden discrimination and insight, to act as a soporific rather than to quicken, to make people insensible to ills which ought not be endured, they render a decided disservice.   Much of contemporary worship, because of these very characteristics, plays into the hands of social reactionaries.

AESTHETIC ENJOYMENT AS WORSHIP.—Beauty, order, and artistry befit approach to God.   Historically, beautiful, stately architecture, music, poetry, drama, and painting, all have been utilized for the expression of the attitude of worship, and it is entirely fitting that the current movement for the recovery of worship should earnestly attempt to enrich worship through their use.   Aesthetic appreciation and enjoyment have sometimes been permitted to become ends in themselves.   Beauty is in itself satisfying, and its enjoyment should be cultivated. The worship of God, if it is to fulfill its personal and social functions, must be something more than the sensuous enjoyment of form and color and sound. These may help to interpret God to the worshiper, but worship should not stop with the sensuous media.

So also with the enrichment of worship by the increasing use of responses, introits, and chants from ancient liturgies. That they have their value is not to be doubted, but dependence upon them as principal sources of the inspirations and insights required by today's worship is a serious mistake. It is at the point of social insight and responsibility that they are themselves most lacking. Only a liturgy that is a fresh outgrowth of the new social vision and social conviction of our times can meet today's requirements.

EDUCATIONAL METHOD IN WORSHIP

To call men and women to worship is not new in the program of the Church. In the language of the New Testament the word "Church" is *ecclesia,* or "assembly for worship." But realization of the values of worship in a program of religious education may fairly be said to be a new thing.

In response to spontaneous impulse, from the very beginning of Christianity Christians have worshiped. Recognizing the essential place of worship in the religious life, our task is to discover how the impulse to worship may be cultivated, and how the full educational values of worship may be realized in experience. How may the values described above be assured? What has educational method to suggest?

TECHNIQUE OF WORSHIP.—As regards group worship, the first requirement is that the leader shall be himself a sincere worshiper, a person who possesses a deep, strong feeling of worship, and not merely a "cheer leader" or a "director" going through the motions. He has something more to do than merely to assemble materials and to lead the group in their use. His added and perhaps greater responsibility concerns what may be called the technique of worship, that which has to do with the setting, the atmosphere, the spirit, and the method of the service. This is a matter in which most lay leaders and, unfortunately, many ministers are both untrained and careless. The brusque, informal, impromptu, often even rude and irreverent manner of the erstwhile leader may conceivably be in place in a "pep" meeting of the Lions' Club, but it is far from fitting in a sincere approach to the presence of God. Carelessness, slovenliness, lack of dignity, haphazard choice of hymns to be sung, are all too common characteristics of what are labeled "worship services." They are destructive of whatever worshipful spirit and atmosphere otherwise might exist.

To be conducive to worship the music and words of the hymns used, and the conduct of the singing, all must have the qualities of dignity and reverence. Many leaders of song in religious meetings apparently do not differentiate between worship and physical exhilaration. If the leader makes conducting a gymnastic exercise, and exhorts the group to "pep it up," and "put life into it," his leading is quite as destructive of the spirit of worship as are raucous, jazzy music and insipid sentimental words. People cannot draw near to God in the spirit and manner of attending a football game. This does not mean that the singing should be dull, listless, and lacking in character. It should appeal to the highest and the deepest in human nature.

Wonder, awe, reverence, the outreach of the soul for God cannot be commanded. Feelings of gratitude and love and the mood of adoration do not come in response to entreaty or exhortation, yet these all are essential. Preparation, order, quiet, and an attitude of reverent anticipation on the part of the leader will do much to create the desired spirit and atmosphere.

FORMS OF WORSHIP.—Our discussion of the content of worship has not meant to convey the impression that any one specific element is essential, at a given time, to the experience of worship, or that participation in a particular order necessarily involves or begets the experience. The wide divergence in forms of worship, even within evangelical groups, ranging from the silent meeting of the Friends to the Episcopal ritual, is sufficient evidence of the former statement. As for the latter, one's own experience abundantly attests that one may participate in an order of worship without really worshiping. The experience of worship is a plus element, that which transcends mere form, to which the form is the external, objective aid. Forms of worship easily become merely *formal*, mechanical acts involving physical attendance, without any deeply personal, creative experience. Genuine worship requires this personal, original, creative participation in which the individual discovers God anew and in which the entire worshiping group is united in a common expression of adoration, petition, and praise.

ORDER OF WORSHIP.—Religious experience through the centuries has developed an order of worship concerning the value of which there is wide consensus of agreement. In terms of the public service of worship the successive steps are: (1) presentation, expressed by the introit, a recognition of God's presence; (2) confession, expressed in the collect or in sentences of confession from the Scriptures; (3) exaltation, finding expression in sentences conveying assurance of God's pardon of the penitent or in expressions of praise such as the *Gloria Tibi* or the *Gloria Patri;* (4) illumination, to which contribution is made by the reading of the Scriptures, the repetition of a suitable creed, the pastoral prayer, and the sermon; (5) consecration, including the offering, a hymn and prayer of consecration, and dedication to a purpose of action.[8]

STIMULI OF WORSHIP.—While the emotions cannot be commanded, willed, or planned, there are stimuli that may be depended upon to evoke emotional response. These include certain kinds of situations, either experienced first-hand or vividly portrayed, pictorially or described in words. For example, if benefits bestowed are described, an example of heroic devotion presented, love freely given portrayed, natural, seemingly almost spontaneous response in terms of attitude is quite certain to follow. Colors, odors, and light are not without emotional effect. Symbols; pictures, both paintings and art glass; and mural decorations that carry religious ideas, if well chosen, are influential aids to worship.

FORMS OF EXPRESSION.—An essential part of the leader's task is that of providing suitable forms of expression. If people are to worship in song or, in other words, if the singing is actually to be a part of an experience of worship, the hymns used, as has already been suggested, must be worshipful, both in tune and words. This principle is often ignored in the choice of hymns. Frequently hymns are chosen whose effect can only be to dissipate the mood and spirit of worship. Instead of aiding worship they effectively prevent it. Their effect spreads to the prayer that has preceded or that follows, so that the intent of the entire service of worship is vitiated by the inappropriate, irreverent character of the songs used. During the past twenty-five years our evangelical churches have been flooded by cheap songbooks, most of them sponsored by revivalists, filled for the most part with music lacking any worshipful quality, and with songs many of which either voice a crude, outworn theology entirely out of place in any program of Christian education or represent a combination of meaningless phrases and sentimental banality. They have been one of the potent influences in banishing worship from the churches.

So far as many of these songs possess a meaningful content their ideology and imagery belong to a past age. They are the expression of a world view which everywhere except in hymnology and in the theology of the illiterate has been abandoned and, being outmoded, has lost its vitality. It is no longer the expression of reality.

We find in this one element of explanation of the weakness of the Church in relation to today's life. Many of those who are engaged purposefully and sacrificially in the effort of building a new world find the worship of the churches within their reach lacking in vitality and sincerity. The reason is found in the fact that the Church persists in its worship in using theological ideology, imagery, and rubrics that are incapable of expressing the social ideals and the aspirations, hopes, and faith of present-day religion.

Too often the social teaching embodied in the sermon, or in a group discussion, has no counterpart in the worship that precedes or follows. Its effect is lessened, frequently even nullified, by the incongruous or contradictory content of the hymns and the prayers.

As with the hymns, so also with the liturgies of the Church. For many centuries they have been concerned almost wholly with the subjective phase of individual experience. For the most part they are almost entirely lacking in any expression of corporate responsibility, social aspiration or social contrition. New hymns, new anthems of praise, new liturgies, new forms of prayer, new orders of worship are required to aid in carrying the content and in undergirding the social teaching of the Christian religion.[9]

SPECIAL WORSHIP PROJECTS.—Our discussion to this point concerns equally the public service of worship and the worship of the adult department of the church school or of other adult groups. No good reason exists for duplicating the service of congregational worship by a similar service as a part of the church-school session. If this is done, the one is almost certain to become for many people a substitute for the other. There are numerous other possibilities.

If a devotional spirit pervades a group assembly, whether of the adult department, the organized adult class, or other adult organization, worship may be expected to spring spontaneously out of the discussions and other activities of the group. Any procedure in times such as these that concerns itself with conserving and developing human values offers possibilities of vital, real worship.

Frequently the organizing center should be a life experience presenting some idea, attitude, or issue which it is agreed by the group as a whole or by the planning committee should be emphasized or developed. The several elements of the order of worship used, such as the hymns, the scripture, the special songs and readings, the dramatization, the discussion or talk by the leader or special speaker, whatever is included, should sustain intimate relationship to this central emphasis, so that the procedure as a whole represents unity essential to effectiveness, the various elements harmonizing like the details of a painting, all of which direct attention to the central figure.

Especially important is it that frequently some specific social value shall be so lifted up through presentation and illumination in an effective emotional setting that it will appeal to the hearts of men and women. If at the same time a clear path is pointed out for expending in action the energy of emotion aroused, the chance of its incorporation into life is perhaps greater than by any other method.

From time to time the adult program should include such special worship projects as an all-musical program; a one- or two-act play; a symbolic service; a lakeside, mountaintop, or other out-of-doors meeting, any one of which may be so conducted as to become an occasion of sincere, spontaneous, genuine worship.

TRAINING IN WORSHIP

There are many men and women who in childhood never learned how to worship. Spiritual beings with inarticulate aspirations and yearnings, many are imprisoned within the walls of sense. Their half-conscious realization of their need of God leads them to the house of worship, but they know not how to pray. How much poorer they are than is their privilege!

> "By how much are men better than sheep or goats
>   That nourish a blind life within the brain
> If, knowing God, they lift not hands of prayer
>   For self, and they that call them friends."

How shall these men and women learn to worship? Are they forever shut out from fellowship with God because as children they never learned to pray? Is there not here an important educational function of the Church, to be exercised through the public service, the adult department, or a specially organized group? Adults who under skillful guidance can learn any one of numerous arts certainly may be expected, if desire exists, to learn the art of worship. It is a mistake to assume that the desire, though unexpressed, does not exist. With many it does exist, and in others it can be created.

USE OF LITURGICAL PRAYERS.—While the use of liturgical prayers has marked limitations, much may be said for the practice. For one thing, it has value in training persons to pray. Rich treasures of devotion exist in the liturgies of the Church, even though, as has been stated, for the most part they are lacking in social content. A program of worship, printed or mimeographed, may be planned for a given month including one or two choice prayers. Or, the prayer alone may be typed or mimeographed and copies distributed to all. The members may then be urged to memorize the prayer, that it may be used as a part of the program without reading. Such a plan, followed for a number of months, accustoms those previously unfamiliar with it to the language of devotion. With a number of such prayers memorized and frequently used, for most persons it should be an easy transition to free, extemporaneous prayer, a transition readily made if the leader recognizes its importance and cooperates in bringing it about. And this transition though simple is exceedingly important. One may memorize and through all the years of his adult life repeat the great liturgical prayers, but if through them he does not so succeed in finding God that he is led to commune with him in words that rise spontaneously out of the depths of his own soul he has not really learned to worship.

There are a few liturgical prayers that have had such an important part in the worship of the Church through the centuries that the religious education of no Christian is complete without knowing them. Such, for example, is the prayer of general confession used by many denominations in the celebration of the Lord's Supper. There are also prayers from the Bible that should be so familiarly known that they can be repeated from memory at any time.

USE OF SCRIPTURE.—Next in importance to prayer in training in worship is the use of great passages of Scripture for the expression of aspiration, yearning after God, faith and trust, confession of sin, praise and thanksgiving, and intercession. The supreme treasury of devotion within the Scriptures is, of course, the Psalms. There are certain of the great psalms that should be the familiar possession of every adult Christian. If they have not been learned in youth, they should be memorized in adult years, for they can be readily memorized by any man or woman. The fact has been commonly overlooked that they are the expression of the emotions not of childhood or of youth but of mature years. Many of their expressions are meaningless to children and some of them are unsuitable for use by children. But they are the utterance of adult experience, the expression of the spiritual hopes and longings, confidence and trust, thanksgiving and praise of the years of maturity, and without them life is infinitely poorer. There are not less than ten of the great psalms that should be known by all. These are the first, eighth, nineteenth, twenty-third, thirty-seventh (vs. 1-11), forty-sixth, ninetieth, ninety-first, one hundred and third, one hundred and twelfth, one hundred and thirty-ninth (vs. 1-18). Other passages of Scripture of inestimable value as treasures of the spirit are the Beatitudes, Matthew 5. 1-12; 1 Corinthians 13; John 15. 1-17; Matthew 7. 7-29; Matthew 25. 34-46; Luke 15. 11-32; Ephesians 3. 14-19; Philippians 4. 8-9; 1 John 4. 7-14.

USE OF HYMNS.—Next to the devotional treasures of the Bible in training adults in worship are the great hymns of the Church, many of which are all too little known. It should be a part of the adult educational program to acquaint men and women with at least some of the hymns that are a priceless part of the spiritual heritage of the race. Among those that should be intimately known by every Christian are:

Adoration, Worship and Praise: "God, the Omnipotent," by Henry F. Chorley; "Nearer, My God, to Thee," by Sarah Flower Adams; "Dear Lord and Father of Mankind," by John G. Whittier; "God of Grace and God of Glory," by Harry Emerson Fosdick; "O Master, Let Me Walk With Thee," by Washington Gladden; "Abide With Me," by Henry F. Lyte; "When I Survey the Wondrous Cross," by Isaac Watts; "In the Cross of Christ I Glory," by John Bowring; "Holy, Holy, Holy, Lord God Almighty," by Reginald Heber.

Consecration, Loyalty, and Courage: "Faith of Our Fathers," by Frederick W. Faber; "Sun of My Soul," by John Keble; "Are Ye Able?" by Earl Marlatt; "Lead On, O King Eternal," by Ernest W. Shurtleff; "O Love That Wilt Not Let Me Go," by George Matheson.

Human Service and Brotherhood: "Where Cross the Crowded

Ways of Life," by Frank Mason North; "In Christ There Is No East or West," by John Oxenham; "O Brother Man, Fold to Thy Heart Thy Brother," by John G. Whittier; "O Master of the Waking World," by Frank Mason North.

The Kingdom of God, Social Aspiration, and Progress: "These Things Shall Be, a Loftier Race," by J. Addington Symonds; "When Wilt Thou Save the People?" by Ebenezer Elliott; "O Zion, Haste," by Mary A. Thomson; "The Voice of God Is Calling," by John Haynes Holmes.

THE PUBLIC SERVICE OF WORSHIP.—Finally, both as offering the possibility of the experience of worship and as a means of training in worship, the public service deserves emphasis. The marked improvement in public worship in ways mentioned above has been chiefly due to appreciation of the values of worship on the part of ministers who have striven earnestly for the enrichment of their services. Their example has influenced others. Doubtless there are many others who lack a proper appreciation of worship, who attach disproportionate importance to other features of the public service, who are deficient in aesthetic sense, and who are ignorant of ways by which the service of worship may be enriched and deepened. But even if the service is cheap and tawdry, crude and spiritually barren, it is not often that a hopeless situation exists. When a minister knows that the leaders and teachers of the church desire a more genuinely worshipful service, unless he is an exception, he will endeavor to provide it. He cannot do it without the approval and cooperation of the congregation, and the help of his leaders, and with this help usually much improvement may be made.

The adult teacher who, without any emphasis upon worship, lectures to a group of men or women on Sunday morning, who thereafter troop out of the church building like a crowd of youngsters escaping from school, is rendering a service of doubtful value. They may be gaining something, but the chances are at least equal that through nonparticipation in the public service they are losing more than they gain.

If it be true, as our discussion has urged, that worship is of central importance in the Christian religion, there is much need today for emphasis upon it. For despite all that has been said and written in recent years on the recovery of worship it is still grievously neglected. Of thousands of our Protestant churches it might almost be said that there is in them practically no worship. Most of the church members and even many of the ministers think and speak of the service of worship as the "opening exercises." The congregation gathers in the "auditorium" of the church to hear about many things more or less religious rather than to commune with God: with the expectation of hearing a thesis discussed, or an essay on a religious theme read, or a doctrine defended, or what not, rather than with the purpose of appropriating power for daily living. An assembly of auditors rather than worshipers, they are listeners to a performance—the performers being the preacher and the paid choir. Their comments are revealing. Ten say to the minister: "I enjoyed your sermon so much today," to one who declares: "You led me today into the presence of God." Twenty exclaim: "The solo (or anthem) today was beautiful" (or "grand," or "just lovely") to one who testifies: "The music today brought me nearer God."

If it be true that in many of our churches there is practically no worship, it is probably a further statement of fact to say there is practically no worship in the lives of a large proportion of church members. Church members who do not come to the public service for worship and who in that service do not actually participate in worship are not likely to worship in their homes, either as a family group or as individuals.

This popular neglect of worship is doubtless a natural out-working of the dominant emphasis in Protestantism upon the reason, the right of private judgment, doctrinal instruction, and the sermon. "The Protestant churches have always exalted the pulpit in the service of the house of God," giving it the central place and magnifying it as the most important part. Church buildings have been thought of primarily as preaching places and have been constructed with preaching in mind. The principal room in the church, in most cases the only room, has been traditionally spoken of as "the auditorium." The training of ministers in theological schools, until recently, has had preaching chiefly in view. With this emphasis pre-eminent in the churches what other result could be expected than the neglect of worship, both public and private.

It is of little avail to emphasize the fact of the neglect of worship, unless we shall be awakened to a realization of what the loss means in our own lives and the lives of coming generations. It means, for one thing, that our religious education is seriously incomplete, and that whatever educative values worship may have are not being experienced by the vast majority of the members of the evangelical churches. An intellectualized religious training and practice, a recreational or leisure-time program, participation from the best of motives in numerous service activities, effort in maintaining and extending an organization, do not provide a substitute for worship. Under these conditions religious education becomes education without one of its most distinctively religious elements. Even more, it is to be doubted whether Christianity in the historic sense of the term will long continue as an aggressive, dynamic force in the world if its adherents lose the realization of communion and fellowship with God.

CHAPTER VII

RELIGIOUS EDUCATION THROUGH SOCIAL PARTICIPATION

THE new language on the lips of the Christians of the first century, recalling Adolf Harnack's statement quoted in our first chapter, "was the language of love. *But it was more than a language, it was a thing of power and action.*"*

Jesus had declared to his disciples that men will be judged on the last day on the basis of their social attitudes and conduct—whether they have given food to the hungry, drink to the thirsty, shelter to the homeless, clothing to the ill-clad, comfort and healing to the sick, and ministry to the imprisoned. Loyalty to him, he taught them, will be interpreted in terms of service to the humblest and most needy of men. There is abundant evidence that his teaching was taken to heart by the early Church. Harnack lists the wide range of social activities under the categories of general almsgiving; maintenance of widows and orphans; ministry to the sick, the infirm, and the disabled; the care of prisoners and slaves; the burial of the poor; and the support of those overwhelmed by calamity or disaster. In more recent centuries the Church has enlisted in behalf of social ministry and social change in numerous areas: the abolition of slavery, prison reform, famine relief, hospital care, and the abolition of child labor.

The process of social participation in which Jesus enlisted his followers was their religious education. The first disciples were adult men and women. They were not given their Christian education in any kind of organized school. They associated themselves with Jesus, at his invitation, becoming participants in his enterprises, engaging in his Way of life.

It is by no means accidental that the Synoptic Gospels are pre-eminently a record of activities of social significance. Jesus seems instinctively to have chosen a new way of living, activity in service, as the method by which the men whom he proposed to charge with responsibility for establishing his Kingdom in the world should be educated in the Christian religion. It is true that by both

* See page 42.

precept and example he trained them in prayer, and that he employed some measure of formal instruction in increasing their store of religious knowledge. But more than anything else he enlisted them in actual tasks, associating them with himself as he went about doing good, cooperating with them in the projects in which he enlisted them, sending them forth on constructive enterprises and later discussing with them what they had done, and why.

REQUIRED: EDUCATION IN AND FOR SOCIAL LIVING.—Adult education, as has been emphasized throughout the preceding chapters, involves a program of action, an education set resolutely to the task of Christianizing the whole of life, both personal and social.

Such adult education as the churches have had in recent decades, alike in its objectives and in its content, as our discussion has revealed, has been knit in with the texture of the past, for the most part in an unseeing, uncritical way. In many local churches it has largely concerned itself with justifying and maintaining the *status quo,* both in religion and in the social order.* In the setting of a disordered and chaotic world, facing new conditions, without scorning the wisdom of the past, adult education should now concentrate directly upon the insistent issues of the present, seeking to develop in the minds not merely of the few but of all men and women an understanding of the critical problems involved in today's life, and undertaking to utilize the vast capacity for constructive building that inheres in the present generation, so largely inert and uncomprehending. This involves a different concept and type of education, an education with a new content and a new emphasis—education for life socially motivated and socially controlled, instead of education for life bent upon individual acquisition.

Formal education has been dominated by the erroneous idea that acquaintance with the subject matter of religion makes people religious, the study of ethics induces ethically motivated behavior, knowledge of the social sciences results in socially desirable conduct. In spite of any amount of evidence to the contrary this idea has persisted. In part, though not wholly because of the dominance of this idea education has been predominantly bookish, a process of schooling, separated from life and the problems of living. In the public schools the elementary tool subjects—reading, writing, and arithmetic—have dominated the elementary grades. As the

* See pp. 54f., 58.

pupil has advanced, reading has expanded into the study of the languages, writing into a study of literature, arithmetic into a study of mathematics. In higher education the natural and applied sciences have been given a prominent place. But none of these as subject matter study impart any considerable degree of understanding of life and its real relationships. They prepare young people in a way to become teachers of subjects, they aid in developing certain skills that qualify persons for jobs, they offer steps in the direction of vocational efficiency, but they do little to fit persons for the supreme business of living.

In the Church and in church schools, *the* Book has been given the central place; pupils, children and adults alike, expected to study its subject matter as "texts" and "lessons." When attention has been directed to the social implication of Bible "lessons," or when other social teaching has been given, too often the process has stopped with the enunciation of abstract social ideals or with offering information concerning unsocial conditions or with exhortations to action, without actually making action an integral part of the teaching and learning experience.

In other words, alike in church schools and public schools education has been predominantly bookish.

There is little bookish learning that is closely related to the ongoing stream of current adult experience. For the most part it is an importation from a world foreign to the learners, much of it an inheritance from ancient times, and what is "learned" consists principally of verbalisms which fail to be so related to the feelings, the attitudes, and the habits of the learner as to affect his ways of living. They are not tied into his neuro-muscular system. They do not lead to action. They remain in the mind, so far as they are retained at all, as they were "learned," vague memorizations, unrelated to the day-by-day problems of living together helpfully, harmoniously, cooperatively as members of a brotherly society.

In contrast, learning is needed that is vital, immediate rather than remote in its connection with the real problems of day-by-day living; learning that supplies knowledge, skills, and attitudes necessary for dealing effectively with problems of personal adjustment, with social and civic problems, and with the problems of world affairs. Learning is called for that reveals the basic causes underlying the unwillingness and inability of the individual to cooperate with others in behalf of the common welfare, underlying the lack of harmony and happiness, the misunderstandings and complexities of adjustments within the home and the community.

The essentials of living, the real materials out of which a well-ordered life may be built, are deep and abiding purposes, an enduring faith in God and men, good will toward all men regardless of race or class, genuine feeling and imagination, strong emotions, abounding hope, fearless courage, a rich and varied assortment of living interests, first-hand contacts with ongoing social processes with insight into their inner meanings, satisfying vocational adjustments, rewarding friendships, consciousness of social responsibilities, sound moral judgments and the ability to govern conduct in accord with them, and well-poised but aggressive action. These basic essentials are not so much outcomes of bookish learning as of life itself and of the experience of living.

EDUCATION AS A BY-PRODUCT OF SOCIAL LIVING.—In other words, the education which the times demand is not something to be given, by any kind of formal procedure, either to children or adults, by teachers and leaders; it is to be achieved by individuals and groups for themselves, and to a considerable extent it will come as a by-product of social living.

For a period of more than a hundred years, in contrast to the prevailing individualism fostered by the capitalist economy and by philosophical and religious influences, a new collectivism has been gradually emerging. Within the past few decades it has developed with cumulative rapidity and power. It has not been imposed, as is so often assumed, by any political party or by the machinations of any group of individuals. It is a by-product of science and technology even as individualism was the outgrowth of philosophical and religious tradition and belief. "The application of science to materials in the effort to meet evolving human needs leads inevitably to cumulative collectivism."[1] For more than a century this inevitable process has been at work, steadily contributing to the development of an order which not only accords with a deep-lying strain in our American tradition, "the American dream," but which also has been for ages foreseen and demanded by prophetic religion.

But individualism has persisted, fostered by education and by trends in our American life that have been contradictory in numerous particulars to Christian ethical principles and social ideals, although most of the time to the majority of persons these contradictions have not been clearly evident. This persistent individualism has permeated education, both secular and religious education, elementary and advanced. Predominant methods of learning and teaching have been for the most part wholly individualistic. Education has involved the serious fallacy that social ends can be achieved by individualistic means, a fallacy that has maintained controlling influence upon educational practice. As a result American culture exhibits a vast amount of individual and group behavior in direct contradiction to Christian social ideals, and a prevailing conduct, particularly economic institutional and personal practice, utterly at variance with the ethical and religious ideals to which as a people we profess adherence.

SIGNIFICANCE OF JESUS' METHOD.—Surely it will be agreed that Jesus' example, as described above, suggests an educational procedure of very great significance for adult religious education today. Whatever one's critical judgment of the present age may be, recognition is due that it is a period of remarkable energy. If ways can be found of taking advantage of the aggressive, dynamic character of the age in the interest of forms of action that are creative in the full Christian sense, a considerable measure of reassurance concerning the future of society may be felt.

THE CENTRAL IMPORTANCE OF ACTION

The principle of education through action finds re-enforcement in the emphasis of psychology on the central importance of will and action.

WILL AND ACTION AS CENTRAL IN LIFE.—An essential and basic fact in the individual and in society is the will to live. Man is a striving animal, and the basic fact of human existence is found in his capacity to do or, as Aristotle declared, the fact that he possesses a natural body endowed with the capacity for life and action. Both mind and body are organized for action, or as James says, "the whole neural organism is, physiologically considered, but a machine for converting stimuli into reactions."[2] The human organism finds its end in action, all consciousness is naturally impulsive, and the mind in all of its experiences finds their completion in some form of action.

There is in this no depreciation of the importance of thought or feeling. On the contrary, action is necessary for the sake of thought and feeling. Not only do they tend to find their fulfillment in action; without some form of expression they are, as it

were, left suspended in midair.   There is here a process of interaction: "the idea, the knowledge content, grows out of, as well as
leads up to, action."

Herein, again, the method and teaching of Jesus are validated
by modern psychology.   His typical invitations to people were:
"Follow me;" "Come ye after me;" "Take my cross upon you"—
varying phrases but in every case an appeal to the will, an invitation
to choose, a command to act.   So also his teaching: "He that willeth
to do . . .   shall know. . . ."

A chief weakness of the program of the Church is that it fails
to make sufficient provision for action.   It rests content with the
proclamation of ideals without making plans for carrying them
out, often, in fact, failing even to indicate the forms of action into
which they should be translated.   The program of Protestantism
continues century after century to be predominantly intellectual,
centering in the sermon, listening to which is primarily an intellectual exercise, with a secondary emphasis upon classes whose
focal point is the presentation of a lesson.   Leaders of the churches
have sometimes gone beyond these traditional activities, undertaking to formulate programs of action, but seldom have they
engaged in any considerable number or for an extended period of
time in determined effort to carry through a significant program of
action.   More often agencies without the Church, such, for example,
as the Labor Movement, have been left to fight the real battles of
social reform, too frequently without any considerable amount of
moral support.

Loyalty to high ideals is demonstrated not by mouthing sentimental praise of them but by doing something about them.   The
American people have long possessed a sentimental regard for
democracy, a sentiment to which the churches undoubtedly have
made large contribution.   But while the ideal of democracy is being
lauded in our churches, the thing itself is being put to death by
political corruption and economic autocracy.   What meaning has
praise of democracy to the factory employee who finds the mill
gate shut in his face by order of corporation directors meeting in
secret session in a distant city?   What content has exhortation to
loyalty to the abstract ideal of democracy to fathers and mothers
whose children are crying for bread?   What weight have empty
phrases about equality and justice in the minds of men who for
years have walked the streets of our cities vainly looking for work,
eating the bitter bread of relief while the reproach of failure gnaws

into their souls? If what semblance of democracy we have possessed passes from us it is not so likely to be because of its violent overthrow by those currently labeled its enemies, as by slow decay for want of substance.

One of the major difficulties in achieving lasting moral reforms is the persisting prevalence of the idea that it is possible to substitute new controlling ideals for old without changing the action tendencies and habit systems of the people. As has again and again been demonstrated, this cannot be done. By legal enactment the unclean spirit may be cast out and the house swept and garnished, but he is soon found to have returned with seven other spirits more wicked than himself, and the last state of that society is worse than the first.

UNITARY RESPONSE NECESSARY.—Education, to be Christian, as has been emphasized at an earlier point in our discussion, must involve development of the total personality. To this end educational programs are required that evoke unitary response. Worship programs and teaching programs that contain no provision for action assure only an incomplete response. Carry-over into action is by no means assured. A program conceived in terms of Christian purposive activity involves the total personality. As chosen, willed activity it is inherently volitional; as purposive it presupposes and involves intelligent choice; and as expressing devotion to a purpose it is deeply rooted in the emotional life. A program that has significant social implications may be readily planned so as to inspire worship and lead naturally to study.

In the literature and practice of religious education in the recent past emphasis has been given to programs of instruction, programs of worship, and programs of service. Programs frequently have been separately planned and have been more or less unrelated. Increasingly a demand for unity has developed. The unpsychological character and resulting ineffectiveness of programs uncorrelated and largely unrelated have become widely apparent. There has been much discussion of correlation. But more is required than superficial correlation, which too often is a mere species of educational carpentry that undertakes to join together existing programs separately planned and variously motivated.

The requirement is for programs that in their essential nature are complete, involving at once the learner's total personality—intellect, emotions, and will, with accompanying and inseparable physical reactions. In a unique sense programs of purposive social action satisfy these requirements. The learner (the individual or preferably the group) surveys the field of social need. A situation is discovered which makes a strong appeal. The situation is analyzed from every possible angle. Possible outcomes, that is, ways in which the needs may be met, are considered. Through reading and study, past experience over a wide area in meeting similar needs is consulted. A course of action (that is, a "project" or "enterprise") is decided upon and diligently followed. The emotions are stirred by a deepening sense of responsibility, social responsibility and responsibility to God for the welfare of fellow men. Intelligent interest, sympathy, attitudes of kindness, helpfulness, and love are developed. In brief, genuine religious education, complete personality development, is in progress. The will is exercised; knowledge is increased; the emotions are appealed to and respond; the entire personality takes on new moral tone.

PARTICIPATION BY ALL REQUIRED.—In the early Church every member was a learner, a disciple. Participation in the functional activities of the local group was universal. In any functioning group, organization with the creation of an organizational overhead of leadership is necessary. In the beginning this represents the functioning of the group as a whole; the group expressing itself through its chosen leaders. As time goes on the leadership tends to become more or less self-sufficient, "acquiring a solidarity of its own apart from the rank and file which created it." The overhead may take on self-interest to such an extent as to cease to express the will and purpose of the larger group.[3] In the Church at large and in local churches an important and difficult problem concerns ways and means of assuring that the organizational leadership shall continuously be of and by and for the entire group, the instrumentality or means through which the whole group functions, and of keeping it from developing into an end in itself. Programs of action, democratically planned, in which all are expected to participate, are one of the most effective means of maintaining unitary group solidarity.

THE CHRISTIAN RELIGION AS THE LIFE OF LOVE.—The central importance of action in religious education may again be seen in the fact that the Christian religion is essentially the life of love. Just this, according to the record of the Gospels, it was to Jesus, a way of life expressive of love: love of God with all the resources of one's being; love of one's neighbor as one's self; and the establishment of a social order in which love is the supreme law, the rule of every man's action. Love, in the Christian sense, even as faith, is in its nature active. Its interpretation as a kind of passive sentiment does it grave injustice. It involves devotion—devotion to God, the loving Father, and to Jesus who has brought God near and made him real to us. But devotion to be real must find ways of expression. The only way men know of actually expressing devotion to God is by social means, ministry to his human children, the service of others, working sacrificially for the establishment of his kingdom; the rule of God actualized in just and loving human relationships. If this be true, Christian religious education consists not so much in transference of ideas or in increase of knowledge as in the enlistment of persons in enterprises which represent ministry to others or which are significantly creative in relationship to the building of the Kingdom of God in the earth.

Herein is a weakness of organized religion. The volitional element is too much neglected. By almost constant repetition in sermon and song the invitation to "come" to Jesus is extended, but all too seldom are men and women offered anything to do in his name that represents significant social achievement. The apparent appeal to the will has been in reality merely a vague appeal to sentiment, devoid of meaningful content. As a result there has been developed in the churches a surplus of almost meaningless sentimentalism. Appeal has been made in sentimental terms and sentimental reactions have been evoked. Visit almost any evangelical midweek prayer service and listen to the songs that are sung, the testimonies that are spoken, the prayers that are offered. What a superfluity of vague, almost mawkish sentimentality often is heard! Is it any wonder that religion seems unreal to many thinking people, or that the churches seem to be losing their hold upon many of those who are engaged in scientific effort for human welfare and social progress?

"I propose to go for the sinking classes, and in doing so shall continue to aim at the heart," declared General William Booth in launching the program of the Salvation Army. But note that at the very moment he declared his intention of aiming "at the heart" the shrewd religious leader was *launching a social program*. The remarkable record of the Salvation Army is sufficient justification of the soundness of his judgment. A program that exhausted itself in the beating of tambourines, pious ejaculations, and highly emotional appeals would never have given the Army the standing it has today. Nor is it likely that a social program, even as practically helpful as that of the Army, would go on indefinitely, propelled by its own momentum, without the re-enforcement of a deep emotional drive.

MOTIVATION OF CHRISTIAN SOCIAL PARTICIPATION

The congregations of the churches for the most part are made up of religiously inactive people. Churches are *auditoriums*, filled, when they are filled, with passive listeners. How may the members of the churches be led into activities that are thoroughly Christian, represent service to men, and involve the application of the principles of Jesus to modern life?

INTEREST IN ACTIVITY.—Fortunately, adults even as children have a natural interest in activity. They are habituated to activity, engaged in doing many things, and readily enlisted in new and additional activities. Interest in significant activities does not have to be laboriously cultivated. It already exists, waiting to be utilized. One reason why many churches do not effectively lay hold on influential people of the community, and engage them wholeheartedly in their membership, is that these churches do not offer worth-while activities in which they may enlist.

There are, of course, exceptions. Some adults are overworked, borne down with too heavy responsibilities, overburdened by care or the mere struggle for existence. This is particularly true of industrial workers, and more true of those in middle life and beyond. When all exceptions have been made, however, there remain many members and adherents of the churches who require only a suggestion that their help is needed, an appeal to existing even though dormant interests, to enlist with wholehearted purpose in activities that are socially significant.

The interest of adults in action is more dependable than that of children or of early adolescents. The interests of children tend to be whimsical; they shift easily and frequently; they may be readily diverted. The interests of adults are more deeply rooted, more permanent in character, less easily changed. In all of this is to be seen both a means of the motivation of social participation and a testimony to the wide usability of service in adult education.

INTERPRETATION OF RELIGION IN TERMS OF SOCIAL PARTICI-

PATION.—Next to the natural interest of adults in action which makes readily possible their enlistment in significant social activities dependence for motivation should be placed upon a more forthright interpretation of religion in terms of social participation. Adult church members are inactive because the Christian religion has so seldom been interpreted to them in terms of social action. Religion defined in social terms, as was emphasized in the opening chapter of this book,* is unfamiliar to the majority of church members. While progress has been made in recent decades it is still true that the social interpretation of religion has only a minor place in the prevailing processes of instruction. Illustration is to be seen in the dearth of hymns of social action and their infrequent use in services of worship. The Church possesses a gospel of social action but for the most part it has been withheld from the people.

ACQUAINTANCE WITH SOCIAL CONDITIONS AND FACTS.—A third element in motivation of social participation is first-hand acquaintance with prevailing conditions. An amazing ignorance of how the majority of people are compelled to live prevails among many of the members of comfortable middle-class churches. In part this is due to a willful blinding of their eyes, but also in part it is because the facts have never been brought to their attention. People become interested in changing unjust conditions which cause privation and suffering when they are brought to see and feel these conditions and are convinced that they can be changed.

EDUCATIONAL VALUES IN EVERYDAY LIVING

"Beyond a doubt," wrote Emerson, "every experience in life is of value to a man." Studying our own past experiences and those of others well-known to us, we may question the truth of the statement. Certainly, all are not of equal value or of value for the same reason. Some experiences have little educative value; others are destructive of ideals, undermine character, tend to disorganize personality, and involve socially undesirable conduct.

It may be agreed that every experience of life is of potential value. What is necessary is that the potential values inherent in particular experiences and types of experience shall be discerned and, second, that the experiences shall be so dealt with that their possible values shall be realized.

* See pp. 56ff.

In adult education it is important that we get away from what Ruth Kotinsky has called "the hampering concepts" of classrooms, textbooks, and lectures. She contends, rightly, that more educational possibilities are involved in buying shoes for the baby than in most of the problems that crowd the pages of textbooks.[4] Yet in the vast majority of cases baby's shoes are bought with no clear recognition by the mother of the problems involved or of the values to be gained through an attempt at their solution.

EDUCATION THROUGH THE CONSUMPTIVE PROCESSES.—By nature we are consumers. The first outreach of the newborn babe is toward its mother's breast. Throughout life we consume in order to live. Most, if not all, values, in one way or another, directly or indirectly, are consummatory. Life, personality, and character are sustained and developed by the consummatory processes of which the consumption of food is only one of many. When we gain our food and shelter, when we breathe the pure air of the out-of-doors, when we gaze upon a gorgeous sunset and feel our whole nature inspired by its beauty, when we so govern our relations with other people that we both benefit them and ourselves, something is happening to us for good. We are becoming stronger and better persons.

The capitalist way of life has perverted consumption, treating it not as an end but as means by which the profit economy can be sustained. It has made production the end, and by so doing has robbed millions of human beings of many of their consumption rights, not only their right to food and clothing, but also their right to life, liberty, and the pursuit of happiness, of self development and education. The consumer economy of Cooperation reverses the order; it treats consumption as an end, which it is, and subordinates production to the rôle of means. In Cooperation the possibilities of self-education through the consumptive processes are restored; men find again a way to the freedom in which the life of the individual and of the group can realize its highest possibilities.[5]

EDUCATION THROUGH THE PROCESSES OF PRODUCTION.—Another result of the reversal of the rôles of consumption and production, making of production an end in itself—the private profit of the owners of the means of production—has been to rob the processes of production of most of their educative values. When the worker owned his own tools of production, his work was a means of self-education. When he became a factory worker, he took his place beside the machine owned by the manufacturer or the corporation, himself little more than a machine.

It is one of the terrible anomalies of modern times that as production through invention and technological skill has gained in rapidity and in extent the workers have been degraded, in many cases skills have deteriorated, and personality has tended to lose its recognizability—the sad degeneration of the *craftsman* to the machine tender. The system has tended to make man merely a thing, so much muscle and brain to be appropriated and used by anybody who had use for it, with no more of human rights than the machine that was being tended.

There is no escape from the fact that the worker is shaped by his work. No more does the potter by clever manipulation mold the bowl by the deft touch of his hand than does the process of production mold the producer in its own image. In vain does modern industrialism point to its material achievements. It cannot distract the sober thought of the world from the truth that "the main product of industry is the worker." In the end it will be judged not by its perfected mechanisms but by what it has done to the men and women in its shops and factories.

When production becomes a means to the end not of the monetary enrichment of the few—the owners of industry—but a means to the end of consumption, serving the needs of all, as it can and will in a cooperative economy, it will once again become one of the great educative means of life.

EDUCATION THROUGH CIVIC AND POLITICAL ACTIVITIES.—Next to the activities of consumption, inseparable from life and living, and of production to the end of necessary consumption, in their claim upon the attention and time of men and women, are the activities encumbent upon persons by virtue of the fact that they are members of society, of organized society in the form of government and of numerous social organizations. It is a sad commentary upon American public life that most of those who mix in politics and clamor for public office, with notable exceptions, are men who have the least sense of social responsibility. Civic interest and some measure of civic activity are the duty of every citizen, and participation in significant civic activities with the purpose of social advance is an effective means of education.

APPLIED DISCIPLINE NECESSARY.—For the educational values

of these and other processes of everyday living to be realized, self-discipline, as has been emphasized at an earlier point in our discussion,* is necessary.   There is no panacea for the ills from which society suffers today, ills that are causing widespread moral disintegration as well as physical privation.   Prescriptions for painless cure in the end avail less than nothing.   Political leaders persist in promising cure through one form or another of government action, most of which are merely ways of treating symptoms and stop short of attacking the roots of the disease.   The people possess the means of cure within themselves: clarifying their own social vision; purifying their motives of the dross of self-interest; organizing groups for cooperative action; strengthening their purpose through struggle; perfecting techniques through practice and ever more practice.   Nothing less than such a process of applied discipline will avail.   The moral and mental fiber that has been weakened by increasing dependence upon help from outside themselves can only be regained by self-confidence and determined self-help.   Disciplined effort that will toughen their sinews and constitute them a people whose strength makes them worthy of a better world is the only process by which the men and women of today can win a social order that exemplifies freedom and justice and the abundant life.   This is a truth with which religion is called upon to challenge the present generation.

SERVICE FOR ITS OWN SAKE.—A caution may be needed at this point lest motives become confused.   Social participation is to be valued for its own sake.   For adults in the church deliberately to engage in service activities for their educative value, or for their leaders to appeal to them to do so, is to reduce Christian education to the level of utilitarian ethics, the motto of much so-called "service" in business: "Service pays."   The Christian man engages in activities of social participation because it is the Christian thing to do, not because it returns dividends.   It has an intrinsic value of its own, like those absolute values—the good, the true, and the beautiful, that stand in their own right and are to be cultivated for their own sake.   So in activities of social participation the idea is not to engage in them as a means of education but because we are Christians and want our lives to exemplify the Christian spirit. But so doing because we are Christian, we take cognizance of the fact that social participation is accompanied by growth.

* See p. 175.

SOCIAL PARTICIPATION AS CHRISTIAN EXPERIENCE

Activities that meet these tests are not only educational; they are definitely Christian. Engaging in them is Christian experience. Social participation of the character of these activities is not mere activity; it is activity lifted to the level of a Christian experience.

The term "expressional activities" has had a prominent place in the literature of religious education within recent years. Too often in practice these have been little more than mere physical activities. As the term frequently has been interpreted it has been simply the physical completion of a process of impressing ideas, a conception, it scarcely needs to be said, that rests upon an outgrown faculty psychology and an outmoded Herbartian pedagogy. The concept of social participation herein emphasized is something far more meaningful than mere expressional activities.

Social participation, moreover, to be Christian, is required to be on a higher level than many so-called "service" activities, such as some of those of organized adult class groups, commercial clubs, and various other organizations. As the term "service" is bandied about in popular speech the word suffers degradation from its Christian meaning. It is interpreted as something that "pays," that "returns the surest of dividends," that "insures success." Service in the Christian sense is its own reward and seeks no other.

FELLOWSHIP WITH OTHERS.—Social participation involves association with others in enterprises which because they are truly social in nature are at the same time Christian. They involve intimate, shoulder-to-shoulder cooperative effort in behalf of significant social ends. Such association is one of the most effective means of re-forming the ideas, the ideals, and the entire nature of the individual. Through fellowship with others in a creative enterprise he is himself recreated. Such fellowship is in striking contrast with much that in our present-day pagan world is popularly called "social fellowship" but which might more properly be termed association for mutual degradation. Motivated as it often is by desire for amusement, sensuous excitement, and nerve stimulation, it leaves its victims fatigued, jaded, despondent, eager to escape their distress by further indulgence.

SHARING THE SPIRIT OF CHRIST.—Jesus so identified himself with those who suffer and are in need that he could say, "When you fed and clothed them ye fed and clothed me." God, he believed and taught, lived in the souls and bodies of the naked, the hungry, and the imprisoned. Whatever in love and kindness is done unto one of these is done unto God. To engage in social ministry is to do Christian work and to share the spirit of the Christ.

In our day a further word needs to be said. In Jesus' day poverty was inevitable. The only way that hunger and cold could be met was by charity. But in present-day society poverty is no longer necessary. Scientific knowledge and technological skill have made it possible for food and clothing and housing to be available for all. Today merely to relieve temporarily particular cases of distress, to temper individual instances of injustice, to ameliorate a few local conditions caused by unchristian principles and practices entrenched in the prevailing social order, falls short of adequately representing the Christian purpose or fully partaking of the spirit of Christ. To be fully Christian today, action must be reconstructive in character. It must penetrate beyond symptoms and surface conditions to causes, and seek to change those causes. When men and women enlist wholeheartedly in activities whose purpose is to create a just human society, then and only then do they fully share the redemptive, re-creative spirit and purpose of Jesus.

FELLOWSHIP WITH GOD.—Cooperative effort of this nature, sharing in the spirit of Jesus, is a process of entering into fellowship with God. There are many who in loving, sacrificial, creative service of their fellows have realized a new and deeper sense of the divine fellowship. Indeed, there are not a few whose first real consciousness of fellowship with God came to them as they gave themselves sacrificially to the service of little children in need, or men and women in distress, or enlisted against heavy odds in a battle against injustice, oppression, or greed.

The adult leader should realize that in all probability among the members of his own group there are those looking to him for guidance in whose lives there is a great void, men and women who if they are ever to be led into fellowship with the Father, must needs experience that fellowship in service to their fellow men. A young man contrasted two preachers: "One is forever trying to explain and define God in terms which often make of him a capricious, arbitrary Divinity; the other is portraying the needs and sorrows of men, seeking to awaken sympathy and love, and to enlist his people in sharing with the Heavenly Father the burden of the sins and woes of humanity in redemptive service." There can be no question concerning which of the two men is exercising an effective ministry in the religious education of his people.

EDUCATIONAL METHOD AND PROGRAM

Enlistment in acts of mercy and help, as was emphasized in the opening paragraphs of this chapter, is not new in the life of the Church. It began as a natural and inevitable result of men and women entering into fellowship, through acquaintance with Jesus, with the self-giving, compassionate Father of mankind. But realization of the values of social participation as an integral element of religious education, has all the newness of a fresh discovery. How may these values be assured? What help has educational method to offer?

In contrast to the prevailing individualistic method, education is required that is social both in the ends at which it aims and the means which it employs. In terms of the reconstruction of society the means involve a community group, a class or club, the adult members of a church, or a local community as a whole studying and discussing their situation or their needs until a course of action becomes clear to them that promises possibility of significant contribution to the remaking of a sector of their world, organizing themselves for action and carrying forward the creative enterprise. In this way life itself becomes education. Learning, wisdom, a philosophy of life, emerge from daily activities.

In other terms, the means may be said to be the wholehearted application of the project principle to adult religious education. But what is required is something more than the use of the "project method" as this has been commonly described in the literature of religious education in recent years, something more than the mere adoption by an adult group of a "project" or a series of "projects." The requirement is that adult Christian education shall be construed in terms of enlisting all the adult members of the church in a comprehensive program of planned, purposive activities within the main stream of day-by-day living—activities designed to remake life in accord with a truly Christian pattern.

EDUCATIONAL CRITERIA OF PLANNED ACTIVITIES.—Perhaps the first suggestion is that activities of social participation should be systematically planned. A significant statement of the criteria to be used in planning is contained in the theory of curriculum developed by the sub-committee on international curriculum of the International Council of Religious Education.[6] Those action projects are declared to be most educative in which persons are purposefully engaged in bringing worthy ends to pass. "The central requirement as to method is that the individual be led into wholehearted activities that help to build the Kingdom of God. Such activities should be (1) suited to the individual's capacity; (2) loaded with problems that raise relations, functions and responsibilities definitely into consciousness, that call for reflection, that require a definite choice between alternatives, and that are capable of indefinite expansion; (3) social and shared; and (4) continuous with the remainder of the individual's experience, so that his religious principles become a controlling factor in the whole of his conduct."

PROGRAM OF CHRISTIAN SOCIAL EDUCATION.—A church should have a program of social participation as systematically planned as its program of worship or its program of formal teaching. In any church where the gospel of Jesus is faithfully taught individuals and groups will be stimulated to respond to human need, but unless systematically planned these responses, while spontaneous, almost certainly will be sporadic, more or less overlapping, and will overlook some of the areas of greatest need.

Responsibility for planning the social action program should be definitely located. Usually this should be a recognized department or committee of the church. If responsibility is assumed by a central group such as the official board or the board of religious education, probably more effective than a standing committee will be the appointment of special committees to deal with specific problems and needs. There is no one best plan of organization. Local conditions should be a determining influence.

In every community some of the factors of the current situation described in chapter three* will be found to exist in one form or another. Other social problems and needs, some doubtless of equal importance, also will be discovered. The responsible group will be well advised to make a preliminary exploratory study of the community. In many cases community surveys made by local social agencies or by agencies of the state or federal governments will be available.

While conditions differ widely in different localities in every community one or another aspect of such problems and needs as the following will be discovered: (1) involuntary unemployment

---

* See pp. 106ff.

of men and women, in many communities in large numbers; (2) discouragement and broken morale due to unsuccessful effort to find work, with accompanying need of moral and spiritual rehabilitation; (3) houses that through age, decay, and lack of repair have become unfit for human habitation; (4) children out of school and of church school because of lack of shoes and clothing; (5) children and adults suffering from undernourishment and malnutrition; (6) persons suffering unnecessarily from disease and ill health due to lack of proper medical care; (7) discrimination in various forms against a particular race or races; (8) corrupt courts, more particularly municipal courts; (9) police practices involving graft, tribute from gambling houses and houses of prostitution, illegal arrest, holding persons in custody without booking, brutality against strikers and persons engaged in peaceful picketing; (10) sweatshop conditions, employment of women in runaway shops and factories, and child labor; (11) bootlegging of liquors and narcotic drugs; (12) school stores selling drugged candies, lascivious pictures and literature to children; (13) factories, mills, and other industrial establishments which discriminate against members of labor unions, compel employees to belong to company unions, or otherwise violate the federal statutes. Social reconstruction is to take place after the manner of the leaven and of the mustard seed. The great work is to be done through undertaking reconstructive measures in a vast number of local situations. Wherever in a local community anywhere there exists a social wrong to be righted, injustice to be corrected, need to be met, there creative effort is to be undertaken.

DEVELOPMENT OF THE PROGRAM.—In practically every community some situation exists upon which attention may be focused, interest stirred, and activity stimulated.

If, as may often be the case, concern is confined to a few persons, possibly to two or three, interest may be extended by organizing a "Know Your Community" or "See For Yourself" trip. Under competent direction let the group visit a sweatshop, a factory or steam laundry where underpaid workers are employed, a migrant workers' camp, a restricted residence district, a slum neighborhood in city or rural community, a jail or prison, a juvenile court session, a coal mine, a group of unfit or condemned houses, homes of persons on relief, or any one of numerous other situations which exhibit acute social conditions. In tactful and skillful ways let the facts be procured and supplied to all those whom it is desired to interest. In some communities contrasting situations may be explored: a rehousing project, a model factory, a modern prison, a resettlement project, a consumers' cooperative, or other significant experiment.

Begin with a recognized need.—The church, of which there are many, that has not engaged in social action as a part of its educational program will do well to start with some point of recognized acute social need and in the beginning confine its effort to this one thing. In this way it will usually be possible to guarantee a degree of unanimity that will insure against sharp disagreement or active opposition within the church during the initial period when a precedent of social action is being established. If either develops, recognize that clash of opinion may be put to educational use. Such recognition often provides a setting for more effective education than would otherwise be possible. The idea, so widely prevalent today, that the Church should avoid all controversial issues, is fallacious in the extreme. Every moral and social issue is controversial, otherwise it would not be an issue. For the church to limit itself either in formal education or in social action to areas in which no difference of opinion exists means for it to abjure its function of education.

Plan the procedure of action.—When a social action project has been decided upon, the next step is that of planning the procedure. Investigation, study, discussion, choice of course of action, and carrying the project through to completion, all should be systematically planned. Definite assignment of responsibilities should be made. When assignments have been carried out, reports should be presented, and the outcomes evaluated.

Enlarge the program.—From such a beginning the program should be gradually enlarged. The scope of social activities of most churches is exceedingly limited. In *Christian Youth in Action,* Frank W. Herriot, after wide inquiry, has listed numerous examples of social action carried out by church groups, chiefly groups of youth and young adults.[7] They include such projects as supplying eggs and milk to a fellow member attacked by tuberculosis; cooperating with a county nurse by providing milk for an orphaned baby, securing work for an unemployed man, carrying on social service work among the deaf, and maintaining a Sunshine Club for unemployed girls including classes in sewing—kindly services of mercy and help, but limited in number and in range, and conspicuously lacking in prophylactic character. With a very few exceptions all were remedial in an individual sense, and in no way reconstructive. The danger is that local churches will be content with projects of this limited character. "These ye ought to have done, and not to have left the other undone."

Examples of the more basic type are to be found. In a number of cities groups of Christian men and women have won battles in behalf of civil liberties that have radically changed local situations. In other communities various types of racial discrimination and exploitation have been overcome. Committees representing groups of churches have been instrumental not only in settling strikes but in materially improving the conditions that gave rise to industrial unrest.

SOCIAL-ACTION GROUPS.—The Church being what it is today, a cross section of the total population, with the conception of religion as an active social force still unfamiliar to the majority of the members,* it is impossible in many cases to enlist the local church as a whole in a program of social action. Groups should be formed in accord with the principles already stated,† constituted of courageous, earnest, socially sensitive, inquiring minds, led by those men and women who are willing to act as Christian pioneers. The least that the church can do is gladly to make a place in its program for such groups.

There are various types of action projects that should be developed as community movements rather than being sponsored by a particular local church. A consumers' cooperative is such a project. Every effort should be exerted to make it a community undertaking. There is no reason, however, why a local-church social-action group should not become the nucleus of a consumers' cooperative, projecting the organization as a community enterprise. A credit union may very well be a local-church project. Many credit unions have, in fact, been organized within churches and have rendered a greatly needed service to the members.[8]

PARTICIPATION OF INDIVIDUAL MEMBERS IN EXTRA-CHURCH GROUPS.—The major part of significant social action in present-day society is being carried on by a wide range of social agencies under federal, state, and voluntary auspices. A large proportion of those engaged in the work of these agencies are members of churches, many of whom not only received from the teaching of the Church the original stimulus to engage in social activities but who also

* See pp. 56f.
† See pp. 195f.

draw from religion much of the encouragement and strength which enable them to persevere under adverse circumstances. The Church is fulfilling its function of social education when it enlists its members in the activities of agencies whose social service is remedial or reconstructive. The local church, as a part of its educational program, should have a list of all such agencies within the local community, should be acquainted with their programs, and should make a systematic effort to enlist its members in their activities. As regards various significant types of social action it is important to recognize that successful outcomes can be achieved only in cooperation with other agencies whose resources of information, personnel, influence, and funds make possible effort on a wide scale. For the most part this holds true of such areas as peace, racial discrimination, labor, housing, and juvenile delinquency.

CONTRIBUTION TO PUBLIC OPINION.—As a part of its program of social education the local church should find and continuously use ways and means of making the enlightened opinions and convictions of its members on significant social issues register in the formation of public opinion in the community at large. This is the more important because of the vast amount of antisocial propaganda constantly disseminated by the public press, the radio, and other commercially controlled agencies. There are many ways in which this can be done, such as resolutions passed by the congregation, the official board, and other groups within the church, published in the local press and otherwise circulated; letters written by individual members to the press; forums on significant issues; plebiscites on the same; and mass meetings in the interest of creating public opinion.

AREAS OF SOCIAL PARTICIPATION

A question remains as to the specific areas within which social participation becomes most significant.

THE HOME AS A CHRISTIAN COMMUNITY.—The life of love must be learned, and the one chief way of its acquirement is sharing a group life in which love rules, thereby learning to govern conduct by the law of love. There can be no better exemplification of social living than is to be found in the group life of those truly Christian homes where in the spirit of kindness, gentleness, sympathy, and cooperation each bears the burdens of all and all cooperate in the tasks of each. In such homes self-giving knows no measure, and love constantly grows because the natural and sure response to love is more love. How ineffective lecture courses and textbooks in comparison with participation in the life of such a family group!

THE CHURCH A CHRISTIAN COMMUNITY.—Just such a family group on a larger scale the church is intended to be. It is a section of the family of God in which the members live together as brothers and sisters in mutual trust, forbearance, and self-giving, each living for all and all for each, seeking to make love as the supreme law effective in all the relations of society in which they participate. If it should be said that there are no such churches, there is but one answer: by so much as any fails of being such a church it comes short of being truly Christian, and in the extent of its failure is to be found the measure of its ineffectiveness in religious education.

As men and women engage cooperatively in action projects whose purpose is their mutual welfare, the improvement of community conditions, and the correction of specific evils in community life—the ultimate goal the remaking of the social order in terms of the Kingdom of God—they become conscious of sharing a common purpose and a common endeavor that is of the very essence of the Christian gospel. In such sharing of purpose and effort as in no other way the life of the church is lifted to a Christian level.

Participating in group life characterized by such social purpose and by warm, genial, vibrant family fellowship, men and women experience values difficult if not impossible of attainment in any other way. Working together, playing together, worshiping together in the intimate face-to-face association of this larger family, a fellowship socially, mentally, and spiritually satisfying, they experience a sense of comfort and security in the midst of a world torn by forces that disrupt old securities. Their individualities are fused in that of the group as a whole; they are inspired by its spirit, partake of its courage, are re-enforced by its strength. Such group association is required for individual personality development. As others are brought into the group life it is an effective means of inspiring in them social ideals and social conduct, thereby making more possible the extension of social values and the achievement of brotherhood outside of the church.

CHRISTIAN ACTIVITY IN THE LARGER COMMUNITY.—It is not enough for men and women to make of the church a Christian community, and through participation in its life, to grow. The obligation is upon them as Christians to share also in the life of the larger community, the rural neighborhood or the city of which they are citizens, and such sharing, through civic and political activities, and through participation in the work of significant social agencies, with the purpose of achieving social advance, as has been said above, is to be recognized as a chief means of Christian education.

Indeed, the educative importance of the local community can scarcely be overestimated. Social participation, the warp and woof of education, is necessarily a local matter.

A principal objective of Christian education, as has been repeatedly emphasized, is the reconstruction of the present social order. As to this there is rapidly increasing agreement. But many are at a loss how to proceed in the direction of such achievement. How can reconstruction be brought about? How is the objective to be attained? The local community is the matrix within which the actual reshaping of the individual through activities in which he participates must take place. It is also in a real sense the matrix for the remaking of the world. The world as a whole is remade only as the local communities of which it is made up are recreated. It is a popular fallacy of social idealists that by some grandiose scheme the world can be transformed at a single stroke. No social reformation is permanent that does not begin with individuals in local communities and from such centers spread toward the transformation of the whole.

There is little reason to believe that thoroughgoing social reconstruction can or will be accomplished suddenly or by wholesale. Many earnest, intelligent people have turned away in recent years from any expectation of social transformation through sudden upheaval, revolutionary change, or any such method as apocalyptic Messianism has stood for in the past. Not but what God could work in such a manner, but that he has not so wrought in the past, nor does such a method seem consistent with what we know of the character of God.

CREATIVE ACTIVITY IN THE ECONOMIC AREA.—The significant areas of Christian action are not to be thought of as exclusively institutional or geographical. Not only in the home, the church, and the local community is social participation in high degree educative, but also, as intimated above in our discussion of education through the consumptive and productive processes, in such phases of living as the economic.

There are few more educative experiences in which men and

women can engage than enlisting in enterprises in which they undertake to organize and conduct their economic activities in accordance with the ethical principles of the Christian religion. There can be no question, for example, but what cooperation offers the principles on which an economic structure of society can be built that exemplifies the ethical ideals of religion. Let men and women engage in organizing, developing, and maintaining a consumers' cooperative, and they find in the undertaking a means both of self-education and of contribution to the reconstruction of the economic order.

A WORLD OUTREACH.—The objectives of Christian education do not stop short of a world-embracing democracy of God. Beginning with the experience of sharing and serving in association with a limited group such as the family and the church, outreach is to be expanded until it includes all humanity. The social consciousness of the individual and the family should enlarge into the group consciousness of the church and the local community, and this in turn to a world-consciousness that knows no boundaries of nation or of race and that is committed to service in behalf of the whole world.

CHAPTER VIII

INTELLECTUAL ASPECTS OF A GROWING
RELIGIOUS EXPERIENCE

JESUS never turned away from the questions of an inquiring mind. He declared it to be the unique privilege of his disciples to know "the mysteries of the kingdom of heaven." He sought to communicate to them the knowledge of God, in which he declared true religion to consist. He made great contributions to the world's thought, giving new scope and significance to man's thought of God, to the nature of man, and to the meaning of human life. In this emphasis upon knowledge, a pronounced emphasis throughout the Gospels, it is made very clear that it is not facts or abstract conceptions which Jesus is concerned to impart, but a kind of life, a sharing of the life of God, which is ethically conditioned. It is the pure in heart who shall see God; it is those who do God's will who know; even as Hosea had declared, those who morally transgress prove thereby their lack of knowledge and their rejection of knowledge (Hosea 4. 1-6). In the teaching of Jesus there is no divorce between knowledge and right conduct; both are aspects of "eternal life," the life which is of God and with God.

KNOWLEDGE AND A GROWING RELIGIOUS EXPERIENCE.—Objectives of adult Christian education made compelling by the situation in which human life is lived today, as has been repeatedly emphasized in the foregoing pages, include (1) growing persons, men and women who in character and conduct increasingly exemplify that righteousness and justice which Christian thought and faith ascribe to God; (2) a society that increasingly reflects in the corporate relationships of men these same ethical qualities; and (3) a developing purpose and ability to share constructively in the ongoing creative process of God's working in his world. How are intelligence and knowledge related to these objectives? What contribution does knowledge have within its power to make to the achievement of righteousness and justice in character and conduct? What is the part of knowledge in achieving a Christian society? What relation does knowledge bear to a sharing of God's creative purpose?

KNOWLEDGE CONTENT OF THE CHRISTIAN RELIGION.—In considering these questions it is well to remind ourselves that the Christian religion rests upon a basis of historic facts. It is the religion of Jesus, an historical Person. Its basic documents, the Gospels and the Acts, are primarily narratives of certain definite, historically attested, happenings. Central in these narratives are the facts about Christ—his birth, the way he lived, his deeds, his words, his death, and his resurrection. Indeed, one of the principal elements of distinctiveness in Christianity as a religion is the importance it attached to these historic facts, and their unique character. Out of these facts of history grow certain convictions, beliefs, ideals, appreciations, and aspirations.

The Christian religion, it has been said over and over again in this book, is essentially an experience. It is a life, a Way of life. But to say this is not in itself enough. It is Jesus' Way of Life. It is an experience conditioned by the convictions, beliefs, ideals, appreciations, and aspirations that have grown out of, and continue ever anew to spring from, the historic facts of the gospel. These must be learned by every new generation. They constitute an important part of the knowledge content of the Christian religion.

Jesus is not an isolated fact in history. He cannot be understood apart from what preceded and followed him. He is the central fact of human history, the climax of an historical process of twenty centuries that preceded, and a fountainhead from which has proceeded much of the history of twenty centuries that have followed. This entire historical process is so essential both to an understanding and an evaluation of Jesus that it should be the familiar possession of every Christian.

It is of significance also to realize that the Christian religion, in its purer form, wherever it has taken possession of the thought life of a people, has begotten increased respect and growing provision for ideas, meanings, power to think, and the development of vigorous intellectual activity.

FUNCTION OF KNOWLEDGE AND IDEAS

Religion concerns the entire personality, which as has been emphasized in our discussion is an integrated whole. Christian experience is the experience of the entire self or person; it cannot be limited to any one aspect of the self. Religion is the inner aspect of all life, the deeper meaning of all experience. Many of the weaknesses of present-day Protestantism result from oversight of this essential nature of religion and of religious experience. With some there is an overemphasis upon the emotional aspect, with the result that religion tends to exhaust itself in emotional expression, often resulting in emotional excesses of one kind or another. Religion that degenerates into mere emotionalism soon brings itself into contempt. Others make religion wholly a matter of moral conduct and humane social relations, with whom it becomes an ethical humanism. With yet others there is an overemphasis upon the intellectual aspects of religion. This type of religion, while it is likely to preserve its respectability, or at least the guise of such, may be quite as barren of the fruits of religion as an excessively emotional type. A cold, formal intellectualism, incapable of deep feeling and human sympathy, bears little resemblance to the Christian religion. While this is true, it is likewise true that without the informed mind the religious life is lopsided. The person of abundant life is he whose mind is well-furnished, its equipment including an ample store of religious concepts, meanings, generalizations, and mental skills. This statement by no means implies that religious knowledge can take the place of emotionalized attitudes, of fine appreciations, of strong purposes, of sacrificial service of others. All of these, and more, are involved in Christian living. But in the face of a current disposition to depreciate "mere information" and knowledge it is important to insist that for abundant living a religiously well-informed mind is essential.

BASIC NATURE OF SUBJECTIVE ACTIVITIES.—Earlier in this discussion it has been said that living is education. Living richly and nobly, engaging daily in the performance of those activities which make up social living, constitutes religious education. But it is also to be remembered that it is out of subjective activities that visible objective activities spring.

There is no more significant factor in the life of any age than its subjective ideas. While it is of prime importance for men and women to be enlisted in significant outward activities in all areas of living—economic, educational, citizenship, recreation, and all the rest—it is quite as important, or even more so, that they shall be engaged in those inner activities of intellectual discernment, valuation, judgment, planning, and choice, from which objective activities come. It would be a superficial type of religious education that would ignore the supreme importance of clear thinking, wide and improved knowledge, spiritual meditation, religious contemplation, aspiration, and longing.

The protest, so generally shared today by progressive teachers, against "content-centered," "material-centered," "knowledge-centered" religious education has grown in no small measure out of the moral and religious barrenness of a so-called religious education that has failed to draw out, to develop, to illuminate, to vitalize, or to empower. Much of it has been a purely transmissive process, a passing over from teacher to learner of bodies of facts, information, and dogmas unrelated to the process of living—dry, lifeless, and impotent. At its worst it has degenerated into mere verbalization —the mouthing of shibboleths, cant phrases, familiar truths, with little or no transmission actually taking place. In some instances the procedure is varied by what passes for discussion, principally simple question and answer; the calling out of familiar facts or statements of dogmatic opinions, few of which are ever changed by the "teaching" procedure. In defense of such a process what can be said?

But when the teacher out of a more profound knowledge or a richer experience says to a responsive individual or group: "Hear now a parable;" or, "My experience has been of this kind;" or, "After meditation and study I have reached the following satisfying conclusion," while he may be said to be transmitting content, is quite as truly sharing experience. In such teaching, experience-centered and content-centered religious education are one. To the extent that the learner actually learns, that is, shares the experience of the leader, the new knowledge acquired is a real experience.

Clearly, in all learning much more than mere physical activity is involved. Emphasis upon activity in its physical aspect may become an overemphasis. "Learning by doing," while an important principle, may easily be seen out of perspective. All-round development of personality is the goal of Christian education, and this demands a foundation of ideas and concepts; the power to think, and to think straight, on moral issues; growth in understanding and in ethical discrimination, and in breadth and depth of knowledge. These objectives are not likely to be realized in any large measure if their inclusion in the scheme of adult learning is left to chance or to attainment as by-products.

That education is a process of response to real-life situations is a valid principle. But it should be realized that an intellectual interest may be and often is a most real real-life situation. It has been sometimes assumed that the learner *always* starts with some immediate problem arising in his own life, and that history, literature, science, come into the process only as means of securing help to solve the problem. Such an assumption is not valid. For example, the reading of Drummond's *The Greatest Thing in the World,* and of the work of Frederick Denison Maurice and Arnold Toynbee for the depressed labor classes of England, led Kagawa to contemplate the misery of the slum-dwellers of Kobe and Osaka and to decide that it was his duty to take up his residence among them. There are many similar instances. Indeed, it may be questioned whether there are not quite as many instances of minds quickened to consciousness of previously unfelt problems through reading and study as of persons who, confronted with immediate real-life problems, reach out into literature for help in their solution.

RELATION OF KNOWLEDGE AND EXPERIENCE.—Knowledge cannot exist apart from experience. There can be no knowledge without a knower. Knowledge is a phase of experience.

Conversely, experience and knowledge cannot be sharply distinguished. "It is impossible . . . completely to separate any experience from our thought about it. Hence pure religious experience, purged of all admixture of idea and belief, is an abstraction as unreal as is pure sensation in psychology. . . . Our actual experience, whether of religion or sense objects, is a life of which thought is a necessary and inseparable aspect."[1] To admit that within the sphere of human life there may be such a thing as bare experience without a cognitive element is to reduce the human mind to somewhere near the level of the jellyfish. At least for all human beings above the level of idiots all experience undoubtedly has some cognitive aspect. The corollary of this is that all knowledge is derived from experience. Knowledge is race experience. All existing knowledge arose first within experience. It is the meaning attached to the activities of individuals and of groups. Arising within experience it turns upon itself and finds its purpose for being in the manipulation and development of other activities.

This is what has come to be known as the instrumental view of knowledge as contrasted to the thought of knowledge as an end in itself. Knowledge is to be esteemed in religious education not so much for what it is in itself as for what it does, not so much for its value *per se* as for its ability to enrich and control experience.

This does not depreciate knowledge, as has sometimes been inferred. Rather, it increases estimate of its value. As a means of interpreting and controlling experience it becomes an indispensable adjunct of living, the means upon which progress in human living depends. Knowledge as content is merely so much inert stuff, one of the things of life, a possession which one may have or do without. As a means of the reconstruction of experience it becomes living and dynamic and creative. "Knowledge as content is dead; knowledge as the record of striving, of thinking, of points of view, of values that at some time have been the indispensable supports of persons who like ourselves have faced for the first time the great adventure of living, with all the risk and romance that such an adventure holds, is instinct with throbbing life."[2]

EXPERIENCE REQUIRES INTERPRETATION.—"Knowledge emerges from experience as meaning." This analysis of the origin of knowledge at the same time points to one of its basic functions: knowledge exercises the function of interpreting experience. And experience, if it is to be of maximum value, requires interpretation.

Take worship as an example. In worship at its best, as we have said, the worshiper experiences God. But worship by no means always purifies conduct, quickens ethical discrimination, promotes social progress. The student of religion cannot pursue his studies far without discovering that much worship is not only not morally helpful but that some of it actually is deadening. It may even be debasing, as worship in some religious practices actually is. Whether worship shall elevate or debase, broaden or narrow, socialize or paganize, depends upon the concept of the God worshiped held in the mind of the worshiper. The worship experience in itself is not enough. It needs to be intellectually conditioned. Even among Christian people a distinct hindrance to worship in enriching experience is the lack of an intelligent, and truly ethical conception of God. Without this it may continue to be, as it has sometimes been in the past, the "opium of the people," a way of escape both from injustices and oppressions that ought not to be endured and from the sense of obligation to deal justly and mercifully even at cost to oneself. The religion of Jesus supplies the concept of God as a personal spirit of goodness and righteousness real fellowship with whom in worship and in work is predicated upon sharing his ethical nature and purpose. What is the meaning of this new experience? How is it to be interpreted? These are questions continually to be kept in mind, insistently and persistently to be raised and answered. This process of inquiring the meaning of present experience and interpreting it in the light of the best experience of the past, a process necessary that the values of experience may be realized, can have but one result—a growing knowledge. And this growing knowledge is religious education—not the whole but an integral and essential part.

FEELING REQUIRES IDEAS.—There is no feeling wholly apart from or destitute of idea; some measure of idea is a part of all feeling. So also as regards feeling and action: feeling is action in embryo. In any existing feeling action is already begun. But that which is merely incipient needs completion: the idea needs to be developed; the action requires to be carried forward.

Religion, as we saw in our consideration of worship, roots in feeling. The most fundamental, as most universal, religious experience is that which finds expression in the sense of awe and reverence and dependence. Moreover, this which is so obvious an element of primitive religion likewise characterizes the highest types of religious experience. Nothing is more characteristic of the religious experience of the prophets and of Jesus than the spirit of reverent awe and profound sense of dependence. But the religious experience which exhausts itself in feeling, whether of awe and reverence, or whatever else, fails of fulfillment. Its intrinsic promise of fruitage suffers blight and inevitable decay.

Worship is of value on its own account. Worship is life, not merely a means to religious living. In worship persons experience illumination, inspiration, strengthening, enrichment. But that the experience may realize its fullest possibilities, that it may go on from strength to strength, and contribute to the growth of complete personality the ideas inherent in worship require to be tended, nurtured, amplified, supplemented, re-enforced, and enriched. The Protestant order of service which includes, along with worship in praise and prayer, the reading of scripture and sermon, finds basis in sound educational procedure if only the possibilities of scripture and sermon are actually realized.

VOLITION REQUIRES INTELLIGENCE AND THOUGHT.—The fundamental importance of intelligence and thought as bases of action cannot be too strongly emphasized. Thinking requires insight, power of discrimination, a high order of intelligence, a knowledge of facts, principles, and procedures. "To think, one must have something to think about—a question, or problem—and facts to think with." There is no necessary opposition between experience and the means for enriching and controlling experience derived from the past. Any form of religious education "that emphasizes experiences, but neglects to provide sources and make provision for the informational and thinking material needed to make these activities as meaningful and intelligent as we know how, is inadequate and partial.   All the more important questions of today require the use of a scientific open mind, free from prejudice, and willing to follow the implications of tested thought wherever it leads."[3]

Knowledge gives dynamic to purpose.   In the long run the intelligent, informed will is the empowered will.

KNOWLEDGE, CONDUCT, AND CHARACTER.—Conduct cannot be wholly disassociated from knowledge.   While it is true that Dewey's oft-quoted dictum, "There is nothing in the nature of ideas about morality, of information about honesty or purity or kindness which automatically transmutes such ideas into good character or good conduct," cannot be disputed, what one does in a given situation depends very largely upon habit and attitude and emotional drive. But it is also true that *in some degree* conduct depends upon what one knows—information previously acquired in relation to the particular situation and knowledge previously gained from experience as to the outcomes of similar actions.

Nor are concepts of truth and right without influence.   They possess a power peculiarly their own.   They not only become permeated with dynamic conviction; they also become infused with an emotional content that gives them power as determinants of conduct.

Not that moral character is constituted of a framework of abstract qualities or traits, a catalog of virtues disassociated from living situations.   On the contrary, moral character is a way of living.   Effective education for character uses concrete material drawn primarily from the person's own experience, and secondarily from current life, history, and literature.   It involves not merely the definition of abstract virtues—a comparatively profitless procedure—but an analysis of life situations with a view to the understanding of the factors involved in them and decision as to what is required in their remaking.   That this process may be carried through there must be some basis for moral judgment.   How can there be deliberative judgment as to Christian outcomes, as to social or unsocial ends, without any basic pattern ideas or concepts of right?

A plea is not here being made for the discredited pedagogical idea that effective teaching involves first inculcating a bit of knowledge or belief, then warming it with emotion, and then applying it in conduct. "The assumption that moral principles are first learned and afterward applied in actual life is a mistaken one; it is in the actual relations and responses of daily life that moral values are revealed and character formed. Honor, truth, goodness, and unselfishness are only words or counters except insofar as they have been embodied in the lives of others or practiced in our own. The depth of meaning they convey depends upon the degree in which they have been experienced."[4] What is being said is that fruitful character education involves reconstruction of experience in the light of those great regulative concepts, those supreme spiritual principles and ideals, validated by racial experience, which find their most dynamic statement in the Christian gospel.

A broader and deeper knowledge also is needed. Where is the man who will not admit the need, for his own health of soul, of enlarging the boundaries of his knowledge? But whether or not one is conscious of his lack it is not too much to say that most men are less useful, less influential and live less satisfying lives than is their privilege because of their ignorance of broad fields of knowledge that lie open before them. The life more abundant includes an intellectual world whose horizons are constantly widening as the years come and go.

The need for growing knowledge is the greater because it is either advance or retrogression, intellectual development or atrophy; there is no such thing as the mind remaining stationary as the years of adult life come and go. The pathetic confession of Charles Darwin is the intellectual life story of many a man and woman who have not to their credit any such record of achievement in a specialized field as had the great scientist: "Up to the age of thirty, or beyond it, poetry of many kinds, such as the words of Milton, Gray, Byron, Wordsworth, Coleridge, and Shelley, gave me great pleasure. . . . But now, for many years, I cannot endure to read a line of poetry. . . . I have also almost lost my taste for pictures or music. . . . If I had to live my life again, I would have made a rule to read some poetry and listen to some music at least once every week; for perhaps the parts of my brain now atrophied would thus have been kept alive through use. The loss of these tastes is a loss of happiness, and may possibly be injurious to the intellect, and more probably to the moral character, by enfeebling the emotional part of our nature."[5]

How superficial, and circumscribed by the physical senses and by things, is the life which lacks insight into the wonders and the beauty of nature, has no feeling for or appreciation of art and music, no enjoyment of literature, no perspective of universal history, no acquaintance with the social evolution of backward peoples during modern times!   Much of the meaning and substance of human existence is comprehended within an intellectual life whose wealth is defined in these terms.   An acquaintance with history gives balance and perspective to the mental life.   Art, music, and painting —all the great disciplines of appreciation—add immensely to the richness of living.

KNOWLEDGE AND SOCIAL PROGRESS.—Ideas and knowledge are tools.   Together with ideals, ideas that have become the objects of desire, they are indispensable means for the development of the Kingdom of God in the earth.

Ideas and knowledge are not materials.   No more can a better world be built of them than can a house be built of hammers and saws and squares.   If carpenters are to build houses, there are four essentials: a plan or *mental picture* of what is to be built; the *materials* out of which the structure is to be fashioned; the *tools* with which the work of building is to be done; and the strength and *skill* with which to use tools and materials.   The Good Society may not be fashioned out of ideas and knowledge, however inspired and true.   The materials of which the structure must be fashioned are the actual stuff of life: the human contacts, strivings, hopes, faith, aspirations, emotions, life situations, experiences, which constitute life, individual and social.   The ineffectiveness in the past of religious education in the churches is in part accounted for by the fact that religious leaders confused means and materials.   They assumed that religious ideas, religious knowledge, are the materials of which the Kingdom of God is to be made.   Hence their dependence upon sermons, lessons, lectures, books.   Ideas and knowledge are means, not materials.   Tools are indispensable but without materials the process of building cannot go forward.   Both are required.

Nothing else can take the place, as means, of ideas and knowledge.   Nothing else is so effective, so powerful in its functioning, both in social construction, and in the destruction that often must precede constructive progress, as a vital idea, a great concept, a dynamic article of faith.   Those who today are skeptical concerning the practical value of religious ideas might well spend a little time reading the history of social progress.   They might discover that, instead of hindering the process, religious ideas and concepts have shaped the course of development and have been the means of guaranteeing its results. "Civilizations have been fashioned, history has been made, human affairs have been shaped by nothing more palpable, or seemingly more practical, than a metaphysical conception of God and of his relation to the world. . . . The story of New England is conditioned by the idea of God held by our Pilgrim and Puritan forefathers. And it was . . . men nourished by such a creed . . . that broke the back of tyranny in the state. . . . And the secret of their pertinacity, of their courage, of their indomitable will, was their belief in a sovereign God and in themselves as the agents of his will. It is of such stuff that heroes are made, and prophets; it is such men that 'subdue kingdoms, obtain promises, and turn to flight the armies of the aliens.' "[6]

Again and again it has been demonstrated that social movements, registered in acts of legislation and otherwise, which seem to demonstrate significant social progress, are like the seed sown in stony soil. They spring up quickly but as quickly wither away unless they are strongly rooted in assured knowledge and deep convictions of the people whose practice is involved. Permanent social results do not come without nourishment from a fertile soil of knowledge and experience.

FUNCTION OF CONVICTIONS AND BELIEF

In discussing the function of knowledge in relation to a growing religious experience we have found ourselves using the term "convictions," which may perhaps suggest the close relationship between knowledge and convictions. The two cannot be disassociated. Conviction, if it is valid, to some extent, though not of necessity wholly, roots in knowledge.

BELIEF AND RELIGIOUS EXPERIENCE.—All religion possesses an essential core of belief. Without convictions as beliefs religion cannot exist. A distinction often made today is that between Christianity as a Way of life, a religion of experience, and Christianity as a system of belief. The emphasis on experience, we contend, is in the interest of vital religion and social progress. But that does not mean that an absolute distinction can or should be made between the two. The Christian experience is conditioned upon certain historical facts, certain associated ideas and basic beliefs, and without these it cannot retain its character as Christian.

To retain validity and vitality, to be a growing experience, the Christian life must be re-enforced by clear, strong, abiding convictions, convictions that develop in strength and depth and scope.

All of this, of course, runs contrary to an emphasis quite generally popular today. How frequently one hears or reads the declaration that what one believes matters little provided one lives the good life. Conduct, not creed, it is said, is of chief importance. In which saying there is an easily recognized fallacy. The question is not one of choice between the two. No necessary alternative is presented. What is required is both right conduct and true belief and between the two there is something of causal connection. For religious experience to retain strength and vitality, to be a growing experience through the years of strain and trial of adult life, nothing less is required than that experience shall be re-enforced by belief that has solid, extensive, reasonable, verifiable, growing content. A religious experience, for example, associated with or dependent upon a crude conception of God, and views of his relation to men contradicted by observable facts, is likely to suffer shocks in the course of years that it will be unable to withstand. The result will be either a discredited experience or the disassociation of religion from real life. The psalmist's figure of the righteous man is one that applies to a vital religious experience: it is "like a tree planted by the rivers of water, that bringeth forth his fruit in his season; [whose] leaf also shall not wither."

DOCTRINE AND RELIGIOUS EXPERIENCE.—Doctrine grows out of religious experience. No sooner has a person had an experience that seems to him to be significant than he undertakes its interpretation. His interpretation, if accepted by others who have had similar experiences, becomes doctrine. As the interpretation of religious experience doctrine is thus inevitable and necessary. It has its own important functions. It is a guide to the individual in the understanding and interpretation of his own experience. It is an aid to him in organizing and systematizing religious ideas. It is an ideational expression of social experience. It is a valuable means of check-up on observations of experience and of interpretation. It is far from infallible, as the history of Christian doctrine, with its innumerable divergencies and contradictions, plainly proves. Religious groups, even great church councils, may err, even as individuals err, in the doctrinal interpretation of religious experience.

With this explanation of their relationship, it is clearly evident that in the Christian life experience is more basic than doctrine. Experience, not doctrine, is the primary factor. Doctrine grows out of experience, not experience from doctrine. The interpretation of the experience follows the experience itself. This is merely to say in other words what Jesus declared: "If any man will do his will, he shall know of the doctrine, whether it be of God." The order is not doctrine and then life, creed followed by experience, but the reverse: life and doctrine, experience followed by creed. Religious education is concerned with the teaching of doctrine, but this is not its first concern. It is concerned first with experience, and second with the interpretation of the experience.

Doctrines are essential as interpretations of Christian experience but they are not a means of begetting Christian experience. The Christian religion is essentially an experience of God, and Christian doctrine grows out of that experience. Religion is begotten not by a process of indoctrination but through an experience of sharing Christian purposes, ideals, and activities. Primary emphasis in religious education, therefore, is to be laid not upon creeds and doctrinal instruction but upon the experience of which doctrine is the intellectual expression. Not only modern education, but the essential nature of the Christian religion as well, demands this emphasis.

Familiar illustration may be found in the case of the first disciples. Peter and John and Paul did not begin with a fully developed doctrine of the Person of Christ. Peter and John responded to his invitation and set out to follow him. In fellowship they came to know him. Their doctrine of the Person grew out of their experience of fellowship. Nor was it greatly different with Paul. Before the day of his vision on the way to Damascus, he had certain fixed notions concerning Jesus of Nazareth, mostly erroneous. It was as a result of that never-to-be-forgotten experience that "in the synagogues he proclaimed Jesus, that he is the Son of God." His sublime declarations concerning Christ in the letter to the Ephesians and in other Epistles were the result of an ever-deepening experience of fellowship with him whom he owned as Lord.

The interpretation of a Christian experience at a particular time, either by an individual or by the group, does not and cannot sound the depths of that experience, nor exhaust its meaning. The Christian experience of a given era is deeper and more significant than is expressed in its doctrinal statement. In this fact is to be found another reason for religious education providing opportunity for new interpretations of experience. Should it confine itself to fixed and traditional interpretations, as in catechetical instruction, it might fail, as has happened again and again in the history of the Church, in promulgating vital and deeply significant meanings of Christian experience newly apprehended by persons of unique spiritual insight. Christian experience is like the pearly nautilus. It refuses to be bound by the interpretations of the past; ever and anon it bursts its old shell of doctrinal interpretation that it may build for itself a house more ample.

Intellectual difficulties with historic doctrines very largely disappear if persons who experience these difficulties may be led to regard the creedal statements not as hard-and-fast definitions to be literally accepted but as the attempt of a particular age to express in words the reality and significance of a vital experience. In this particular religion parallels science. The scientist does not regard scientific law as final and complete, but as a tentative statement, as exact and full as present knowledge permits, but subject always to development and verification in the light of newly discovered data. Thus understood creeds of the past continue to be significant, and may be used in testimony of fellowship in sharing with believers of other centuries the experience of life with God.

The weaknesses and evil effects growing out of an over-emphasis upon intellectualism in religion have been emphasized in preceding chapters. But these should not lead to the inference that there is no place in religious education for belief. The basis of the existing difficulty lies very largely in a lack of understanding of the relationship pointed out above, a difficulty that modern psychology and pedagogy should enable us to overcome.

The function of information is similar to that of doctrine. It is not to be sought or conveyed for its own sake. There is such a thing as religiously significant information. Certain information possesses definite value, but this value is found not in itself but in the relation it bears to experience. It is a means by which individuals and groups are enabled to interpret their experiences and thereby to understand and control them.

RELIGIOUS BELIEF AND SOCIAL CONVICTIONS.—The great dynamic social convictions that have had and continue to have so large a part in changing the world root in religious beliefs. They are the outgrowth, for the most part, of men's conception of God, his nature and purpose for his world, his relationship to men and man's answering obligation to him.   Today there is a tendency to try to maintain and enforce social ideals and convictions while neglecting the basic Christian beliefs from which they were originally derived.   There is good reason gravely to question how long such a process can be continued.   To retain vitality and power, even in the life of a single adult generation, social convictions need constant re-enforcement from the religious springs from which they were originally derived.

FAITH AND RELIGIOUS EXPERIENCE.—Commonly, "belief" and "faith" are used as synonymous terms.   While this practice finds justification in the fact that faith has an intellectual content, its intellectual element is but one of three principal aspects.   Faith as presented in the life and teaching of Jesus is essentially dynamic and active.   It is a principle of energy: an outward thrust upon the basis of one's convictions as though one knew them to be really and demonstrably true.   Faith expresses itself in action, but it does not stop there.   It goes beyond action to the formulation of conviction growing out of action, namely, belief.   Finally, faith embodies an attitude of trust, repose of the mind in God.

The relation of faith to a growing religious experience is to be seen in each of these aspects, more particularly perhaps in the fact that being essentially active faith finds its fulfillment in a continuous effort to establish all the relationships of life on the Christian pattern—the relationship of the individual with God, of person with persons, and of groups of persons with individuals and with other groups.

INTELLECTUAL NEEDS OF ADULTS

In general terms some of the chief ways in which intellect serves religious experience have been set forth, ways which under all circumstances and at all times retain validity.   But at this point another question is suggested.   Are there special needs growing out of the situations which adults confront in today's living?   Do the new factors and new conditions described in an earlier chapter, together with the compelling objectives which have been urged, present new needs?

REQUIRED: A NEW MIND.—Mr. and Mrs. Hammond, writing of the period of the rise of the factory system in Great Britain, record this significant insight: "It was not merely that the evil was greater. . . . It was that men still saw with the eyes of their grandfathers and that they were busy polishing the life of the slum, when a race that was vigorous and free in its mind could have put an end to it."[7] The characterization is peculiarly applicable to our day. The conditions now existing in America do not bear testimony to a high degree of intelligence, understanding, and Christian purpose applied to the social and economic order. They give evidence rather, not only of dominance of the motive of private profit, but of lack of basic intelligence and understanding, of creative imagination, and of vigorous purpose.

Social reconstruction must be guided by mind. The present situation presents a complexity that is baffling. There is no easy way out. The old slogans, the catchwords of the past, the treatment of symptoms by legislation, naïve trust in superficial panaceas, vested ignorances and institutional stupidities, all are pathetically inadequate as means of solution of existing problems.

Nor is social salvation to come by any mere shift of power from one party, group, or class to another. Increasing numbers of people pin their faith to a transfer of industrial and political power from the beneficiaries of privilege to the workers. "If workers bring into industrial control nothing better in the way of a philosophy of power than the present concepts of capitalists and employers, the net gain will be zero."[8] What is required is a new mind coming to birth from the travail of today's suffering, tribulation, and need even as the Christian mind of the first century—what Paul calls the mind of Christ—was born out of the sore tribulation and need of the religious, social, and political breakup of the first century.

Does the Church of today really want this new mind? Is it willing to pay the price of the application of the mind of Christ to the total life of society? This is one of the most crucial questions that can be asked. And the answer in the light of the attitudes of the majority is, "No!" No, because religious men, and more especially official religious leaders, know that critical thought is merciless to privilege, dangerous to established institutions, and indifferent alike to economic, political, and ecclesiastical authority. Knowing these things, they fear the critical mind as they fear few other things.

But the changed mind will come, if not in one way then by another. Men and women living in a country that has the traditions of freedom and democracy, of equal rights and justice for all possessed by America will not continue to endure conditions that now prevail. Either as a result of a sweeping cataclysmic movement such as violent revolution or by the gradual, peaceful method of education under influence of the Church, the school, and other agencies which influence public opinion. The possibility exists of the change being effected by these other agencies, even though the Church refuses or neglects to take its part.

WIDER SOCIAL INTELLIGENCE.—A necessary element in the new mind required by the exigencies of the times is a wider social intelligence. The declaration of Reinhold Niebuhr that the average American does not possess sufficient intelligence to criticize the social order in which he is a participant[9] is undoubtedly true of members of the Protestant churches. Coupled with this generally prevalent social illiteracy among many church members is an apparent lack of desire and even unwillingness to face social conditions as they really are. Comprehensive social intelligence is necessary, intelligence that embraces a knowledge of the facts, as nearly as possible *all* the facts and conditions affecting the total social life of the people of America, together with ability and willingness to face the significance of these facts for individual and group conduct. Involved, therefore, in the achievement of the new mind are ways (1) of widening the acquaintance of men and women with social facts and conditions; (2) of awakening the mind to all of the issues involved, and (3) of facing issues as they arise and thinking each one through in terms of how it may be met in a Christian way.

NEW CREATIVE IDEAS.—To be effective in controlling conduct religious concepts must be clear and sharply defined. So far as traditional religious terminology lacks in clearness and definiteness, so far as it does not possess the ring of reality, it is without dynamic for living. Many words and phrases which in the days of their origin expressed realities of experience have lost for many in our day their vital meaning. They are like old coins, sentimentally cherished, but with this difference: they are kept in circulation under the delusion that they are still coins of the realm with all their former purchasing power. A chief responsibility of religious education is that of filling with vital social content, expressing in modern speech, and determining for personal and social conduct and character the implications of such great Christian concepts as love, brotherhood, and cooperation that are the common possession of the people of the churches.

Democracy, it has been said, cannot exist without the continuous emergence of new, critical reconstructive ideas.[10] The statement is even more true for vital religion. Prophetic religion always is dissatisfied with past achievement, impatient with the present. The contrast of existing conditions with the divine ideal is so glaring that the religious teacher always is under compulsion to bring forth new meanings of religion in its application to current living. In a changed and changing world the interpretation of religion, if it is to be effective, cannot be the same as it was a generation ago. For one thing, today's world is infinitely more complex. To solve its problems—as old in some of their aspects as human society, in other aspects as new as the newest machine—new ideas, new knowledge, new social planning are required. Industry with its extortionate profits and its less-than-living wage, its overproduction and its unemployment; agriculture with its inadequate return for labor invested, its so-called overproduction in the face of hundreds of thousands of undernourished men, women, and children; politics with its professionalism, its gang rule, and corruption of the electorate; organized religion with its inferiority complex in the presence of the extravagant assumptions of science, its too frequent appeal to dead dogmas and disregard of live issues, its subservience to power and wealth and its tendency to think of religion as something to be enjoyed rather than to be used, its complacency and neglect of new educational instruments; science a house divided against itself, a method which insists too often on assuming the rôle of philosophy, an instrument without vision as to the end for which it is to be used—all these need ideas and ideals; ideas, purposive; ideals, spiritual; to which religion and only religion can give birth.

RESISTANCE TO PROPAGANDA.—A third necessary element in the required new mind is ability to detect and resist propaganda.[11] As never before in their history the American people today are beset by the clamor of a multitude of voices, each determined to bring about specific action. Most of the propagandists are not concerned about the merit of the claims which they advance or whether the ends advocated are socially desirable. Their concern is wholly that of convincing the public mind in the interest of selfish advantage. The press, the radio, the newsreel, the lecture platform, and even the pulpit and the public schools are used as instruments. The propagandists include not only individuals but political parties, commercial associations, labor unions, farm organizations, patriotic societies, and a multitude of other organizations, including some that label themselves as religious. The result is hopeless confusion—conflicting counsel, utter contradictions claiming equally high authority of truth and right, claims and counter claims, charges and counter charges without limit. In the face of this interminable confusion the average person is helpless, in many cases not even realizing that he is a victim of propaganda or, when he realizes somewhat the extent of deliberately misleading information, wholly at a loss how to detect propaganda when he hears it.[12]

The evil in propaganda is not limited to the degree of its falsity; it inheres in the misuse of educational method and in the fact that propaganda invariably is charged with emotion, and almost always with prejudice and bitterness.

A CHRISTIAN PHILOSOPHY OF LIFE.—The new mind which the age requires must needs be characterized not merely by a wider social intelligence, new creative ideas, and ability to detect and resist propaganda, it must represent a comprehensive, basic philosophy of life. Significant diagnostic insight into today's situation is expressed in the statement of John Haynes Holmes: "Our world is disintegrating inwardly, as it is collapsing outwardly, because it has neither a structure of thought nor an ideal of life in things basic to man's experience upon this planet." Just this: a structure of thought grown out of the soils of their own personal experience and the experience of the modern world, a structure of meaning that under the inspiration of the Spirit has emerged from life as it is being lived today, with all of its newness, its complexity, and its difficulty, which comprehends the Christian understanding of life expressed in terms relevant to the situations within which life is necessarily being lived, is a supreme need.

A large proportion of the men and women of our churches possess no such life philosophy. For men of an earlier generation the theology of Protestant orthodoxy represented a satisfying philosophy. To many, probably a majority of their descendants, it no longer does. The dogmas central and basic in the historic creeds of the Church, popularly known today as the "fundamentals" of Christianity, have for many lost their vitality. They have become for them unreal, lifeless, and almost if not quite meaningless. Their rehearsal in creedal statements and in hymns used in church worship has a hollow sound; they seem to them to have no correspondence with their actual experiences of living.

It is vain to hope that any theology of traditional type can satisfy the need. A "distinguished theologian," unnamed, is quoted by J. H. Oldham as expressing unqualified dissent from the

claim that it can do so, maintaining: "Nothing could be more per-
verse . . . than to suppose that the hope of the world lies in
theology with its intellectualism, its abstractions, its remoteness
from life, and its barren controversies."[13] What men and women
require is not a structure of thought built by armchair philosophers
or theologians from laboriously accumulated learning, though
learning is integral to it; nor from abstract knowledge, as such,
though knowledge also is an integral factor. It is, rather, as Oldham asserts, "the fruit of spiritual insight and understanding . . .
silently born in the minds of multitudes of plain men and women
as they loyally endeavor to do the will of Christ in the ordinary
circumstances of their lives."

A structure of thought or philosophy of life thus conceived,
it seems hardly necessary to say, is not something settled and fixed,
to be imposed by a process of authoritative instruction. It cannot
be developed by transmitting authoritative doctrines or beliefs by
the Church or by any teacher to "pupils." It is essentially a process
of discovery, of evaluation, of inner growth in which the teacher
or leader of the individual or of the group is the guide, the friend,
and the counselor.

WHAT KNOWLEDGE IS OF MOST WORTH?

From the foregoing discussion the conclusion is not to be drawn
that content of knowledge and belief has no valid place in adult religious education today. On the contrary, there is great need for new
emphasis upon its importance. It is not a question of whether
knowledge is required but, rather, what knowledge is of most worth?

A structure of thought born of the experience of today's world,
yes, but with the experience of the past not ignored. There are
those whose attitude toward the past is almost one of contempt.
They are impatient of any suggestion that past experience has produced any worth-while result in terms of dependable knowledge and
belief or that the race possesses an inheritance of verifiable convictions. Their point of view finds expression in such statements
as these: "Every life is a new voyage of discovery. No one has a
dependable chart. The past has revealed no creed or moral code
worthy of our adherence." Concerning such a point of view it is
probably sufficient to say that one who feels compelled to look
upon the experience of the past with contempt has no reason to
look upon the future with anything but despair. If there are no

certitudes growing out of centuries of experience of the past, little of meaning or significance can be expected to emerge from the experience of the present or the future.

The content for which we plead in adult Christian education is not differentiated from life; it is identified with experience—the experience of the present, and the experience of the past so far as it is found relevant to today's life.   Convictions, belief, knowledge which have grown out of past experience and by test verify their authenticity for present-day living find their function in re-entering present experience as means of enrichment, guidance, and control.

THE CHRISTIAN KNOWLEDGE OF GOD.—The ultimate fact in religion is its reference to a Supreme Power.   A distinctive feature of all historical religion with the possible exception of Buddhism has been its central emphasis upon some form of God concept.   A second has been the effort to come into a growing understanding and into right and satisfying relationship with the Divine.   No religion has ever risen above the level of the God or gods with whom fellowship has been sought.   Hence the importance in religious education of the knowledge of God.   *"Visio Dei vita homines,"* a saying that comes down to us from the past—the life of man is his vision of God—is as true today as it has ever been. The vast expansion of knowledge in recent decades constitutes a call to the men of today to enlarge their understanding of God and of his purposes in humanity and the world.   Only in the confidence that we can achieve some apprehension of the will and purpose of God can we possess the courage and patience to face the new demands and exacting tasks that the modern world brings.   "The urgent need of today is that the thought of the Church about God should be brought into harmony with the expanding knowledge of the world.   In proportion as we open our minds to a larger understanding of God's purpose and ways in the light of growing knowledge and of the events of the present may we expect . . . to gain new strength for our tasks."[14]

It would be difficult to overestimate the seriousness of the disposition, all too prevalent in evangelical religious circles, to hold on to inherited concepts of God which are far more pagan than Christian—a tendency for which prevailing practice in adult religious education cannot wholly absolve itself from responsibility. Devotion to a mechanical scheme of Bible study, with an accompanying disproportionate emphasis upon picturesque narrative material, has fastened early Hebrew conceptions of Jehovah as a "God of wrath," a "God of vengeance," a "jealous God," a "man of war," so firmly upon the minds of multitudes of church members that Jesus' teaching of "the Father" has sufficed only to modify in minor degree the earlier, pre-Christian conception. All too frequently Christians have failed entirely to advance beyond the primitive conception, or elements of the primitive conception have remained in the mind as survivals alongside Jesus' teaching, with a resulting utterly confused conception in which contradictory attributes abound. How common, indeed, it is to hear imputed to God motives and attitudes expressly declared by Jesus to be unworthy even of children of the Heavenly Father!

UNDERSTANDING AND APPRECIATION OF THE LIFE AND TEACHING OF JESUS.—Next in importance to a developing knowledge of God is a growing understanding and ever-deepening appreciation of the personality, life, and teaching of Jesus. The two, in fact, are so interrelated that the one cannot be said to be secondary to the other. "He that hath seen me hath seen the Father." It is chiefly through Jesus that we gain our concept of God. In this much more is involved than an idea of God. The even more important thing is that in Jesus God has revealed himself; in him we are brought face to face with the transcendent reality of God. Christ is the purpose and the power of God, and in him these are made available for our utilization in the development of personality and the remaking of society.

The great commandment of Jesus is that men should love God, and their neighbors as themselves. "Thou shalt love the Lord thy God with all thy heart, and with all thy soul, and with all thy mind. This is the first and great commandment. And the second is like unto it, Thou shalt love thy neighbor as thyself. On these two commandments hang all the law and the prophets." The Church has proclaimed this teaching, but it has failed to inculcate an intense and passionate belief in the principle and to interpret its application in concrete terms. As a result there is lacking in most of the members of the Church a compelling, passionate conviction that the principle of love enunciated by Jesus constitutes the utter and final truth regarding men's relations with one another in social, economic, and industrial life.

There is need today, as ever there has been, for men and women of saintly character. But more than saintliness of character is required under modern conditions. A large part of a man's life today is that by which he acts as an owner of property, an employer or employee, a member of a corporation. What does the law of love require of him in these relationships? Perhaps the question of all questions in a day of compulsory social change is, What does the law of love require in terms of the organization and methods of industry and commerce, of production and distribution, of national aims and policy? This the Church must discover and teach.

THE CHRISTIAN CONCEPT OF MAN.—Of scarcely less importance than the knowledge and understanding of God is a Christian estimate of man. The supreme value that Jesus placed upon human personality has been stressed throughout our discussion. His evaluation of man seems to root in certain tacit convictions concerning human nature: (1) human nature has the capacity of unlimited moral development; (2) men likewise possess the capacity of fellowship with an ethical God—of sharing the life of God; and (3) there is in human nature that which will respond to the goodness and love of God, and to the confidence and active good will of their fellows.

Jesus knew what was in man. He was under no illusion concerning the frailty of human nature, of its moral perversity, of the depths of degradation to which it often descends, and of the cruelty and brutality of which it is capable. But he refused to despair of man, not only because of his confidence in a good God, sufficiently powerful to overcome the evil of men and to redeem them from their sins, but also because of his confidence in them.

The moral perversity of human nature is not something to be minimized or overlooked. "For the good that I would I do not; but the evil which I would not, that I do." For the truth of this declaration no man needs look farther than within his own heart and life. His personal experience supplies abundant evidence to satisfy his mind. And that not alone individually, but socially. "We must . . . face the fact that we do, individually and collectively, oppose, resist, and undo our own work of social upbuilding."[15] But this is only one aspect of human life, and for a man to allow it to dominate his thought of himself and his evaluation of his fellows means for him to undermine his own morale and all confidence in or determined effort for the building of a better world.

THE KINGDOM OF GOD.—In recent decades in American Christianity the concept of the Kingdom of God as a social ideal—an

ideal which requires that the values of human personality be placed
above all others, demanding that every person shall be treated as an
end in himself and never as a means to some other end—has been, as
John C. Bennett declares, "a great unifying and liberating conception . . . which gave a fresh mandate to the Church. . . ."[16]

At first regarded as a rediscovery of the original teaching of
Jesus, in more recent years there has been increasing agreement
among Biblical theologians that the conception expressed in the
term "building the Kingdom of God" has little or no historical
foundation.[17] Nevertheless, the hope and the conviction grows in
devout hearts, including more than a few scholarly believers, that
the goal of human history is the Kingdom of God, meaning a human
society which by virtue of being human will not be perfect but
which will in no small measure represent in its relationships, its
attitudes, and its working the love and the righteousness of God.[18]
We believe in God, the Father. And because God is the Father we
have a sure confidence that his purpose is to create a human family
in which men shall live with one another not as enemies or competitors, either actual or potential, but as friends, cooperators, and
brothers.

This hope of the coming Kingdom expressed in one or another of several divergent forms has been a dominant idea in
American Christianity from the beginning of the life of the nation,
never more so than in these troubled years.

A basic requirement for a growing religious experience is a
cause so great and so difficult of fulfillment that it challenges the
utmost of faith, courage, and effort of which human nature is capable. Christians find such a cause in the Kingdom of God. Even
though the history of all the past may suggest that all history may
fail to realize it, nevertheless its vision lures men on—inspiring,
stimulating, and strengthening them, and giving to the history of
the past and of the present whatever supreme meaning it is possible
for human history to have.

KNOWLEDGE AND USE OF THE BIBLE.—The Bible is a transcript
of significant religious experience. As such it is of unique value for
the enrichment and control of present experience. To this, multitudes of men have testified in the past, a witness borne by many
in contemporary life. For adults this significance is increased by
the fact that it is a repository of *adult* religious experience. Whatever it may be made to mean to children and youth, it has increased
possibilities of inspiration and guidance for the mature, and reas-

surance and solace for the aged. Only the adult can sound the depths of the experience the book records. To appropriate all that it has to offer requires a lifetime. "I come back again and again to the Bible," declares a great Christian leader. "I turn aside from it at intervals to quench my thirst at other springs. But invariably I return to that which more than any other is to me a wellspring of life."

The Bible deserves to be known and understood. The pre-eminent place which it is universally acknowledged to hold in literature and in religious history is such that no one who neglects it can rightfully claim to be a well-educated person. To be ignorant of the Bible is to be religiously illiterate. To the extent that it prevails today religious illiteracy holds serious implications both for culture and for character. What is needed is not a revival of the Bibliolatry of early Protestantism, but an intelligent under-standing of the Bible and its teachings, an understanding which it is no small part of the responsibility of the Church to impart.

CHAPTER IX

METHOD IN ADULT LEARNING

"HE seated himself, and when his disciples came to him, he proceeded to teach them. . . ." There are in the Gospels few instances of what appears to be formal instruction. This clearly is one.

The followers of Jesus are here called "disciples," that is, learners. As in the first century so in the twentieth, those who follow the Christian Way may rightly be expected to possess inquiring, receptive minds. But how are they who answer to this description to be taught? How may the adult teacher inspire and deepen in men and women the desire and purpose to learn? How may he most effectively cooperate with them in learning?

FORMAL INSTRUCTION IN ADULT CHRISTIAN EDUCATION.—Religious education unfortunately has been considered by many as exclusively a process controlled by formal teaching techniques or methods of instruction. Thus to identify education with instruction, or with the authoritative imposition of ideas, exalts the intellectual element above the volitional and emotional elements, and has the unfortunate effect of making religion chiefly a matter of acquiring information and ideas *about religion*—a narrow and inadequate conception. The preceding chapters of this book have set forth a broader and more comprehensive view. The fact that no sharp line of differentiation may be made between process and method has been emphasized. Method has been presented in terms of all ways by which the leader and teacher cooperates with persons in the direction of achieving a fully developed Christian personality and a Christian society.

The vital question for the teacher is not, What method shall I use in teaching this lesson? Effective adult teaching is seldom, if ever, achieved through this approach. The more significant question is: How can I assist in bringing about desirable changes in the thinking, the beliefs, the attitudes and relationships, the conduct and character of these men and women?

In some colleges and theological schools, as well as in non-institutional agencies of leadership education, there has been a tendency for religious education to assume almost wholly the form of method and organization.   This tendency has been reflected in the predominance of courses concerned with organization and administration and with methods of teaching.   In the practice of some directors of religious education it has found expression in an overemphasis upon organization and methods.   Such emphasis usually accompanies an idea of content as a given quantity of material or knowledge to be taught and absorbed, the one most important factor being the "methods" by which the knowledge may be transmitted.   Thus "methods" are emphasized as over against "content," as a result appearing to be, as in reality they are, mechanical, artificial, unrelated to experience, lifeless.   Religious education of this character soon reveals its superficiality and weakness.   Concerning this type of emphasis upon methods one may not only say with Kant that form without content is empty, but also that it is powerless.   Its barrenness tends to bring discredit upon the whole movement.

THE PROBLEM OF INDOCTRINATION.—Traditionally, instruction is a process of passing on knowledge from teacher to learner, and such "transmissive" teaching is in more or less disrepute in progressive education today.   It is characterized as "authoritarian," "anachronistic," "lacking in dynamic," "feeble," "a survival."   And, doubtless, all of these characterizations are deserved by much that passes for religious instruction.   It should be borne in mind, however, that the Christian religion is historically conditioned.   It rests on a basis of historical facts.   If education is to be Christian in the generally accepted sense of the term, a considerable element of transmission is a necessity.   There is no way by which the entire body of religious knowledge which forms the historical basis of Christianity can possibly emerge anew from immediate experience as meaning.   It can only be experienced as content.   For its possession by every new generation we are utterly dependent upon a process of transmission.   An education which definitely separates itself from the Christian tradition, the essential basis and method of which would be precisely the same if Christ had never lived, may be able to prove itself creative, but why call it Christian?

The issue of indoctrination came to the fore in education in the twenties, sharply stated in the question: Has indoctrination any rightful place in education?   As the issue was commonly discussed indoctrination was interpreted as the imposition by a person (the teacher), or a group of persons, in the name of authority, of a more or less rigidly defined body of doctrines, beliefs, or standards of conduct and action. In contradistinction, it was urged, education is a process of reconstruction of experience, under guidance. Against indoctrination, thus defined, liberal thought—both religious and social, strongly reacted negatively.

In more recent years it has come to be more clearly recognized that all education inevitably involves a considerable element of imposition. Even without the will so to do common life impresses a common stamp. So also with the conscious process of education. Today, as always in the past, education aims at the inculcation of chosen attitudes, ideals, loyalties, values, and beliefs. Always also, whenever education is a guided process, the factor of selection enters—the choice of situations or experiences to be dealt with, social facts to be presented, truths or ideals to be emphasized, the type of interpretation given. Accordingly, therefore, as Coe has said, "It is not within our power to determine whether education shall be both transmission from the past and response to the present —it is bound to be in some measure each of these—but we can select one or the other of them as the primary function, and we can make either of them contributory to the other . . . the Christian teacher's practical dilemma takes this form: Shall the primary purpose of Christian education be to hand on a religion, or to create a new world?"[1]

PURPOSES OF INSTRUCTION.—In his endeavor to aid the learners to achieve the objectives of Christian education the teacher will therefore use techniques of formal instruction as means by which he will guide men and women in acquiring: (1) essential religious concepts and meanings, knowledge and beliefs; (2) habits of reflective thinking and of study and investigation; (3) skills that are significant in religious living; and (4) appreciations, aspirations, attitudes, and ideals.

SOME CONDITIONING FACTORS OF LEARNING AND TEACHING

ADULTS ARE EDUCABLE.—A large number of experiments in recent years within the field of adult learning prove that many adults are both plastic and teachable in all mental functions. Adult ability to learn, it appears on the basis of experiments thus far conducted, is very nearly as great as that of the late teens. In the case of adults of superior intellectual ability the difference between the late teens and the early forties in ability to learn a logical, systematic subject is very small. Similarly, experiments with adults of inferior intellect show between the ages of twenty and forty a very slight decline in ability to learn. The decline from the highest point of ability to learn, in the early twenties, to about forty-two years, is "only about thirteen to fifteen per cent for a representative group of abilities," while "ages twenty-five to forty-five are superior to childhood, and equal or superior to early adolescence in general ability to learn."[2]   These experiments verify the findings of Meumann, recorded much earlier, to the effect that the learning ability of children of the *Volkschule* is less than that of adults; and that the adult of forty-six has a greater learning ability than school children in the best years of their development.[3]

The net results of Thorndike's studies are conclusive evidence that in general adults possess ability to learn easily and rapidly, and might learn much more than they do; that almost anything is learnable at any time up to fifty; that "adults learn much less than they might partly because they underestimate their power of learning, and partly because of unpleasant attention and comment"; and "that adults learn less than they might because they do not care enough about learning."

There have been very few studies on ability of persons over fifty to learn. Thorndike declares "there can be little doubt that at some time between twenty and ninety the inner developmental forces which make the ability to learn wax give place in most persons to other inner influences which make it wane. But the time of their onset and the course they pursue is not known."[4]   He also presents evidence indicating that at about fifty-five "the net result of changes in general energy, interest in one's work, and ability to improve is a regression in achievement." There are, however, a sufficient number of specific instances on record, of persons of fifty-five, and much beyond, making marked progress in learning, to support the thesis that for many people even old age offers possibilities of mental growth. A single example, of many, may be set down here. A college professor testifies that his mother, whose attendance upon school ceased when she was eleven, and who was married before she was sixteen, graduated from the Chautauqua Institution after she had raised a family of nine children, and that in her old age she had become as well informed as any one of her college-trained sons or daughters.

DEFICIENT MOTIVATION.—It is clear from the foregoing that age, at least up to fifty, in itself is a minor factor in learning. Excluding the factors of capacity, decreased amount of time available, and somewhat lessened energy, the most important factor in adult learning is increase in the desire to learn. Adults do not learn because they lack sufficiently strong motives for learning. "The ordinary American of today has at twenty-five in large measure supplied his demand for learning. . . . If the offerings of all the schools in the world were available for him in a free evening school beside his home, he would be unmoved by most of them, either because he does not and never did want them, or because he tried learning things like them and did not find the game worth the candle, or because he has already as much of them as he wants. . . . Thereafter he restricts learning to matters which are to his economic advantage, or which meet desires evoked by new situations, like the emergency of war or the invention of the radio, or which gratify desires which were thwarted in youth. In the competition with other ways of spending time, learning weakens relatively year by year as we satisfy one craving after another of those which need learning to satisfy them."[5]

This being true, a chief problem of the teacher of adults becomes that of broadening, deepening, and enriching existing interests and of supplying other sufficiently strong incentives for learning.

The teacher of children knows that her first and basic task is to get acquainted with her pupils, or, as one has said, "to learn her pupils." It is equally true in teaching adults that success in motivation depends upon an intimate knowledge of the persons whom one is attempting to guide. The wise teacher will not so much as mention "I.Q.'s" and "intelligence tests" by name. Moreover there are few if any tests that attempt to rate intellectual ability or knowledge which lend themselves to use with adults in the church school. Nevertheless, through personal acquaintance, conversation, observation of responses in group discussion, the teacher will attempt to form a reliable judgment of the intellectual capacity and range of knowledge and interest of each member of the adult group.

Again, the teacher of children has learned that improvement in motivation is accomplished more than in any other way by celebrating successes. She has observed the quiet and sure reaction of children to praise. She has forsworn scolding, urging, driving, and depends upon encouraging, commending, praising. In their response to commendation adults are but children of larger growth. Why not apply the same principle to adult teaching? A well-known educator has said that the successful supervision of teachers is principally "the art of commendation." So also with the motivation of adult learning in religious education.

Beyond these elemental principles how may motivation for learning activities of a wider range and on a deeper level be developed? Adult teaching probably presents no more difficult problem than this. A first step involves discovering needs from which interests may be developed. Various techniques may be used for this purpose, such as: (1) a check list; (2) attitude, personality, and knowledge tests; (3) casual conversations, and under some circumstances formal interviews; (4) group discussion of carefully selected issues. When needs have been revealed, specific techniques may be used: (1) *Watch for leading-on opportunities.* Very often by skillful manipulation one interest may be made to lead on to others. (2) *Take advantage of readiness.* An address by a widely known leader, a crisis in the community, the nation, or the world, or some striking current event, may be made the means of creating a new interest. (3) *Develop associated learnings.* No doctrine, belief, or historical event is an isolated phenomenon. Always there are associated items which illuminate and are an aid to understanding that which is the object of interest. These associated particulars of whatever nature may be so presented as to develop into wider interests.

The teacher of religion, whether of children or of adults, possesses an additional potent means of motivation, all too little utilized, in the very nature of the Christian religion. The Christian is one who is seeking constantly not only to grow in grace and the virtues of the Christian religion but also "in knowledge of the truth."

CLOSED MINDS.—There can be little doubt that the adult mind, especially beyond middle age, is less open to new ideas than that of younger persons. Thorndike reports the results of one inquiry in which thirty-nine persons forty years old or older, and forty-three persons from thirty to thirty-nine years old, answered questions concerning common religious beliefs and certain prejudices. The majority of those who held the beliefs named, and the prejudices, changed them, but *almost all who changed did so under forty.* While the comparatively small number of persons involved in this test, and the negative form of the questions (changing or giving up beliefs), make this particular inquiry of slight significance as concerns ability and willingness to accept new ideas, it must be said that the test confirms the common observation of many who as teachers have contact with men and women. On the other hand, it seems true, though again this impression is not validated by scientific tests, that young adults, persons of twenty-five to forty, are less defensive and less impervious to change of mind than are adolescents.

LOW-GRADE MENTALITY.—In 1920 approximately six per cent of the population of the United States over ten years of age were illiterate. Of the 4,931,905 illiterates, 3,084,733 were native born, and 1,847,172 were foreign born. Of the total, 3,006,312 were white and 1,925,593 were Negroes. Illiteracy has various roots: one is subnormal mentality; a second is lack of educational opportunity; a third is economic.

There are hundreds of thousands of men and women (any exact estimate is impossible) included within the membership and constituencies of the evangelical churches, who are uneducable as the public schools define education. A few of them were never enrolled in the public schools. The large majority entered but were eliminated between the second and sixth grades. A fundamental cause of elimination was their low intelligence level. Approximately, twenty of one thousand pupils who enroll in the public schools are on the border line of feeble-mindedness. Their intelligence quotient in the Stanford Revision of the Binet-Simon tests ranges between 70 and 80. A second group, approximately one hundred and fifty of one thousand pupils enrolled, possess an intelligence quotient of 80 to 90. These cannot go beyond about the eighth grade. For the men and women of these two groups there is not much that adult religious formal instruction can do. Their range of attainment in religious knowledge is subject to the same limitation as operated in their elimination from public school.

LIMITATIONS OF FORMAL INSTRUCTION

Formal instruction has other limitations also.

LIMITED TRANSFER.—Formerly it was quite generally assumed in religious education that moral and religious truth, if stated, could be depended upon to carry over into conduct and character. The assumption was based upon a theory, seldom explicitly stated, that it is only necessary, in order to transfer knowledge to another, to get him to listen. Quite generally prevalent in general education, the notion was taken over by religious education and to this day underlies prevailing practice in adult teaching and is commonly believed to justify it. Psychology knows, on the basis of experiment, that the amount of actual transmission accompanying mere telling is extremely limited. If the current practice of depending upon exhortations, talks, lectures, and sermons, as means of religious instruction, might be subjected to processes of thorough, accurate test, there can be no doubt that reliance upon them would appreciably diminish.

The limitation affecting transfer not only emphasizes the importance of lessening the proportionate place given to transmissive methods, but of correspondingly increasing a more vital and direct attack upon present experience. Instead of giving so much of our time to the attempt to transfer to adult minds certain truths, hoping that they will be stored up to be later applied, let us undertake to assist men and women to analyze, understand, and improve those things in which they are at present engaged, thus in some measure avoiding separation of knowing and doing and of doctrine from Christian experience. This is not to admit that religious education has no place for formal instruction as such. It has, as we believe we have shown. But since that place is less than it has traditionally been held to be; since the actual amount of transmission effected is likewise less; and since formal instruction may easily become, as it often has become, a fetish—cramping activity and dulling thought and ethical discrimination, teachers should refuse to be bound by so inadequate a method.

A MIXTURE OF TRUTH AND ERROR.—Coe has made clear how, due to inherent psychological defects of method, formal instruction inevitably hands on not only what is good in our concepts— doctrines, and word-symbols of ideals—but also what is bad in their content *as understood* by the hearers of our sermons and class lectures.[6] Instruction, as such, does not involve the development and use of discrimination. Its characteristic attitude is: Here is the true, the good; take it as I give it to you. But what the recipient "takes" may be not at all what is offered in the teacher's own understanding of it; what is taken is content interpreted in the light of what he sees as well as hears, and what he has seen through the years. A Christian is a "saved" person, says the teacher. The interpretation attached to "saved" is the kind of character possessed by those whom the hearer has known who profess to be Christians and the sort of behavior they have exemplified in daily living.

BONDAGE TO "UNIFORM LESSONS."—Under existing conditions in a large majority of Protestant churches perhaps the greatest limitation of adult education is the prevailing bondage to the use of the "Uniform Lesson" and the obsolete teaching procedures associated with it. The church school is the only modern institution laying any claim whatsoever to being "educational" which in its predominating curriculum *makes no provision for progress in learning.* In their use of "Uniform Lessons" adult groups move perpetually in circles. By their own confession, given utterance in the materials they use, adult classes are those who "are ever learning and never coming to a knowledge of the truth." Endless repetition, cycle after cycle, is their record of failure to make progress.

A second element of limitation in the "Uniform Lesson" system is the fact that it makes no provision for individualized instruction or for selection of subject matter chosen on the basis of interests and needs of groups. It assumes that all adults of all ages are alike in their needs. It offers them all the same dose administered in the same way. Then we wonder why the health of the patient does not improve!

In part, of course, this willingly endured bondage to "Uniform Lessons" is due to perpetuation of the traditional Protestant dogma of the Bible as the sole and sufficient textbook of religious education. But only in part. One wonders how long the "Uniform Lesson" system would retain its place if it were not the source of financial profits to denominational boards and publishing houses? The inevitable defense that these profits are for benevolent religious use has, of course, no validity as an argument in Christian education. Shall the Church rob its people of adequate vital education in the Christian religion for the sake of funds with which to meet its Christian obligations?

GENERAL PATTERN OF INSTRUCTION

THE HERBARTIAN METHODOLOGY.—Since Christian education involves, as one element, the transmission of a body of knowledge, historical subject matter, attention should be given in adult education to the methodology built upon the foundation laid by Herbart.* While it is essentially a pouring-in process, and does little

* See pp. 94f.

to stimulate creative thinking, even those who have least use for it agree that the formula does more or less closely approximate the process of inductive thought, and that the technique of teaching built upon it, which dominated the theory and practice of normal schools during the last generation, marked an advance in imparting knowledge.

Freely to admit that religious knowledge has a necessary place in Christian education and that the Herbartian methodology should be the familiar possession of the teacher by no means signifies unqualified acceptance of the contention that knowledge constitutes the center of the learning process or that education is to be identified with instruction.

Few would contend that the procedure of instruction in adult teaching should follow in any rigid way the so-called "five formal steps" associated with the name of Herbart. As presented in standard treatises on pedagogy the Herbartian technique is one worked out for teaching children, immature and untrained minds assumed to be uninterested in the material and, because of immaturity, limited in capacity. It involves definite, exact, formal planning of lessons and represents a teacher-pupil relationship in which initiative rests with the teacher. For mature, trained minds it is wasteful of time and tends to dull interest, thinking, and application. An infantile method of teaching is not necessary in teaching those adults who represent a high level of intelligence and general education.

"Spoon feeding of predigested material" is a feature which has tended to bring discredit upon the church school and the adult Bible class. Certainly, there are many adult groups for whom formal instruction should be not so much the presentation by means of an elementary-school technique of brief "lessons" of limited scope as a process of making accessible and introducing to alert, capable minds significant treatises in which religious learning and experience are stored. To guide men and women in the discovery and use of logically organized presentations of Christian knowledge and belief and in gaining understanding and utilization of them, and at the same time to develop an appreciation of this mode of presentation in preference to the traditional elementary mode of teaching, should be an element in the teacher's objective.

It is to be noted also that the Herbartian pattern, frequently called the "inductive-development" method, involves working up by a succession of steps through induction to deduction. Such a logical process has value provided the material of instruction includes unfamiliar laws or principles to be mastered. In this case the Herbartian method offers a series of distinct details or particulars which leads to the general conclusion in the form of a rule, principle, or formula to be applied. "By wise selection and presentation of details, the teacher may set before learning minds such material as will make possible the comprehension of generalizations that have been evolved through many years, or even centuries of human experience. Instruction is thus provided with a method that makes thorough and efficient learning possible."[7] In adult religious teaching, however, in many cases the principle or truth given expression in the lesson is familiar, and in a general abstract way accepted. What is required is not so much coming to an intellectual understanding of an unfamiliar principle through a logical process, as the working out of the significance of a formally accepted principle in terms of its meaning for today's life and its actual application to life in creative ways. If a logical distinction is to be made, it is more a matter of deductive thinking than of induction.

The adult teacher, therefore, will use both induction and deduction. Disavowing in practice rigid teacher domination, seeking to develop the spirit of cooperation in search for truth, he will recognize instances in which a process of finding, examining, and comparing specific cases, and drawing from them general principles, rules, or laws is a needed procedure. This is especially true in view of the fact that so many principles of conduct long accepted on authority are now questioned or rejected. To the extent that he does utilize the Herbartian pattern he will look upon it, not so much as a succession of exact "steps," as a series of processes not to be rigidly or mechanically used. Each will be recognized as having significance in the process of instruction, to be given more or less attention in connection with the presentation of any well-defined unit of subject matter.

The five successive steps, or aspects of instruction, may be briefly considered:

Preparation.—There are various ways in which the mature learner may be "prepared" for the presentation of the knowledge or truth which it is desired to bring to attention. Formally stated, preparation has three phases: (1) the awakening of interest, or increasing interest already existing; (2) recalling more or less familiar ideas pertaining to, and with which to interpret, the new; (3)

stating the aim.   Usually, as a help in stimulating thinking, the aim should be stated in the definite form of a problem.   Knowledge results from thinking, and persons do not think unless their minds are confronted with an issue.   It should be remembered that "aim" includes the teacher's general aim; the teacher's specific aim; and the learner's aim.

The teacher, in many instances, lives on a different intellectual level from that of many of the members of his class.   More than theirs, probably, his is a world of thought and ideas.   He is a student of books; possibly they are not.   His vocabulary may be literary, scientific, or theological; theirs, none of these.   Abstract terms are meaningful to him; to them they may have little meaning or none. Their vocabulary is unscientific; their thinking concrete and empirical.   *Preparation* is a matter of the teacher and the members of his group getting on some common ground of understanding.

Presentation.—Commonly in adult-class teaching the teacher lectures to the class.   This should not be the invariable practice for reasons to be stated later.   Learning is an active process, and the more purposive cooperation and participation throughout by the members of the group, the more effectively learning takes place. By giving attention to the matter: agreeing upon assignments, referring individual members to sources, commenting on different points of view presented in different sources, indicating various possible lines of investigation, making various members responsible for reports on specific phases of the topic, much more general participation than is usual can be secured.   One of the greatest causes of weakness in adult-class teaching is the unvarying habit of many teachers of presenting material without effort on the part of the members of their classes.   They pour showers of words upon the ears of passive hearers and naïvely assume that learning is in process.

An important part of presentation is the bringing in of examples and illustrations.   The question is, what experiences have the members of the group had or what are they familiar with that will help in the understanding and mastery of this principle or truth?   Apt, illuminating illustrations not only quicken interest; they may contribute much to understanding.   There is, however, no virtue in the mere multiplication of illustrations.   Several specific examples contribute to learning, provided they are varied, each illustrating a different aspect of the truth.   Sufficient time should be spent in analyzing the illustrations or other material presented to make sure that the point intended to be emphasized is grasped.

With the predominant emphasis now being placed in many quarters upon discussion and problem-solving the teacher may be misled into thinking that good teaching procedure requires that every new idea must be drawn out of the experience of the members of the group even though evidence is not lacking that the idea is not present. No more profitless would be an attempt to draw blood from a turnip than a prolonged effort to evoke particular ideas or the statement of problems when neither the ideas nor problems are present.

Association.—Knowledge is of little or no value unless it is related to experience. Presentation aims to get the new knowledge before the mind and get it understood. If it is to be understood it must be interpreted in the light of past experiences and articulated with future activities. Association stresses the relating of the new material to experience, past, present, and future.

Association, it is evident, is not a clear-cut segment in the teaching process; it begins during the step of presentation and continues into the step of generalization. It is a point in the general procedure at which discussion is particularly useful.

Generalization.—This step, which involves the formulation of the material into a general proposition, a principle, definition, rule, or law, is the culmination of the inductive process. If the material does not lend itself to any such statement, a well-organized summary is desirable.

Invariably, the members of the group should be expected to formulate the principle or the summary. In skillful teaching the generalization comes to the members of the group as their discovery. This step, therefore, is at once a test of the teacher's skill in the preceding part of the procedure and of the learners' grasp of what has been presented and their ability to integrate it with their experience. While the burden at this point is upon the learners, the teacher is not absolved from responsibility of guiding the learners in the formulation of their statement in satisfactory terms. The superficial teacher and the teacher who estimates success in teaching in terms of the extent of his own verbosity are inclined themselves to make the generalization. Since generalization should never be omitted, if any unavoidable time exigency forbids the working over of the learners' statement, the teacher may formulate it.

Application.—Herein is the final test of religious instruction, the step which determines whether the material is merely a collection of pious-sounding words or the expression of significant truth which shall re-enter experience to enrich and reconstruct it. Was the aim of the lesson stated in the form of a problem? The application involves exploration of the extent to which the principle which has been agreed upon, or the summary, may be utilized in the solution of felt problems or in the interpretation and understanding of conscious intellectual or moral difficulties. A too-prevalent weakness of formal instruction is that application, which should consist in actually doing something about the situation, usually stops short of action and consists merely in saying what should be done. The really effective teacher makes the application a leading-on procedure that culminates in significant action.

The teacher of rich experience and wide learning also has an opportunity at this point of rendering a distinctive service to the members of his group through developing the wider applications of the truth. In this, again, is a test of effective teaching as contrasted with shallow, lifeless, restricted instruction. The poor teacher restricts application to a narrow, traditional range. The good teacher relates the truth to new, varied, and broad areas of thought and life.

PROCEDURES IN FORMAL INSTRUCTION

Of general types of formal instruction there are perhaps three which are best adapted for use in the churches in adult groups: (1) lecture; (2) lesson or textbook discussion; (3) problem-project or seminar. In a particular instance a combination of two or even all three of these types may be used.

There are various books which list and describe "methods" of teaching. For this reason the discussion here of only three procedures may be disappointing to some. Sound teaching techniques grow out of ways of learning, and basic learning procedures, as we have stated earlier, are relatively few. Adult teachers should not be deceived by enumeration of so-called "methods" which are nothing more than devices or tricks of the trade. There is wide diversity in terminology but if one knows the basic learning types, he will not be confused by mere differences in labels.

THE LECTURE AS A TECHNIQUE OF INSTRUCTION.—In a considerable proportion of adult classes the groups are so large that any other procedure than lecturing or preaching is almost impossible. The larger classes range from fifty to three hundred persons; the largest have five hundred, even a thousand, in a few instances as many as fifteen hundred in attendance.

The lecture in adult religious education more often than not might better be labeled a lay sermon. A popular definition of a sermon is "an oral address to the popular mind, upon religious truth contained in the Scriptures, and elaborately treated with a view to persuasion." A more apt brief description of the procedure used in the average adult class it would be difficult to frame. In evaluating the lecture for use in formal instruction, therefore, one should not base conclusions upon the procedure commonly used in adult classes.

Disadvantages of the lecture.—That the lecture has certain very obvious disadvantages is evident from widely prevailing criticism in educational circles. (1) *In itself the lecture involves no requirements of thought or of study.* It is purely a pouring out process without any provision for the reception, understanding, and use of the knowledge poured out. At its worst it has been satirized thus:

> "Good morning, fool,
> Once every week
> You hold us helpless while you speak.
> Well, here we are, your hundred sheep,
> Tune up—play on—pour forth—we *sleep*."

This satirical rhyme suggests a second disadvantage of the lecture: (2) *There is involved in it no assurance of attention.* Often men and women come to the group sessions with minds preoccupied with cares, responsibilities, and interests unrelated to the subject to be presented. Whether or not the teacher delivers his lecture well, they may or may not receive the intended instruction. The lecture method neither insures attention, nor affords a means by which the lecturer may assure himself that what he is endeavoring to teach is being learned.

(3) *The lecture involves no procedure by which the instruction conveyed is integrated as a permanent element in conduct and character.* Even if attention is present in maximum measure mere telling and hearing do not constitute education. What is heard must be used, and for that the method makes no provision. Listeners remember but a small proportion of what they hear. The lecture method may take account of the principle of repetition, and

through frequent hearing the truth uttered may become familiar; but if it is merely filed as unused information, there is no education.

(4) *The lecture of the teacher competes with the sermon of the minister.* If the "lesson lecture" is a lay sermon, as we have said is often the case, two sermons are offered in succession, a diet that tends to surfeit many persons. Evidence the large number of members of lecture classes who do not attend the public service of worship. If the teacher is an able lecturer, his lectures may surpass the pastor's sermons in teaching values, and on this basis alone the choice of the absentees may be justified. But are there not other real values, both religious and distinctly educational, in the public service of worship which are thereby missed? Apart from this consideration, the situation created is not a happy one.

(5) *The lecture method tends to make decreasing demand upon the teacher.* One easily becomes habituated to talk. Silent listeners who attend from a sense of obligation make upon the lecturer no requirement of preparation. Fluency of speech and expenditure of physical energy in delivery may be mistaken for significant teaching. Many adult class lectures are nothing more than desultory utterance.

Values of the lecture.—Despite very real disadvantages, the lecture has certain significant values. Among these should be mentioned: (1) *The lecture permits a large number of persons to share benefit of the teaching of the best qualified teachers.* Thoroughly qualified teachers of religion are few. Even the professional ministry suffers from the lack of capable, well-educated pastors. Not many churches possess within their membership a sufficient number of men and women of education, training, and personality to supply the need for teachers and leaders if the groups are small. The exceptional teacher can accomplish greater results in life and character using an inferior method than the poorly equipped teacher using a superior method.

Large class groups do not seem to be *per se* detrimental to effective learning. To the contrary, a series of fifty-nine fully or semicontrolled experiments involving 108 classes under twenty-one instructors in eleven departments of four colleges of the University of Minnesota indicates that large classes incite all types of students to higher levels of attainment. "The experiments involved 5,879 students—4,025 in large classes, and 1,854 in small. Direct man-to-man comparisons were made upon 1,288 pairs of students, carefully matched as to intelligence and scholarship. The final criterion was student achievement as measured by tests and examinations, most of which were objective. In forty-six of the experiments, or seventy-eight per cent, a more or less decided advantage accrued to the paired students in the large sections. . . . At every intelligence level the paired students in the large sections excelled their mates in the small. . . . Class size seems to be a relatively minor factor in educational efficiency measured in terms of student achievement. . . . If true teaching is less a matter of educating people and more a matter of giving them guidance and practice in educating themselves, large classes may prove to be ideal educational institutions."[8]

(2) *The lecture is an economical means of supplying information.* Where the total amount of time involved is a material factor, as is undoubtedly the case in adult education, the lecture method has a marked advantage. A given amount of information can be acquired by a group more quickly through listening to a lecture than in any other way. The expenditure of time involved in consulting sources and in organizing and classifying the material is confined to one person—the lecturer, who within a limited period may convey the results of long investigation and study. Under existing conditions in many communities the lecture is the only way by which information on certain subjects may be gained. The sources of information are not available to the large majority of the class members.

There is some experimental evidence that the immediate recall of subject matter is facilitated by the lecture. In a series of carefully controlled experiments over a three-year period aiming to determine the relative effectiveness of the lecture and class-discussion methods of teaching, the experimenter found that in three of the five experiments on the immediate recall tests the group score distinctly favored the lecture as over against the class discussion. A total of 158 teaching periods were involved in the experiments including 510 persons. The subject matter was chiefly education and psychology. In all five experiments the delayed recall tests favored the class discussion method. The experimenter concludes: "It would seem clear, then, that the lecture is relatively better suited to the immediate recall of subject matter and the class-discussion method better adapted to its retention."[9]

(3) *Under certain conditions the lecture is superior to the discussion method in phases of learning measured by tests.* Experi-

mental studies of method have not been sufficient in number to yield conclusive data. There is some evidence that adults tend to do better work, as measured by examinations, under the lecture method. Spence and Watson experimented with the lecture and discussion methods with two groups of graduate students in educational psychology. In both sections examination results favored the lecture method.[10]

(4) *The lecture is often of value as a means of supplementing other techniques of teaching.* Sometimes it is the best way to get appreciation and desirable mental attitudes at the beginning of a course. It is desirable, frequently, as means of supplying information needed at a certain stage, or stages, of a discussion course.

The problem, therefore, would seem to be not whether the lecture is superior to other methods of instruction but, rather, under what conditions will the lecture produce most effective results? In what situation is it desirable, and in what not desirable to lecture?

Prevalence of the lecture.—It is to be feared that the predominant use of the lay sermon, or so-called class lecture, in adult class teaching is not to any considerable extent based upon a careful evaluation of this as compared with other possible methods. It is the traditional method, and tradition in religious practice is hard to overcome. Most adult teachers tend to follow the line of least resistance. Again, for the adult leader habituated to its use, it makes less demand upon the teacher's time than any other method. Little time or effort is required for preparation.

Making the most of the lecture.—While the lecture does not intrinsically make as great demands upon the teacher and the class members as some other techniques of instruction, this weakness may be in large part overcome by earnest purpose on the part of the teacher and cooperative effort on the part of the listeners. There is no good reason why any teacher should be content with merely "delivering" a class lecture. He may supplement his oral statement by the use of outlines, charts, and blackboard. He may lead the group in a discussion of the subject following the formal lecture. He may cite references for reading and study; assign in turn to different members of the group the preparation and reporting of a summary of the lecture.

The lecturer may ask and expect the members of the group to cooperate by (1) maintaining an active attitude during the lecture; (2) listening thoughtfully, understandingly, and critically; (3) preparing for the lecture by studying the topic in advance; (4) taking notes on the lecture; (5) supplementing the lecture from their own experience.

There is considerable educational opinion to the effect that the possibility of making the lecture an effective instrument of teaching depends upon the lecturer rather than upon the method. The lecture and the personality of the lecturer cannot be separated. Some are able to do their best teaching by means of the lecture; others are unable to use it effectively not so much because of inherent defect in the instrument as because of lack of ability to lecture well.

Lesson Discussion.—Doubtless, a majority of adult-class teachers who do not lecture, if questioned, would say that they use the discussion method. If pressed for an exact description of the procedure followed, it would be found that the method actually used is the asking of questions by the teacher and answers by the members of the group with frequent interpolation of comment by the teacher and a few of the members. Occasionally questions are asked by members of the class. This practice might more properly be classified under the head of "question-and-answer method," or "recitation," than discussion. It is neither group discussion, as this method is elsewhere described in this book, nor in any proper sense lesson discussion.

It is a carry-over into adult teaching of the traditional recitation procedure formerly used in the elementary grades of the public school, and in high schools. Almost invariably little group spirit or cooperative effort is in evidence. The attitude of the teacher acts as a deterrent. Too often the teacher assumes all responsibility for the group's learning. He does most or all of the preparation and wholly determines the procedure. The class members have only to be acquiescent; what is done and how it is done is not in any sense their enterprise. Only in a few exceptional persons is found any marked enthusiasm, keenness, or seriousness of purpose of learning. The rehashing of material more or less familiar to all present develops slight response in those in attendance. The class assembles; the members take their seats after exchanging friendly greetings with a few fellow members and await the teacher's initiative. No one has a fresh discovery to report; no one has had a new vision of a great truth; no one has found a new source of inspiration which he is eager to report to fellow seekers after truth. The responsibility is not theirs; it belongs to the teacher. Some members of the group are called upon and respond, usually perfunctorily. With his questions, comments, and fragmentary lectures, the teacher does most of the talking. The end of the hour arrives; some mention of the next "lesson" may be made, accompanied by an exhortation to study it faithfully, and the class is dismissed. Whereupon many of the members gather in knots and break out into animated conversation about things which concern them or activities in which they are engaged.

In contrast with this there is a procedure which lends itself to use in adult religious teaching and which possesses definite instructional values. It may perhaps be more accurately designated by the term *lesson discussion,* or textbook discussion, than by any other. *It differs from group discussion as later described* in that it centers discussion in a "lesson," the essential meaning of which is to be interpreted, appropriated, and applied, while group discussion begins with a felt need, or a life situation containing a problem element.*

Lesson discussion as a procedure may follow the general pattern of the Herbartian methodology as outlined above. A few points deserve special emphasis:

Spirit of cooperation.—Of first importance is development of the spirit and attitude of cooperation, a feeling of "we-ness" and a sense of group enterprise. The possibility of mutual helpfulness is emphasized by the teacher, and division of labor agreed upon by the class members. Exploration of the lesson subject, if it is to be thorough, will involve reading of both up-to-date treatises written from the most modern viewpoint and some of the older standard works. Plans for locating, consulting, and reporting upon available materials are formulated. Skillful questioning reveals the problems associated with the content of the lesson and plans are made for their consideration. Discussion locates some specific experience or general area of experience to which the truth of the lesson is related.

Possible sources of significant information on religious subjects are almost innumerable. The pity is that so few of these sources are known to most of the adult members of our churches. The paucity of religious literature, particularly books, in the

---

* See Chapter X.

homes of church members is pathetic. What money is spent by them for literature is mostly for ephemeral reading material—newspapers and other periodicals of little value. The adult teacher during a period of years by skillful direction, persistent urging, and wise counsel can lead many to build up small select home libraries. Not everything need depend upon individual initiative: adult classes and departments may be led to start reference libraries to which additions may be made from year to year. In connection with each course studied several of the best books on the subject may be purchased and used for supplementary reading on agreed topics.

Class participation.—The degree of success in lesson discussion is in proportion to the extent to which the group feels responsibility for and takes initiative in carrying the procedure of discussion forward. The formal question-answer type of reciting has gone, replaced by conversation and guided discussion. There is no mere parrotlike repetition of what has been read. Without restraint or constraint members of the group give their versions of the subject or state concisely viewpoints gathered from their reading. One will make a statement supplementing that of another. Disagreements as to facts, interpretation, and opinion will develop, but contention or debate will be absent. The skill of the leader will be shown in encouraging the critical-minded, problematic attitude, but at the same time guiding the discussion by analysis, definition, discrimination, and citing of evidence. He will avoid settling questions by authority; rather, he will lead the group in thinking its way through to a group judgment.

In discussing high-school teaching Parker says, "The common practice of using the class period for mere repetition of material learned in the textbook is one of the most pernicious sources of waste and lack of interest to be found in schools." This is even more true in adult-class teaching where, in most cases, the subject matter is familiar from repeated usage. Instead of such procedure he suggests that the teacher should raise questions which stimulate active thinking, because they involve (1) interpretation, (2) criticism, (3) supplementing, or (4) application. Adults are often both slovenly and lazy in thought. Many are entirely willing to let others do their thinking for them. Not infrequently they deceive themselves by assuming that incoherent statements, mere repetition of words, involve thought. By checking up on careless statements, calling for facts in substantiation, appealing to the experience of others, the teacher may do much to break up such habits and to stimulate reflection.

Use of resources of experience.—Many of the so-called "lesson expositions" and "lesson comments" in the teachers' magazines and religious textbooks are merely logically organized summaries of the subjects treated.   They lack richness of detail, and merely state generalizations in the form of conclusions, rules, or laws, instead of supplying a large number of experiences from various areas of living from which through a process of inductive development the desired generalizations may be derived.   If, therefore, teaching is to be vital, much depends upon the ability and skill of the teacher in drawing upon the rich resources of experience represented within the group, and bringing them to bear upon the subject under consideration.

Weaknesses of lesson discussion.—In practice, lesson discussion has certain obvious weaknesses: (1) *It is nothing more than a re-citing of the facts or principles of the lesson.*   Too often the teacher expects merely a repetition of the statements of the lesson text and "lesson helps" traditionally used.   He is apparently fully satisfied with the mere rehearsal of the words without evidence of understanding or of ability to apply the words to today's life situations and problems.   The repetition of a verbal formula in the realm of religious knowledge and belief is no proof either of knowledge or faith.

(2) *Lesson discussion tends to encourage uncritical acceptance of traditional formulas.*   There is nothing in the recitation pattern, as such, to stimulate inquiry, the critical mind, or creative thinking.   So marked is the tendency to accept uncritically the lesson statements and the lesson writer's point of view that in many instances any disposition to question is met with prompt expression of group disapproval.   The general effect becomes that of endorsing and re-enforcing the *status quo* in religious creed and social practice.

(3) *Weaknesses of the group-discussion (problem discussion) procedure also appear.*   As these are stated at length elsewhere* it is not necessary to go into detail at this point.   The garrulous tend to monopolize the time.   The discussion easily becomes irrelevant.   If the loquacious, as sometimes happens, are the more shallow-minded, the discussion readily becomes insignificant or

* See pp. 324ff.

tedious and demands no mental effort on the part of the majority of the group.

Values of lesson discussion.—These weaknesses are not necessarily inherent. (1) *Lesson discussion may enlist the activity of all members of the group.* In this it has an obvious advantage over the lecture. As a medium of instruction used by an alert, skillful teacher it does just this. No members of the group are permitted to be merely passive onlookers; they are expected to exercise their insights, their understanding, and their capacity of reflective thinking by helping in the formulation of statements of fact, of value judgments, and in solution of problems of application. Explanations are called for where meanings are not clear. Obscure points are cleared up. New applications of the truth are made to present-day conditions.

(2) *The ability of clear, pertinent, forceful statement is developed.* To be able to state succinctly and clearly in contemporary verbiage an important truth or moral principle is a worth-while ability. Lesson discussion may be used to do this and to develop the power of reflective thought.

(3) *Lesson discussion at its best has marked socialization values.* Attention is sustained by the give-and-take of the discussion. Mind kindles mind. New resolutions are formed. Moral earnestness is developed. Purposes of service are created. Vital, creative teaching is taking place.

Requirements of the teacher.—The conduct of such a lesson discussion is no easy task. It lays upon the teacher difficult requirements: (1) *The teacher must be mentally alert.* He must possess vital insights, keen ethical discrimination, dependable moral judgment. He must know the historical backgrounds out of which the lesson came, and be able to distinguish between the temporal and the abiding elements of the statement. He must know how to stimulate thought and expression. Few procedures are more profitless than a slow-moving, dull, listless lesson discussion.

(2) *He must have high standards,* particularly as respects precision and understanding in statement. "General and indefinite answers should be discouraged. He should be suspicious of statements which fail to give evidence of reflective thinking. . . . The purpose is to educate and not just to get questions answered."

(3) *Skill in questioning is necessary.*—In what is probably the most important treatise of ancient times on education, the *Republic,* Plato says: "Then you will enact that they [the rulers]

shall have such an education as will enable them to attain the greatest skill in asking and answering questions." However important as a qualification of rulers, it certainly is a requirement of good teaching in using lesson discussion.[11]

PREACHING AS AN EDUCATIONAL METHOD.—One searches current educational literature, both textbooks and periodicals, in vain for an evaluation of preaching as an educational method. For the most part, in educational circles, preaching is ignored as an educational influence. The *Educational Index,* indexing educational periodicals, over a ten-year period, (1929-38), contains not one reference to preaching. Considering that for three hundred years of Protestantism preaching has not been merely one of many methods but *the* method of adult religious education, this fact speaks volumes.

When not ignored, more often than not in the professional literature of education preaching is depreciated. Such statements as these are more or less common: "Is preaching a valid method for exerting wholesome influence upon the behavior of human beings? The answer, in view of those portions of modern psychology where substantial agreement may be found, must be an unmistakable negative. Preaching is not only inadequate, but as currently practiced, it is an inhibition to more valid methods of changing conduct."[12] "Preaching began and has continued to be maintained by the churches as an instrument of social change and of social control. As such it has ceased to be effective." Occasionally depreciatory statements are voiced by the clergy as, for example, this from W. R. Inge: "Nothing can be more futile than to try to fill rows of narrow-necked vessels by throwing a bucketful of water over them."[13]

"His word was with power." More than twenty times, in different connections and in varying phrase the writers of the first three Gospels bear this testimony concerning the preaching and teaching of Jesus. If today preaching is ineffective in changing the ideas and the lives of men, to the extent that it is without power to inspire, to challenge, to create faith and hope and courage, to send men forth to rebuild the broken-down structure of society, it is not because the method is *per se* valueless but because those who use it are themselves lacking in power and skill. "Preaching," says Phillips Brooks, "is the revelation of truth through personality."

Preaching when it is effective is persuasion, reassurance, chal-

lenge, incitement to action.   It appeals both to the intellect and to
the emotions.   Has Protestantism today no word of God to declare?
Has it nothing but sentimental chatter, literary essays, mild moral-
istic exhortation, popularized psychology to preach?   Has it no
longer the spiritual insight and the ethical conviction to answer
in convincing terms the age-long inquiries which men anew today
are making about God, human obligation, and mankind's social
destiny?   When preaching again takes to itself the prophetic
function of religion—as it is doing in the ministry of some present-
day preachers—when by the clarity and depth of its own conviction
it is able to focus the thought of congregations upon the problems
of today that cry out for Christian solution, arousing awakened
consciences of men and women to grapple with the vast social
wrongs of today's life, it will again become an instrument of
heightened educational significance, recognized as such.

The nerve of power of Protestant preaching has been cut by
its subservience to the economic motive and prevailing practices of
a dominantly materialistic civilization.   Says Paul Tillich, "Protestantism does not possess an independent culture apart from
capitalistic society."[14]   If this is true, it has lost its prophetic genius
and function.   Prophetic preaching from the days of the eighth-
century prophets has done more than merely to give support to the
prevailing culture, to those ways of thinking and living which
characterize current society.   In the best examples of today it
does not separate itself from the ongoing stream of current experience, but in the name of God it challenges those elements of the
prevailing culture that cannot stand the test of high ethical principles and ideals, calls upon men to change their thinking, their
ways of living, and the very structure of the society of which they
are a part, and by so doing it aids the stream of experience to cut
new channels and to flow in a different direction.

Preaching that answers to this description is not an easy nor
comfortable method to use.   It makes all but impossible demands
upon the preacher.   But by these demands it stimulates the development of his own personality in vitality and strength.   It
possesses all of the values while at the same time it is subject to
all of the disadvantages described as characterizing the lecture.
Of the many difficulties which it presents one of a practical character arises from the wide range of educational level within the
congregation.   How can the preacher challenge the attention of
well-educated men and women without becoming unintelligible

to the unread, the unlearned, and the undiscerning? How can he
challenge and give direction to the thinking of the awakened or
partially awakened younger men and women without giving
offense to those who are wedded to the idols of the *status quo,*
to whom the folklore of the prevailing social system is sacred?
Narrow and straitened is the way and few are the preachers that
find it.

SPECIAL METHOD IN LEARNING AND TEACHING.—In addition to
the procedures thus far discussed there are certain others which
merit fuller presentation than limits of space permit.

Much to be deplored, considering the significant place drama
once had in the life of the Church, is its neglect as a means of
learning and teaching in modern times. Not only as a method of
instruction but even more as a means of developing attitudes and
appreciations, dramatization deserves a place among the primary
procedures of religious education. Long recognized on the basis
of observation, psychology now enables us to understand how and
why it is that one who plays a part, in assuming bodily postures
and facial expressions and in performing certain acts becomes
identified in emotions, purpose, and experience with the character whose part is played.

For dramatization as it has been used by many churches in
recent years little that is good can be said. Too often it has not
been so much the use of an art as its degradation. Many so-called
plays and dramatic entertainments have been cheap, tawdry, and
crude. More often than not they have been burlesques, devoid of
any true artistry, destructive of good taste in art, literary style,
and spiritual values. Usually the actuating motive has been commercial—the raising of money, an activity to which a good purpose
has not been sufficient to lend either skill or helpful moral purpose. Often the most significant result has been to cheapen the
church and all for which it stands in the thought of many people
in the community. Exception is found in a select few highly
creditable plays and pageants produced under church auspices, a
list that is gradually increasing as a growing number of churches
come to an appreciation of the drama as an educational method.

A significant value of the dramatic method is the release
which the individual and the group gain from the limitations of
their environment, individual and social. Desires, impulses, and
purposes long denied expression find release with a resulting
stimulus to personality and character.

For its possibilities to be realized (1) the use of drama must be purposive—both the leader and members of the group must know for what ends dramatization is being used; (2) the technique of production must be studied and the production must satisfy the requirements, in literary form and dramatic value, of good drama; (3) the play must be suited to the needs and capacities of the players; and (4) it must possess positive moral and religious values. If as not infrequently happens the dramatization is lacking in spontaneity, if it involves slavish memorization and drill, and rigid routine of performance, its distinctive values fail of realization and it becomes no more than any other formal method.

What is to be said concerning reading as a method of religious education? At nineteen Luther Burbank read Darwin's *Varieties of Plant Life*. He got from it a new idea, and it shaped his entire life. "The whole world seemed based on a new foundation when I laid down that book." Many young adults have had similar experiences. The Gray-Munroe investigation, too limited in scope to be taken as a basis of broad generalization, would seem to show that the average adult spends about ninety minutes a day in reading. Newspapers and magazines are read very much more than books. The study indicates that books are read by approximately fifty per cent of the people.[15] One has only to mark the paucity of books, either secular or religious, in the average home, to be convinced of the accuracy of this study. Reading is at present not widely influential as an educative force in religion for the reason that the average adult does so little of it. What limited reading is done is of little value because of its ephemeral character. Newspapers and magazines predominate. Much newspaper reading is occupied with accounts of crime, and with the sports and market sections, which monopolize the larger proportion of space, with less attention given to social and political movements, editorials, travel, and articles of opinion. Of the magazines the sensational story magazines are more widely circulated than the higher-grade monthlies. In the reading of books the lightest grade of fiction is most popular. Nevertheless, systematic reading may be made an effective procedure in adult religious education. There are various types of reading purpose. In fact the word "reading" is a blanket term covering a number of "significantly different activities. The attitudes, purposes, and procedures of one and the same man are significantly different when he reads, for instance, the 'funny paper,' a novel, or a contract between himself and a building contractor." We are here discussing reading as a means of gathering information, accumulating knowledge, and supplementing the limited treatment of the courses or other source materials in use. If, the motivation of learning being present, as a part of the process of guidance (1) definite topics, problems, or interpretations are assigned; (2) sources of interesting, understandable material are cited; and (3) a requirement of a report on what has been read is made, reading may become one of the most valuable aids of supplementing formal instruction.

DEFECTS IN CURRENT PROCEDURES.—All of the procedures of formal instruction which have been described are subject in current practice to certain easily discernible defects, most of which can be remedied by dint of diligent effort. A summary of defects observed in the teaching of young adults in colleges as reported by fifty-four persons is made by Crawford under eighteen heads.[16] Ten of the most important defects listed are: (1) defects of personality and temperament; (2) defects associated with propaganda, dogmatism, and violation of freedom; (3) careless and unsatisfactory organization of materials; (4) lack of study and keeping up with the age; (5) failure to be practical; (7) failure to make teaching interesting; (8) lack of personal interest in members of classes; (9) lack of variety in teaching procedures; (10) defects of method in class lectures. All of these defects hold for adult religious education.

Whatever final evaluation is placed upon formal instruction, in itself it cannot be said to constitute a sufficient instrument with which to meet the urgent needs of the present situation. That it may and should be used more effectively and to better ends than it is being used few will dispute. To too great an extent dependence in education has been placed in it. Other and more creative techniques are required.

CHAPTER X

ENRICHING EXPERIENCE THROUGH
DISCUSSION

IN the name of loyalty to Christ the Crusaders succeeded in gaining possession of his sepulcher but they discovered in the end that it was only an empty tomb: they had lost contact with their Leader through the spirit and method by which they sought to serve him.[1] Other instances abound, by no means all in medieval times. Religious education in Protestantism has sometimes lost the very spirit and heart of the Christian religion because of its method. Too often it has been merely a means of inculcation of dogma, traditional concepts from which life has long since departed. A primary need in contemporary adult education is that the present-day implications for individual and social life of the vital principles of the Christian gospel shall be developed. One of the most important ways by which this may be accomplished is reflective thinking through a process of group discussion in which learners are brought face to face with the necessity of solving real-life problems, thinking through actual life-situations by a process of analysis, weighing of alternatives, and choice of outcome.

WHAT IS GROUP DISCUSSION?—Like many other words in common use, discussion has a variety of meanings. To one it suggests debate, formal or informal, between two or more persons. By another it may be understood to be practically synonymous with conversation. Yet another, thinking of an address delivered, may refer to a speaker's discussion of a subject. In this book, with adult Christian education in mind, *organized discussion is presented as a means of purposive reconstruction of life situations through cooperative thinking.* That is, we are here concerned primarily with three things: (1) A life approach to adult education rather than a subject approach; (2) a procedure in which a group of persons by general agreement engage; (3) which procedure, while not rigidly fixed, has certain understood characteristics and conforms to a more or less well-defined methodology.

Cooperative thinking is not a modern device. Always since

the dawn of civilization it has characterized the common life of families where love, mutual sympathy, and cooperation have prevailed. It is an assumption, also, underlying the deliberation and speaking "when moved by the Spirit" of the Quaker meeting. It is closely akin to the method of scientific inquiry.

Experience, as was pointed out in a preceding chapter, may or may not be significant. In life as commonly lived it is quite as likely as not to be meaningless and barren. That it may become meaningful and fruitful it is necessary that different points of view shall be brought to bear upon it; that it shall be looked at from different angles, reflected upon, and interpreted in the light of other experiences. In organized discussion, just this process may take place. The various members of the group each make their contribution and through the cooperation of all the experience under review is lifted from a more or less commonplace, or little understood segment of living, to a significant level.

Doubtless the most striking example of the effective and far-reaching influence of discussion in remaking the life of a people is to be found in the Folk Schools, schools for young adults, of Denmark. Largely through their influence a nation has been transformed; a "sullen, suspicious peasantry, averse to all progress" has been changed into an intellectually alert, morally strong, spiritually awakened, cooperative people. The conception of the Folk Schools originated with the Danish hero and prophet, N. F. S. Grundtvig, but its most effective realization in practice was in the work of Kristen Kold. It was left to him to develop Grundtvig's ideas into a method and an institution that met the deepest needs of the common people of Denmark. "He saw the necessity of *awakening* his countrymen before he could succeed in *enlightening* them. . . . He considered the acquisition of external knowledge as quite secondary, believing that a young man with an awakened and illumined inner life could easily acquire the information he needed. The aim of the school was to approach the soul of the pupils through the living word (spoken with spirit from heart to heart) and thus to awaken a life which would never cease growing. . . . The great thing for us is the free meetings. . . . We do not give lectures. . . . All must be mouth, eyes, ears—the only real way from heart to heart. We speak about widely different matters: religious, historical, political, social, physical, and so on. But always the point is a man standing freely and speaking Danish to his countrymen."[2] Even though the quotation does not contain the word, it would be difficult indeed to write a more apt or accurate characterization of the educational significance of discussion.

VALUES OF GROUP DISCUSSION

Organized group discussion enriches experience by awakening the mind, by developing skill in reflective thought, and by stimulating action. Skill in thinking is achieved only by practice in thinking. Practice in thinking may be provided by a series of group-discussion experiences in which the members constantly confront questions and arrive at conclusions on difficult problems.

REALIZES UPON EXPERIENCE.—Persons do not learn from experience merely by having experiences. Many people live their lives day after day without turning their minds upon their experiences; they allow themselves to become dull, unseeing, unresponsive to the very life they are leading. Not infrequently, not merely ordinary experiences, but experiences of the most profoundly significant character are undergone without realization of their significance. Or, the experience may be participated in mechanically, almost as unconsciously as a complicated machine participates in an involved operation. One who has observed the motions of a linotype machine, for example, has a good illustration of what often takes place when the mind of a man carries through an experience involving delicate and difficult operations without either the separate elements or the experience as a whole coming into clear consciousness or becoming the subject of reflection.

As we have seen, it is even within the power of experience to distort life and to dwarf and deform personality. Experiences are educative only as they are seen in a true perspective, for what they are, and an intelligent attempt made to discover and utilize their meaning and value. Discussion may be a valuable means to this end. It brings to bear upon a particular situation the varying points of view of different persons.

STIMULATES THOUGHT.—When discussion is entered upon as a group undertaking, a real cooperative enterprise, each member feels himself challenged to make some contribution. His mind is stimulated to play upon his own experience, and aspects and meanings come to light of which he had not before been conscious. This challenge to thought is an important factor.

In cooperative thinking the intellectual resources of the group become the assets of the individual, and thereby a widely extended range of ideas is opened up to the individuals composing the group. "A group of people, engaged in dialectic, can, like a pack of hounds, follow up the most promising idea that occurs to any one of them."   Not only is the range and variety of ideas extended, the multiplicity of ideas in itself stimulates intellectual activity.

Young people ought to learn to think as a part of their training, but at this point public schools, and even the college, often signally fail.   President E. D. Burton, writing on the business of a college, said: "A college ought . . . to teach [its students] to think, not to follow precepts, not to practice an art according to fixed methods, or to play a game according to the rules of the game, but to observe facts, to set them in relation to one another, to view them dispassionately, to draw conclusions from them. The impulse to do this is inborn; but it needs encouragement, development, practice, intensification.   The thinker, dispassionate but acute, is one of the world's great needs."

To refer again to the Folk Schools of Denmark: one who has recently studied their service to adults remarks that while they do not assume that a person who comes to them has a "mind" of a particular quality, they do undertake to awaken whatever "mind" that person may have brought with him to the school, and they offer that "mind" "the chance that it needs to escape from the trivial, the glittering, the sordid, and the moribund in its environment, into life and growth."[3]   This is precisely the service that discussion is well fitted to render.

In its challenge to thought, and its expectation that the members of the group will express their own opinions and reach their own conclusions, organized discussion offers a marked contrast to the usual procedures in adult-class teaching.   The implications of these characteristics are far-reaching.   They affect not merely individual experience but national character.   "How can we have a vital democracy," a religious leader well asks, "if our educational agencies are intent not upon opening minds but upon closing them in the interest of propaganda or dogma?"   If democracy is to be a creative power, making for moral integrity and spiritual vitality in the citizenship, education must be set free and it must stimulate growth from within.

Bryce, in his *Modern Democracies*, describes the Athenian assembly: "After the assembly the voters walked away in groups, talking over the speeches.   They had been made to feel that there are two sides to every question, and they argued these with one another. Socrates, or some other youth, who had been listening to Protagoras or Georgias, overtook them on the way and started fresh points of discussion." "This," says Bryce, "was political education."[4] It was political education, and it was moral education as well. It was a process of formation of individual and national character. Both depend upon vitality and strength of conviction. Such conviction grows out of reflective thought based upon a free and open consideration of all sides of the questions that spring from immediate experiences—experiences as old as the race but also as new as every fresh generation.

DEVELOPS FACILITY OF CRITICAL JUDGMENT.—The conditions under which we live today demand facility of critical judgment. Has there ever been a time when paid propaganda existed to the extent that it now exists? Whether it be newspaper, magazine, or book, one may scarcely be sure that the subject matter is not some subtle form of propaganda. Such conditions demand the ability to sift and weigh evidence, to discern specious forms of argument, to detect exaggeration and misstatement, to recognize and resist appeals to prejudice. The inability of the present adult generation to retain mental force and calm in the face of highly organized, nation-wide propaganda had a striking illustration in the development of the mind to war within the memory of many now living. Lesser illustrations readily come to mind. A critical-mindedness able to withstand organized propagandism is demanded. Otherwise our civilization, good and bad elements alike, is at its mercy.

The truly critical mind is creative. Critical-mindedness does not merely function negatively. As we have pointed out in a preceding chapter, there is great need in our time of creative thought in Christian ethics. Among those who express willingness to take the mind of Jesus as the norm there is no general agreement on what is right. Our civilization is vastly more complicated and more closely interrelated than that of the first century. The question, What would Jesus do? finds no simple and easy answer as regards multitudes of situations which Jesus never confronted. Even if we may agree on a statement of principle as representing the mind of Jesus, it is by no means clear how that principle is to be applied in widely varying situations. In three chief areas of our modern life—economic, racial, and international relations—

equally wise and earnest followers of Jesus disagree on what is the Christian thing to do in particular situations. It can neither be said that there is universal agreement among evangelical Christians either as to exactly what are the basic principles of the Christian gospel or how these principles are to be interpreted in concrete terms of social ethics and personal conduct. The need, therefore, for creative Christian minds is one of the greatest of the needs of our times. Until we get expression of judgment on concrete issues in wide areas of our modern life upon which Christians can be brought to agree there is little chance of marked progress in the creation of a Christian world.

DEVELOPS INNER AUTHORITY.—Dependence upon external authority involves no development of personality. It is a passive, noncreative attitude. Development of personality results not through the imposition of authority, whether religious, political, economic, or what not, but through a process of building up an inner authority.

Organized discussion in developing moral conviction and ability of critical judgment contributes to the formation of a conscience which becomes an inner authority. There is probably no greater need in the life of individuals and of the Christian Church today. Conviction and conscience are lacking. Many of the old sanctions have lost their authority and new ones have not been built to take their place.

There are those who demand the right to think for themselves; they are unwilling for others to do their thinking for them. They develop their own philosophy of life. They create their own creeds. They formulate their own codes of conduct. They are willing to do these things cooperatively, for they realize—some dimly, some keenly, their need of help. They will receive help and receive it gladly if that help comes out of experience. They refuse to receive it in the name of outer authority. Organized discussion under Christian guidance becomes, therefore, one of the most effective ways of developing the inner authority necessary to make the Church that moral and social power required if it is to do its part in redeeming social and national life from bestiality and paganism.

SOCIALIZES EXPERIENCE.—Discussion may be made an effective means of socializing experience. Individual experiences are shared by the group. The experience of one becomes the experience of many. People enter into one another's lives and thereby come to share one another's joys and to bear one another's burdens. They become in very truth members one of another.

Discussion also may be made a significant means of broadening the application of ideals to attitudes and practice. Ideals are learned not in the abstract but in particular concrete situations. Christian education involves a process of extending the application of ideals to ever-widening areas of life. Often a man who is kind, sympathetic, loving, and cooperative within the area of family relationships may exhibit little of these attitudes in community relations, and in business may show himself hard, unfeeling, and uncooperative in relations with employees and competitors. Under skillful guidance discussion may bring persons to the realization that integrity requires the application of particular ideals not merely to one or to a few but to all areas of life, and also may reveal what such application requires in areas where they have not hitherto been applied.

CREATES NEW EXPERIENCE.—The statement "discussion enriches experience" scarcely expresses fully what takes place in discussion at its best. Discussion may be said to create new experience. "A creator takes life apart—his own mental life included—and puts it together again in new arrangements. More accurately, he dissociates some part of life and then reassociates some of the fragments with others in his possession, so that the result is something new and unified and important. Sometimes two bits of life that are utterly colorless and inconsequential when standing apart become startling and momentous when brought together. If just the right units enter into the computation, the whole may be infinitely more significant than the sum of the parts."[5] Here again is an apt description of what takes place in organized discussion at its best. Out of the dissection of experience, analysis, interpretation, and rearrangement, there comes an experience that is essentially a new creation. Just how the movement proceeds out of which a new experience arises has been thus stated: "A says something. Thereupon a thought arises in B's mind. Is it B's idea or A's? Neither. It is a mingling of the two. We find that A's idea, after having been presented to B and returned to A has become slightly, or largely, different from what it was originally. In like manner it is affected by C and so on." Commenting on this statement by Follett, says Sheffield, "B's" idea has been affected by the others, so has C's, so that all three ideas come to interact not as distinct psychic units but each as an interpenetrated system of idea-factors and feelings."[6]

CHARACTERISTICS ESSENTIAL TO CREATIVE DISCUSSION

In a single sentence, characteristics essential if group discussion is to be creative are admirably stated by Lindeman: "Small groups of aspiring adults who desire to keep their minds fresh and vigorous who begin to learn by confronting pertinent situations; who dip down to the reservoirs of their experience before resorting to texts and secondary facts; who are led in the discussion by teachers who are searchers after wisdom and not oracles —this constitutes the setting for adult education, the modern quest for life's meaning."[7]

EXPERIENCE CENTERED.—Much of what passes for religious discussion is not discussion of religion at all; instead, it is mere clashing of opinion or debate about controversial doctrines. It centers not in experience but in opinions rooted in tradition. To be effective in enriching experience organized discussion must concern itself with experience. It may ask and answer questions such as these: What are the religious values of this particular experience? In what way is this experience religious? How is religion related to this experience, or this experience to religion? Is this experience an evidence that religion is working in life or that it has failed to work? How has it modified this experience? If it is not at work, why not? How may it be made to work more effectively?

As no other method of teaching, discussion may be experience-centered. No two people approach any problem with exactly the same background of experience. Every person who takes part in the discussion, by virtue of participation is a different person than before, for experience is in some measure modified by the discussion. In a sermon or lecture there is no response required on the part of the listener, and often, therefore, no modification of experience.

Discussion, when it is vital, involves thinking. Vital thinking, in turn, is a phase of action. It finds its stimulus in problems and needs, and its goal in change or modification of conduct and action. There is a popular idea that thinking precedes action.

It would be more nearly true to the facts to say that more often real thinking takes place within action. Many religious teachers —teachers of children and teachers of adults, proceed on the theory of presenting abstract ideals, that is, a principle, an idea, a belief, warming them up with an emotional association, and expecting that later when an appropriate situation occurs they will be applied. Discussion begins with a problem situation, or with an enterprise, involving problems, in which the members of the group are participants, and as it moves forward toward the solution of these problems discovers principles and formulates ideals, developing a realization of their value and some skill in their use.

A COOPERATIVE UNDERTAKING.—Organized group discussion presupposes agreement among the members of the group that the procedure is actually to be a cooperative undertaking. The purpose is mutual helpfulness and mutual achievement. No member of the group, in group discussion at its best, undertakes to impose his views upon the others. The prevailing attitude is that of seeking to learn rather than seeking to convince or win. No one permits himself to retain any kind of defense mechanism. This cooperative purpose, operating in an atmosphere of mutual confidence and sympathy, is essential. A determination to win the group to one's own particular point of view is a distinct hindrance to group thinking. It has a tendency to draw the group into argumentation, to close minds to new evidence, and to act as a preventive to the discovery of new truth.

The members of a discussion group come together to face a common problem with a desire to find a solution, expecting that each member of the group will have some contribution to make to it. Each becomes a participant in the process with the purpose of making a contribution, but also with a desire and purpose of receiving from the others. Each contributes his ideas, convictions, experiences, not in a spirit of forcing them upon others but willing to see them restated, modified, and enriched.

Herein is an essential difference between group discussion and debate. Debate is a conflict of conclusions already arrived at and tenaciously maintained by opposing speakers. As speakers align themselves on two sides of the question listeners are likely to take one side or the other of the controversy. The tendency is to regard the debated subject not so much as a problem which they are to think through under the guidance of the debaters as a battle. As for the debaters themselves, their attitude tends to become contentious. Each attempts to score on his opponent. There is no common expectation that those on the losing side will have, following the debate, a cooperative attitude or be won to a purpose of action in accord with the decision.

This is not to say that debate is without value. In its recognition of orderly rules of procedure debate marks a significant advance in conflict of opinions. "Rules of order . . . make mere force take a back seat; . . . they make it possible for the last man to be heard. They provide for pause, a second thought, amendment and postponement; they enable minorities actually to modify the thinking of majorities, and they are an instrument of a genuinely common will—a will proved to be common by the loyal acquiescence of minorities in final decisions by vote."[8] Recognizing clearly all of these values of orderly debate, it is still evident that it opens up no such opportunity for progress in thought as is afforded by group discussion.

There are marked differences also between group discussion and the forum method. In a forum the lead is taken by some one person chosen on the assumption that he possesses knowledge and experience of special significance. Responsibility is borne wholly by the speaker for supplying information, stimulating thought, and carrying forward the process of thinking within the group. There is little opportunity for real discussion. Questions or objections are encouraged, and in replying the speaker attempts to guide thought, but because of the setting and the number present in the group there is no such interplay as characterizes effective group discussion nor the same extent of participation. It is not in the same sense a cooperative group experience.

The cooperative attitude that should dominate group discussion is well described in a characterization of the newer spirit in college teaching. "The desk and the raised platform are gone from our midst. Gone also is the gulf fixed between professors and students, across which, by tradition, long-distant communication has been conducted. Our favorite classroom arrangement provides a table with a dozen chairs around it. About the table students and teachers gather, discussion ranges back and forth and up and down, and the visitor who looks in upon the session sometimes has to look twice in order to distinguish the teacher from the students. . . . This informal relation has been encouraged by intimate association in government, social entertainment, and physical recreation. We doubt if any curricular arrangement or administrative machinery can be effective unless it promotes this kind of friendly intercourse between teachers and students. By means of such informal, personal relations, the older and the younger learn from each other, real problems come out for discussion, real obstacles in the way of wise and happy living are attacked and perchance removed."[9]

The Christian quality of group discussion is evidenced by its cooperative character. The Christian religion lays emphasis upon the inherent worth of every individual, a principle which implies a contribution by every individual to the group. Group discussion as a process builds upon this principle.

In some quarters a disposition has been evidenced to belittle group discussion as an educational method on the ground that members of the average group have nothing to contribute. Such a statement is a two-edged sword; it is a poor defense of lecturing and preaching that persons who have been listening all their lives to lectures and sermons have nothing to say that is worth saying. Moreover, as Woodrow Wilson testified, such a statement is untrue: "Some of the most penetrating questions that I have ever had addressed to me came from some of the men in the audience (at Cooper Union) who were the least well-dressed, came from the plain fellows, came from the fellows whose muscle was daily up against the whole struggle of life. They asked questions which went to the heart of the business and put me to my mettle to answer them. I felt as if those questions came as a voice out of life itself, not a voice out of any school less severe than the severe school of experience."[10]

The cooperative character of group discussion secures for the benefit of all the contribution possible from the wealth and resourcefulness of the best-furnished minds. Not only is each individual by the process of give-and-take stimulated to better thinking than he is capable of, deliberating alone, but the combined result is more than the possible contribution of any one or two members.

ATTITUDE OF DISCOVERY.—Discussion, as herein described, differs from the methods of adult teaching in common use in that it does not aim primarily at increasing enthusiasm for convictions already held, or at indoctrination, or even disseminating factual knowledge. It is essentially a cooperative effort toward the discovery of the meaning of experience. A college teacher, stating what he believes to be the demands made upon education today by college students, sums these up in the declaration that what they most want is direct and immediate assistance in dealing with vital personal, social, and spiritual problems of their own experience. These also are demands made by adults, particularly men and women in early adult life, of the church and of religious education —demands which traditional methods of teaching are doing little to meet, but which organized discussion is admirably fitted to supply.

One may have to travel far and search diligently in books in order to discover the essential significance of a particular experience. Life is not logically or methodically arranged like a textbook. It is full of complications, contradictions, and unexpected changes. If the road traveled by the student is one on which the weekly way stations are "subjects" or "lessons," designated by persons who have no acquaintance with him, the way may be very long before he makes any discovery that is of paramount, immediate concern in its bearing on his experience. But, if, as is presupposed in the adoption of organized discussion as a teaching-and-learning technique, the procedure starts not with a "subject," "topic," or "lesson," but with an actual life situation or group of related situations, the significant aspects of the experience, or at least what are believed to be such according to the judgment of the members of the group, are likely very soon to begin to appear. The starting point of the discussion may not be the particular experience of paramount concern, but even so it is an easy and quick transition from the suggested life situation to that which is central in the concern of any member of the group.

SPIRIT AND ATMOSPHERE OF FREEDOM.—Yet another essential to success of group discussion is that it shall be conducted in the atmosphere of freedom. For the procedure to be fruitful in largest measure not only must the discussion be free from external restraint and compulsions but the members must free themselves from emotional tensions and so far as possible from the inhibitions of prejudices and fixed beliefs. They must bring to the discussion open minds and an expectation of learning.

Against such an attitude of open-mindedness there are those who urge that some issues certain to be raised in a discussion group are not in any proper sense open questions; "they are not even debatable." The answer is that by open-mindedness is meant readiness to listen, willingness to weigh evidence without prejudice, and, if it is needed, to present reasons fairly. In this sense open-mindedness should be universal. Truth does not need the protection of high, impenetrable walls marked "No entrance to the public."

Open-mindedness is a none-too-prevalent attitude among adults. The testimony of many college teachers agrees with that of the professor who, offering a course on basic but concrete social problems, found that his class of young men and women were so ruled by preconceptions, prejudices, and uncritical opinions, so given to dogmatic assertion and judgment on the basis of socially inherited sentiments, and so lacking in open-mindedness and objectivity, that fruitful class discussion of problems involving conflict of interests and sentiments could not advance. If this situation is one frequently found to prevail among students in their late teens and early twenties, it is even more prevalent among adults of middle age and beyond. In some groups closed minds and a spirit of dogmatism will be found to be so marked as to make the use of discussion in a vital sense impossible. The discussion leader should be awake to the probability of this contingency. An exploration, in advance, in the form of an opinion test will reveal to some extent what he must be prepared to meet. Two or three introductory sessions with lectures and discussions on the scientific attitude and method and on open-minded quest for new truth should serve in some degree to modify existing attitudes and to prepare the way for free, open-minded discussion.

Confidence in the value of organized group discussion assumes the capacity and the right of common people to think, to weigh evidence, and to decide for themselves—assumptions, as was stated earlier, historically fundamental in Protestantism, foreign as they may be from the prevailing situation in many evangelical Protestant groups. Whereas in organized discussion it is understood that every member of the group has full right to his interpretation even though it may represent an opinion directly opposed to that of the leader in many adult Bible classes it is assumed that the teacher of the class is in possession of truth of which it is his office to secure unquestioning acceptance. He speaks as an oracle whose word is not open to question. An assumption of organized discussion is that "we learn little from those who agree with us, but a great deal from those who differ with us."

The creation of the necessary atmosphere of freedom is aided by the leader's attempting to secure expression of opinion from every member of the group and encouraging every person to trust his own experience.

A discussion which has the characteristics that have been described takes on the aspect of an adventure in the sharing of experience. There is no attitude of reservation or of withholding but, rather, the bringing of all resources of experience to bear upon the search for meanings and values. The current runs deeper than the mere expression of opinion and of feeling. The process becomes an exploration of the depths of the totality of experience to which each has made his contribution.

TECHNIQUE OF ORGANIZED DISCUSSION

Much has been written in recent years of the "discussion method," often with the assumption of a new discovery, a kind of educational panacea, guaranteed to fit all situations and certain to be creative in result. Misleading and unfortunate is this tendency to define "the discussion method" as a rigidly defined procedure, a highly refined technique, an exact step-by-step process, invariably to be used, and always productive of desired results in thinking and living. There is no such "method."

Creative cooperative thinking may take place under a wide variety of circumstances and in the use of various procedures. It is very desirable that these various procedures, successfully used in specific situations, suggestive for other situations, shall be experimentally used. But no one of them should be set forth in rigid terms as *the method.* Underlying the several procedures a general pattern may be discerned, subject to varied adaptation in detail, of wide usefulness, what Sheffield has called "a little map 'of a complete educative process.'" Succinctly stated, following Dewey's description of the way a conclusion is reached in orderly thinking, the process proceeds through the following stages: (1) a problematic situation involving an experience of a felt difficulty; (2) the location and definition of the difficulty, breaking the problem into its elements, or analysis of the situation into its factors; (3) listing of possible solutions, or outcomes, or alternative courses of action, a stage of procedure which involves opportunity and obligation of extensive exploration of current and past experience; (4) tentative adoption of solution, the result of evaluation, involving decision or choice, a stage which may involve advance chiefly through reasoning or through action or conduct; (5) experimentation, including observation and testing, leading to verified choice, acceptance of conclusion, belief, or course of action, and habituation.

This general pattern, we repeat, is not to be thought of as a one, two, three, procedure through which every discussion is to move. "Any particular new conviction, it is true, is not really wrought into the mind of the learner . . . except as the matter is (1) experienced; (2) faced as a problem; (3) dealt with in the light of new facts and discriminations, and (4) satisfactorily acted on. . . . But many matters are too large and complex to be moved through in this fashion. With them, one's learning experience may start at a later phase—say, with a speech, a prejudice-test, a passage of reading, or an experimental project."[11] Any of these stages may, in a particular instance, be regarded as a more or less separate and distinct unit of experience of sufficient importance to be dealt with as such, in which case a different type of discussion procedure will be called for.

Emphasizing that the general pattern described is not to be regarded as a series of formal steps, we proceed to a fuller exposition.

STATEMENT OF THE PROBLEM.—Much depends upon the description of the situation, or the statement of the problem, to be discussed. The starting point necessarily is a concern, a particular experience or problematic life situation, in which the majority of the group have a vital interest. Usually, it may be assumed, the members of the group know in advance what this situation or problem is. But invariably a wide range of preparation or lack of preparation for its consideration is represented. In most adult class groups, as conditions prevail today, a majority of the members will have made no specific preparation, while a small minority in all probability will have given considerable time to previous thought and study.

It is important that the situation, or problem, shall be definitely and clearly stated. Each person should be aware of the problem as it appears to other members of the group. Frequently an apparently simple situation appears differently to different people. A question which clearly states a problem for one person may not carry the same connotation to another. There are numerous ways in which the situation may be brought clearly into consciousness. Some of the best are these:

An incident from current life may provide the starting point.

Better yet, several brief incidents involving the same problem may be presented. A natural beginning is the telling, by various members, of the way or ways in which the situation or problem has been for each an actual experience. This creates a sense of reality, and identification with actual life. Out of the several statements a composite picture of the situation or experience should arise in which important details are filled in, thus constituting a more typical and complete whole than the statement of any one person offers.

These may be accompanied by pertinent questions from the leader intended to sharpen formulations of the problem. It may be necessary to follow up one or more of the initial questions in order to get the problem fully, clearly stated.

The problem may be stated briefly by the leader or some other well-qualified person. Emphasis should be placed on the importance of brevity and clarity of statement. Also, it should be understood that the statement is intended solely as a formulation of the problem.

Brief statements may be formulated in advance by two or more members of the group, rather than a single statement. This plan is to be preferred when the problem is quite certainly one that presents different aspects to different persons. It is also desirable when the situation is one concerning which the experience of the group is limited. An objection to this plan is the amount of time consumed in a step purely preliminary. It is also difficult, sometimes, to make the transition from these more or less formal statements to free discussion.

Formulations of the problem from significant sources may be read by the leader. These statements should be brief and challenging. Great care should be exercised that they are germane, and particularly that they do not complicate the problem by introducing extraneous elements. Significant sources include authorities whose statements may be quoted, and investigation of the facts of a situation.

A well-prepared historical introduction may be prepared in advance and read. This applies only in the event that the problem is one which has an historical background, consciousness of which is an important element in its consideration. The reading of the historical introduction usually should precede the statement of the problem by the leader, or by others.

Tests are available which serve effectively to open up certain problems. Their use often is a means of quickening interest and stimulating thinking, creating alertness and questioning. A test is of no value unless the leader knows how to interpret the result for the particular group with which it is used in terms of the situation or problem to be discussed.

It should be clearly recognized that the problem is not satisfactorily stated until it has become a real situation for every member of the group. An issue which everyone recognizes to be a vital issue must be involved.

ANALYSIS OF THE PROBLEM.—A beginning having been made in the statement of the situation or problem, next in order in the process of clear and effective group thinking is the breaking down of the problem into its constituent factors.

It is doubtless true that our life today, more than that of any preceding era, presents situations which are extremely complex, involving, in many instances, numerous factors which at different times and places appear in almost innumerable variety of combinations. In spite of this, many choices and much action are of the nature of undiscriminating, mass response, a kind of hit-or-miss affair, the result more of a chance impulse, or general undifferentiated reaction, than of weighing the various elements, and intelligent, moral choice. The situation seen only as a blur, the response is of the same sort.

In a complex situation certain factors may be important and others comparatively irrelevant. Analysis involves discovering all factors, weighing their significance, canceling those that are unimportant, and emphasizing those that are vital. Discrimination in analysis is an essential element in reflective thought.

This step marks the transition from uncontrolled, random or haphazard, hazy thinking and action to discriminating, critical, reflective thought and deliberate choice. It should not be hastened. The fact that the leader sees the factors of the problem is no assurance that the members of the group discern them. The group should analyze the problem for itself. It is of great advantage to set down the various factors, as they are discovered, on a blackboard.

LISTING OF POSSIBLE SOLUTIONS.—A next stage in the procedure of group thinking is the listing of possible solutions of the problem, or courses of action constituting outcomes. This involves a moving out or projection of thought, a proposed advance in action, variously involving supposition, conjecture, hypothesis, suggestion, or proposed action. To the extent that this step is thoroughly considered a comprehensive list of alternatives, representing wide variety, will be presented. The enumeration, or listing, of possible solutions is not something that can be well done in any extempore fashion. It involves search of present experience, and of the experience of the past. Each is of such importance as to demand separate although necessarily brief elaboration.

(1) *Search of personal experience.*—The question to be raised by the leader at this point is: What suggestions of possible solutions are supplied by the experience of the members of the group? Have various members previously confronted similar or identical situations? What was done? The answers should be in very specific, concrete terms. This step, also, of the procedure should not be hurried. The statement of experiences by various members will enable fellow members to recall half-forgotten experiences and will lead them to see other experiences in a new light. Every effort should be made by the leader to call out diverse and varied suggestions. At this point creativity in thought has its first opportunity.

(2) *Search of contemporary experience.*—No discussion group should consider itself self-sufficient. No matter how rich and varied the experience of its members, it should be stimulated to reach out beyond its own circle to explore a range and depth of experience lying beyond its own group horizon. There are various ways in which this may be done. Interviews may be arranged with persons thought to have contributions, and reports brought in. Books and periodicals covering a wide range of contemporary thought and experience, current events, history, opinion, surveys, biographies, all may have something to contribute. Preliminary use may also be made at this point of resource persons, men and women who possess special experience on the matter in hand.

(3) *Search of past experience.*—Nor is the age in which we live self-sufficient. The past has great contributions to make to any survey of experience. Individual experience is of one piece with race experience. Our problems may present themselves in new guise, but basically few are different from problems with which the race has struggled in every age. Out of the past may come some of the most significant suggestions of possible courses of action. Unfortunately, tradition often acts only to hamper, restrict, and bind, but the past has other than this negative contribution if its experience is thoroughly explored.

EVALUATION AND CHOICE.—Also important in the general pattern of group thinking is evaluation of all proposed solutions of the problem, or courses of action, and deliberate choice.

Here, again, personal experience, other contemporary experience, and past experience, should be called upon for contributions. The question should be asked: What light does personal experience shed on choice of alternatives? This is a question which should be persistently urged. Tactfully, urgently, insistently, the leader should press for the contribution of each member. The leader should be on his guard against too easy assent to a judgment forcefully presented. Varying points of view are represented in every group, and every effort should be made to get them expressed.

Sooner or later the point will be reached where need is evident for help from outside the group. The need may be for information not possessed by any member of the group, for help in evaluation of a particular suggestion, or for aid in any one of numerous directions. Group discussion by no means makes books and expert opinion unnecessary. Rather, it brings them to bear on felt needs. Members are impelled by newly awakened interest and newly developed consciousness of need to seek out the sources of help.

One of the chief weaknesses of the discussion technique as commonly used is failure to make provision for the discovery, collection, and presentation of new and unfamiliar facts. Frequently a discussion is carried through to a conclusion without taking into consideration an immense amount of factual information which, although readily available, lies entirely outside the range of knowledge and experience of members of the group.

When the need for additional information becomes apparent the group may be divided into committees for investigation and report, each committee being assigned to make a thorough and impartial search for all available facts within a specific area. In some instances it may be sufficient to make assignments to individuals rather than to committees, but always important is assurance of the collection and presentation of all possible pertinent facts and information.

The stage of evaluation and choice is the second point at which resource persons, experts and authorities, are of service. Their presence is not an occasion for a lecture or address unless a very specific need has developed for comprehensive information or for an elaborated judgment, which only a lecture can supply. Usually the service to be rendered will be that of answering specific questions or expressing opinions on specific phases of a proposal.

A resource library is a valuable adjunct of group discussion. Its value will be enhanced by the preparation of reading and study lists with annotated references to various volumes. If the group session is of sufficient length to permit periods of study, alternating with discussion periods, or if the library is located in an accessible reading room to which members may repair between sessions, the leader may insert slips indicating especially significant passages. Assignments for reading may be made in the group sessions with report to be made at the succeeding meeting.

At this step, also, a blackboard helps. If the principal proposals are indicated in substance, standing continually before the eye, the mind is free to give itself wholly to the weighing of comparative values and the thinking through to conclusions, without the otherwise necessary effort of trying to recall from time to time what has been said.

Not always will even a tentative conclusion be reached in the process of evaluation. Some problems are of such complexity and importance that a lifetime's effort is involved in the attempt to find a solution. Group discussion does not offer an easy and quick means of arriving at the solution of age-long problems. The group should be freed of the delusion that if no consensus of judgment is quickly reached, the procedure followed has been of no value. Concerning some problems the greatest service to be rendered to unthinking people is an awakening to their seriousness.

Usually, however, it may be expected that a tentative solution to the problem, on which the group agrees, will be reached, and discussion should be continued until this goal is attained.

TESTING OF CHOICE, AND HABITUATION.—A fifth and concluding stage of the general procedure consists of an experimental testing of the outcome, verification, and the formation of habit through repeated choice. In this final stage the result arrived at is subjected to proof; its validity demonstrated in practice. The outcome of experimentation may, of course, be negative, in which case the fourth step of evaluation and choice will be repeated.

A group procedure that follows the general pattern described is discussion, but it is more than discussion; it is a vital process of reflective thinking, discrimination, choice, and action that eventuates in new experience creative in influence upon character and personality.

SUMMARY.—A significant summary of the values of group discussion is contained in the statement of twenty men and women, members of a discussion group studying the history of modern education:[12] (1) "Allows many members to contribute something to the presentation. . . . (2) Has the advantage of spontaneity, freshness, enthusiasm. (3) Pays tribute to initiative and individuality. (4) Enables class and instructor to clear up misconceptions. (5) Arouses and keeps interest. . . . (6) Stimulates thinking—when students themselves are discussing things, they usually think. Even those who don't speak, think. (7) Causes out-of-door interest and observation. (8) Helps persons to express themselves. . . . (9) Not dogmatic; expression of opinion is free. Gives each individual the right to express his own opinion. (10) In harmony with the modern tendency of group participation. (11) New angles and opinions are brought out . . . which others, including the leader, have not thought of. The scope of the course is broadened by introducing the experiences of members of the class. (12) Perhaps the most significant point . . . is that the student is actively engaged in what would otherwise be a two-hour nap. . . . Shows the instructor the interests of the class and how the students think. . . . Put persons on a freer social level, a social factor not to be overlooked. . . . (18) Fosters a spirit of tolerance for each individual's opinion. . . . (19) Supplements book knowledge by personal experiences and observations. (20) Encourages mental alertness and assimilation, rather than absorption and memory. . . ."

CONFERENCE PROCEDURE

A variant of organized discussion as described in the preceding pages is what has come to be known as the "conference" or "seminar." By some the term "problem-project technique" is used. Many of the values of organized discussion inhere in the conference.

CHARACTERISTICS.—Essential characteristics of the conference are much the same as of organized discussion. It differs from the ordinary techniques of instruction in that much more initiative is taken by the members of the group. The leader cooperates with the members in the discovery and statement of a common problem or problems; counsels with them as to sources of information; and guides them in seeking to arrive at solutions. It differs from organized group discussion as described above in that the problems in which the procedure centers usually are those which have to do predominantly with intellectual aspects of experience.

PROCEDURE.—A first step is discovery of or decision concerning the problems on which conference will center. There are various ways of doing this. A problem questionnaire may be used, or a check list of problems, or interviews with individual members of the group, or a preliminary group problem discussion. The task of discovering basic problems representing real and vital interests is somewhat complex and difficult, to which careful attention should be given.

Problems to be studied having been determined, allocation by choice may be made either to individuals or to groups. If the group is large, division may be made into committees of five to ten persons on the basis of interest, each committee to take a particular problem for investigation, study, and report. Reports, whether by individuals or committees, may be made to the entire group, discussed, and, if desired, reformulated. There are numerous possible variations of this general procedure.

It will be found advantageous for the members of the group, approximately ten to twenty in number and not more than twenty-five, to be seated around a large table. The chairman, named in advance by a committee or elected by the group at the first meeting by a process that provides opportunity for selective choice, should announce the purpose of the conference briefly, and present either on a mimeographed sheet or on a blackboard the problem or problems to be discussed.[13]

CONDITIONS OF USE.—Employment of the conference method will be found profitable when (1) the members of a group have common problems; (2) for which they share a desire to find solutions; (3) in seeking which they are willing to pool their common experience; (4) and in the search make an earnest attempt to think together. The method is essentially one of the sharing of experience, not that of a group of persons being instructed by a teacher or leader.

PURPOSES.—Various purposes may be served by the use of the conference method. A few of those for which it is best adapted are: (1) Training in ability to analyze problems and to explore the meaning of experience. (2) To develop agreement as to policies to be followed by persons bearing common or similar responsibilities, as for example, the several officers of a church or other organization; the pastors of a given community, or the Christian business men of a community. (3) "To work out common practice." (4) "To improve cooperation between department heads." The conference method will be found especially valuable in areas of experience and action in which subject content, textbooks and guidance manuals are lacking.

Certain risks and limitations of the conference or seminar procedure are suggested by Lindeman: "A conference . . . may get out of hand; it may lead in directions where authoritarians fear to go; it may result in sharp differences and open conflict; and it may fail. Many adults . . . find it difficult to adjust themselves to it. . . . All of their past experiences and their total habit-systems lean in the opposite direction. . . . There are those who function effectively only when the spotlight shines on them; there are others who dislike to have their ideas challenged, and still others who are inhibited by their individualism, by their inability to behave as collaborating members of a group. For these and many other reasons a conference which begins with problems instead of pronouncements may fail. But why should this deter us? Have we been so successful in the use of traditional and non-educative methods as to shrink from probable failure through experimentation?"[14]

FUNCTIONS AND QUALIFICATIONS OF THE DISCUSSION LEADER

The leader, whether of organized group discussion or of a conference procedure, is primarily a guide and helper of persons, not merely a teacher of subjects and books. His functions relate more vitally to the members of the group—their thinking, their understanding, their cooperation, and the enrichment of their experience than to a subject or problem of discussion.

SECURES CLEAR STATEMENT OF THE PROBLEM.—The leader's first responsibility is for a clear and definite statement of the situation or problem for discussion. While the group itself is the final arbiter of the statement as satisfactory, much will depend upon the clearsightedness of the leader, and his ability to uncover obscurities, fallacies, indefiniteness, and other possible deficiencies. Formulation of a clear, definite statement is by no means so simple or easy as may be supposed. For one thing, what is seen clearly by some to others may be obscure. The meaning of some words is colored by association, by misinformation, by prejudice. "Socialism" is such a word; "fundamental" is another. Even so familiar and oft-used a word as "faith" may convey different meanings to different people. When a word or phrase appears in a statement of a problem which evidently carries different meanings to different persons, or which with some causes strongly emotional reactions, the leader should not be satisfied until a restatement has been formulated that is apparently clear to all and in the thought of all carries the same meaning.

GUIDES THE DISCUSSION.—A second important function of the leader is that of guidance. This responsibility may be partially likened to that of the pilot. He steers the ongoing movement in order to clear the eddies, avoid sandbars and shallow waters, hidden rocks and shoals, and to insure progress. Unlike the pilot, the discussion leader does not have in mind a predetermined goal toward which he directs the course of the procedure.

Guiding the discussion involves holding the procedure to the point of real issues. Almost invariably some word or chance remark will supply a cue to some person with a single-track mind who will immediately get going on his pet idea. Such talk should not long be suffered. Resort to parliamentary "out of order" is not necessary. The leader should break in, courteously asking precisely how the talk bears on the issue under consideration, or requesting that the statement be brought in at a future time when it is pertinent.

An allied responsibility is that of curbing the garrulous talkers. Always there are one or more persons who talk more freely than others, who lack ability unaided to curb their garrulity, or who always want the last word whether or not they have any real contribution to make. The leader's skill is tested in preventing such persons from monopolizing the time, and accomplishing this effectively without discourtesy or harshness. Irrelevant talk is the shoal on which many a discussion goes aground.

Guidance also involves the responsibility of supplying new starting points or recalling the thinking to overlooked issues. Not infrequently discussion finds itself in a blind alley, where further progress seems impossible. In such a situation it becomes the function of the leader, by a question, a suggestion, a quotation, or otherwise, to start the group on a new trail. A similar responsibility devolves when a highly emotional outburst, usually colored by prejudice, has interrupted the process of orderly thinking. Timid persons are too fearful to proceed. Some may have been swept off their feet by the tempest of feeling. Others are silent, not wishing to precipitate heated controversy. The skilled discussion leader, dispassionate, clearsighted, and calm, comes to the rescue, and by restating the contention in a more reasonable manner or by recurring tactfully to a more vital issue, re-establishes the mood of open-minded discussion.

Unless unusually equipped with factual information the leader should assemble and bring with him to the group session a body of essential factual data as a resource when possible differences of opinion develop as to facts. An alternative plan is to arrange for the presence of an authoritative resource person who can be called upon, when occasion demands, for a statement of facts.

Additional preparation desirable involves the planning in advance of an outline, preferably in question form, of the discussion procedure for the session. While it is impossible for the leader fully or accurately to forecast the development of the discussion he should be able, through careful thought, to discover where the most vital issues are likely to appear and also where the sharpest conflicts probably will develop. To be even partially forewarned is to be forearmed for successful guidance.

At intervals progress is aided by a summary. Usually, the leader should summarize the discussion. Occasionally he may call upon another to do it. A good summary takes account of the different points of view that have been presented and states the consensus of judgment.

GUARDS AGAINST DOMINATING THE DISCUSSION.—While the leader guides the discussion, he zealously guards against making his convictions the dominating factor. He is more concerned about showing himself impartial and fair than in presenting his personal judgment. More important than assuring that his own point of view is strongly presented is his responsibility of getting all the different points of view clearly stated and understood. He neither imposes his personal conviction upon the group nor throws the weight of his influence on one side of the discussion in order to assure its prevailing. He does not take sides. He interprets to the group what is being said, if anything giving more attention to the point of view that has been timidly or obscurely presented.

Very important is it, when an opinion has been hesitatingly expressed or obscurely stated, for the leader to come to the rescue saying, "Yes, your point is ———," thus making clear and forceful what otherwise might have been passed by without attention.

Most leaders of discussion do too much talking. They find it easier to make pertinent statements than to draw them out from members of their groups, and they yield to the temptation to dominate. This tendency is easily detected by members of a discussion group, and with most persons evokes a negative reaction, in many cases so strong as to constitute a deterrent to participation. If the leader is consciously on the lookout for those who are not sharing in the procedure, he will not be so likely to jump in whenever a gap appears. An additional precaution, as well as a positive aid to those of more limited experience, is afforded by placing quotations of source material, in advance, in the hands of some of the members, to be called for when needed.

INDEPENDENCE AND INITIATIVE REQUIRED.—It is evident that a large degree of open-mindedness is a necessary qualification of the successful discussion leader, but this does not mean that an effective leader may not have strong, compelling convictions, nor does it imply lack of initiative. In fact, more of independence and resourcefulness are required in a discussion leader than in a teacher who follows a prescribed course. There is no easy falling back upon the authority of textbooks and lesson-helps. An inner authority, the contribution of experience, and self-confidence born of test are necessary qualifications.

LIMITATIONS OF ORGANIZED DISCUSSION

Valuable as creative discussion is in enriching experience, in adult religious education it is necessary that it shall be supplemented by other learning-teaching techniques. We shall be helped in evaluating group discussion as an educational procedure by frankly recognizing some of its more marked limitations.

HOBBY-RIDING.—In practice, group discussion probably suffers as much from hobby-riding as any other one cause. In nearly every group will be found one or more loquacious persons, frequently with single-track minds, fond of arguing, sometimes strongly egotistical and intolerant, who insist on being heard.

Sometimes the hobbyist's attitudes are such that his mind-set may be overcome. Frequently, however, his hobby-riding grows out of mental limitation, nearly or quite impossible to overcome. Because of this limitation, to him the solution of practically every problem reduces to a single simple formula, in pursuing or defending which he becomes emotionally tense and fanatically intolerant of all other suggestions. The only thing necessary is "conversion"; or the source of all evil is the "liquor traffic"; or the sum of all iniquities is "card-playing." Whatever the hobby, the rider's highly wrought insistence on it, on the one hand, or any attempt on the part of the discussion leader to hold him within bounds, is likely to create an emotional tenseness that counteracts openness of mind and impartial weighing of evidence and inhibits free participation on the part of many.

TENDENCY TO PERSONIFICATION.—Many adults, either through intellectual limitation or long custom have become habituated to thinking almost wholly in terms of persons and ignoring impersonal factors and forces. This seems almost to be an inherent limitation of many minds. Evidence is seen in animism and anthropomorphism in religion. Illustrations of this basic tendency are found in the frequency with which group discussion assumes the form of criticism of particular persons or of attack upon propositions which are strongly colored by association with certain persons. This common handicap to fruitful social thinking, says Sheffield, is what Overstreet calls "social animism," . . . "the tendency to personify the forces—economic, cultural, psychological, which have given rise to a situation, and to treat it as melodrama, with the capitalist, the bolshevist, or the pacifist, gathering all the mischief-making into his one personal rôle. This makes the solution of the difficulty merely a question of how to defeat some designing villain. It loses sight of the network of impersonal causes which must be understood and mastered if we are to achieve social control and enlightened redirection."[15]

This easy reference of all difficulties to persons and solution of problems through their defeat or elimination is likely to be accompanied by an inability or unwillingness to read, study, and undertake real research. It is difficult to attach a requirement of study to the discussion technique, for it disavows the pressure of external authority, and unless the inner purpose and disposition are present, imperative is lacking. The coming together of a group of persons who are uninformed and who have within themselves no compelling impulse to pursue investigation, and at the same time a tendency to personify all problems, does not provide a promising situation for profitable group discussion.

CIRCLE TALKING AND SIDETRACK DISCUSSION.—A difficult phase of the discussion leader's task is to steer a middle course between the group's moving in a circle and following a tangent. Unless a high degree of both skill and tact is shown by the leader, the discussion is likely either to proceed in circles and arrive nowhere, or follow a tangent and end in a blind alley.

Particularly in instances in which the thought of a majority of the group moves in a deeply cut channel the very momentum of group pressure is likely to interfere with the clarity of the leader's perception of the real issues, or even sweep him off his feet. In practice, it must be admitted that in discussion main issues are often lost sight of or obscured while the procedure proceeds irresistibly on a tangent.

It must be confessed that many adult groups, including a large proportion of Bible classes in which "the discussion method" is said to be used, merely engage in a free talkfest around a topic. This has been known to happen even in a college classroom! If any considerable proportion of participants engage in more or less superficial, pointless talk, and no way is discovered by which nonsignificant participation can be prevented, the procedure inevitably moves in a circle and the limit of time is reached with the company having arrived nowhere as a group and, with many, more confused in mind than when they came.

To say that such procedures as these have little in common with a real group discussion in which eager minds, pursuing an urgent quest, press forward together in orderly thinking toward the formation of a group opinion enlightening and satisfying, does not constitute a sufficient answer.

A LIMITED DYNAMIC.—Persons, in many cases, have need for release and renewal in the emotional and volitional depths of their natures—depths to which group discussion seldom penetrates with regenerating power. This is not to say that *vox populi* may not sometimes be *vox Deus,* but only to acknowledge a limitation of the discussion technique. Added significance, because of its source, attaches to a statement of the *New Republic:* "There is no evidence so far as we know that group discussion or any analogue to it in the life of a religious fellowship is adequate to liberate the individual from the bondage which is imposed on him by the impurities of his own heart or by his habitual dissipation of his vital energy."[16] Selfish interest, sexual tension, domestic malad-justments growing out of personal idiosyncrasies, are ever-present causes of impotence of human effort and of unsocial, sinful conduct.

When group discussion has done all that it is capable of doing in purifying the springs of action and empowering volition, adult education still has with it a considerable part of its problem of developing in men and women that selflessness and purity of motive, that drive and energy in pursuit of spiritual ends, and that sacrificial devotion characteristic of Christian personality at its highest and best. Group discussion has great values, and its service to adult education has never yet been fully utilized, but it is by no means a panacea, and it should not be looked to, as is sometimes urged, in an exclusive sense as *the* method of Christian education.

CHAPTER XI

EDUCATION THROUGH CREATIVE LEISURE

"THE wisdom of a learned man," declares an ancient writer, "cometh by opportunity of leisure." Following this observation, he states what has been one of the most baffling educational problems of past ages: "How can he get wisdom that holdeth the plow, . . . that driveth oxen and is occupied in their labors . . . so every carpenter and workmaster, that laboreth night and day. . . . The smith also . . . and the potter." As if to emphasize the seriousness of the problem, he concludes by paying tribute to the indispensability of the laboring masses: "Without these cannot a city be inhabited, . . . they . . . maintain the fabric of the world."[1]

THE CHANGED MODERN PROBLEM.—Now, for the first time in the world's history, the form of this ancient problem is changed. For that large proportion of adult men and women employed on a fixed schedule of hours per week there remains over and above the hours required for refreshment and sleep a considerable surplus of time to be profitably occupied. The working week has been reduced from eighty-four hours in 1840 to forty-four hours in 1940, with an acceptance in theory of the forty-hour week, or less, for the future. For many others than those on a fixed schedule there has been a corresponding reduction. For many housewives, though far from all, changes in the techniques of housekeeping, the introduction of mechanical aids, and the broadening of the program of education of children, the drudgery of overlong hours of housework has been relieved. It is estimated that adults working forty-four hours per week and sleeping eight hours out of twenty-four have left for other purposes fifty-five per cent more time than is devoted to routine employment. No longer is the difficulty one of making time available for education. Rather, it is that of making unoccupied time contribute to the accumulation of wisdom and the enrichment of life.

The new problem has still another aspect. Our prevailing economic order ordains enforced unemployment for vast numbers of men and women. Its extent has been elsewhere stated.* Even

* See page 109.

328

proponents of the present order admit that due to increased efficiency of industry, displacement of hand labor by machines, and consequent disparity between production and consumption, widely extended unemployment, if not a permanent condition, will remain for long years to come. "What do you do in your spare time?" the social worker asked the unemployed man. He replied, "All of my time is spare time." The problem of unoccupied time is vastly increased in complexity and difficulty when the total time of adults is unoccupied. That which mankind for ages has sought, even battled for, the substance of the dreams of poets and seers—the opportunity of leisure for the common man at last is at hand. But, alas! it comes more as a threat than as a boon.

THE CREATIVE USE OF LEISURE

The profound social changes of the past one hundred years have given men immensely more leisure and more unoccupied time, but they have not as yet resulted, at least not for the many, in any considerable increase in freedom, relaxation, recreation, or happiness. With a surplus of time upon our hands such as civilized man has never before known, we do not know what to do with it. For unoccupied time in such large proportion we are not prepared, as L. P. Jacks has declared, either biologically or by education. How this unoccupied time is used will in no small measure determine the quality of future civilization.

THE NEW PROBLEM.—This, then, is the new problem: how utilize the largely increased amount of unoccupied time in ways that contribute to the enrichment and development of personality, and to social welfare?

The problem is obviously complicated by certain facts now quite generally recognized. For men and women who work under the high pressure and trying physical conditions characterizing modern industry, and to a considerable extent business also, the kinds of leisure activity sought are means of escape, ways of release from stress and strain, activities calculated to make one forget. Concerning this more will be said later.

A second group of facts involves the effects of unemployment. The human organism, as the result of the long evolutionary process, is keyed to physical and mental activity. In mind and body it begins to degenerate the hour activity ceases. With no preparation for the profitable use of idle time, the unemployed are in a serious plight.   Many spend the unoccupied time, forced upon them, in stagnating physically, mentally, and morally.   The common testimony of social workers brought into professional relationship with them is that they are almost totally lacking in resources for utilization of their vacant days and weeks and months.   Mostly they sit and wait and brood—hoping vainly that something will happen. Their idleness contributes chiefly to a steadily increasing burden of worry, despondency, and hopelessness.   With some these attitudes breed despair, with others vice or crime or both.   They are "a multitude at a loose end; with no initiative or faculty of invention to fill the empty days; with no skill of their own beyond that which went out of use and began to decay when employment ceased."[2]

PHILOSOPHY OF CREATIVE LEISURE.—Leisure is a term commonly all too loosely used.   Much that has been spoken and written in recent years about "the new leisure" is almost wholly beside the point.   The connotation of leisure is freedom from tension and worry, a condition in which both body and mind are at ease, an adjustment to one's environment and to life itself which is pleasurable and satisfying.   It is a misuse of the term to apply it either to those who are involuntarily unemployed, suffering from consequent deprivation, burdened with fear and with worry concerning others dependent upon them for bread, or to those for whom the reduction of working hours means a corresponding reduction of income below the level of a decent living wage.   Properly used, the term is distinguished by the following criteria: (1) both its original incentive and its fulfillment are to be found in the individual himself rather than in the coercions of the social and economic order; (2) it involves activities or states different from those forced upon one by his vocation or station in life; (3) it is "at least compatible with, if not conducive to, physical, mental, and social well-being"; (4) it possesses the capacity of relatively permanent interest.[3]

Understood in this sense, the distinction commonly made between leisure and labor very largely disappears.   Leisure is not idleness.   It is far removed from the shallow banality of the useless pastimes of the idle rich.   It is equally far removed from the slow rusting away of the moral fiber of the unemployed.   It is response to the urge to creative activity which in some degree exists in everyone.   It involves those activities which to the persons engaging in them seem to be real life, in which they experience the thrill of being alive and expressing their real selves creatively. Human nature presents infinite variety. Consequently creative leisure finds its expression in numberless ways—ways that are neither labor in the sense of toil nor the kind of play that represents more or less aimless activity, but partakes of the highest quality of both work and play.

There is much in common between creative leisure and recreation. In the true sense recreation is re-creation. It is engaging in activities which recreate body and mind and the higher powers of both. In recreation at its best the play of life is lifted to the level of re-creative activity.

USE OF IDLE TIME.—With such an ideal the prevailing use of idle time offers striking contrast. A vivid picture, though far from complete in detail, is presented by Jerome Davis: "During their playtime some thirty million Americans will be tooting and bouncing along the highways in all sorts and varieties of gasoline-propelled vehicles. Other thousands may be sitting on narrow little wooden benches watching eighteen men intermittently run around a field, now and then diving into the dust at the feet of someone trying to catch a ball. Still other millions are sitting in darkened rooms watching a stream of light play on an aluminum screen. They sit entranced at what purports to be the secret lives of millionaires, bandits, murderers, and prostitutes, not to mention cowboys, wild-west Indians, and a variety of others."[4]

Significant progress undoubtedly has been made in recent years in the profitable use of leisure time, some elements of which will be emphasized later in this discussion. But room for improvement yet remains. There are vast numbers of men and women of the more intelligent class, many of them influential in the professions, successful in business administration and industrial management, the people as one has said "for whom pictures are painted, books are written, music is composed and performed," who are to be found during much of their leisure time "desperately intent upon the chance composition of a hand of cards, to the exclusion of humor, wit, sense, spirit and all the other proper elements of civilized social intercourse."[5] This is one of the most favorable aspects of the picture. At the worst these and others may be found indulging in pastimes in taverns, cocktail lounges, gambling halls, and elsewhere, compounded in varying measure of excitement, degrading indulgence, tawdry sentiment, banality, and sheer imbecility. "Frank, riotous indecency would, in many cases, be more tolerable, for it would at least have a savor of vital human nature, even if a rank, disagreeable savor."[6]

PRESENT CONDITIONS AFFECTING ADULT LEISURE AND RECREATION

The situation thus briefly characterized requires further exploration.

LIMITED RECOGNITION OF SIGNIFICANCE AND NEED.—The American people have not yet fully recognized the significance of leisure or the values of recreation. Many are so obsessed with material, capitalistic ideals of success and with ambition for material gain and the building of a fortune that they tend to define the profitable use of time exclusively in these terms.

The situation, to be understood, also requires to be viewed against the historical background. The dominating Puritan and pietistic influences in religion prevailing in the past, characterized by austerity, sternness, and a negative social attitude, contributed to a view of life that frowned upon recreation, regarding it in all its forms as akin to frivolity, and inimical to religion. The *Discipline* of 1792 of the Methodist Episcopal Church contained the following paragraph: " . . . We prohibit play in the strongest terms. The students shall rise at five o'clock, . . . summer and winter. . . . Their recreation shall be gardening, walking, riding, and bathing, without doors, and the carpenters', joiners', cabinet-makers' or turners' business within doors. . . . A Master . . . shall always be present at the time of bathing. Only one shall bathe at a time; and no one shall remain in the water above a minute. No student shall be allowed to bathe in the river. . . . The student shall be indulged with nothing that the world calls play. Let this rule be observed with the strictest nicety; for those who play when they are young, will play when they are old." While marked change of attitude has taken place in all of the evangelical churches, there is yet a holdover from the former Puritan negative attitude that is frequently in evidence, particularly in the views of older adults. Many men and women do not know how to play and are inclined to view with at least mild disapproval those who make any form of recreation a habit.

EFFECTS OF MECHANICAL WORK.—Immense benefit, actual and

potential, have come to mankind through the mechanization of the processes of industry and other forms of labor. But these gains have been very largely offset by corresponding losses for which compensation must in some way be found. Machines and innumerable kinds of labor-saving devices have taken out of work much of physical drudgery, and wear and tear upon muscle and man's physical frame. But they have also robbed many forms of work of all creative zest, of the necessity of skill, of its novelty, color, and joy, and in its place left dull, mechanical grind, fatiguing monotony without a soul. There yet remain numerous arts and technical processes which demand intelligence and a high degree of skilled workmanship, but for that major portion of the operations of industry, business, and commerce in which machines have been substituted for hand labor efficiency demands close concentration upon a monotonous routine, elimination of distractions and variation in effort, a rigidly controlled artificial work environment, insistence upon speed, subordination of personality, and in varying degree the reduction of human beings to the status of automatons. Arthur Pound, in *The Iron Man,* has given us a picture that is duplicated in thousands of modern mills and factories employing great masses of human beings. "I watched a man shove metal rings across six inches of space to a guide from which they were taken automatically through the machine.... That was his job from morning until night, his pay depending upon how many slotted rings passed inspection. Eyes concentrated on his little platform, he missed not one revolution of the wheels, which were grinding out his life, even as they ground out the goods. Economically, he was part of the machine—an automatic feeder, who chanced to be flesh and blood and mind.... So far as the great majority of the workers are concerned, modern industry presents this phenomenon—the dulling of the mind—on a scale unequaled in extent, and to a degree unequaled in intensity, by anything on record in history."[7]

Such a process as this, it must be recognized, is a species of drudgery which runs directly counter to man's nature, keyed as it was by his Creator to spontaneous, creative activity. It is a kind of labor devoid of capacity of exciting any deep or genuine interest; it is toil robbed of meaning, which in turn robs the worker of any sense of real participation in a creative process, taking from him all incentive to the development of any of the higher skills which he is capable of developing. From this point of view is it too much to say, as a distinguished British educator and writer has said,

"Of all the wrongs that have ever been done to labor, I count that the greatest which came into being when the efficiency of the machine took the place of personal skill as the foundation of industrial prosperity. A greater calamity has never fallen on the human race. . . ."[8]?

The saving element lies in the fact that an opportunity is offered, not yet widely recognized, of recovering by creative leisure, through utilization of the hours that machines have freed, the skill and recuperative joy that the processes of mechanization have destroyed.

When it is considered that a large proportion of the men and women in industry enter it in adolescence—many of the past generation and some even today in later childhood—and that monotonous machine operation tends through repression to kill spontaneity of spirit, it is not to be wondered at that life is so dull, so lacking in aspiration and idealism, for multitudes of men and women. "Why do you get drunk?" a stockyards worker was asked. "Because that's the quickest way out of Packing-town," was his answer. On which E. A. Ross comments: "Small wonder that people who scrape pig bristles sixty hours a week and live in mean, dingy little houses, looking out across stretches of mud, cinders, or car tracks, should seek the ruddy glow of saloon good fellowship and drink to forget."

DOMINANCE OF PASSIVE AMUSEMENTS.—The debilitating, dulling effect of mechanization is a contributory factor in the prevalence of passive forms of amusement and recreation. The extent to which "spectatoritis" prevails in America has never been duplicated except possibly in the attendance upon the gladiatorial shows of Rome in the period of her decadence. At a single prize fight in Madison Square Garden, New York City, one hundred thirty-five thousand spectators paid more than two million dollars for their seats. The combined seating capacity of the stadiums of six leading American universities is four hundred and thirty-five thousand persons. There are in the United States more than twenty-two thousand moving-picture theaters attended each week, according to statistics of the Motion Picture Producers and Distributors of America, by approximately seventy-seven million people, of whom sixty-six million are young people of fourteen years and over and adults.

Doubtless these and other passive amusements may be said to bring not only a thrill to jaded nerves but also a certain amount of nervous release from the deadening effect imposed upon men and women by a coercive social order.   But there is in most of them not at all the kind of release of nervous tensions required in the interest of health of body and mind nor any contribution to the development of personality.   Not in any basic physiological or psychological sense can they be said to be recreative.

COMMERCIALIZATION OF RECREATION.—As is evident from the foregoing paragraphs recreation in America to a considerable extent has degenerated into an area of life exploited for profit by so-called commercial enterprise.   The list of exploiting agencies is a long one, including in addition to those already mentioned, drinking taverns, roadhouses, pool halls, cabarets, skating rinks, dance halls, bowling alleys, vaudeville, burlesque, and regular theaters, and numerous others.   The President's Research Committee on Social Trends estimated the annual expenditures for moving pictures, cabarets and night clubs, radio, and entertainments for which an admission charge of seventy-five cents or more is made at somewhat more than ten billion dollars.   If all forms of amusement, entertainment, and recreation were included, this amount probably would be doubled.   Moreover, the conclusion reached as the result of a study made in 1932 by *Business Week* probably still remains true: "The outstanding feature of the picture of pleasure expenditure by the American consumer during the last ten years is the dominant and relatively increasing importance of the commercial or professional kinds of recreation as contrasted with the private, personal, or individual varieties."[9]

Concerning these aspects of the current situation the following observations are pertinent.   A large proportion of our adult population are permitting themselves, through the influence of specious, alluring advertising and senuous appeals of various kinds, to be "led by the nose" into spending both their time and money on forms of amusement and recreation, falsely so called, the best of which are lacking in positive re-creative values and the worst of which are vicious and degrading.   Commercialization without question has contributed to the debasement of popular taste, the demoralization of moral standards, encouragement to crime, and the inculcation of shallow, false ambitions.   To a considerable extent commercialized amusements and recreation have fallen into the hands of the less scrupulous and even vicious elements of society.   In no small measure this has been due to general indifference to the need for positive forms of recreation on the part of the better elements of society and to the critical, negative attitude of the churches. To permit the normal desires of people to be prostituted to greed for profit is to contribute to the death of the creative spirit in man.

CONDITIONS IN RURAL AREAS.—Recreation among adults in rural communities is even less general than in urban centers. Especially for women, farm life tends to be monotonous. For the many farmers' wives who, in addition to housework, care for the garden, mow the lawn, feed the pigs, and milk the cows, the drudgery involved not only causes undue fatigue but tends to undermine health. Recreational activities are few, limited chiefly to infrequent picnics, occasional visiting, some form of music (though there is little organized musical production), reading, and fancywork. With the exception of a comparatively few communities there is conspicuous lack of organized athletics, boating, swimming, floriculture, use of the camera, and camping, for all of which country life abounds in possibilities. It is the exceptional community that provides public facilities for organized play and recreation such as playgrounds, tennis courts, baseball fields, rural parks and picnic grounds, and swimming pools. Fraternal orders are numerous, though less popular than formerly; they possess sociability and have some recreational value. The one-room rural school has practically no recreational function either for children or adults. In the program of the township consolidated school, especially the high school, recreation has a growing place with a tendency toward development of social-center functions, though most of them still lack gymnasiums, adequate auditoriums, and well-equipped playgrounds.

PARTICIPATION BY THE CHURCH.—The use made by men and women of their unoccupied hours has become a matter of practical social concern, and in this concern the Church increasingly shares. Lying back of the baffling industrial and economic problems that plague society today is the equally difficult or possibly even more difficult problem of maintaining the morale of the masses. If men decay, if the physical, mental, and moral deterioration so noticeable in many individual cases within the ranks of the unemployed, families upon relief, the sharecroppers and tenant farmers, becomes general these other problems are certain to prove more and more insoluble. Creative leisure and re-creation, in the interest both of maintaining and of improving the quality of personality of men and women, in the present situation assume first-grade importance, a fact that the churches gradually are coming to realize.   Increasing recognition by the Church at large of its recreational function is numbered by *Social Trends* among the three most important changes in religious organizations in recent years.[10]   The new conviction is taking form in such statements as that of the Oxford Conference: "Leisure time has become one of the most serious educational problems. . . . The new leisure presents an opportunity for adult education on a large scale which Christians are called upon to promote, and for adult Christian education in which the Church should actively participate."[11]

Practice lags behind conviction.   Churches in larger towns and cities in many cases make more or less provision for recreation for children, but as yet very few possess an organized recreational program for adults.   Where church gymnasiums exist they are utilized, as a rule, exclusively by the children and young people.   The few socials, bazaars, and suppers held are in most churches money-making activities, though the custom of at least an annual fellowship dinner is growing.   An increasing number of the larger churches are equipped with a social hall, usually with a stage, in addition to a dining room and kitchen.   Many possess moving-picture machines; a few have outdoor facilities such as tennis courts. Growth also is to be noted in the maintenance of musical organizations for young people and adults, principally orchestras and chorus choirs.

As a rule, recreational facilities and organized programs for adults are entirely lacking in village and rural churches.   There are entire counties with from sixty to ninety rural churches where not one possesses a gymnasium, dining room, kitchen, tennis court, chorus choir, or orchestra.

INCREASED RECREATIONAL FACILITIES.—In general, however, there has been phenomenal increase in recreational facilities in recent years.   Hundreds of urban communities have become sufficiently convinced of the values of play and recreation to provide through taxation facilities for wholesome recreational opportunities for adults and children.   Most numerous are such facilities as museums of various kinds, art galleries, public libraries, parks and playgrounds, golf courses, tennis courts, picnic grounds, and swimming beaches.   In a few isolated instances communities have dared innovations such, for example, as a community handicraft shop with facilities for working in wood, iron, and textiles, together with provision for elementary training.

THE PHYSICAL BASIS OF THE GOOD LIFE

With this general background before us it is important to consider what significance adult leisure and recreation have from the standpoint of the objectives of Christian education set forth in preceding chapters.

UNITY OF BODY AND MIND.—A natural point of beginning is found in the physical basis of the good life. The efficient functioning of the total personality in terms of mental activity, emotional balance, social relations, and work is necessary to the more abundant life. Such functioning is impossible without a strong, healthy, efficient physical organism. Many persons have proven themselves able to overcome the handicap of a weak, crippled, or diseased body, but they are the exception. As a rule, effective everyday living is closely co-ordinated with physical well being.

The differentiation commonly made between mental activities and physical activities is not a true distinction. All activities are both mental and physical. No activity of the mind can be carried on independently of the body. Whatever its nature it requires the participation of the brain and the neural system, thus involving the body. Poise, strength of purpose, and power of will all have in part a physical foundation in the cells and the controlling nerves of the body. Physical well-being is basic both to the efficient functioning of the mind and to the development of the personality as a whole.

IMPORTANCE OF A RIGHT ATTITUDE TOWARD HEALTH.—The unity of body and mind emphasizes the importance of a right attitude toward health. No one who is concerned with living a productive life can afford to be indifferent to health, for upon his physical condition depends not only his own efficiency but the welfare of others. The wife and mother, for example, who is subject to digestive disorders, headaches, or miscellaneous unnecessary aches and pains is permitting remediable physical conditions to produce irritation, friction, and emotional disorder within the household. Innumerable maladjustments in personal relationships within and without the home are due, more than to anything else, to such easily remedied conditions as faulty diet, lack of sufficient amount of the right kind of exercise, and unnecessary fatigue due to lack of sleep. Medical examination of any group of adults, apparently in good health, almost invariably reveals a minority enjoying exuberant health and a majority suffering from more or less serious disorders of one kind or another.

A leading woman's college, insisting that right health attitudes are essential in the development of personality, confronts all young women entering as students with questions such as these: Are your health habits good or bad? What is your attitude toward diet, posture, fatigue, relaxation, shoes, play, and recreation? Are you a physical "illiterate" or have you skills at your command? Have you developed ways of spending your leisure time wisely? What are your hobbies? A similar list, only more extended, might well be brought periodically to the attention of all adults.

A SIGNIFICANT PHASE OF EDUCATION.—So widely recognized have these considerations become in recent years that numerous colleges and other agencies such as the Y.M.C.A. and Y.W.C.A. have made education in health a primary element in adult education. Barnard College, for example, asserting that physical education is a phase of education, "education from a different point of view, but education nevertheless," indicates something of what it means to be physically educated in the following list of questions: "(1) Do you know your own strengths and weaknesses, your own potentialities? (2) Are your body mechanics good insofar as it lies within your power of accomplishment? (3) Do you know the food needs, rest needs, and the activity needs of your body? (4) Have you certain neuromuscular skills for use for pleasure, for relaxation, for safety? (5) Do you know how to live so as to function at your *optimum* as well as at your maximum? (6) Have you at your command the necessary facts regarding your body and its functioning and can you apply these facts? (7) Have you valuable knowledge regarding sports and games and physical activities—knowledge of values, as well as knowledge of rules and techniques? (8) Have you formed certain mental, physical, and emotional habits which will enrich your living? (9) Have you acquired the proper attitudes toward play, health, recreation, relaxation, sportsmanship, and human relationships? (10) Have you acquired certain appreciations of these; also of music, art, and of social relationships which will make for finer living?"[12]

What is to be desired is not physical education as a supplement or addition to general education but, rather, co-education of body and of mind, the development of the two as an inseparable unity; an educational art exemplified in Greek education at its best in which physical culture and the culture of the mind were combined in an inseparable whole, in which having brought their bodies under the control of intelligence, they developed not only perfect physiques but the capacity of creative thought and a remarkably high degree of artistic expression.

AIMS OF PHYSICAL EDUCATION.—Some of the specific objectives that should determine a program of physical education for adults are such as these: (1) Development of right attitudes toward physical activity, interest in and appreciation of activity for its own sake as a foundation for good physical habits. (2) Activities that will develop and maintain a well-poised body, good muscle tone, proper organic functioning, and neuromuscular adjustment and control in the interest of bodily vigor and positive health. (3) Corrective exercises to remedy physical defects and handicaps. (4) Activities that will develop skills both of utilitarian value and productive of satisfaction and joy.

In our day new medical knowledge and scientific methods of treatment keep alive many physical weaklings and defectives who in earlier generations would have succumbed. The Greeks systematically exposed defectives to death. Today every resource of science is utilized to keep them alive. But merely to keep life in their bodies is not enough. The Christian ethic demands out of regard for their own happiness and usefulness to society and for the future welfare of the race that every available method shall be used to develop health and strength. Defective bodies tend to reproduce defectives. Note the physical types in evidence wherever crowds congregate—the flat chests, the stooped shoulders, the shuffling gaits, the protruding bellies, and the enormous girths. Human material of these kinds bodes no good for the future of the race. The prevalence of neurasthenia and of other neuroses, of habits of unnecessary anxiety, and the increase of minor mental disorders and of insanity, supply additional reasons for concern. Physical education cannot make short persons tall or oversized people small, but it can strengthen the physically enfeebled and reduce the flesh of the obese. It can straighten stooped shoulders, fill out the chest, give a good carriage, and impart animation, grace, and sprightliness to the walk. It can develop physical vigor, give muscular and nerve tone, improve respiration and the circulation of the blood, stimulate digestion, build right habits of bodily functioning, and create a foundation for emotional and mental health and vigor.

PHYSICAL EDUCATION PROGRAM.—The preliminary physical examinations of men called out by the draft of the Great War indicated that approximately one fourth of the young men of America were unfit for war service. Training camps by systematic training methods brought tens of thousands of men up to par, increased their weight, developed their muscles, straightened their backs, strengthened their heart and lung action, and otherwise contributed to bodily development. Such a program is quite as necessary for the service of peace as for the service of war.

Under some auspices there should be provided in every community a program or programs available to every adult including three principal elements: health teaching, physical activities, and recreation.

The instructional program should make provision for the teaching of facts, ideals, and habits. The facts presented should be simple, concrete, and practical, with a thoroughly scientific basis. Essential factual material is easily available in public health bulletins of the federal government, state and municipal agencies, and public welfare organizations. Adults need to be warned against quackery and fake health literature of which an immense amount is in circulation in free pamphlets and widely distributed books, and also against the specious, false advertising that prevails in newspapers, magazines, and radio broadcasts. The program should include as a minimum basis of health education the fundamental facts of personal hygiene, information on nutrition, foods, and balanced diets, and a practical working knowledge of the body and the mind. It should inculcate definite health standards and ideals, and should equip men and women with a knowledge of means of spending their leisure time in ways that contribute to health of body and mind.

The physical-activities program should offer regular, systematic activities adapted to the physical requirements of individuals. It should supply means of overcoming remediable physical defects and bad health habits. It should build bodily strength and vigor and provide the means of acquiring skills in sports, games, and rhythmical activities. In many cities physical-activities programs are offered by the Y.M.C.A. and the Y.W.C.A., and in some by industrial and business organizations. In smaller towns and villages they are all but universally lacking.

Finally, the recreational program should plan systematically for play and for the utilization of available recreational facilities.

MORAL AND RELIGIOUS VALUES OF RECREATION

For the purpose of our discussion it is not enough to establish the fact that the good life has a physical basis. It is of equal or perhaps greater importance to discover the positive moral and religious values which inhere in recreation. What significance does recreation have from the standpoint of adult Christian education?

INCREASED PHYSICAL EFFICIENCY.—The Christian religion requires men and women to live at their highest and best. The Christian life is the more abundant life not in any merely material sense but in terms of the functioning of the total personality. It brings to the individual this challenge: Are you going to drag through life only half alive—dull, drowsy, mentally stagnant, continually ailing in body, or are you going to keep yourself so mentally alert, so physically fit, so spiritually vibrant that you give the best self of which you are capable to everything that you undertake?

Mechanized work and the tension of competitive business tend to induce physical dullness and fatigue. These in turn generate care, worry, and despondency, thus lowering the bars of moral resistance. They undermine high thinking and efficient action. They prevent men and women from being their best selves and doing their best work. Play and recreation are effective means of overcoming fatigue and of restoring depleted energy. They are allies of rest and sleep in the ministry of physical and mental restoration. They revitalize the nerves and counteract the effects of the stress and strain of the shop and store and office. They are means of re-creation.

Differentiation should be made between recreation and amusement. Recreation involves the expenditure of energy, physical or mental, or both, although the exertion is pleasing and recuperative. Amusement requires little or no exertion, either physical or mental. Contributing as it does to relaxation it, as well as recreation, has an office to perform. For many life is so complex and so busy that what is most needed is not activity so much as complete relaxation. Forms of amusement are to be desired that offer relaxation without excitement and strain and without accompaniments that are morally objectionable.

ENRICHMENT OF LIFE.—A characteristic of our age is the definition of wealth in material terms. The degree of absorption of the American people in the production and acquisition of material goods probably exceeds that of any other nation or age. Many seem utterly indifferent to the aesthetic and the beautiful, and the fine arts are neglected by all except a few. "Into the task of making the world beautiful, of making life sweet and agreeable to those who live in it, but little of our energy is directed. 'So feverish and yet so mechanical, so interesting and yet so unlovely,' the age . . . subordinates living to the process of gaining a livelihood, regards artistic creation as a superfluous frivolity, and considers industry, commerce, inventions, and wealth the only serious occupations of men."[13] Many are they who are engaged in a mad striving for material gain, and members of the churches are but little if any different in this regard from the unchurched populace.

Recreation offers in some measure an opportunity for the cultivation of a love of beauty and an appreciation of the aesthetic, and to this extent opportunity for the spiritual refinement of life. It must be admitted that the forms of recreation which most generally prevail do little for the enrichment of life. Far too often they exalt the crude, the ugly, the bizarre; sometimes even the risque and the openly immoral. Instance the ordinary movie theaters, the cafés and taverns, the dance halls and roadhouses everywhere to be found. Even when class or club or guild within the local church essays the rôle of entertainer it is too often content with the crude, the cheap, and the tawdry, sometimes—be it said to its shame—descending almost to the vulgar. Sometimes also churches endeavor to capitalize the recreational interest by seeking to make it a source of financial income, joining in this way the ranks of the agencies that commercialize amusement.

But all this is not as it should be. It is the function of recreation to stimulate imagination and creativity, to add to the zest of living and to contribute variety and color, sweetness and beauty to life. It enlarges the range within which personality functions. It is required, as John Dewey says of play and art, "to take care of the margin that exists between the total stock of impulses that demand outlet and the amount expended in regular action. . . . [It keeps] the balance which work cannot indefinitely maintain. . . . [It is] required to introduce variety, flexibility, and sensitiveness into disposition."[14]

PRACTICE IN SOCIAL LIVING.—Play is essentially social. It creates a sense of fellowship, a feeling of togetherness and of relaxed congeniality. Certain group games and folk dancing perhaps more than anything else have these effects. The playing group tends to be fused into a consciousness of oneness on a plane of equality. Distinctions of class, of race, and of economic status tend to disappear in the common fellowship. Recreation, in thus teaching people to play together, is at the same time teaching them to live together harmoniously and cooperatively.

There is a growing tendency in recreational programs to consider the community as the unit, the attempt being to bring *all* the people together in a common interest, in neighborliness, and in understanding. Denominational divisions unfortunately make it impossible for the Church to do this with any large degree of effectiveness. A recreational program under some general auspices may make a significant contribution to the sense of community. For a large proportion of the people the activities of a consumers' cooperative and, in an industrial neighborhood, a labor union may be made to have this same value. To the extent that all such attempts are successful the spirit and essence of democracy is promoted and men and women are fitted to function as citizens of a real democracy.

DEVELOPMENT OF COMPLETE PERSONALITY.—Recreation in contributing in ways that have been indicated to physical health and vigor, to physical efficiency, to the widening of interests, and to the socialization of the individual aids in the development of complete personality. But it is within its power to aid also in other ways. In the life of the child play is the principal instrument of growth. It has been declared by psychologists that without play there would be no normal cognitive life, no healthful development of affective life, and no virile development of volition. In what play does for the child may be seen an index of its possible contribution to the adult. There are many occupations in which adults engage so routine and restricted in their nature as to afford almost no opportunity for free expression, for initiative, or for individual decision. Recreation under conditions of freedom offers opportunity for manifold forms of expression. It is not too much to say that what men and women do in their leisure hours is a major influence in forming character and determining personality.

THE LIMITS OF RECREATION.—Without detracting from anything that has been said, we feel under the necessity of suggesting that it would be a serious mistake to put upon recreation a burden heavier than it can bear. The moral and religious values of recreation are real, but it is impossible for it wholly to redeem men and women from the curse of intolerable industrial conditions. There are conditions of labor in mills and mines, in factories and on farms, so contrary to all the demands of human nature as to be dehumanizing in their effects. With throat and lungs eaten by poisonous gases, other organs diseased by penetration of subtle chemicals, nerves worn to a ragged edge or bodies taxed to the point of utter exhaustion, it is folly to think that intermittent hours of leisure can repair the damage. To be truly creative leisure must be correlated with a work life that is other than destructive in its effects. Where an oppressive, exploitative economic system dwarfs and enfeebles the bodies of men and destroys their souls, no recreational program can provide salvation. Both social welfare agencies and the Church must recognize that the Coney Islands, taxi dance halls, moronic movies, burlesque shows, and saloons are effects as well as causes.

FORMS OF CREATIVE ACTIVITY

Marking our insistence on the moral and religious values of recreation, there are doubtless those who are disposed to ask for something more specific. What forms of recreation possess in any considerable degree the values that have been described? And what are their comparative values?

Doubtless, it has already become clear that we have been using the term "recreation" in a broader sense than is commonly understood. Included are not only the games played by adults—tennis, golf, gymnasium games, and such sports as fishing, canoeing, and others, but also all of the skills, crafts, and hobbies in which men and women find satisfaction and joy, together with the fine arts as avocations—music, painting, amateur photography, and many others. Many examples might be given. A teacher during his leisure hours does beautiful wood inlay work. Another makes French Provincial furniture. A minister is skilled in working with leather. A woman has become proficient in the art of Japanese flower arrangement and delights in teaching the art to others. A British Ambassador to the United States, himself skilled in handcraft, insists that almost anyone can, if he tries, become a first-class craftsman in some branch or other. He says, "Anyone of us taking up as a hobby, . . . carving in wood or stone, iron work, pottery making, stained-glass making, bookbinding, tapestry making, carpet weaving, and the like, . . . might become a really good craftsman and leave behind us something whereby we might be remembered."[15] He adds that one can contribute much to his own happiness and to the happiness of the world generally if he will learn not only to appreciate beautiful things but also to create them within the measure of his capacity. And the capacity exists. Who can doubt that in the American people there exists a vast reservoir of latent skill, skill in endless variety, as yet unborn or unused, but waiting to be developed?

Defined in broad terms, recreation has multitudinous forms. A study of the spare-time activities of one hundred and sixty adults, made as a part of the Cleveland Recreation Survey, revealed one hundred and eight different activities, of which some of the more popular were reading, attending theater, visiting, travel, music, walks or hikes, motoring, camping, and baseball. Some of the more important forms of recreation are conspicuous by their absence from this list. A more extensive survey would reveal a much larger list. Even this limited catalogue, however, covers a wide range of activities, some primarily intellectual, others aesthetic, others physical, yet others social, while still others cannot be so sharply classified. How can so many different activities be evaluated? The problem is too complex to permit within our necessary limits anything more than a partial and somewhat superficial consideration. For its complete solution far more extensive and thorough scientific study is required than has yet been made.

MUSIC AND THE FINE ARTS.—To an exceptional degree the fine arts fulfill the requirements of desirable leisure pursuits from the standpoint of individual and social development and well-being. They are permanently interesting; they afford opportunity as almost nothing else for release and relaxation; and under proper conditions they contribute directly to physical and mental health and to all-round personality development. There is an abundance of scientific evidence to substantiate the claim that music offers an effective integrative experience. Harry A. Overstreet tells of the effect produced when, having joined an orchestra, he first participated: "I can still recall what happened within me as, at the signal from the piano, we all fell to. It probably was pretty poor music, but for me it was a transporting experience. I seemed to be lifted into something beyond myself, to be swung along in a rhythm that made me suddenly powerful and free. . . ."[16] A chorus is also a significant means of fusing a crowd into a single unified whole.

Drama is one of the fine arts. In recent decades there has been a reawakening to its educational and social values. The making and production of a play offers an exceptional opportunity for the development of the spirit of cooperation and of the sense of inter-relationship. Consciousness of interdependence is created and realization of the common pursuit of a single aim.

While in the beginning of the new movement churches were slow to recognize the new evaluation of the drama, they have not been able to ignore the testimony of educators, and recent years have witnessed on the part of many a remarkable change of atti-tude. Something akin to impetuosity has characterized the turning to dramatic activities by some general organizations of the denom-inations and some local churches. The rapidity of the shift has not been without its unfortunate features. When drama fails to attain the artistic quality and the skill of the fine arts, its educa-tional value fails to be realized. Not that it is necessary for drama, in order to be educational, to be able to meet all the tests of a "finished" dramatic production, presented with the aid of elab-orate equipment and stage effects. On the contrary single, spon-taneous presentations with a minimum of stage setting and cos-tuming may be very effective. Often, however, it has happened that dramatic activities presented in local churches have been so mediocre, bizarre, and tawdry, so lacking in artistic quality, that for the participants they have been not only valueless as an educational experience but have offended and alienated persons of culture and refinement. A trained leadership in the use of drama is now being raised up by the churches. This is greatly needed. The service of drama and its continued use by the Church depends upon the skill and ethical discrimination of its sponsors. That it may be made one of the most significant and widely useful means of reli-gious education may not be doubted. That it may be given a fair chance to prove its value plays that are lacking in literary merit and crude in technique should be excluded. The church that can-not do a worthy thing in dramatic presentation had better forego public performances until at least a reasonable degree of discrimi-nation and skill have been developed.

HANDICRAFTS.—Another form of activity that offers unexcelled opportunity for education through creative leisure is handicraft work. So closely allied is it to the essence of play that the association of the term "work" with it may be fairly questioned.

Handicrafts fall into two general categories: those in which the man or woman plans and creates something needed by himself or those dependent upon him; and, second, those in which he patterns and fashions something not so much for utility's sake as for the sake of expressing a creative idea. Examples of the first classification, handiwork in which the craftsman makes what he himself or his family requires for use and uses what he makes are a dress, a tent, a canoe, a household utensil, or a dwelling house. Examples of the second are a wood inlay, a wrought iron shadow picture (a form of handiwork in which the Chinese excel), a wood carving, a lacquered bowl, a piece of embroidery, a vase of pottery, or any one of innumerable other works of art. The two categories are not sharply separated but merge, the one into the other. Such handicrafts offer an opportunity for one to invest his highest gifts of mind and his finest skill of hand, to test his powers, and in so doing really *to live*. A thought akin to this apparently was in the mind of the unknown ancient writer who closes the paragraph quoted at the beginning of this chapter with the significant words, "and in the handiwork of their craft is their prayer."

An advantage of handicrafts is that they can be used in adult education with persons of all levels of intelligence and formal schooling. There are many adults to whom book learning makes little or no appeal. They cannot be enlisted in classes for formal study or discussion, but they do find satisfaction in working with their hands. In the wide variety of possible handicrafts something can be found which everyone not only can do, but can do well enough to become for him a means of creative leisure. Moreover, handicrafts have strong potentialities of concomitant learnings. Enlist a person in a handicraft in which he is interested and he may readily be encouraged to make inquiry, to read, and to engage in discussion as means of widening his knowledge and increasing his skill.

Handicrafts often reveal unsuspected abilities. They are not only a means of developing latent skills, but also of leading the individual to discover latent powers of which he himself has been unconscious. Of all the services education can render to the adult few are greater than just this of self-discovery with consequent liberation of energies and building up of self-respect and self-confidence, qualities which widespread unemployment has destroyed in so many thousands of human beings. "I have been told by so many employers that they have no use for me that I had come to believe that I was of no use to anybody, including my family, and myself," said a middle-aged man who after a few weeks of encouragement and training became a skilled woodcarver producing articles of original beauty and of utility as well.

Increasingly handicrafts are being used as a therapeutic means, not only of bringing physically handicapped persons into better adjustments but also in the treatment of mental cases, as also are music, drawing, dramatics, and folk dancing. They have made an indispensable place for themselves in hospitals and sanitariums.

Finally, it should be emphasized that to work with his hands, patiently, affectionately, and skillfully with materials is a character-forming discipline of significant value. One of the serious counts against the profit economy is that its dominating motive stresses profit at the expense of quality, a fact illustrated by hundreds of items used in daily living, and emphasizes the price an article will bring rather than its intrinsic value, both of which have a subtle destructive influence upon character. In handicrafts respect for the object with which one is working steadily grows as the work proceeds. Concentration, patience, skill, self-control, the power to hold the ideal or pattern with which one began, likewise grow. And the growth of these constitute nothing less significant than the development of character and personality.

TEAM, GROUP, AND MASS GAMES.—In finding relaxation from the strain of factory, office, and household work group gymnastics are of marked value. They afford the muscular coordination, the big-muscle activity, and the stimulus to organic functioning so seriously lacking in the prevailing sedentary occupations. It is easy for adults thus engaged to lose motor ability to do many things natural in childhood and youth which may be regained within limits through group gymnastics, with an accompanying sense of physical well-being and increased strength and vigor, all of which are contributory to normal mental and social adjustments.

Worthy of inclusion among the arts is the folk dance, in which a growing interest has been manifest in America in recent decades. An outgrowth of the occupations and social ideals of the people, a means of free expression and of finding pleasure in rhythmic movements of the body, it has been in the past communal in nature, a way by which young and old, men and women of all occupations, gained an experience of social unity. In these respects it presents a marked contrast to the modern formal dance which has been aptly described as "a most unsocial phenomenon," reflecting that overstressing of the individual inherent in our competitive civilization and exhibiting some of its typical cruelties.   Even a heterogeneous crowd of sophisticated moderns may within a short time under skilled leadership be transformed by folk dances and games into a joyous community, happy in one another's company, having a good time together.   Folk dancing moreover is healthful exercise, giving as it does activity to the big muscles, stimulating the circulatory and respiratory systems and developing bodily freedom, coordination, and control.

EDUCATIONAL METHOD

The detailed discussion of method, particularly on the side of organization, is outside the limits of this book.   Certain general considerations, however, are necessary.

RECREATIONAL PROGRAM REQUIRED.—Impulse to play and capacity for re-creation are inborn in normal human beings.   But this inborn ability, as other inherent capacities, does not in the majority of adults find really creative expression without external stimulus and guidance.   Of this fact the prevailing forms of amusement and recreation offer convincing evidence.   If it is to find such expression, a recognized place in the educational program must be given to recreation.

Ideally the expression and satisfaction of creative impulse should be found in the daily round of vocational tasks.   Unfortunately, not only is this opportunity not afforded but physical and mental energies are so exhausted by routine that a dead weight of lethargy and indifference is encountered in any attempt to enrich unoccupied hours.   Attempts to enlist adults in such types of creative leisure as have been described are almost certain to be met with frank avowal of disinterest or the excuse, "We have no time." Movies, lodge meetings, card parties, and what not lend questionable credence to the plea.   Under these circumstances education through creative leisure, left to chance, will find small place in the lives of most men and women.   A well-planned program with the weight of the church's influence back of it can undoubtedly enlarge that limited place.

IMPORTANCE OF RIGHT STANDARDS.—The most significant contribution of the Church can perhaps be made at the point of the formulation and maintenance of standards for creative leisure in positive and constructive terms. The comparative uselessness of a merely negative attitude has long been demonstrated. People are the victims of the ill effects of harmful amusements and recreation, in part at least, because of lack of ideals. They indulge themselves blindly, unconscious of the moral and spiritual deterioration which they are undergoing.

Standards should involve tests such as these: Does a given form of recreation contribute to physical health and strength? Does it contribute to health recognized as mental and emotional as well as physical? Does the total personality—mind, emotions, and personality—find satisfaction in each activity? Does the program as a whole lend itself to complete integration with the educational program of the Church as a whole? Are the recreational activities offered sufficiently numerous and varied to appeal to all the adults of the church and make possible participation by all?

UTILIZE COMMUNITY RESOURCES.—Churches led to give consideration to the importance of education through creative leisure will in most instances find themselves apparently balked by limitation of means and facilities. Our discussion is not intended to carry the implication that the church itself is obligated to provide all of the necessary means and facilities. The problem is more one of conviction of need and of insight into the character of the program required by present conditions than one of facilities. Why build more buildings, gymnasiums, playgrounds, and other paraphernalia until available facilities are fully utilized? A group of parents and teachers prepared a list of available recreational facilities in their city—with surprising result. At the very least every church can know the worth-while recreational opportunities of its community and supply guidance to the men and women who through its influence are moved to utilize their free time in rewarding ways.

CHAPTER XII

LIFE IS THE CURRICULUM

AS discussion of the aims, content, and method of adult Christian education has moved forward it has become evident that what has been known in the past as the curriculum, in the light of the changing social and religious situation has taken on new and enlarged meaning. No longer does the aim of religious education inherited from the Protestant Reformation—to teach the Bible, as the authoritative Word of God, and Christian doctrine, the systematized truths of the Bible—prevail as a sufficient objective. No longer is curriculum to be conceived merely as a system of "lessons," a block or series of blocks of historical subject-matter divided into smaller blocks, "lessons," set out to be "learned."

When Christian education was regarded wholly as a process of instruction, principally instruction in a body of historical subject matter (the Bible) and in doctrines elaborated upon the basis of passages from the Bible, the curriculum naturally was thought of as a system, or organized body, of Bible lessons and lessons in doctrine. Now that Christian education is recognized to be the process of achievement, through continuous growth, of an integrated personality effectively functioning in the reconstruction of our present-day world into a Christian society, the concept of curriculum acquires new breadth and depth and richness of meaning.

THE PRESENT ADULT CURRICULUM.—Practice, as might be expected, lags far behind advanced theory. The adult curriculum actually in use in a majority of churches represents a carry-over from the past. It has not yet been modified to any considerable extent by recent developments in the theory of Christian education. As in the past probably the predominant purpose is that of imparting Biblical information. True, in many cases, this purpose is supplemented by other objectives, but the curriculum is still considered by the laity and by many ministers to be a system of study courses, in periodical or textbook form, made up of a consecutive series of blocks of material, or "lessons," to be studied. Right conduct is believed to result from the acquisition of knowledge of the Bible and its teachings embodied in "lessons." In order to assist this carry-over of knowledge to experience and conduct the "application" of the "lesson" is accompanied by a period of worship without any very clear or definite conception of relation between the two. Frequently the prayers contain a petition for divine aid in putting the "lesson" studied into practice.

In local churches in addition to adherence in practice to these traditional ideas such weaknesses may be observed as: (1) lack of clearly conceived, definite aims and objectives of the adult education program; (2) almost total lack of provision for social participation as a recognized part of the curriculum; (3) lack of appreciation of the place and values of worship as an integral part of the educational program; (4) a corresponding lack of recognition of the place and values of creative leisure-time and recreational activities; (5) duplication, overlapping, and competitive nature of organizations for adults within the church; (6) lack of recognition of the religious educational values of, and of any attempt at correlation with, extra-church community organizations and activities for adults; (7) lack of integration of the adult educational program with the total program of the church.

Certainly, the need for clear conceptions of the adult curriculum and of its method, organization, and content is very great.

WHAT IS THE CURRICULUM?

Much of the discussion of the foregoing chapters has direct bearing upon the nature, form, and organization of the curriculum. Let us undertake to make explicit some of the more important implications.

COMPLEXITY OF ADULT EXPERIENCE.—While in every age the experience of men and women has involved perplexing problems, never before has human life presented such complexity as today. Some of the complicating factors that characterize present-day living have been pointed out in an earlier chapter.* For most persons the number of these factors increase as the responsibilities of adult life come upon them. The vocational, avocational, and social experiences of individuals and groups are both more varied and complex than those of adolescents and far more so than those

_____
* See p. 106ff.

of children. This is a fact that has never yet been given due consideration in the planning of curricula. In practice the curriculum materials commonly offered adults represent a narrower range and less variety than those for either young people or children. It is essential that the complexity of adult experience shall be taken into account in planning adult curricula.

ALL EXPERIENCE OF RELIGIOUS SIGNIFICANCE.—Religion in the Christian sense, we have contended, is not tangential to life, but integral with life. It cannot be isolated, or restricted, to a single area of experience. Since persons according to the Christian view are of supreme worth, all experiences that in any way affect personality are of religious significance. All the activities and relationships of life are to be evaluated in terms of their effect upon persons. Every experience in life may be faced religiously and, this being done, is lifted to the religious level.[1]

This contention is re-enforced by the psychological principle of the unity of personality. In whatever one does the whole person is present. In many acts apparently only a partial reaction of the human organism is involved, but in truth the whole personality is affected, though in varying degrees. Just as in a sincere act of worship the whole man, the entire psychophysical organism, is involved, so also in as commonplace and mundane acts as eating one's breakfast and buying or selling the articles of food constituting a meal the moral and the spiritual aspects of personality are involved even as is the body. From this standpoint also there is no experience of everyday living that is without religious significance.

PRESENT EXPERIENCE OF PRIMARY CONCERN.—It is significant that Jesus seemed primarily concerned with the current needs in the lives of the persons with whom he came into contact. The same characteristic is seen in his teaching; most of it grew directly out of life situations or experiences of his hearers, and more often than not dealt with the understanding, control, and reconstruction of the experiences, and with the motives, purposes, attitudes, and conduct of the persons concerned. All of which suggests that the guiding clue in the construction of curricula is to be found within the experience of the individual and group. It is to be determined more by the present needs of persons than by preconceived conclusions as to the inherent worth of traditional materials.

In the past responsible curriculum makers have directed first attention to materials which they believed should be included in the curriculum because of their value *per se*. They have selected materials which declare a truth, enforce a duty, or exalt a virtue without inquiring whether as "lessons" they meet a present need of the particular individuals and groups expected to use them. This procedure followed, in many cases the "lessons" chosen have not connected in any significant way with live interests or crucial needs of the persons for whom they have been intended. Moreover, the assumption that the "teaching" will be stored away for use when a situation to which it is apropos presents itself has proven in practice to be for the most part ill-founded.

In contrast the procedure suggested in preceding chapters of our discussion is the exploration of the actual day-by-day experiences of persons for discovery of their needs as growing persons and as responsible participants in a progressively developing society. Particular experiences are selected to be dealt with because of the needs they reveal, their problematic character, or their strategic relation to major issues in personal growth and social progress.

This is not to suggest that while the curriculum centers in the present experience of individuals and groups, it should be wholly limited to it. Education involves the creation of problems and needs as well as the solution of those consciously present. The experience of many adults is impoverished by their environment and by the conditions under which they have been forced to live. What they need perhaps more than anything else is that their lives shall be broadened and enriched, that they shall be introduced to a new and different world offering new experiences, different in quality from anything previously known. In these cases the curriculum should be made the means of initiating desirable types of experience.

EXPERIENCES INVOLVING SOCIALLY SIGNIFICANT ACTIVITY ESSENTIAL.—The most educative experience for men and women is participation in processes of significant activity in which real issues are at stake. As men and women become conscious participants in vital social enterprises, growth, that is, education, takes place, and it is a question whether to any appreciable degree it takes place anywhere else. In other words, development in character and personality occurs as a by-product of participation in actual Christian living. "The moral person is not abstractly good, but good for something. He is a part of a busy, constructive, creative program. . . . The virtues are not treasures to be won, but attitudes toward the actual situations men and women have to face."[2]

The mere manipulation of ideas apart from participation in significant activity does not even prepare for participation in some indefinite future. What it does prepare for, if anything, is the kind of ineffective well-wishing that so often finds futile expression from the mouths of indifferent Christians. The ineffectiveness of presentation and manipulation of bare ideas and ideals lies in their failure to evoke response in action. "The question is sharply raised whether it is possible to teach morality and religion apart from the actual situations in which one is called to live his life morally and religiously. . . . If morality and religion are to be taught effectively, that is, so that they will function in the conscious and purposive direction of experience from within, they must be taught as an integral part of the responses that are made to day-by-day actual, concrete, and typical situations that life presents to the learner, with the relations, functions, and responsibilities that they involve."[3]

It is important to recognize in this connection that, in fact, the carry-over of a bare idea or ideal is impossible. What is presented as an idea is, in fact, always an idea in a given setting of persons, environment, institution, and occasion, from all of which the idea takes color, and to the total impact of which the person addressed responds to whatever extent response is made. It is the speaking person, as well as the idea to which he gives voice, the group and their attitudes, together with the larger setting of the whole in prevailing public opinion and in social situations, to which the person reacts.

It should also be realized that an intellectual interest may and often does directly connect with a socially significant experience. Activity is not to be conceived merely in physical terms, nor are life situations to be thought of only as involving physical activity. Intellectual interests, we need again in this connection to remind ourselves, are real life situations.*

A SUCCESSION OF ENTERPRISES OR PROJECTS.—When curriculum is conceived in these terms, in particular instances it takes the form of a succession of enterprises or projects rather than a logical arrangement of subjects or blocks of subject matter. Not that ideas, concepts, and different types of knowledge essential to

---

* See pp. 249f.

the growth and enrichment of experience are ruled out of the projects undertaken. By no means. They are definitely included, but primary emphasis is placed upon the carrying forward of enterprises, out of which social insights, social appreciation, social loyalties, and social habits may be developed. Study also is called for, but study in which information, ideas, and ideals are integrally related to problems which the projects present.

A reason for the project type of curriculum, in addition to those already suggested, is that it is difficult, if not impossible, to develop virtues in the abstract. It is possible to influence men and women to be just in given concrete situations, but in an attempt to teach justice as an abstract virtue there is no assurance of carry-over to concrete situations in daily living; in conscious practice of just acts there can be no question but what justice is learned.

Yet another reason why the experience type of curriculum is of special significance in our times, apart from the fact that didactic teaching has been so overloaded with dead wood of ritualized content, is that in a period of drastic social change the new experience cries for analysis, understanding, and guidance in the light of fundamental values.

INCLUSIVE OF ALL AREAS OF LIFE.—If it be true that all experience is of religious significance, it is important that the curriculum shall include experiences from the entire range of living. This also is a principle which finds illustration in the example of Jesus. In his teaching he dealt with situations from practically every area of life.[4] If the whole of life is to be Christianized, the curriculum of Christian education cannot stop short of including all areas and activities of living within its scope.

Our discussion in earlier chapters has emphasized the moral and spiritual importance of the economic area. It is doubtless at this point that exception will be taken. Justification for including the area of economic relations in the curriculum of religious education is found in the fact that all economic conduct involves human welfare. "In every bargain that I make, in every article that I use or consume, I traffic in human energies as well as in things; I relate myself to the health and happiness of men and women whom I have never seen; I take part in making their children what they become."[5] A second objection is that the inclusion of experiences from such areas as the economic, health, and vocation tends to make the curriculum of religious education identical with that of general education. All education, whether general or religious, has to do with the whole of life. The distinction is found in the difference in objectives and goals, in motivation, in interpretation of experience and in frame of reference.

WITHIN THE LEARNER'S RANGE OF CAPACITY.—By general agreement one of the greatest advances made in religious education in recent decades is the recognition of the right of those of limited capacity to be provided with curricula within the range of their interests, needs, and capacities. The principle has been chiefly applied in terms of capacity as defined by age, that is, that curricula for kindergarten children, for example, shall be determined by the capacities of children of four and five years. But the principle also applies to capacity defined in other terms than age. In an organized curriculum the materials and activities selected should be within the range of the capacity and the experience of the learners. The members of an adult group in their relations within the family, the church, the community, vocational associations, and elsewhere confront a wide variety of situations. For them grading involves the selection of experiences in terms of the groups' capacity to master them, with provision for progression as understanding and the ability to deal effectually with situations grows.

PLANNED TO INCREASE SOCIAL INTELLIGENCE.—It is of special importance, in view of the new situation, that the curriculum of adult education include activities that will quicken social insight and increase social intelligence. Materials are required that will equip men and women more clearly to understand, appreciate, and evaluate changes that are under way; the forces that are compelling these changes, and in relation to them to act in the interest of the common welfare.

To produce the kind of intelligence required for the building of a Christian world religious education must lead men and women to acquaint themselves with all those economic, political, and other conditions that violate the spirit of love and brotherhood, and on the positive side with all the contemporary enterprises that have been undertaken in behalf of social welfare, social justice, a cooperative economic order, and a world society. In many instances the point of beginning may well be a study of social conditions, institutions, and economic and political practices within the immediate community. The need for this is obvious. Do the men and the women of our churches know the conditions under which their fellow members and neighbors labor in stores, factories, and other industrial establishments—the hours of labor, wages received, conditions of light and heat and ventilation, sanitary conditions, the profits made by the owners on the bona fide investment of capital? Do they know the inside working of the municipal government? Do they know the facts concerning juvenile delinquency and how juvenile offenders are dealt with? For many, these and similar elementary facts represent an almost wholly unexplored area.

INCLUDING PARTICIPATION IN SOCIAL RECONSTRUCTION.—The exploration of issues and acquainting minds with facts is not enough. The way to build a new world is to begin building. If basic structural changes in the economic order are to be achieved by peaceful means, there must be action by Christians within the existing order consciously aimed at effecting change. While local churches as such doubtless should not sponsor group experiments or specific projects of economic reconstruction, they can and should encourage their members as Christians to do so, at the same time making explicit and clear the principles to be followed.

LIFE IS THE CURRICULUM.—What, in the light of these principles, is the curriculum? "Fundamentally," as Coe has said, "the curriculum is a course of living, not a course in supposed preliminaries to real life."[6] Or, as Bobbitt has stated, "the current activities of high-grade living twenty-four hours each day, and seven days each week are the curricula."[7] In the broadest sense the experiences of persons, whether as members of the Church or as members of the community, in the whole range of relationships and activities of life, constitute the curriculum of adult education.

However, a definition as broad as this is not applicable when Christian education is considered as an organized process, into which the element of guidance enters. It fails also to make clear that certain situations, experiences, and activities have greater significance for Christian education than others. In this more limited sense the total educational program is the curriculum. The Church's curriculum of Christian education for adults consists of experience under guidance for the accomplishment of desired ends, namely, "all the activities and enterprises which the Church provides, uses or recognizes for the purpose of contributing to the religious welfare of men and women and the moral and spiritual improvement of group life."[8] It includes experiences of fellowship, of worship, of study and discussion, of stewardship, of participation in the Christian missionary enterprise, and of all projects sponsored by the Church for the common welfare, for social reconstruction, and the building of the Kingdom of God.

ANALYSIS OF EXPERIENCE

Obviously, if life is the curriculum, Christian education ideally should deal with all the experiences of life for their reconstruction and enrichment in terms of Christian principles, values, and ideals. But this is impossible. The Church as the agency of formal Christian education under the limitations that determine its program cannot deal with more than a fraction of total experience.

The importance of religion entering all areas of living as a factor for definition of values and control of conduct, and of Christian education actually dealing with experiences distributed throughout all areas, has been previously emphasized.* How may it be assumed that this will be done? How can it be guaranteed that the curriculum shall include experiences selected from the total range of everyday living?

The wide variety of experiences embraced within adult living on first thought seems to present such diversity as to defy analysis. Moreover, the totality of experience includes not merely objective situations but also a wide range of subjective experiences—wishes, feelings, values, ambitions—the whole content, in fact, of the inner life. And it is with the total experiencing person, not merely with objective situations and responses that Christian education has to do. A clue to possible analysis, however, is found in the fact that most experiences fall within the two broad general classifications of functions and of relationships. A man or woman as a person has a wide variety of functions; daily living is made up in large part of activities which are functional. Besides, every person is more than an individual; he is a member of various groups—the family, for example, and among others the community, the nation, and the world. Out of these relationships a wide variety of experiences springs, experiences having to do with relations of individuals to individuals, individuals to groups, groups to groups.

CLASSIFICATION OF FUNCTIONS.—It is probably impossible to

* See pp. 171ff.

differentiate functional areas in any thoroughly satisfactory way. Every specific unit of experience is complex, so complex as to defy simple classification. Moreover, every experience runs into or overlaps other experiences in such ways as to make separation or isolation for the purpose of exact classification impossible. Various schemes of "categories," "divisions," or "areas" have been used, none of which is entirely satisfactory.[9] The following classification based upon that suggested by the Educational Commission of the International Council of Religious Education is perhaps as satisfactory as any that may be suggested:

1. *Specifically religious activities.* In a special and unique sense religious, such as cultivating religious insights; practicing the presence of God; attending church services and participating in public worship.

2. *Health activities.* Activities upon which physical well-being depends; mental attitudes, understandings, appreciations, and skills related to physical and mental health.

3. *Intellectual activities.* Activities involved in mental development and efficiency, cultivating native gifts, broadening the mental horizon, increasing the range of interests, deepening insight into life—its meaning and worth.

4. *Economic activities.* Activities involved in the business and economic relationships of everyday living, use of money, purchase and sale of goods; use of commodities; relations to production and consumption.

5. *Vocation.* Functions involved in vocation—duties, obligations, and responsibilities pertaining to vocation; creative activity in developing vocation, making it increasingly vital and serviceable.

6. *Citizenship.* Functions as a citizen—duties, obligations, and responsibilities; using citizenship creatively in the interest of a more Christian social order.

7. *Recreation.* Use of leisure time; making play recreative; ways and means of amusement.

8. *Sex, parenthood and family life.* Function of reproduction; maintaining a sane, wholesome sex life; duties, obligations, and responsibilities of life as a member of the family.

9. *Friendship.* Relations with intimate, friendly associates; activities in being a friend; maintaining wholesome friendships, using friendship creatively.

10. *Aesthetics.* Appreciating, cultivating, and enjoying the beautiful.

11. *General life in the group.* Functions and activities involved in membership in various special social groups; using group relationships creatively.

CLASSIFICATION OF RELATIONS.—For the most part the relations involved in normal adult living may be classified under the following categories: (1) personal relations; (2) family relations; (3) church relations; (4) neighborhood relations; (5) wider-community relations. The experiences with which Christian education is concerned arise in the exercise of the several functions listed above within these various relationships.

A TYPICAL ANALYSIS OF ADULT EXPERIENCE

A large number of concrete situations within each of the areas named above is involved in adult living. That the extent of opportunity and responsibility of adult religious education may be more clearly realized we shall attempt a sample listing of adult experiences within a typical area.[10] Since specific objectives emerge most clearly and definitely out of actual life-situations it is not possible in connection with such an analysis to do more than supply a tentative statement of objectives.

No attempt is made to present anything more than a typical list of experiences within the selected area. Limitations of space would prevent presenting a complete list, even if it were otherwise possible. It is not possible. Data do not exist for a scientifically complete list of life situations within any given area. Such a list complete and accurate today would be incomplete and inaccurate tomorrow. Typical situations are construed in terms of being crucial from the standpoint of their Christian significance, and of being difficult of control in a Christian manner. Typical situations such as these may not be said in themselves to constitute the curriculum. They are curriculum material in the sense that they may be used as a means of uncovering actual life situations of the members of an adult group. In Christian education it is of first importance to discover and utilize actual experiences of members of the teaching-learning group. The list may be of value also in suggesting the variety and range of experiences with which adult religious education may deal, and with which it must deal if religion is to be related to the total area of living.

ADULT EXPERIENCE WITHIN THE AREA OF ECONOMIC ACTIVI-
TIES.—1. *Personal relations:* (a) Relation to employer or to employees. (b) Source of income of employer (individual or corporation). (c) Amount of salary in proportion to salaries of other
workers (including basis of determination). (d) Distribution
(use) of income. (e) Investment of savings. (f) Relation of consumer to producer, or of producer to consumer. (g) Division of
the consumers' dollar. (h) Proportion of return, as "profit" to
capital. (i) Adulteration of products. (j) Purchase and use of
products of child labor. (k) Purchase and use of products of
sweated labor. (l) Lack of economic security; unemployment;
business reverses; strikes; wages; working conditions; collective
bargaining; arbitration.

2. *Family relations:* (a) Joint account and distribution of
responsibility for expenditures. (b) Wife and children employed.
(c) Allowances to children. (d) Accounting for expenditures. (e)
Family councils on expenditures (budget). (f) Expenditures on
the home: furniture; labor-saving equipment; library, etc. (g)
Investing in education of children. (h) Personal belongings of
members of the family. (i) Wages of servants in the home and
of laborers serving the home.

3. *Church relations:* (a) Support of the Church; stewardship;
systematic giving; proportion of income. (b) Contributing to missions and other church benevolences. (c) Special contributions,
church building, special causes. (d) Attitude and expression of
the Church on economic questions. (e) Salary of pastors. (f)
Salary of employees of the Church. (g) Taxation of church property. (h) The Church as employer and investor.

4. *Neighborhood relations:* (a) Support of community enterprises. (b) Payment of taxes (income tax; property tax; personal
property taxes; special assessments). (c) Public opinion on economic problems. (d) Community attitude toward wage-earners.
(e) Salaries of public officials. (f) Poverty in the community. (g)
Family breakdown under economic stress.

5. *Wider-community relations:* (a) Public opinion on the distribution of wealth. (b) Public attitude on labor unions. (c)
Tariff barriers between nations.

OBJECTIVES WITHIN THE AREA OF ECONOMIC ACTIVITIES.—The
general objective of Christian education within the area of economic activities may be agreed to be substantially this: To develop

a growing insight into the meaning of work and an appreciation of its possible contribution to the development of personality; to develop a realization that the principles and ideals of the Christian gospel apply as fully within the area of economic activities as within any other area of living; to inspire a growing purpose to make all labor creative, so far as is humanly possible, and to do away with all aspects of economic activities and relationships that are destructive of human values; to develop a growing understanding of the Christian uses of money, property, and the industrial process, and a corresponding purpose to conform personal and social action thereto; to replace the motive of private profit by that of service, and the method of competition by cooperation; to make all economic activities and relationships serve the common good.

A tentative statement of *specific objectives*, it may probably be agreed, should include among many others the following: (a) Knowledge of the economic requisites of physical and moral health.   (b) Acquaintance with the social results of poverty.   (c) Acceptance of the principle of the supreme value of personality and the consequent dominance of personal rights over property rights.   (d) A growing ethical insight and discrimination in particular situations.   (e) A willingness to sacrifice to help less fortunate and needy persons.   (f) Making investments in particular cases in the spirit of service.

CURRICULUM AND METHOD

Curriculum, we have said, is experience under guidance for the achievement of desired ends.   Method may be said to be the ways by which resources are utilized to achieve ends.   In terms of religious education method may be defined as ways of reconstructing experience to accomplish desired moral and religious ends.

CURRICULUM AND METHOD INSEPARABLE.—Thus defined, it becomes impossible sharply to differentiate curriculum and method.   The one merges into the other until they are seen to be inseparable.   In content the curriculum of Christian education consists of experiences of everyday living undergoing reconstruction; while from the standpoint of method it consists of the procedures by which these experiences are reconstructed.   Teacher material, in form, is not merely subject matter to be taught; it is also guidance in method: guidance in assisting the teacher to locate significant experiences, in determining objectives, in discovering possible ways of reconstruction, including source materials, and in evaluating outcomes. Daily, persons utilize thought and effort in directing their resources and manipulating materials to achieve desired results. Good method is that which with maximum efficiency utilizes available resources to achieve desired objectives.

Curriculum thus conceived as including both content and method is not less concerned with one than with the other. If either becomes its exclusive or even predominant concern, curriculum becomes one-sided and comparatively ineffective. Experience, whether present or past, without method of interpretation and enrichment, lacks meaning and result. When method is made the exclusive object of concern, it becomes mechanical and increasingly nonproductive.

Able religious leaders in the past have given much attention to the preparation of adult courses and textbooks under the impression that content thus prepared and set-out-to-be-learned alone constitutes worthful curriculum, ignoring the fact that the lives of the men and women for whom the "lessons" were written contain reservoirs of content in day-by-day experiences which remain neither understood nor utilized, and that what these persons most need are methods of making the most of the resources they have ready at hand.

Others have given themselves to organization, methods, and devices of adult work, reducing religious education to the level of mechanics, oblivious of the complex and difficult experiences amid which men and women flounder and, almost equally, of the importance of acquainting them with rich experiences of the past in the light of which their problems may be solved and their lives guided. Curriculum to be of major effectiveness must concern itself both with content and method.

RELATION OF THE TEACHER TO CURRICULUM AND METHOD.—
When curriculum is conceived as experience undergoing guidance, the teacher's rôle, as already stated, becomes far more than that of a lecturer or instructor in printed lessons. He is the counselor and guide of the adults with whom he is associated as teacher in all phases of their experience. He concerns himself in cooperating with the members of his group in carrying through those activities which promise most in achieving desired objec-

tives in character and personality. He does not merely take subject matter more or less arbitrarily prescribed by tradition and administrative arrangements and make it the subject of "explanation," "exposition," and "application." Instead, he cooperates with men and women in exploring their experiences, analyzing them, considering their possible outcomes, seeking light and help from past experience, determining courses of action, and trying out these chosen paths.

The teacher's responsibility extends beyond the range of present experiences of the members of his group. His method involves bringing about conditions under which enrichment and control of experience are possible. Although, since he is dealing with adults, he may not have the same opportunity of leading his class members into new experiences as has the teacher of children, he should consider the extent to which this is possible and attempt to do it whenever needed to whatever extent is possible.

In addition to enlarging the range of experience, it is the teacher's part to help people to sense the significance of the experiences they are undergoing, raising problems which they do not sense of their own accord, guiding them to the sources of wisdom, or giving them the information which they need to solve their problems intelligently or to engage in projected enterprises successfully.[11]

RELATION OF THE LEARNER TO CURRICULUM AND METHOD.—With curriculum and method thus interpreted, the adult learner has a largely increased share in the determination of both. Under the former procedure the curriculum was authoritatively determined by others and handed over to the learner to be appropriated. Under the new procedure the learner ceases to be a passive recipient of the content of the curriculum and becomes a determining factor in relation both to curriculum and method. "Since knowledge is the primary factor in the control of experience, method is chiefly determined by the way in which knowledge emerges from experience in the form of organized meaning and by the way in which it re-enters experience as a factor of control. The acquiring of clear and complete concepts is only the first step in the learning process. The vastly more important part of the learning process is the acquisition on the part of the learner of the insights and skills by which such concepts become effective in the control of character and conduct."[12]

Method is of special concern to the adult learner because in a much more marked degree than in the case of children the responsibility is upon him to learn the best ways of accomplishing desirable objectives. "This involves certain ways of meeting situations of one type, and other ways of meeting those of a different type. It involves the ability to recognize the factors in a situation, the ability to gather and utilize data which are necessary for the most effective meeting of situations—it involves, in brief, the learning of the shortest road toward the discovery and attainment of a desirable goal."[13] Children may not be expected to possess these personal resources in large measure, nor can it be said that all adults are conscious of their possession. At least, in tactful ways they should be reminded that they are expected through the years to have developed such resources; otherwise, how do the passing years contribute to skill in living? At any age the practice of turning one's mind upon one's own experience may be begun, and even old dogs may learn new ways of performing and thereby of gaining desired rewards.

TYPES OF METHOD.—With method recognized as an essential element of curriculum the question of the range or scope of the adult curriculum becomes in part one of extent and variety of method types to be utilized. In a particular instance choice of method will depend upon judgment, based upon experience, as to the way in which the experience undergoing reconstruction may be dealt with most fruitfully. Among the major emphases of our discussion to this point which may be conceived as types of method are the following: (1) Choice of central motive and purpose, a basic essential in Christian education.* (2) Christian fellowship, an exceedingly potent means of creating atmosphere, remaking attitudes, deepening purpose, changing conduct, and thus developing personality.† (3) Worship, a means of bringing impulses, desires, and purposes in line with that central purpose which the Christian understands to be the will of God.‡ (4) Wholehearted purposive activities, preferably self-initiated, in which men and women may express Christian purpose in planning, carrying out, and evaluating enterprises believed to be significant in building a Christian social order.§ (5) Formal instruction as a means of

* See pp. 152, 164f.
† See pp. 49, 203, 235.
‡ See pp. 204, 208.
§ See pp. 237ff.

acquainting adults with important information and significant knowledge.* (6) Group discussion as an effective means of stimulating reflective thinking in problem solving.† (7) Educative recreation and play as significant ways of utilizing leisure time in development of personality and social attitudes.‡

Other types of method also have been briefly discussed. When all have received consideration it will be realized that, again, from the standpoint of method, the curriculum of Christian education is as broadly inclusive as life itself. Every enterprise and process which deserves a place within the organized life of the church, and every activity and influence within the total life of the community which the church may utilize in developing personality, will be recognized as a part of the total curriculum. Not only the teaching of Bible "lessons" but the sermons, the pastoral calls, participation in choir or choruses, the social events under church auspices so far as they present opportunities of fellowship and service, plans of recreation—all, so far as they are or may be made educational in the Christian sense, are included within the curriculum.

METHOD WITHIN THE AREA OF ECONOMIC ACTIVITIES.—Recurring to the analysis of adult experience within a typical area—the economic—question may be raised as to types of method applicable to a particular area such as this. A program of adult Christian education within the area of economic activities may include: (1) The formulation of a code of Christian principles for business and industry. (2) The study of biographies of men who have used business and industry as means, not of private gain, but of development of personality. (3) The cultivation of a spirit of worship in the carrying forward of socially motivated economic experiments. (4) The discussion in church-school groups of problem situations in economic activities. (5) The undertaking of community projects involving the application of Christian principles to particular economic activities. (6) Projects involving the attempt to create public opinion and to influence existing public opinion on such subjects as labor organization, the right of collective bargaining, the international influence of high protective tariffs, minimum wage for women, the abolition of child labor; the organization

---

* Chap. IX.
† Chap. X.
‡ Chap. XI.

and promotion of a consumers' cooperative, or a producers' cooperative; the organization and promotion of a credit union.

CHOICE OF METHOD.—How, in a particular instance, is choice of method to be made? Effective method may not be determined either arbitrarily or by rule. It grows out of insight into and analysis of the nature of the situation. What are the needs of the men and women concerned? What are their problems, both those of which they are keenly conscious and those which are not isolated and defined? What are the areas of living to which religion has not been related? What are the day-by-day experiences which should be enriched by Christian meaning or remade after a more truly Christian pattern? It is in the light of answers to such questions that adults should make choice of method in a specific instance.

The responsibility of the leader to guide the group in the selection of lines of activity that challenge real interest, purposive participation, and wholehearted effort is one that tests both his ethical acumen and his skill in leadership. To what needs and problems are the members of the group sensitive? To what neglected and overlooked areas can they be made sensitive? How overcome the traditions, prejudices, taboos, and plain ignorance which defines the limits of curriculum in terms of prescribed blocks of Bible verses? These and other similar questions to which no ready-made answers can be given emphasize the difficulty of the leader's task.

NEED FOR IMPROVED METHOD.—The time is at hand in the life of the evangelical churches when all religious leaders, not only those in official positions but all pastors and lay leaders, should realize keenly the utter necessity for improved method in Christian education. The comparative ethical failure of those methods and procedures upon which the churches have relied in the past, the inclusion within the membership of large numbers of people whose ideals and practice are no whit higher than those of multitudes outside, the widespread failure of religion to function effectively in the conduct of men in their commercial, industrial, social, and political relationships, within the local community, the nation, and in international affairs, as evidenced by destructive, conflict-breeding competition, injustices, oppressions, dishonesty, greed, and corruption so generally prevalent—all emphasize the imperative need for improved method if organized Christianity is to do its part in the development of a better order.

CURRICULUM AND SUBJECT MATTER

The dominance of subject matter in the curriculum in the past requires consideration of the question of the place it should occupy in the present-day curriculum of adult Christian education.

WHAT IS SUBJECT MATTER?—It is important, first, to clarify the concept. Historical subject matter is recorded experience. At some time—yesterday, last year, or perhaps five thousand years ago—it was alive, an integral part of present, vital experience. It lived in the thought, the purpose, the feeling, and the deeds of a living, acting person or group of persons.

When once this is clearly realized, there does not seem to be any good reason to consider subject matter as limited to past recorded experience. Neither the time element nor the fact of the recording of the experience is especially significant, although the recording of a particular experience doubtless means that at the time it seemed specially important. Present experience would seem to possess quite as good a claim to be considered subject matter and to be utilized as subject matter as a recorded experience of thousands of years ago. Only the quality, the value, of an experience gives it significance.

Viewed as experience subject matter is of different kinds. It may be a segment of the present life-stream of the individual, or of the common experiences of the group. It may be a segment of the past experience of the individual or the group. It may be a block of systematized, recorded knowledge (historical subject matter), a segment of race experience which is a part of the heritage from the past of the living generation.

PRESENT EXPERIENCE AS SUBJECT MATTER.—The first or primary type of subject matter is the present life-stream of the learner. It may be said to be made up of a succession of life situations within the various areas defined by the relations and functions of his life as it is being lived. Concerning the significance and value of present experience, and the necessity—if religious education is to be effective either in forming individual character or in reconstructing the social order—of dealing with the actual situations of day-by-day living, our discussion already has had much to say. All that has been said applies to present experience as subject matter, and need not be repeated.

PAST EXPERIENCE AS SUBJECT MATTER.—The second type of

subject matter is constituted of the past experience of the learner and of other living persons—experience which has not yet become historical subject matter. It is the net result in knowledge, attitudes, habits, and skills acquired by the learner in the process of living, and the results of others' living accessible to him. It is evident that this type of subject matter is more abundant and reliable in the case of adults than of children and young people. For those who have lived a rich, abundant life it is a resource of very great significance, capable of much larger and varied use than it has had in traditional practice.

PAST EXPERIENCE OF THE RACE AS SUBJECT MATTER.—The third type of subject matter is constituted of the experiences of past generations of men. While conditions under which we live our lives today are in various respects different from those of former times, many of the relations and functions of life are identical or similar. Many of the problems faced today have been faced by successive generations of mankind. The outward aspects of the life of society have greatly changed, but many of the typical, basic experiences of individual and group living are much the same. The record of the religious experience of former generations is accessible in sacred literature, art, architecture, customs and institutions, and other forms of record, constituting a vast repository of invaluable subject matter.

FUNCTION OF SUBJECT MATTER.—In a given learning-teaching situation all three of the types of subject matter described may be utilized: factors in the situation undergoing reconstruction; unrecorded experiences of the learner and of other persons; and past experience in the form of systematized records.

The function of subject matter thus comprehensively defined is that of re-entering experience as an element of enrichment, reconstruction, and control. It is utilized not as so much information or knowledge to be acquired and stored away for possible future use, but is immediately and directly related to the ongoing process of life, utilized as a means whereby living becomes different from what it has been in the past or what it otherwise would be in the future.

While this is a different conception of the nature and function of subject matter than has commonly prevailed in the past, it is one which gives it much wider, more practical, and more dynamic use.

PLACE OF THE BIBLE IN THE ADULT CURRICULUM.—The Bible entered into our national history and influenced the early development of our American institutions in unique ways. While it was not always intelligently used, there are few historians who question the power of its influence. Nor is its service yet complete. The men and women of today need to know the Bible. They need the consciousness of God in their lives and in the life of the nation which it inspired in men of earlier generations. They need the quickening of social conscience which it is capable of creating. They need the moral courage, and the faithfulness in service to humanity which many in the past have drawn from it. Because of the lack of these qualities which many possess, their lives are poorer than they need be, and they are far less useful to the Church and to society than otherwise they would be. All of which gives point to the statement that more effective ways of drawing upon the resources of the Bible for personal enrichment and growth, and for stimulus in social progress, are sorely needed.

Does an experience curriculum as we have described it offer such a new and significant approach? Many hold that it does. Under wise and skillful use, it is confidently believed, a more penetrating study of the Bible and a more vital appropriation of its values for life and living may be secured than in any other way.

Viewing the matter superficially this may not seem to be the case. To some doubtless it will always seem, because a block of Bible verses is not week by week set out to be learned, that the Bible is being displaced. But are these "lessons" in any real sense "learned" by any large proportion of those for whom they are rather blindly prescribed? An idol would be shattered for many people if they could be brought to realize, first, that the selection of these Bible lessons in systematized form is made on the basis of presuppositions which, however deeply they may be ingrained in the minds of those who make the selection, exist scarcely at all in the minds of most of the younger adults of those for whom the selection is made; second, that the organization of these Biblical materials is in accord with a principle or interest which may be, and often is, extrinsic to the lessons themselves; and third, that these Bible lessons are always accompanied by interpretative notes upon which major attention is usually centered instead of upon the Bible text. In contrast with this procedure an experience curriculum guides the learner directly to the Bible in an intensive first-hand effort to discover what it has to offer in the carrying forward of his plan, the solution of his problem, or the remaking of his experience.

USE OF OTHER HISTORICAL SUBJECT MATTER.—What is true of the Bible is also true of various other types of historical subject matter. It has been found, for example, that the carrying forward of a project in some instances has utilized material which in the traditional subject classification would be located under ten or twelve different heads. In other words, while subject matter no longer constitutes the exclusive content of the curriculum, the conclusion is not to be drawn that it is depreciated or overlooked.

Doubtless early attempts in the use of an experience curriculum leave much to be desired in perspective, balance, and comprehensiveness. First attempts do not often produce finished results. There is nothing in the theory of the experience-centered curriculum as such which necessitates lack of balance or perspective. On the contrary a primary characteristic is its breadth of scope as compared with a subject curriculum. It is as broad as life, as comprehensive as human experience.

Nor do these qualities of breadth and comprehensiveness compel an atomistic curriculum. They make such a result possible; probably even tend in that direction, but by no means necessitate it. If examples may be found which suggest a mosaic of relatively isolated units of experience, the whole apparently destitute of design, integration, or unity, they should serve as demonstrations of what an experience curriculum should not be. They certainly do not illustrate what need be or should be.

The experience curriculum affords the adult leader an opportunity of different kind and extent than he has had hitherto—the chance, without feeling that he is violating the rules of the game or departing from a prescribed path, of seizing upon a burning interest, a crucial test, a baffling problem at the very hour it emerges in consciousness and dealing with it on the spot. What teacher who has realized such an opportunity and taken full advantage of it has not felt a sense of achievement which has given "teaching" an entirely new significance in his thinking? Certainly, there is a tremendous advantage from the standpoint of vital, dynamic teaching in the full opportunity given by the experience curriculum of dealing first-hand with immediate life situations.

ORGANIZATION OF THE CURRICULUM

The primary purpose of organization within the Church is to provide the conditions under which Christian education as an organized process may be most effectively carried on. It is a means of control and guidance. Thus defined organization becomes a form of method; one might almost say indistinguishable from method. Much of what has been said above under method is equally applicable, therefore, to organization.

THE PROBLEM OF ORGANIZATION.—It becomes evident at this point that the problem of organization of the curriculum for effective adult Christian education is a difficult creative task. Organization is to be determined by its purpose, the maximum contribution to the development of Christian personality and of a Christian society. The criteria for judging organization is the extent to which it serves this purpose. This much is clear. Difficulty arises from the fact that all the activities of living have some relation to this objective. The major proportion of these activities are entirely outside the scope of possible planning and direction of the church. Many are planned and directed by more or less closely related agencies such as the Y. M. C. A., the public library, women's clubs, "service" clubs, social welfare agencies, and many others. Is the adult curriculum of the church to be thought of as merely one of these many programs? Or is it to be conceived as a comprehensive program including those of all closely and loosely affiliated agencies? If the latter, is the church to limit its specific activities to areas neglected by these other agencies, or is it to overlap by duplicating some activities? To what extent should the church relate itself to these other agencies in order to influence the determination of their activities in accord with its great objective? How should it proceed in order to make its influence most effective?

An extended discussion of these questions is probably more properly in place in a book on the organization and program of the church. Here, at least there should be recognition that they are involved in the problem of organization of the curriculum, and not to be sharply separated. Also the judgment should be recorded that for the church to plan its curriculum in such highly specialized terms that within its program are included only activities not offered by any other agency would unduly limit and restrict it, and almost inevitably in the course of time narrow the popular conception of its function.   On the other hand, to plan a program which takes account of all activities of all educational and social agencies, provides for all neglected areas, and completely integrates the whole, is usually undesirable if not impossible.   Practical possibility would seem to lie between the two extremes.

EXPLORATION OF NEEDS.—In any event the point of beginning in organizing the adult curriculum is an exploration of the interests, needs, and capacities of the adult constituency.   In the past attention has been almost wholly centered upon "lesson courses." Unbelievable as it is, practically the one question considered has been: Shall a particular group use the "Uniform Lessons," or "an elective course," and if the latter, which of a limited list of electives?   If the problem of organizing the adult curriculum is to be seriously attacked, the horizon of exploration must be immensely widened and the point of beginning must be not alone historical subject matter but the subject matter of individual and group experience.   Such questions as these must be asked: What are the problems and issues which are proving particularly baffling in the experience of the men and women of this church and its constituency?   What are the issues around which local interest and discussion are now centering?   What are the live areas in contemporary thought and experience to which the men and women of the church are unconscious?   What are the issues within these areas which because of their timeliness are of immediate concern? What are some of the typical life situations of men and women of the church?   This list of questions might be indefinitely extended.

FACTUAL DATA REQUIRED.—Such an exploration of needs presupposes a background of factual data covering a wide range. American adult life is cosmopolitan, not merely from the standpoint of race, but also from that of cultural level, religious and social heritage, and economic status.   Communities differ widely in the number, variety, popular appeal, and program of their religious, educational, and social agencies.   Doubtless there are still American communities to be found where, in addition to the home, the church is the only organized educational agency claiming the allegiance of any considerable number of adults.   Far more numerous are the communities where literally scores of agencies vie with one another in bidding for the time of men and women—lodges, clubs, societies, associations, and what not, involving their members in an endless variety of activities and programs, some significant, some disintegrating and harmful, some merely meaningless.

In the community where the curriculum is being organized is the church practically the sole educational and social agency other than the school and the home? Has it a dominating place among numerous agencies? Does it have to compete strongly for interest and attendance with other agencies? Who are the members of the church and its constituency? Is the church group homogeneous or not? What are the racial backgrounds of the people? What cultural levels are represented? What leadership skills are represented and in what lines of activities? Are the members strongly class conscious? What attitudes are represented: as to race relations? community cooperation? interchurch cooperation? international relations? What characterization may be made: as to sensitivity to live social problems? ethical issues? current moral problems? What factions, "sets" cleavages, exist? What group prejudices? What taboos, fixed customs, traditions, growing out of the past history of the church or the community? What has been the curriculum of religious education in the past? Has it moved in a single groove for a generation or more? What attempts have been made to alter, enrich, or broaden its scope? What facts are available concerning results of these attempts?

Within recent years a number of surveys of the churches of particular communities have been made. Very little use has been made of them, although they represent a large investment of money and energy. One reason is that church programs are not planned in detail interdenominationally within communities. This should be done, and in many communities a beginning can be made in this direction. Whether in cooperation or proceeding alone, the local church should make thorough studies along the lines indicated above and then proceed to plan its program in the light of the results of these studies.

EVALUATION OF CURRENT PROCEDURES.—The third step in organizing the curriculum may well be a frank, thorough evaluation of current procedures. In most churches the adult program is taken for granted. In the early years of the present century the organized-class movement brought new interest, a quickening influence, increased activity, and greatly accelerated growth. Within two decades the movement reached its climax and since has gradually declined. Many of these organized classes linger on, but comparatively few maintain a vital program. Within recent years the United Christian Adult Movement has been inaugurated on broad lines, under able interdenominational leadership, and is taking root in a growing number of local churches.

Tact, ingenuity, and enterprise are necessary in the process of evaluation. A wide variety of instruments, chiefly in the form of tests and measurements, have been devised for use with children and young people, but few for use with adults. Some planned primarily for younger persons may be adapted; some possibly may be used practically unchanged.[14] Chief dependence, however, must needs be placed on frank facing, by local adult leaders, of the results or lack of results accruing from the program in use. Results which they themselves have gained or failed to gain will be an index to what is happening in the lives of other men and women.

PLANNED PROGRAM OF CURRICULUM UNITS.—The fourth step in organizing the adult curriculum is the actual planning of the activities for a specific year or portion of a year. Not that a year's program is to be thought of as rigidly fixed. In a real sense the program should be continuous, and continuously in the making. But it is important that an outline of the program for the year should be democratically planned by a responsible local group. Preferably the group should consist of representatives of all the adult agencies of the church, plus two or three members at large.[15] Such an outline should indicate some degree of correlation between the program of the church and other educational agencies of the community; it should indicate major and minor emphases in the work for the year; and it should include an extensive list of possible activities chosen in the light of the exploration of needs, the factual data reviewed, and the evaluation of current procedures. The list should be considered suggestive, not obligatory.

In preparing its outline the planning group will be confronted by the problem of grading. To what extent should curriculum units be planned in terms of the several adult age groups —young adults, middle age, and elderly men and women? Recognition should be given to the desirability of three types: (1) Curriculum units of such wide appeal and general interest as to be adaptable for use by a group of adults of all ages. (2) Curriculum units dealing with dominant interests and experiences peculiar to some one age group. (3) Curriculum units whose appeal is to special interests independently of age.

When completed in outline form, the program should be presented for consideration, amendment, and approval to the several organizations by their respective representatives and in turn to the responsible educational board of the church. Finally it should be presented in printed or mimeographed form to a meeting of the entire adult constituency. The adoption of projects and courses by existing groups should be wholly by voluntary action on their own part. New groups may be formed on the initiative of the general committee or leaders chosen by them, while yet other groups may take form spontaneously. The general committee will probably desire to strongly urge a few major activities on the basis of its exploration, its sense of needs, and its judgment of the capacity of particular groups to carry important projects through to a successful issue.

CRITERIA OF SELECTION.—Serious consideration should be given by groups to the selection of curriculum units. The criteria suggested in our discussion of religious education through social participation* are equally applicable to the curriculum as a whole. At the most no more than an infinitesimally small proportion of the total range of possible units of experience can be dealt with by an individual or a group. Obviously, care should be used to choose those which promise to be most fruitful in their contribution to the objectives of Christian education.

———

Our discussion of adult education draws to a close. Adult education, as became clear in the historical survey of Chapter II, is not a new thing in the life of the Church. Always the Church has been an educational institution. The early Church began as a fellowship of disciples who had been with Jesus and had learned of him. His example as a teacher so strongly influenced his followers that as soon as the fellowship of believers took organized form the Church gave attention to teaching, organizing schools for the purpose of preparing converts for membership and for the training of leaders and teachers. In later expansion of the Church Cathedral Schools became prominent and influential institutions, performing an invaluable service in instruction of new members and in the education of lay leaders and of the clergy. The great medieval universities were the direct outgrowth of the educational interest and concern of the Church.

In the Reformation education as well as religion experienced a new birth. Education as a function of the State took its rise as a

———

* See pp. 237f.

part of the Reformation movement.   During the Colonial period
in America and for some time thereafter all education was definitely religious.   With the gradual secularization of public-school
education the Church began again increasingly to assume responsibility for education in religion.   The growing sense of obligation
has not been limited to the religious education of children.   The
earliest institutions for higher education in America were Church
foundations, and zeal for the founding of denominational colleges continued through the whole of the eighteenth and the
nineteenth centuries.   The Church is today, in the totality of its
impact upon life, the most influential institution in the world for
adult education.

Analysis of our contemporary society presents, as we have
seen in the course of our discussion, an exceedingly disturbing
picture; almost complete secularization; the lack of any dominant
integrating center; decreasing influence of the Church; class divisions strongly accentuated; economic insecurity growing through
a period of decades; the prevailing economic structure "sin infected"; the spirit of narrow nationalism waxing steadily stronger
—all of these conditions contributing to a growing sense of dis-
illusionment, futility, and helplessness, and to the development
of a philosophy of pessimism, a theology of human helplessness,
and attitudes of discouragement and social dependence.

In order to counterbalance these tragic conditions society
needs from a Christian point of view a spiritual rebirth.   Repentance and regeneration are required.   Society must again find its
integrating center in God and in the purpose of building his
Kingdom in the earth; it must itself be remade after the Christian
pattern.

New social orientation and deeply religious motivation of
individuals and of society at large is necessary.   The objectives of
living must be made to transcend material ends, and individual
and group effort must both be dedicated to the service of humanity.

Reconstruction of the economic order is required through
the substitution of the service motive for self-interest; through
substitution of the method of cooperation for that of competition;
through the destruction of corporate (monopoly) control and the
substitution of economic democracy, involving withal provision
for the physical foundation of the good life for all.

The "American dream" of a democratic society in which all
persons have an equal right to life, liberty, and the pursuit of

happiness must be made a reality. It can only come through a fraternal brotherly society, without antagonistic class divisions, and the discovery of new and practical ways of social living.

A Christian society requires international cooperation. The world must become a family of nations. Each member of the family must have access to the sources of raw materials and to markets and within the international family differences must be settled not by war but by friendly arbitration.

Leadership capable of creating the new way of life does not seem to be available. The forces most sensitive to the social situation and most effective in the use of techniques of control are very largely outside of the Church and to a large extent, also, indifferent to the resources of religion. The Church seems illy equipped to play its part in the social reconstruction that the times demand.

What, under these circumstances, is required? Many things. One answer, though doubtless not the sole answer, is the kind of vital, aggressive program of adult Christian education outlined in the successive chapters of this book.

From the period of its beginnings in the ministry of Jesus the Christian Church has looked to the common people for the creative source of moral, religious, and social advance. What is now required in the development of a Christian society is that the members of the Church shall be brought to see the goals and led to advance toward them with intelligently conceived, determined purpose. When these basic essentials are developed as group qualities, from within the group will emerge the leadership required for common advance.

Always the Church has been confronted with a task of huge magnitude. Never have the difficulties seemed less than insuperable. In these particulars the situation in which the Church finds itself in our generation is not radically different from that of other periods of its history. The early Christians whose collective life found organizational expression in the Church revived a waning hope in human hearts. They planted in old and outworn soil new religious and social ideals. While an old order was disintegrating, they laid the foundations of a new. Surrounded by the evidence of a decaying civilization, they became the builders of a new world. This they were able to do by the help of God even though the Church fell far short of being a perfect instrument. What has been done can be done!

APPENDIX

REFERENCES AND NOTES

The following references and notes locate quotations and indicate sources of supplementary material. In some cases, also, differing points of view are cited. While intended for all careful readers, they will be found to be of special value to teachers and leaders using this book as a guide for group study.

INTRODUCTION

1. Interim Report of the Committee on Adult Education on Industrial and Social Conditions in Relation to Adult Education (H. M. Stationery Office, London, 1918), p. 3.

2. As early as 1923-24 the *American Labor Year Book* (Vol. V) listed the following agencies as having a place in the movement: The Ladies Garment Workers; the United Labor Education Committee; the Rand School of Social Science; the Department of Education of the Pennsylvania Federation of Labor; the Amalgamated Clothing Workers; the Trade Union College, Washington, D. C.; The Chicago Classes of the Women's Trade Union League; the Boston Trade Union College; Amherst Classes for Workers; the Cooperatives; the Workers' College of Seattle; the Workers' Education Bureau of America; and the Brookwood Labor College. To these should be added a considerable number of trade-union schools and classes.

3. Quoted by B. Y. Landis and John D. Willard in *Rural Adult Education* (The Macmillan Company, New York, 1933), page 100.

4. Kilpatrick, William H., Ed., *The Educational Frontier* (D. Appleton-Century Co., New York, 1933), p. 141.

5. Noffsinger, John S., Correspondence Schools, Lyceums, Chautauquas (The Macmillan Company, New York, 1926).

I. THE CHURCH TODAY

1. W. W. Sweet, *Story of Religions in America* (Harper & Brothers, New York, 1930), p. 322.

2. Ernest Barker, in *Church and Community* (Willett, Clark & Company, Chicago, 1938), p. 43.

3. *The Mission and Expansion of Christianity* (G. P. Putnam's Sons, New York, 1908), Vol. I, p. 141.

4. F. R. Barry, *The Relevance of the Church* (Charles Scribner's Sons, New York, 1936), p. 46.

5. ". . . there is no ecumenical conception of the Church which can be accepted by all the churches or even by a large majority . . . the various conceptions of the Church do not merely supplement one another . . . they also contradict one another." W. A. Visser

'T Hooft, *The Church and Its Function in Society* (Willett, Clark & Company, Chicago, 1937), p. 80f.

6. Art., "Sects and Churches," *The Christian Century*, July 3, 1935, pp. 885ff. The distinction between the "sect" and the "Church" given prominence by Ernst Troeltsch in his *Social Teachings of the Christian Church* (The Macmillan Company, New York, 1931), is discussed at some length by F. Ernest Johnson in *The Church and Society* (The Abingdon Press, New York, 1935), Chap. III.

7. Cf. A. N. Whitehead: "Protestant Christianity, so far as concerns the institutional and dogmatic forms in which it flourished for three hundred years as derived from Luther, Calvin, and the Anglican Settlement, is showing all the signs of a steady decay. Its dogmas no longer dominate; its divisions no longer interest; its institutions no longer direct the patterns of life." *Adventures of Ideas* (The Macmillan Company, New York, 1933), p. 205. With this statement K. S. Latourette seems to be in complete disagreement: "The Church has never been so vigorous and so widely influential in the affairs of men as in the nineteenth and twentieth centuries." *Church and Community* (Willett, Clark & Company, Chicago, 1938), p. 17.

8. *The Oxford Conference, Official Report,* J. H. Oldham, Ed. (Willett, Clark & Company, Chicago, 1937), p. 182.

9. Responsibility for this situation rests more upon the schools than upon the churches. Cf. C. A. Ellwood, ". . . the nonmaterial phases of our culture have as yet not been materially advanced by our educational system. The general level of our culture still remains so low that our masses are ignorantly unappreciative of science, art, government, religion, and even morals." *Man's Social Destiny* (Cokesbury Press, Nashville, 1929), p. 152.

10. Additional Report of the Section on Church and Community, *The Oxford Conference, Official Report,* p. 175.

11. *The Oxford Conference, Official Report,* p. 108.

12. For specific substantiation of this statement see *The Beliefs of 700 Ministers,* George H. Betts (The Abingdon Press, New York, 1929).

13. Hornell Hart, in *Recent Social Trends* (Whittlesey House, McGraw-Hill Book Company, Inc., New York, 1934), p. 1013.

14. Supporting data may be found in *Religion Among American Men,* Committee on the War and the Religious Outlook (The Association Press, New York, 1920).

15. *The Oxford Conference, Official Report,* p. 105f.

16. Much remains to be done in the field of the psychology of adult learning. The outstanding character of the contribution of Thorndike in *Adult Learning* (The Macmillan Company, New York, 1928), and in his other books, is generally recognized. However, the fact remains that an adequate basis for adult education in psychology and social philosophy is yet to be developed.

17. *The Church and Its Function in Society* (Willett, Clark & Company, Chicago, 1937), p. 171.

18. Some would contend that it is not the obligation or the function of the Church to improve society. In Lutheranism there is a tendency to regard the Church and the world as unrelated spheres of action and to hold that the gospel concerns only the salvation of the individual soul, not the redemption of society. This view is not by any means that of all Lutherans, and it is held by some members of all Protestant churches.

II. OUR PROTESTANT HERITAGE

1. This is set forth in what has been characterized as the most beautiful of all of Luther's works, *The Liberty of the Christian Man,* a book the reading of which is essential to an understanding of the Protestant Reformation.

2. The development barely outlined in this paragraph is described in thorough detail by Max Weber, *The Protestant Ethic and the Spirit of Capitalism* (Charles Scribner's Sons, New York, 1927); R. H. Tawney, *Religion and the Rise of Capitalism* (Harcourt, Brace & Company, Inc., New York, 1926); and Ernst Troeltsch, *The Social Teaching of the Christian Churches* (The Macmillan Company, New York, 1931). Brief but illuminating discussions may be found in *The Social Gospel and the Christian Cultus,* Charles Clayton Morrison, Chap. V, "The Social Expansion of Christian Ethics" (Harper & Brothers, New York, 1933); and in *Statesmanship and Religion,* Henry A. Wallace, Chap. II, "The Spiritual Adventure of the Reformers" (Round Table Press, Inc., New York, 1934). Weber holds that Protestantism, particularly in its Calvinistic and Puritan form, is the parent of capitalism. With this view Tawney partially agrees. McNeill declares in *Christian Hope for World Society* (Willett, Clark & Company, Chicago, 1937), p. 193, that "no such simple statement" as is made by Weber can be accepted. H. Richard Niebuhr holds that the two were interacting phases of a developing culture, at the same time calling attention to the suggestion of Wuensch in his *Evangelische Wirtshaftslehre* that while Calvinism may have affected industrialism strongly, "rationalism is more likely to have been responsible for the parentage of capitalism." See *The Social Sources of Denominationalism* (Henry Holt and Company, New York, 1929), p. 288.

3. The doctrinal content of Protestant catechisms of the period is indicated by the title of a typical example, "*A Catechism;* On the Grounds and Principles of Christian Religion . . . wherein the Summe of the Doctrine of Religion is comprised, familiarly opened, and clearly confirmed from the Holy Scriptures. . . ." By Richard Mather (1650).

4. The popular idea that the Roman Catholic Church represents within itself complete unity in contrast to the many divisions of Protestantism is erroneous. There have been many controversies and

numerous parties and orders within Catholicism, but the central authority of the pope has been sufficient to prevent a breakup of the institution.

5. Other influences also contributed to the development in America of the private profit economy, e.g., the settlement and development of the New World was almost wholly an achievement of individual enterprise, isolation and the self-sufficiency of family units contributing to independence and individualism. Also, as in Europe, bankers, merchants and tradesmen, whose interest and power inhered in property accumulation gradually gained increasing political control and interpreted the essential function of the State as the protection of private property and the maintenance of the sanctity of contracts. Out of this grew the business philosophy, expressed in the maxim *caveat emptor,* which disavowed responsibility for the general welfare and regarded society as a legitimate area of exploitation.

6. This is not a necessary interpretation of the distinctive Protestant doctrine of justification by faith. The point is that the doctrine was so misinterpreted as to give credence to the idea that it is possible for men to gain a valid assurance of salvation through a private contact with God which ignores their participation in sins of the corporate life which, according to the teaching of Jesus and the Hebrew prophets, alienates God from men. Cf. Harry F. Ward, *Which Way Religion?* (The Macmillan Company, New York, 1931), p. 145f.

7. Quoted from Albert Parker Fitch, by Charles A. Ellwood, art., *Religious Education,* May-June, 1931, p. 421f. So, also, Ellwood: "Protestantism . . . was an individualistic movement, and it broke to pieces the old social order. It fostered individualism both in religion and in the economic life. Second, it was relatively unconcerned with the social order, because its emphasis was subjective. Third, it promoted theological-mindedness and other-worldliness and neglected the teachings of Christ for the Old Testament and the Pauline Epistles. All of this gave pagan economic tendencies their chance. Individualism rose to a mighty tide. . . . Exploitation of the weak became the basis for the prosperity of nations as well as of individuals." *Ibid.,* p. 422f.

8. Charles Clayton Morrison, *The Social Gospel and the Christian Cultus,* p. 154.

9. Cf. H. Richard Niebuhr: "The ethics which it [Methodism] had in mind was not the social ethics of the Sermon on the Mount, but the sober, individual ethics of 'The Serious Call' and of Moravian piety; . . . the hope of a thoroughgoing social reconstruction was almost entirely absent. . . . Apparently Wesley believed that the justice of a cause was quite secondary in the eyes of God to the personal purity of its defenders. In the rules for the band societies . . . their members are to abstain from evil, especially from buying or selling on the Sabbath, tasting spirituous liquors, . . . backbiting, wearing needless ornaments, . . . and taking snuff and tobacco. . . . In the much greater moral problems involved in the new social relationships

brought about by the industrial revolution or present in the age-old relations of the classes, Wesley and Methodism had no real interest." *The Social Sources of Denominationalism*, pp. 64ff. Cf., however, Francis J. McConnell's estimate of the social contribution of the Wesleyan movement and its part in mitigating the horrors of the industrial revolution in his interpretative biography, *John Wesley* (The Abingdon Press, New York, 1939), Part IX.

10. Cf. Charles Clayton Morrison, *The Social Gospel and the Christian Cultus*, p. 149.

11. Melancthon, *Corpus Reformatorum*, Vol. XI, p. 273.

12. Paul Monroe, *History of Education* (The Macmillan Company, New York, 1907), p. 550.

13. Cf. William Clayton Bower, *The Curriculum of Religious Education* (The University of Chicago Press, Chicago, 1925), Chap. II.

14. Cf. Rexford Guy Tugwell and Howard C. Hill: "One immediate effect of the new inventions was poverty and suffering for the working classes. . . . The generation from 1800 to 1830 marks the lowest point in the welfare of the British working class, . . . in many respects in all history. . . . In the factory towns of Northern England entire families were huddled in damp, poisonous cellars at night, and for fifteen or eighteen hours a day were driven at the most wearing kind of labor in the mills and factories. . . . Wages, and consequently allowances for food and clothing, were incredibly small." *Our Economic Society and Its Problems* (Harcourt, Brace & Company, Inc., New York, 1934), p. 34f.

15. For a fuller treatment see Edmund B. Chaffee, *The Protestant Churches and the Industrial Crisis* (The Macmillan Company, New York, 1933), Chap. VI, "Slavery and the Rise of the Social Classes."

16. The Communistic Manifesto of 1848, by Karl Marx and F. Engels, has been one of the most widely influential documents of modern times. No one who desires to be informed concerning the forces at work in contemporary society can afford to be ignorant of its content.

17. Cf. George A. Coe, "It is not possible to speak of 'the' Protestant type of religious education. For not only are there many sorts of Protestantism, but within each Protestant body, at least within the larger bodies, variety, ferment, fresh experimentation are characteristic, and consequently at times the strain of conflicting convictions. . . . Protestant education is a conglomerate, several different types being found side by side, even within the same denomination." *A Social Theory of Religious Education* (Charles Scribner's Sons, New York, 1917), p. 304.

III. PRESENT COMPELLING OBJECTIVES

1. This conviction has been expressed both by social and political scientists and by religious groups. Representative of the latter is a statement by the Social Order Committee of the Philadelphia Yearly

Meeting of the Society of Friends: "We hold that the framework of accepted laws and usages which we call the social order is . . . not beyond human control, but can be shaped to such ends as we have the will to achieve."

2. In early America the attainment of this goal was a cherished hope all but universal. Now, in the face of the actual possibility of achievement, the contention is being brazenly advanced by some that an impoverished life, poverty, and cultural deprivation is inevitable for all except a privileged few.

3. Variously known as "'capitalism," the "profit-system," the "price-and profit system," the "profit economy," and by other terms. There is, as the *Encyclopaedia Britannica* states, no fully satisfactory definition of the term. "Although nothing is more evident than the thing," it is so interrelated with other aspects of society that it cannot satisfactorily be separately defined. The *Britannica* describes capitalism as "the world-wide modern system of organizing production and trade by private enterprise free to seek profit and fortune by employing for wages the mass of human labor" (Fourteenth Edition, Vol. IV, p. 801). Economic authorities generally agree that the essence of capitalism is the unrestricted acquisition or accumulation of material wealth, motivated primarily by the desire for profit, to which all other relations and considerations are subservient. Beginning as commercial capitalism, the system has passed through several successive stages including as the major later developments industrial capitalism and the present finance capitalism or corporatism.

4. *Consumer Income in the United States* (National Resources Committee, Washington), p. 2.

5. It is declared, for example, that the Bell Telephone System has suppressed nearly thirty-five hundred such patents. See *Resistance to Adoption of Technological Innovations,* Bernhard J. Stern, National Resources Committee, 1937.

6. Cf. *Conclusions and Recommendations,* Commission on Social Studies of the American Historical Association (Charles Scribner's Sons, New York, 1934), p. 18.

7. *The Oxford Conference, Official Report* (Willett, Clark & Company, Chicago, 1937), p. 90.

8. For substantiation in detail of this statement see *Dynamite,* by Louis Adamic (The Viking Press, New York, 1934).

9. The dissenting opinion by Chief Justice Hughes declared that the majority opinion reverses a cherished principle of American government.

10. Cf. statement of the Commission on Social Studies, American Historical Association, *Conclusions and Recommendations,* p. 12.

11. Cf. *The Chart of Plenty,* Harold Loeb (The Viking Press, New York, 1935).

12. For an illuminating, brief discussion of this question see the

pamphlet *Property,* by Kirby Page (Industry Series, No. 14. Eddy and Page, 347 Madison Avenue, New York).

13. As F. Ernest Johnson convincingly argues, to make either social or individual teaching of Christianity a derivative of the other runs counter to the Biblical, historical, and psychological evidence. "Self and society are complementary terms, . . . the social content of his [Jesus] gospel was fused with the personal." *The Church and Society* (The Abingdon Press, New York, 1935), p. 43.

14. Cf. William Clayton Bower, *Character Through Creative Experience* (The University of Chicago Press, Chicago, 1930), p. 43.

15. Cf. the statement of the Committee on Social-Economic Goals, National Education Association, *Journal of the N. E. A.,* January, 1934, pp. 7, 8.

16. Other particulars are named elsewhere in this and other chapters. An admirable summary is contained in a paper written by R. H. Tawney in preparation for the Oxford Conference from which quotations are made in *The Church and Its Function in Society,* W. A. Visser 'T Hooft and J. H. Oldham (Willet, Clark & Company, Chicago, 1937), pp. 194, 195, 197.

17. This interpretation of the teachings of Jesus, it should be understood, is directly counter to the contention of the premillennialists, who have no hope of betterment of the world through human effort.

IV. CHARACTER AND PERSONAL RELIGIOUS LIVING

1. Gardner Murphy, *General Psychology* (Harper & Brothers, New York, 1933), p. 538.

2. Gardner Murphy, *Ibid.,* p. 60ff.

3. Cf. C. K. Ogden, *The Meaning of Psychology* (Harper & Brothers, New York, 1926), p. 238.

4. Cf. H. A. Carr, *Psychology* (Longmans, Green and Co., New York, 1925), p. 280; R. S. Woodworth, *Psychology,* Third Edition (Henry Holt & Company, Inc., New York, 1934), p. 338; Gardner Murphy, *General Psychology* (Harper & Brothers, New York, 1933), pp. 75, 92.

5. Cf. Ernest J. Chave, *Personality Development in Children* (University of Chicago Press, Chicago, 1927), p. 115. The entire chapter (V) will be found helpful.

6. Georgia Harkness, *The Recovery of Ideals* (Charles Scribner's Sons, New York, 1937), p. 48. As an example of dangerous emotional loyalty, not rooted in authentic knowledge, and in fact largely based on false ideas, Miss Harkness cites the devotion of most Americans to the capitalist system.

7. Among contemporary writers, of those in whose books may be found a discussion of religion in terms of attitude toward the universe are B. F. Streeter, D. C. MacIntosh, and W. E. Hocking.

8. William McDougall, *Introduction to Social Psychology* (John W. Luce and Co., Boston, 1914), p. 19.

9. For example, Karen Horney. Cf. her *The Neurotic Personality of Our Time* (W. W. Norton & Company, Inc., New York, 1937), p. 34. The book as a whole should be read in substantiation.

10. Cf. Murphy, Murphy, and Newcomb, *Experimental Social Psychology* (Harper & Brothers, New York, 1937), p. 509.

11. William McDougall, *Introduction to Social Psychology*, p. 93.

12. *Influencing Human Behavior* (The People's Institute Publishing Company, New York, 1925), p. 147f.

13. Cf. statement on "the definition of sin," John C. Bennett, *Social Salvation* (Charles Scribner's Sons, New York, 1935), p. 6ff.

14. With this statement some disagree. Cf., for example, Rufus S. Jones's contention that religion is one of three basic "drives" or "urges" along with hunger and sex, in *The Testimony of the Soul* (The Macmillan Company, New York, 1936), p. 50.

15. George Albert Coe, *The Psychology of Religion* (University of Chicago Press, Chicago, 1916), p. 152.

16. This is discussed at length by Pratt, *The Religious Consciousness* (The Macmillan Company, New York, 1920), Chap. VIII.

17. Many of the poems of Browning are "dramatic renderings of these decisive hours of passion and energized will."

V.   CHRISTIANIZING THE WHOLE OF LIFE

1. "To help, in his own sphere, to rebuild society is the lifework of every Christian. It is to be foreseen, studied, planned for in the true professional spirit, and with the same regard for technical proficiency that one looks for in a lawyer, a physician, or a mining engineer." George A. Coe, *A Social Theory of Religious Education* (Charles Scribner's Sons, New York, 1917), p. 70.

2. Cf. statement, General Conference of the Methodist Episcopal Church, 1936: "The Christian conscience declares that the continuance of these conditions is sinful in the sight of God, and the Christian Church summons its membership to the task of saving us from our sins. . . . Because of the differences of opinion as to method, and the sincerity and standing of the individuals arguing the cases at issue, we do not pass judgment on techniques."

3. This same emphasis is being made by others than religionists. Cf. the contention of Aldous Huxley that reform must begin in the souls of individuals who are willing to remake themselves and willing then, in turn, to form small groups to put into practice on a small scale the ideals which they advocate for society as a whole. *Ends and Means* (Harper & Brothers, New York, 1938), Chap. X.

4. A consideration of social inertia would involve recognition of different types, e.g., internal, resistance to change of existing patterns of

activity within a particular group; and external, resistance to change of the group's relationship to other groups.

5. The United States Commission on Industrial Relations, 1912, Final Report.

6. A legal stronghold of wage slavery of which much is made in the name of personal liberty by reactionary interests is so-called "freedom of contract." For example, a young woman out of work, the sole support of her aged parents, applies for employment, in answer to an advertisement, to a department store. The manager takes advantage of her inexperience and of "surplus labor supply" and offers her five dollars a week. Because of the extremity of her family she accepts. The law labels this procedure a "contract" and it "protects" the person's "liberty" to take as low a wage as he will. This so-called "freedom of contract" is purely a legal fiction. What it amounts to in this, as in millions of cases, is liberty to starve.

7. Witness the development and present status of the Cooperative Movement, not only in the United States but more especially in Great Britain, in the Scandinavian countries, and in other nations of the world. For statistical data consult recent issues of *The Peoples Year-book*, issued annually by the Cooperative Wholesale Society of Great Britain.

8. Distinction should be made between the type of social ownership represented by Producers and Consumers Cooperatives and that represented by state (or municipal) ownership. The former offers a *de facto*, realizable ownership with more direct personal participation in management and a greater sense of personal responsibility. For a more extended discussion see James P. Warbasse, *Cooperative Democracy* (Harper & Brothers, New York, 1936), p. 107ff.

9. Against this type of collectivism Walter Lippmann presents a convincing case in *The Good Society* (Little, Brown & Company, Boston, 1937). He argues that (1) national and international economic planning and dictatorship is in principle a reversion to the old method of mercantilism with its regulation of all industry by patents of monopoly and privileged guilds under which society was dominated by poverty and stagnation; (2) it is a method practicable only for purposes of war or other acute emergencies; (3) its operation would necessarily depend upon universal and permanent compulsion; and (4) it would not only result in enslavement but would also inevitably curtail production and lower standards of living.

10. Le Cour Grand-Maison, Catholic member of the French Chamber of Deputies, quoted by Thomas Mann in *The Coming Victory of Democracy* (Alfred A. Knopf, New York, 1938), p. 62.

11. Is it possible to teach the Christian religion in abstract terms? The effort is constantly being made in preaching and adult group teaching, but how much actual teaching really takes place? Cf. Chapman and Counts: "If divorced from the currents of life, neither religion nor morals can be successfully taught. The inevitable conse-

quence [of such a separation] is that the religious experience appears but a pale and ethereal phantom among the riches of that colorful world" in which men feel and will and labor. *Principles of Education* (Houghton Mifflin Company, Boston, 1924), page 359. Cf. also John C. Bennett: "The preaching of general goals . . . will get its sharpness and become more than a series of platitudes if it is linked with the most specific statement possible about present evils. . . ." *Social Salvation* (Charles Scribner's Sons, New York, 1935), p. 122ff.

12. For a discussion of the ineffectiveness of transmissive education see *What Is Christian Education?* George A. Coe (Charles Scribner's Sons, New York, 1939), particularly Chap. III, "Why We Fail."

13. A cohesiveness, Ruth Kotinsky suggests, that has "some meaning in terms of outdoor purposes, so that their indoor deliberations have relation to an intelligent cooperative attack on the problems at hand." Cf. her statement in *Adult Education and the Social Scene* (D. Appleton-Century Co., New York, 1933) p. 186.

VI. CHRISTIAN EDUCATION THROUGH WORSHIP

1. *Worship* (Association Press, New York, 1917), p. 8.

2. For a brief elaboration of this analysis of individual prayer see introduction to the author's book, *Challenge and Power* (The Abingdon Press, 1936), pp. 17-21.

3. Cf. H. N. Wieman, *Methods of Private Religious Living* (The Macmillan Company, New York, 1929), p. 122f.

4. *Religious Education,* Vol. XX (February, 1925), p. 349. Georgia Harkness states the same value in psychological terms in saying, "Prayer opens the subjective receptors of personality to the directing and vitalizing power of that which lays demand upon us for the purification of life" *(The Recovery of Ideals,* p. 73). A somewhat similar statement is made by H. N. Wieman: "Stated very simply, we may say that religion releases human energy by adjusting the individual in such a way that . . . God shapes the organs of the body and the impulses of the heart to the end of maximum constructive behavior." *(Methods of Private Religious Living,* p. 45.)

5. *Modern Man's Worship* (Harper & Brothers, New York, 1934), p. 258.

6. Cf. George A. Coe: "I do not say or think that the enrichment of worship that is taking place is simply and solely mental involution or flight from reality. But I do say that we are in danger, precisely through the increasing worshipfulness of our worship, of dissociating our elevated sentiments from their proper integration with sturdy and creative purposes." *What Is Christian Education?* (Charles Scribner's Sons, New York, 1929), p. 170.

7. *Religious Education* (University of Chicago Press, 1928), p. 293.

8. For more thorough discussion of the order of worship consult

Von Ogden Vogt, *Art and Religion* (Yale University Press, New Haven, 1921); Odgers and Schultz, *The Technique of Public Worship* (The Methodist Book Concern, New York, 1928), Chap. IV.

9. Cf. Charles Clayton Morrison, *The Social Gospel and the Christian Cultus* (Harper & Brothers, New York, 1933), Chap. II, "The Social Orientation of Worship."

VII. RELIGIOUS EDUCATION THROUGH SOCIAL PARTICIPATION

1. E. C. Lindeman, *The Meaning of Adult Education* (New Republic, Inc., New York, 1926), p. 152.

2. William James, *The Principles of Psychology* (Henry Holt & Company, Inc., New York, 1931), Vol. II, p. 372.

3. Cf. M. F. Follett, *Creative Experience* (Longmans, Green & Co., New York, 1924), p. 217.

4. Cf. *Adult Education and the Social Scene* (D. Appleton-Century Co., New York, 1933), p. 45. Also E. C. Lindeman: What is the right pair of shoes to buy—right with respect to the shape of the baby's foot; with respect to the mother's income; the kinds of material of which babies' shoes are made? Is the price right: Were the persons who made the shoes and the salesman who sold them paid a living wage? (*The Meaning of Adult Education*, p. 175.)

5. Elaboration of some of the ideas expressed in this and preceding paragraphs; together with a significant study of the subjection of consumer functions by the capitalist economy, and of the philosophy of Cooperation, will be found in *The Decline and Rise of the Consumer*, by Horace M. Kallen (D. Appleton-Century Co., New York, 1936).

6. Cf. *The Development of a Curriculum of Religious Education*, Research Service Bulletin No. 5 (The International Council of Religious Education, Chicago, 1928), p. 38ff.

7. *Christian Youth in Action*, by Frank W. Herriot (Friendship Press, New York, 1935).

8. The service rendered by Credit Unions under direct church auspices as an agency for savings and as a means of providing credit for those otherwise without it has no lack of precedent. The Montes Pietatis, founded in the fifteenth century, loaned money to those in need (*Catholic Encyclopaedia*, 1911, art., "Montes Pietatis"). John Wesley, in 1746, established among the early Methodist societies a "lending stock" for small loans which was successfully maintained for many years. In Europe very many Roman Catholic parishes have parish Credit Unions, particularly in Belgium. The first Credit Union in the United States is believed to be that organized in Saint Mary's parish (Roman Catholic), Manchester, New Hampshire. In recent years many Catholic and some Protestant churches have developed successful Credit Unions.

VIII.   INTELLECTUAL ASPECTS OF A GROWING RELIGIOUS EXPERIENCE

1. Edgar Sheffield Brightman, *Religious Values* (The Abingdon Press, New York, 1925), p. 9.

2. William Clayton Bower, *The Curriculum of Religious Education* (Charles Scribner's Sons, New York, 1925), p. 54.

3. Frederick G. Bonser, *Twenty-sixth Yearbook* of the National Society for the Study of Education (1926), Part II, p. 61.

4. Jerusalem Meeting, International Missionary Council, Vol. II, *Religious Education* (International Missionary Council, New York, 1928), p. 50.

5. *Life and Letters of Charles Darwin* (D. Appleton & Co., New York, 1887), p. 81.

6. Raymond Calkins, *The Christian Church in the Modern World* (The Macmillan Company, New York, 1924), p. 109ff.

7. J. L., and Barbara Hammond, *The Rise of Modern Industry*, Third Edition (Harcourt, Brace & Co., Inc., New York, 1926), p. 228.

8. Cf. E. C. Lindeman, *The Meaning of Adult Education* (New Republic, Inc., New York, 1926), p. 37f.

9. The contention of Reinhold Niebuhr in *Moral Man and Immoral Society* (Charles Scribner's Sons, New York, 1932), is that more is required than increase of social intelligence and religiously inspired good will to establish justice and harmony. "Conflict is inevitable, and in this conflict power must be challenged by power" (p. xiv).

10. Cf. J. K. Hart, *Adult Education* (Thomas Y. Crowell Company, New York, 1927), p. 117.

11. The origin of the term "propaganda" is significant. It originated from the "Congregation of Propaganda" of the Roman Catholic Church, an association of Cardinals established in 1622.

12. Valuable aids in helping people to detect and analyze propaganda are the publications of the Institute for Propaganda Analysis, Inc., 132 Morningside Drive, New York, N. Y.

13. *The Church and Its Function in Society* (Willett, Clark & Company, Chicago, 1937), p. 151.

14. Jerusalem Meeting, The International Missionary Council, Vol. II, *Religious Education,* p. 9ff.

15. George A. Coe, *A Social Theory of Religious Education* (Charles Scribner's Sons, New York, 1917), p. 181.

16. *The Church Through Half a Century* (Charles Scribner's Sons, New York, 1936), p. 115.

17. Cf. C. H. Dodd, *Parables of the Kingdom* (Charles Scribner's Sons, New York, 1936), p. 206; also, *History and the Gospel* (Charles Scribner's Sons, New York, 1938), p. 181 *et al.*

18. It should, however, be said that a considerable number, including not only premillenarians but others, some of whom are eminent Christian scholars, hold that this goal lies beyond human history, to be attained only through the power of a transcendent God; that the dominant forces of this world are demonic and that within this present world there are no forces either human or divine which can be depended upon for the significant improvement of human society. See, for example, *The Kingdom of God and History* (Willett, Clark & Company, Chicago, 1938).

IX. METHOD IN ADULT LEARNING

1. *What Is Christian Education?* (Charles Scribner's Sons, New York, 1929), p. 28f.

2. Edward L. Thorndike, *Adult Learning* (The Macmillan Company, New York, 1930), p. 147.

3. *Okonomie und Technik des Gedachtnisses*, 1908, pp. 267-69.

4. Edward L. Thorndike, *Adult Learning*, p. 131.

5. Edward L. Thorndike, *Adult Learning*, p. 151.

6. *What Is Christian Education?* p. 46ff.

7. M. J. Stormzand, *Progressive Methods of Teaching* (Houghton Mifflin Co., New York, 1924), p. 72.

8. Report by Committee on Educational Research, University of Minnesota, 1926-27. Quoted in *Association of American Colleges Bulletin*, Vol. XIV, No. 5, p. 390ff.

9. Charles L. Bane, "The Lecture vs. the Class-Discussion Method of College Teaching." *School and Society*, Vol. XXI, No. 532, p. 300ff.

10. Ralph B. Spence, "Lecture and Class Discussion in Teaching Educational Psychology." The *Journal of Educational Psychology*, Vol. XIX, No. 7, p. 454f.

11. The adult teacher will do well to study the principles of good questioning. These are briefly stated by Betts and Hawthorne, *Method in Teaching Religion* (Abingdon Press, New York, 1925), pp. 224-26; at greater length by Horne, H. H., *Story Telling, Questioning, and Studying* (The Macmillan Company, New York, 1916), p. 62ff.; Parker, Samuel C., *Methods of Teaching in High Schools* (Ginn and Co., Chicago, 1920), p. 465ff.; and Strayer, G. D., *The Teaching Process* (The Macmillan Company, New York, 1911), p. 114ff.

12. E. C. Lindeman, address before the American Country Life Association, November, 1924.

13. *The Spectator*, Vol. 135, p. 687.

14. Quoted by Jerome Davis, *Capitalism and Its Culture* (Farrar & Rinehart, Inc., New York, 1935), p. 257.

15. William S. Gray and Ruth Monroe, *The Reading Interests and Habits of Adults* (The Macmillan Company, New York, 1929).

16. *School and Society*, Vol. XXVIII, pp. 497-502.

X.   ENRICHING EXPERIENCE THROUGH DISCUSSION

1. Cf. E. Stanley Jones, *Christ at the Round Table* (The Abingdon Press, New York, 1928), p. 11.

2. From an address by Holger Begtrup, reported in Bulletin XXX of the World Association for Adult Education, p. 32f.

3. Art., "The Plastic Years," by S. K. Hart, in *The Survey*, Vol. LVI, p. 55.

4. James Bryce, *Modern Democracies* (The Macmillan Company, New York, 1929), Vol. I, p. 72.

5. R. W. Brown, *The Creative Spirit* (Harper & Brothers, New York, 1925), p. 3.

6. A. D. Sheffield, *Joining in Public Discussion* (George H. Doran Co., New York, 1922), p. xif.

7. E. C. Lindeman, *The Meaning of Adult Education* (The New Republic, Inc., New York, 1926), p. 11.

8. George Albert Coe, *Motives of Men* (Charles Scribner's Sons, New York, 1928), p. 236.

9. *Association of American Colleges Bulletin*, Vol. XIV, No. 5, p. 409.

10. *The New Freedom* (Doubleday, Page and Co., New York, 1913), p. 39.

11. A. D. Sheffield, *Creative Discussion*, Third Edition (Association Press, New York, 1933), p. 40.

12. H. H. Horne, University Students on the Discussion Method, *School and Society*, Vol. XVI (August 19, 1922), p. 218ff.

13. For a more detailed description of the conference procedure see Conference Method in Education, *The Phi Delta Kappan*, Vol. XVII, No. 1, pp. 24-48.   See also Round Table Conference Method, *Association of American Colleges Bulletin*, Vol. XIV, No. 5, p. 426.

14. *Journal of Adult Education*, Vol. I (1929), p. 144.

15. A. D. Sheffield, *Creative Discussion*, Third Edition, p. 37f.

16. Quoted in Editorial, *The Intercollegian*, June, 1928, p. 258.

XI.   EDUCATION THROUGH CREATIVE LEISURE

1. Ecclesiasticus 38. 24-34.

2. L. P. Jacks, *Education Through Recreation* (Harper & Brothers, New York, 1932), p. 13.

3. Cf. G. A. Lundberg, *Leisure, a Suburban Study* (Columbia University Press, New York, 1934), p. 19.

4. *Capitalism and Its Culture* (Farrar and Rinehart, Inc., New York, 1935), p. 261.

5. Cf. Alvin Johnson, "Youth and Human Conservation," in *Civilization and Enjoyment*.   Edited by Baker Brownell (D. Van Nostrand Company, Inc., New York, 1929), p. 35f.

6. Henry Arthur Jones, *Patriotism and Popular Education* (Chapman and Hall, Ltd., London, 1919), p. 36.

7. *The Iron Man in Industry* (The Atlantic Monthly Press, Boston, 1922), pp. 42f., 51.

8. L. P. Jacks, *Constructive Citizenship* (Doubleday, Doran & Co., Inc., Garden City, N. Y., 1928), p. 112.

9. Issue of July 13, 1932, p. 20.

10. *Recent Social Trends* (Whittlesey House, McGraw-Hill Book Company, Inc., New York, 1934), p. 1019.

11. *The Oxford Conference, Official Report* (Willett, Clark & Company, Chicago, 1937), p. 137.

12. *Syllabus for Physical Education* (Barnard College, New York, 1938), p. 7.

13. Chapman and Counts, *Principles of Education* (Houghton Mifflin Co., Boston, 1924), p. 302f.

14. *Human Nature and Conduct* (Henry Holt & Company, Inc., New York, 1930), p. 160.

15. Quoted by A. H. Eaton, *Handicrafts of the Southern Highlands* (Russell Sage Foundation, New York, 1937), p. 306.

16. *A Guide to Civilized Leisure* (W. W. Norton & Company, Inc., New York, 1935), p. 58.

XII. LIFE IS THE CURRICULUM

1. *The International Curriculum Guide*, Book One, *Principles and Objectives of Christian Education* (The International Council of Religious Education, Chicago, 1932), p. 53.

2. *Character Education Methods, The Iowa Plan* (Character Education Institution, Washington, D. C., 1922), p. 1.

3. William C. Bower, *The Curriculum of Religious Education* (Charles Scribner's Sons, New York, 1925), p. 55.

4. For example, the following: health, Mark 2. 1-12; parenthood, Luke 11. 11-13; general family relations, Luke 8. 19-21; economic relations, Luke 12. 13-34; vocational relationships, Luke 5. 3-10; group relations, Luke 9. 46-48.

5. George A. Coe, *A Social Theory of Religious Education* (Charles Scribner's Sons, New York, 1917), p. 105.

6. *A Social Theory of Religious Education*, p. 98.

7. *Twenty-sixth Yearbook* of the National Society for the Study of Education, Part II (Public School Publishing Co., Bloomington, Illinois, 1926), p. 43.

8. The International Curriculum Guide, Book Four, *Christian Education of Adults*, p. 8.

9. The following may be noted: (1) The Commission of the National Education Association on the Reorganization of Secondary

Education in 1918, with the totality of pupil interests, needs, and activities in view, stated the main objectives of education as health, command of fundamental processes, worthy home membership, vocation, citizenship, worthy use of leisure, and ethical character. (2) Bobbitt, in *How to Make a Curriculum* (Houghton Mifflin Co., Boston, 1924), classifies experience into ten major fields: a. language activities, social intercommunication; b. health activities; c. citizenship activities; d. general social activities, meeting and mingling with others; e. spare-time activities, amusements, recreation; f. keeping oneself mentally fit; g. religious activities; h. parental activities, the upbringing of children, the maintenance of a proper home life; i. non-vocational practical activities; j. labors of one's calling. (3) Soares in *Religious Education* (The University of Chicago Press, 1929) treats of the areas involved in "six great interests": a. play; b. work; c. money; d. art; e. worship; f. knowledge.

10. Under auspices representing the best available educational experience there should be made comprehensive lists of typical life situations of adults, together with statements of what are agreed to be Christian responses. Such lists should not be understood to be final or authoritative but subject to revision in the light of growing experience.

11. Cf. *The International Curriculum Guide,* Book One, p. 21.

12. From a preliminary statement prepared for use in preparation for the Jerusalem Meeting of the International Missionary Council.

13. *The Development of a Curriculum of Religious Education* (Research Service Bulletin No. 5, The International Council of Religious Education, Chicago, 1928), p. 18.

14. For available instruments for use in evaluating procedures of adult Christian education address the Adult Department, International Council of Religious Education, 203 North Wabash Avenue, Chicago, or your denominational headquarters.

15. While this statement seems to lodge total responsibility for the curriculum on the local group it is to be recognized that a very large part of the effort involved in curriculum planning is beyond the resources of any local church. The necessity is obvious for (1) central curriculum planning agencies, both interdenominational and denominational; (2) specialists to prepare outlines and plans for curriculum units of various types; (3) publication agencies to make available to local groups a wide variety of printed materials.

BIBLIOGRAPHY

INTRODUCTION

Cartwright, Morse A., *Ten Years of Adult Education*. The Macmillan Company, New York, 1935.

Ely, Mary L., Ed., *Adult Education in Action*. American Association for Adult Education, New York, 1936.

Hart, Joseph K., *Adult Education*. Thomas Y. Crowell Co., New York, 1927.

Hewitt, Dorothy, and Mather, Kirtley F., *Adult Education, A Dynamic for Democracy*. D. Appleton-Century Co., New York, 1937.

Kotinsky, Ruth, *Adult Education and the Social Scene*. Part II, Criticism of the American Movement for Adult Education. D. Appleton-Century Co., New York, 1933.

Landis, Benson Y., and Willard, John D., *Rural Adult Education*. The Macmillan Company, New York, 1933.

Rowden, Dorothy (Ed.), *Handbook of Adult Education in the United States*. American Association for Adult Education, New York, 1936.

I. THE CHURCH TODAY

Athearn, Walter S., *Character Building in a Democracy*. The Macmillan Company, New York, 1924.

Bacon, Benjamin W., *The Teaching Ministry for Tomorrow*. Yale University Press, New Haven, 1923.

Bennett, John C., *Social Salvation*. Charles Scribner's Sons, New York, 1935.

Brown, Charles R., *The Honor of the Church*. The Pilgrim Press, Boston, 1922.

Brown, William Adams, *The Church in America:* A Study of the Present Condition and Future Prospects of American Protestantism. The Macmillan Company, New York, 1922.

Calkins, Raymond, *The Christian Church in the Modern World*. The Macmillan Company, New York, 1924.

Cavert, S. M., *The Church and Industrial Reconstruction*. The Association Press, New York, 1920.

Coe, George A., *What Is Christian Education?* Charles Scribner's Sons, New York, 1929.

Coe, George A., *The Motives of Men*. Chap. VIII, "The Dilemma of Christianity." Charles Scribner's Sons, 1928.

Committee on the War and the Religious Outlook, *Religion Among American Men*. The Association Press, New York, 1920.

Committee on the War and the Religious Outlook, *The Teaching Work of the Church.* The Association Press, New York, 1923. Part I, "Why the Church Must Be a Teacher."

Douglass, H. Paul, and Brunner, Edmund S., *The Protestant Church as a Social Institution.* Harper & Brothers, New York, 1935.

Dole, Charles, *Religion for the New Day.* B. W. Huebsch, Inc., New York, 1925.

Ellwood, Charles A., *Christianity and Social Science.* The Macmillan Company, New York, 1924.

Ellwood, Charles A., *Man's Social Destiny.* The Cokesbury Press, Nashville, 1929.

Faunce, W. H. P., *The Educational Ideal in the Ministry.* The Macmillan Company, New York, 1908.

Fitch, Albert Parker, *Preaching and Paganism.* Yale University Press, New Haven, 1920.

Glover, T. R., *Jesus in the Experience of Men.* The Association Press, New York, 1921. Chap. IX, "The Church Compromising." Chap. XII, "The Church Triumphant."

Harkness, Georgia, *The Resources of Religion.* Henry Holt & Company, Inc., New York, 1936. Chap. IV, "The Impotence of the Church."

Hart, Joseph K., *Adult Education,* Thomas Y. Crowell Company, New York, 1927.

Hutchinson, Paul, *The Ordeal of Western Religion.* Houghton Mifflin Company, 1933.

Jacks, L. P., *The Lost Radiance of the Christian Religion.* The Lindsey Press, London, 1922.

Johnson, F. Ernest, *The Church and Society.* The Abingdon Press, New York, 1935.

Kilpatrick, William H., *Education for a Changing Civilization.* The Macmillan Company, New York, 1928.

Leiper, Henry S., *Christ's Way and the World's.* The Abingdon Press, New York, 1936.

Lynd, Robert S., and Helen M., *A Study in Contemporary American Culture.* Harcourt Brace & Company, Inc., 1929. Part V, "Engaging in Religious Practices."

Oldham, J. H., *The Oxford Conference, Official Report.* Willett, Clark & Company, Chicago, 1937.

O'Shea, Michael V., *Social Development and Education.* Houghton Mifflin Company, New York, 1929.

Parks, Leighton, *The Crisis of the Churches.* Charles Scribner's Sons, New York, 1922.

Peabody, Francis G., *Religious Education of an American Citizen.* The Macmillan Company, New York, 1917.

Peters, Charles C., *Foundations of Educational Sociology.* The Macmillan Company, New York, 1925. Chap. XI, "The Church as an Educational Agency."

Sheppard, H. R. L., *The Impatience of a Parson.* Richard R. Smith, New York, 1928.

Stanley, Oliver, Ed., *Essays on the Meaning and Purpose of Adult Education.* Oxford University Press, Oxford, 1923.

Swift, Arthur L., Jr., *New Frontiers of Religion.* The Macmillan Company, New York, 1938.

Tittle, E. F., *What Must the Church Do to Be Saved?* The Abingdon Press, 1921.

Visser 'T Hooft, W. A., and Ollham, J. H., *The Church and Its Function in Society.* Willett, Clark & Company, Chicago, 1937.

Williams, Charles D., *The Prophetic Ministry for Today.* The Macmillan Company, New York, 1921.

Yeaxlee, Basil A., *Spiritual Values in Adult Education.* Oxford University Press, London, 1925.

President's Research Committee on Social Trends, *Recent Social Trends in the United States,* Whittlesey House, McGraw-Hill Book Company, Inc., New York, 1934.

II. OUR PROTESTANT HERITAGE

Adams, John, *The Evolution of Educational Theory.* The Macmillan Company, New York, 1922.

Allen, A. V. G., *The Continuity of Religious Thought,* Houghton Mifflin Company, New York, 1884.

Bower, William Clayton, *The Curriculum of Religious Education,* Charles Scribner's Sons, New York, 1925. Chaps. I-IV.

Brown, William Adams, *The Church in America.* The Macmillan Company, New York, 1922. Chap. VIII, "The Old Religion in the New Intellectual Environment."

Coe, George Albert, *A Social Theory of Religious Education.* Charles Scribner's Sons, New York, 1917.

Cubberly, E. P., *The History of Education.* Houghton Mifflin Company, Boston, 1920.

Graves, Frank P., *A Student's History of Education.* The Macmillan Company, New York, 1915.

Hart, J. K., *Adult Education,* Thomas Y. Crowell Company, New York, 1927. Chaps. I-III.

Hart, J. K., *Democracy in Education.* D. Appleton-Century Co., New York, 1918.

Hearnshaw, F. J. C. (Ed.), *The Social and Political Ideas of Some Great Thinkers of the Renaissance and the Reformation.* G. G. Harrap and Company, London, 1925.

Köstlin, Julius, *Life of Luther.*   Charles Scribner's Sons, New York, 1904.

McGiffert, A. C., *Protestant Thought Before Kant.*   Charles Scribner's Sons, New York, 1911.

McNeill, John T., *Christian Hope for World Society.*   Willett, Clark & Company, Chicago, 1937.   Chap. VIII, "The Social Outlook of the Reformers"; Chap. X, "Christian Education and Modern Thought."

Mathews, Shailer, *Christianity and Social Progress.*   Harper & Brothers, New York, 1934.

Monroe, Paul, *Textbook in the History of Education.*   The Macmillan Company, New York, 1917.

Niebuhr, H. Richard, *The Social Sources of Denominationalism.*   Henry Holt & Company, Inc., New York, 1929.

Reisner, Edward H., *Historical Foundations of Modern Education.*   The Macmillan Company, New York, 1927.

Tawney, R. H., *Religion and the Rise of Capitalism.*   Harcourt, Brace & Company, Inc., New York, 1926.

Troeltsch, E., *Protestantism and Progress.*   Williams and Norgate, London, 1912.

Wallace, Henry A., *Statesmanship and Religion.*   Round Table Press, Inc., New York, 1934.

————, *The Social Function of the Church* (C. O. P. E. C. Commission Report, Vol. XI), Section IV, "Preaching and Teaching; Aim, Scope and Method."   Longmans, Green & Co., London, 1924.

III.   PRESENT COMPELLING OBJECTIVES

Ames, Edward S., *Religion.*   Henry Holt & Company, Inc., New York, 1939.   Chap. XIX, "Religious Education."

Bennett, John C., *Social Salvation:* A Religious Approach to the Problems of Social Change.   Charles Scribner's Sons, New York, 1935.

Bobbitt, Franklin, *How to Make a Curriculum.*   Houghton Mifflin Company, Boston, 1924.   Chap. I, "Preliminary Survey"; Chap. II, "The Objectives."

Bower, William C., *The Curriculum of Religious Education.*   Charles Scribner's Sons, New York, 1925.   Chap. IV, "The Curriculum as Enriched and Controlled Experience."

Bower, William Clayton, *Religion and the Good Life.*   The Abingdon Press, New York, 1933.   Chap. V, "The Spiritual Reconstruction of Experience."

Chase, Stuart, *A New Deal.*   The Macmillan Company, New York, 1932.

Committee on the War and the Religious Outlook, *The Church and Industrial Reconstruction.*   Association Press, New York, 1920.

Chap. VII, "What Individual Christians Can Do to Christianize the Industrial Order"; Chap. VIII, "What the Church Can Do to Christianize the Industrial Order."

Davis, Jerome, *Capitalism and Its Culture.* Farrar & Rinehart, New York, 1935.

Deissmann, Adolph, *The New Testament in the Light of Modern Research.* Richard R. Smith, New York, 1929. Chap. VI, "The Religious Value of the New Testament."

Dennis, Lawrence, *Is Capitalism Doomed?* Harper & Brothers, New York, 1932. Conclusion, pp. 307-317.

Ellwood, Charles A., *Man's Social Destiny.* The Cokesbury Press, Nashville, 1929. Chap. II, "The Resources of Mankind."

Jacks, L. P., *A Living Universe.* George H. Doran Co., New York, 1924. Chap. I, "Education and Religion in a Living Universe."

Kilpatrick, William H. (Ed.), *The Educational Frontier.* D. Appleton-Century Co., New York, 1933. Chap. II, "The Social-Economic Situation and Education."

Knudson, Albert C., *Present Tendencies in Religious Thought.* The Abingdon Press, New York, 1924. Chap. III, "Experience as a Basis of Religious Belief."

Lansbury, George, *Your Part in Poverty.* B. W. Huebsch, Inc., New York, 1918.

McAfee, Cleland B., *The Christian Conviction.* The Macmillan Company, 1926. Chap. III, "The Christian Conviction in Its Personal Origin."

Overstreet, Harry, *We Move in New Directions.* W. W. Norton & Company, Inc., New York, 1933. Chap. VII, "The Challenge to Education"; Chap. VIII, "The Fivefold Wisdom."

Polakov, Walter N., *The Power Age:* Its Quest and Its Challenge. Covici, Friede, New York, 1933. Chap. XII, "Parting of the Ways"; Chap. XIII, "In Conclusion."

Rugg, Harold, *The Great Technology.* The John Day Co., Inc., New York, 1933.

Soares, Theodore G., *Religious Education.* The University of Chicago Press, Chicago, 1928. Chap. VII, "Education as Directed Experience."

Thomas, Norman, *Human Exploitation in the United States.* Frederick A. Stokes Company, New York, 1934.

Vieth, Paul H., *Objectives in Religious Education.* Harper & Brothers, New York, 1930.

Ward, Harry F., *The New Social Order.* The Macmillan Company, New York, 1919. Part I, "Principles of the New Order."

Ward, Harry F., *Which Way Religion?* The Macmillan Company, New York, 1931. Chap. II, "The Need for an Ethical Religion."

IV.   CHARACTER AND PERSONAL RELIGIOUS LIVING

Betts, George Herbert, *Teaching Religion Today*.   The Abingdon Press, New York, 1934.   Chap. V, "The Drives Back of Conduct and Character."

Bower, William Clayton, *Religion and the Good Life*.   The Abingdon Press, New York, 1933.

Bower, William Clayton, *Character Through Creative Experience*. The University of Chicago Press, Chicago, 1930.

Burnham, William H., *The Wholesome Personality*.   D. Appleton-Century Co., New York, 1932.

Calkins, C., *Some Folks Won't Work*.   Harcourt, Brace & Company, Inc., New York, 1930.

Gilkey, James Gordon, *Managing One's Self*.   The Macmillan Company, New York, 1932.

Groves, Ernest R., *Personality and Social Adjustment*.   Longmans, Green & Co., New York, 1931.

Harkness, Georgia, *The Recovery of Ideals*.   Charles Scribner's Sons, New York, 1937.

Hartshorne, Hugh, *Character in Human Relations*.   Charles Scribner's Sons, New York, 1935.

Horney, Karen, *The Neurotic Personality of Our Time*.   W. W. Norton & Company, Inc., New York, 1937.

Ligon, Ernest M., *The Psychology of Christian Personality*.   The Macmillan Company, New York, 1935.

Overstreet, Harry, *About Ourselves*.   W. W. Norton & Company, Inc., New York, 1927.

Patrick, G. T. W., *Psychology and Social Reconstruction*.   Houghton Mifflin Company, New York, 1930.

Symonds, Percival, *Diagnosing Personality and Conduct*.   D. Appleton-Century Co., New York, 1931.

V.   CHRISTIANIZING THE WHOLE OF LIFE

Bower, William C., *Character Through Creative Experience*.   The University of Chicago Press, 1930.

Coe, George Albert, *A Social Theory of Religious Education*.   Charles Scribner's Sons, New York, 1917.

Coffin, Henry Sloane, *A More Christian Industrial Order*.   The Macmillan Company, New York, 1920.

Coffin, Henry Sloane, *Some Christian Convictions*.   Yale University Press, New Haven, 1915.   Chap. I, "Religion."

Ellwood, Charles A., *The Reconstruction of Religion*.   The Macmillan Company, New York, 1922.   Chap. VIII, "Religion and Economic Life."

Hodgkin, Henry T., *The Way of Jesus*. Doubleday, Doran & Company, Inc., New York, 1923. Chap. II, "Prevailing Standards in the Present Social Order."

Jacks, L. P., *Ethical Factors of the Present Life*. The Williams and Wilkins Co., Baltimore, 1934.

Knox, Raymond C., *Religion and the American Dream*. Columbia University Press, New York, 1934.

Lynd, Robert S., and Helen M., *Middletown:* A Study in Contemporary American Culture. Harcourt, Brace & Co., Inc., New York, 1929.

Lynd, Robert S., and Helen M., *Middletown in Transition:* A Study in Cultural Conflicts. Harcourt, Brace & Co., Inc., New York, 1937.

Macintosh, Douglas C., *Social Religion*. Charles Scribner's Sons, New York, 1939.

McNeill, John T., *Christian Hope for World Society*. Willett, Clark & Company, Chicago, 1937. Chap. XIV, "Economic Idealism in the Industrial Era."

Niebuhr, Reinhold, *Does Civilization Need Religion?* The Macmillan Company, New York, 1927.

Oldham, J. H. (Ed.), *The Oxford Conference, Official Report*. Willett, Clark & Company, Chicago, 1937.

Tawney, R. H., *The Acquisitive Society*. Harcourt, Brace & Company, Inc., New York, 1920.

Ward, Harry F., *Our Economic Morality and the Ethics of Jesus*. The Macmillan Company, New York, 1912.

Weber, Max, *The Protestant Ethic and the Spirit of Capitalism*. Charles Scribner's Sons, New York, 1927.

VI. CHRISTIAN EDUCATION THROUGH WORSHIP

Bower, William C., *Religion and the Good Life*. The Abingdon Press, New York, 1933.

Brightman, Edgar S., *Religious Values*. The Abingdon Press, New York, 1925.

Brown, William Adams, *The Life of Prayer in a World of Science*. Charles Scribner's Sons, New York, 1927.

Byington, Edwin H., *The Quest for Experience in Worship*. Doubleday, Doran & Company, Inc., New York, 1929.

Calkins, Raymond, *The Christian Church in the Modern World*. The Macmillan Company, New York, 1924. Chap. VII, "The Worship of the Church."

Dearmer, Percy, *The Art of Public Worship*. A. R. Mowbray and Company, London, 1919.

Dearmer, Percy, *The Church at Prayer*. James Clarke and Company, London, 1923.

Dickinson, Edward, *Music in the History of the Western Church.* Charles Scribner's Sons, New York, 1902.

Duchesne, L., *Christian Worship:* Its Origin and Evolution. The Macmillan Company, New York, 1919.

Fiske, G. W., *The Recovery of Worship.* The Macmillan Company, New York, 1931.

Fitch, Albert Parker, *Preaching and Paganism.* Yale University Press, New Haven, 1920. Chap. VII, "Worship as the Chief Approach to Transcendence."

Harris, Thomas L., *Christian Public Worship:* Its History, Development, and Ritual for Today. Doubleday, Doran & Company, Inc., New York, 1929.

Heiler, Friedrich, *The Spirit of Worship.* Hodder and Stoughton, London, 1926.

Herman, E., *Creative Prayer.* George H. Doran Company, New York, 1925.

Hocking, William Ernest, *The Meaning of God in Human Experience.* Yale University Press, New Haven, 1912.

Hoyt, Arthur S., *Public Worship for Non-Liturgical Churches.* George H. Doran Company, New York, 1911.

Hylan, John P., *Public Worship.* Open Court Publishing Company, Chicago, 1905.

Jones, Rufus S., *New Studies in Mystical Religion.* The Macmillan Company, New York, 1927. Chap. III, "Mysticism and Religious Education."

Lyman, Eugene William, *The Experience of God in Modern Life.* Charles Scribner's Sons, New York, 1918.

Meland, Bernard E., *Modern Man's Worship.* Harper & Brothers, New York, 1934.

Morrison, Charles Clayton, *The Social Gospel and the Christian Cultus.* Harper & Brothers, New York, 1933.

Mudge, E. Leigh, *The God-Experience.* Caxton Press, New York, 1923.

Parker, Fitzgerald Sale, *The Practice and Experience of Christian Worship.* The Cokesbury Press, Nashville, 1929.

Pratt, James Bissett, *The Religious Consciousness.* The Macmillan Company, New York, 1923.

Schlater, J. R. P., *The Public Worship of God.* George H. Doran Company, New York, 1927.

Soares, Theodore Gerald, *Religious Education.* The University of Chicago Press, Chicago, 1928. Chap. XIV, "Worship as an Organizing Experience"; Chap. XV, "Education in Worship."

Sperry, Willard L., *Reality in Worship.* The Macmillan Company, New York, 1925.

Steere, Douglas V., *Prayer and Worship.* The Association Press, New York, 1938.

Stolz, Karl R., *The Psychology of Prayer.* The Abingdon Press, New York, 1923.

Streeter, Burnett H., et al., *Concerning Prayer:* Its Nature, Its Difficulties and Its Value. The Macmillan Company, London, 1921.

Vogt, Von Ogden, *Art and Religion.* Yale University Press, New Haven, 1921.

Vogt, Von Ogden, *Modern Worship.* Yale University Press, New Haven, 1927.

Wieman, Henry N., *Methods of Private Religious Living.* The Macmillan Company, New York, 1929.

VII. RELIGIOUS EDUCATION THROUGH SOCIAL PARTICIPATION

Bower, William C. (Ed.), *The Church at Work in the Modern World.* University of Chicago Press, Chicago, 1935.

Calkins, Raymond, *The Christian Church in the Modern World.* The Macmillan Company, New York, 1924. Chap. V, "The Church and the Social Conscience."

Herriott, F. W., *Christian Youth in Action.* Friendship Press, New York, 1935.

Johnson, F. Ernest, *The Church and Society.* The Abingdon Press, New York, 1935.

Johnson, F. Ernest (Ed.), *The Social Work of the Churches.* Department of Research and Education, Federal Council of the Churches of Christ in America, New York, 1930.

Kotinsky, Ruth, *Adult Education and the Social Scene.* D. Appleton-Century Co., New York, 1933. Chap. II, "Schooling as Life, and Life as Education."

Luccock, Halford E., *Christian Faith and Economic Change.* The Abingdon Press, New York, 1936.

Mathews, Shailer, *Christianity and Social Progress.* Harper & Brothers, New York, 1934.

Myers, James, *Religion Lends a Hand.* Harper & Brothers, New York, 1929.

VIII. INTELLECTUAL ASPECTS OF A GROWING RELIGIOUS EXPERIENCE

Bode, Boyd H., *Modern Educational Theories.* The Macmillan Company, New York, 1927. Chap. XI, "The Ideal of Culture in a Democratic Society."

Bower, William Clayton, *The Curriculum of Religious Education.* Charles Scribner's Sons, New York, 1925. Chap. VIII, "The

Origin and Function of Knowledge"; Chap. XIII, "Historical Subject Matter."

Brigham, Carl C., *A Study of American Intelligence.* Princeton University Press, Princeton, 1923.

Brightman, Edgar S., *Religious Values.* The Abingdon Press, New York, 1925. Chap. X, "Philosophy and Religious Education."

Brown, William Adams, *Beliefs That Matter:* a Theology for Laymen. Charles Scribner's Sons, New York, 1936.

Calkins, Raymond, *The Christian Church in the Modern World.* The Macmillan Company, New York, 1924. Chap. VI, "The Teaching of the Church."

Coffin, Henry Sloane, *Some Christian Convictions.* Yale University Press, New Haven, 1915. Chap. II, "The Bible."

Lewis, Edwin, *A Manual of Christian Beliefs.* Charles Scribner's Sons, New York, 1927.

McAfee, Cleland Boyd, *The Christian Conviction.* The Macmillan Company, 1926. Chap. IV, "The Christian Conviction Concerning God." Chap. V, "The Christian Conviction Concerning Man." Chap. VI, "The Christian Conviction Concerning Salvation."

McDowell, William Fraser, *Making a Personal Faith.* The Abingdon Press, New York, 1924.

Rall, H. F., *A Faith for Today.* The Abingdon Press, New York, 1936.

Soares, Theodore G., *Religious Education.* The University of Chicago Press, Chicago, 1928. Chap. VIII, "Education Through Organized Knowledge."

Weigle, L. A., and others, *The Teaching Work of the Church.* The Association Press, New York, 1923.

Youtz, Herbert A., *The Affirmations of Christian Belief.* The Macmillan Company, New York, 1930.

IX.   METHOD IN ADULT LEARNING

Betts, George H., and Hawthorne, Marion, *Method in Teaching Religion.* The Abingdon Press, New York, 1925.

Burton, William H., *The Nature and Direction of Learning.* D. Appleton-Century Co., New York, 1929. Problem 4A, "Is There Any Value in the Herbartian Formal Steps?"

Chapman, J. C., and Counts, George S., *Principles of Education.* Houghton Mifflin Company, Boston, 1923. Problem 23, "What Methods Should Control the Conduct of Instruction?"

Earhart, Lida B., *Types of Teaching.* Houghton Mifflin Company, Boston, 1915.

Gray, W. S., and Munroe, Ruth, *Reading Interests and Habits of Adults.* The Macmillan Company, New York, 1929.

Horne, Herman Harold, *The Leadership of Bible Study Groups*. The Association Press, New York, 1914.

Kelly, Robert L. (Ed.), *How We Teach*. Association of American Colleges Bulletin, Vol. XIV, No. 5 (November, 1928).

Kilpatrick, William H., *Foundations of Method*. The Macmillan Company, New York, 1925.

Overstreet, Harry A., *Influencing Human Behavior*. The People's Institute Publishing Co., New York, 1925.

Stormzand, Martin J., *Progressive Methods of Teaching*. Houghton Mifflin Company, Boston, 1924. Chap. III, "The Inductive Development Technique and Its Limitations."

Strayer, George D., and Norsworthy, Naomi, *How to Teach*. The Macmillan Company, New York, 1917.

Thorndike, Edward L., *et al*, *Adult Learning*. The Macmillan Company, New York, 1930.

Waples, Douglas, and Tyler, R. W., *What People Want to Read About*. University of Chicago Press, Chicago, 1931.

————, Members of the Faculty of the Divinity School of Yale University, *Education for Christian Service*. Yale University Press, New Haven, 1922.

X.   ENRICHING EXPERIENCE THROUGH DISCUSSION

Bower, William Clayton, *Character Through Creative Experience*. The University of Chicago Press, Chicago, 1930. Chap. VII, "The Steps of Self Learning."

Bowman, Leroy C., *How to Lead Discussion*. Womans Press, New York, 1935.

Coe, George Albert, *Motives of Men*. Charles Scribner's Sons, New York, 1928. Chap. XXVIII, "Release Through Cooperative Thinking."

Dewey, John, *How We Think*. D. C. Heath and Co., New York, 1910. Chap. VI, "The Analysis of a Complete Act of Thought."

Elliott, Harrison S., *Group Discussion in Religious Education*. The Association Press, New York, 1924.

Elliott, Harrison S., *Why and How of Group Discussions*. The Association Press, New York, 1924.

Elliott, Harrison S., *The Process of Group Thinking*. The Association Press, New York, 1928.

Ewing, R. L., *Methods of Conducting Forums and Discussions*. The Association Press, New York, 1926.

Gruenberg, Sidonia M., *The Discussion Method in Parent Education*, The First Yearbook.—National Congress of Parents and Teachers, Washington, D. C., 1930.

Jones, E. Stanley, *Christ at the Round Table.* The Abingdon Press, New York, 1928.

Kilpatrick, W. H., *Foundations of Method.* The Association Press, New York, 1925.

Moulton, Phyllis M., *What Is Group Discussion?* The Inquiry, New York, (Pamphlet).

Pfleiderer, W., *World Conference on Adult Education,* Cambridge, 1929. World Association for Adult Education, London, 1930. "Methods in Extensive and Intensive Adult Education."

Sheffield, A. D., *Creative Discussion.* The Association Press, New York, 1933. Third Edition. (Pamphlet)

Sheffield, A. D. (Ed.), *Training for Group Experience.* The Inquiry, New York, 1929. III. Discussion as the Redirection of Experience.

Sheffield, A. D., *Joining in Public Discussion.* George H. Doran Company, New York, 1922.

Winchester, B. S., *The Church and Adult Education.* Richard R. Smith, New York, 1930, Chap. IV, "The Clash of Opinion."

XI. EDUCATION THROUGH CREATIVE LEISURE

Cabot, Richard C., *What Men Live By.* Houghton Mifflin Company, Boston, 1914.

Chapman, J. Crosby, and Counts, George S., *Principles of Education.* Houghton Mifflin Company, Boston, 1924. Problem 16, "How May Education Enrich the Recreational Life?"

Davis, Jerome, *Capitalism and Its Culture.* Farrar & Rinehart, New York, 1935.

Eaton, A. H., *Handicrafts of the Southern Highlands.* Russell Sage Foundation, New York, 1937. Chap. XX, "Adult Education Through Handicrafts."

Gates, H. W., *Recreation and the Church.* University of Chicago Press, Chicago, 1917.

Heaton, K. L., *Character Building Through Recreation.* University of Chicago Press, Chicago, 1929.

Jacks, L. P., *Constructive Citizenship.* Doubleday, Doran & Company, Inc., Garden City, New York, 1924. Chap. VIII, "The Greatest Skill of the Greatest Number"; Chap. IX, "The Hatefulness of Labor"; Chap. X, "Vitalized Leisure."

Jacks, L. P., *Education Through Recreation.* Harper & Brothers, New York, 1932.

Kotinsky, Ruth, *Adult Education and the Social Scene.* D. Appleton-Century Co., New York, 1933. Chap. VI, "Worthy Leisure and Labor."

Wayman, Agnes R., *Education Through Physical Education.* Lea and Febiger, Philadelphia, 1928.

XII. LIFE IS THE CURRICULUM

Bower, William C., *The Curriculum of Religious Education.* Charles Scribner's Sons, New York, 1925.

Bower, William C., *The Living Bible.* Harper and Brothers, New York, 1936.

Coe, George A., *A Social Theory of Religious Education.* Charles Scribner's Sons, New York, 1917.

Cobb, Stanwood, *The New Leaven.* The John Day Co., Inc., New York, 1928.

Kilpatrick, William H., *Education for a Changing Civilization.* The Macmillan Company, New York, 1926.

Rugg, Harold, and Shumaker, Ann, *The Child-Centered School:* An Appraisal of the New Education. World Book Company, New York, 1928. Chap. VIII, "On Planning the Curriculum in Advance."

Soares, Theodore G., *Religious Education.* The University of Chicago Press, Chicago, 1928. Chap. IX, "The Meaning of Curriculum."

Yeomans, Edward, *Shackled Youth.* Little, Brown & Company, Boston, 1921.

————, *The Twenty-sixth Yearbook* of the National Society for the Study of Education, The Foundations and Technique of Curriculum Making. Public School Publishing Company, Bloomington, Illinois, 1926. Part I, "Curriculum Making: Past and Present"; Part II, "The Foundations of Curriculum Making."

FOR GROUP DISCUSSION

I. THE CHURCH TODAY

1. From the standpoint of their effect upon the life and work (function and program) of the Church, what are the most important changes that have taken place in recent decades?

2. In what ways has the Church made most significant growth during the past half century?

3. Why is the Church to be considered one of the most basic institutions of human society?

4. What are the most significant contributions made by the Church to American life?

5. What evidences exist of a decline in recent decades in the prestige and influence of the Church in the national life?

6. Why has not the development of social conviction and concern within the churches made more rapid progress?

7. What are some of the chief causes of the growth of secularism in recent times?

8. What constitute some of the most important elements in an educational program adequate to the needs of the Church today?

II. OUR PROTESTANT HERITAGE

1. What teachings or practical achievements of Martin Luther have special significance for our times?

2. What should be considered the chief elements in the Protestant Reformation?

3. By what process did the Bible become the center of Protestant education?

4. What were some of the chief influences leading to the development of sects within Protestantism?

5. In what ways did Protestantism foster and in what ways modify the early developments within the new capitalism?

6. What seem to you to be the chief influences modifying the traditional Protestant aim of religious education?

7. In religious education, as you have come into contact with it in recent years, what has been the predominant aim?

8. In what ways are the outcomes of traditional religious education to be considered unsatisfactory?

III. PRESENT COMPELLING OBJECTIVES

1. What new factors in today's life seem of greatest significance in relation to the objectives of Christian education of adults?

2. If you were asked to eliminate the least important of the eight factors described in Chapter III, which would you discard, and why?

3. Which of the factors named might be less serious today if Christian education had been more effective in past decades?

4. In what ways does the concept of God which people hold influence the content of education?

5. How can religion be made a more potent factor in transforming both individual character and society?

6. After studying this chapter (Chapter III), what would you list as the distinguishing marks of a Christian society?

7. What is necessary in order that the church may become more effective in developing a Christian society?

IV. CHARACTER AND PERSONAL RELIGIOUS LIVING

1. What are some of the principal evidences of increase of personality disorders among adults in contemporary life?

2. What are some of the reasons why it is important to understand the physical bases of disposition, attitudes, and conduct?

3. Why are the emotions a matter of concern in adult education?

4. Of the numerous factors influencing human conduct which, as a general rule, are the most dynamic?

5. What positive bases of social conduct exist in original human nature?

6. Why are habits of great importance in the determination of character and personality?

7. What are some of the most obvious difficulties in achieving unity and integration of life and character under present-day conditions?

8. What do you consider to be the chief contributions of the Christian religion to the achievement of the highest type of character and personality?

9. What are some of the ways frequently overlooked by which men and women may come into a fellowship with God, ways that are vital and transforming in their effect upon character?

V. CHRISTIANIZING THE WHOLE OF LIFE

1. What are to be considered necessary elements in an effective technique of achieving Christian personality today?

2. In a group discussion on ways of combating crime a layman made the statement: "It is folly for the business or professional man who is solicitous for maintenance of moral standards in the community to think that he can turn over to preachers and church-school teachers the teaching of morals and religion when his own business or profession or industry is so conducted as to contradict in practice the moral ideals preached and taught on Sunday." Was the speaker justified in making such a statement? Why, or why not?

3. What are the chief characteristics of a Christian society?

4. Does the teaching program of the local church (or churches) with which members of the group are associated point out specific steps to be taken in achieving a Christian society? If not, should it do so?

5. What are some of the principal ways by which the resources of the Christian religion for motivation for social change may be made available?

6. What is the explanation of the fact that persons who are Christian in certain relationships and areas of living are very unchristian in others?

7. In *Information Service,* the editor in an article entitled "Toward an Understanding of the Economic Crisis," says, "It would seem incumbent on the lay leadership of the churches, who also largely constitute the leadership of business, to study the pressing economic issues of this hour not merely as members of an economic class but as representatives of a Christian system of ethics." In the spirit of this suggestion discuss from a Christian standpoint various ways that are proposed for changing the structure of the social order.

8. How can adult religious education be made effective in bringing about basic changes in personal living and in the structure of the social order?

9. What are some of the principles of which account should be taken in any attempt to improve adult religious education?

VI.   CHRISTIAN EDUCATION THROUGH WORSHIP

1. To what extent in the public services of your church do the members of the congregation engage purposefully and earnestly in worship? To how many, in your opinion, is the experience of worship real and satisfying?

2. Is due emphasis placed upon worship as central in the public service? If not, why is this not done?

3. What is the significance of the emotional aspect of worship?

4. Why is it important to think of worship as an experience integrated with life as a whole?

5. What are the indispensable elements entering into the content of worship?

6. What do you consider to be the chief educational values of worship?

7. How may public worship be made more effective as a means of Christian education?

8. What is needed in order that the emotion and passion generated in worship may be more effectively applied to the Christianization of society?

9. What part may the adult leader and teacher have in enriching the public service of worship?

10. What methods do you consider most effective in training adults in worship?

VII.   RELIGIOUS EDUCATION THROUGH SOCIAL PARTICIPATION

1. What is the significance of the fact that the Synoptic Gospels are pre-eminently a record of activities of social significance?

2. What have been the chief characteristics of adult education under church auspices in recent decades?

3. What are some of the principal evidences of the central importance of action in human life?

4. Why has the Church not made larger provision for action in its program?

5. How may more of the members of the churches be led into activities that represent basic social reconstruction?

6. What significant possibilities of education inhere in a cooperative consumer economy?

7. By virtue of what tests does social participation become Christian experience?

8. How and where should a beginning be made by the local church in developing a program of Christian social education?

9. What should be considered a minimum program of social participation for any church?

VIII.   INTELLECTUAL ASPECTS OF A GROWING RELIGIOUS EXPERIENCE

1. In what ways does the New Testament emphasize the importance and value of knowledge?

2. What seems to you to be the function of knowledge in the Christian life?

3. What is the relation of knowledge to social progress?

4. How is religious experience served by belief?

5. What arc some of the special intellectual needs of adults growing out of present-day conditions?

6. How may resistance of adults to propaganda be built up?

7. What knowledge should be considered of most worth to the Christian?

IX.   METHOD IN ADULT LEARNING

1. Why has authoritarian teaching ("transmissive education," or "indoctrination") become an issue in education?

2. What are some of the chief limitations of formal instruction?

3. How are the Christian attitudes such as friendliness, sympathy, faith, and gratitude developed in the lives of people? What relation has instruction to this process?

4. Why do the "Uniform Lessons" retain a dominating place in adult religious education in the churches?

5. Under what circumstances can the general pattern of the Herbartian method be used to advantage in teaching adults?

6. Of a class of young adults answering a questionnaire, seventeen declared the "best" teacher they had ever had used the lecture method and eight said the "poorest" teacher used the lecture method. What is the interpretation of these answers?

7. Everything considered, do you regard instruction an effective method of enriching and deepening religious experience?

8. In what ways and to what extent does instruction aid men and women in making Christian decisions concerning moral and social issues involved in daily life in industry and business? What is the evidence?

X. ENRICHING EXPERIENCE THROUGH DISCUSSION

1. What values of discussion is it possible to realize in a group of average adults?

2. What are the indispensable characteristics if discussion is actually to be creative?

3. Why is debate of less value than creative discussion?

4. Why is discussion as commonly practiced in adult groups so often unfruitful?

5. Under what conditions is the "conference" or "seminar" procedure to be preferred to group discussion?

6. What are the most essential functions of the discussion leader?

7. What, in practice, have you found to be the most serious limitations of organized group discussion? How can these limitations be overcome?

XI. EDUCATION THROUGH CREATIVE LEISURE

1. What are the chief new factors affecting profitable use of unoccupied time?

2. What do you understand to be the proper meaning of leisure?

3. In the community which you know best what are the most significant conditions affecting recreation of adults?

4. In what ways has the attitude of the Church toward play and recreation reacted on your own thought and life?

5. Why should physical education be considered to be a significant phase of education?

6. What are the chief moral and spiritual values of recreation?

7. What forms of recreation possess these values in largest degree?

8. In what ways have the lives of men and women whom you have known been impoverished by lack of right kinds of recreation?

9. What contribution can the Church be expected to make to education through creative leisure?

XII. LIFE IS THE CURRICULUM

1. What are the prevailing conceptions of curriculum among the adult leaders and teachers whom you know?

2. Why and in what ways does it seem necessary to modify the traditional concept of curriculum?

3. What seem to you to be the values of conceiving the curriculum of Christian education as consisting of all the experiences of living?

4. Why may we not conceive of the Church's curriculum of Christian education as so constituted?

5. What are some of the necessary steps of practical procedure in formulating an adult curriculum for use in the local church?

6. When curriculum is conceived as experience under guidance for the achievement of desired ends, what are to be considered the most important functions of the adult teacher?

7. Under this concept of curriculum what seem to you to be some of the more important types of method?

8. What is the place of subject matter in the experience curriculum?

INDEX

INDEX

A

Action: central importance of, 225ff.; interest of adults in, 230; intelligence and thought as bases of, 252f.; vital thinking a phase of, 306

Activities, planned: educational criteria of, 237f.; in the economic area, 244, 363ff.

Activities, subjective: basic nature of, 248f.; totality of experience includes, 360

Activity, creative: forms of, 345ff.

Adult: when is a person an, 157; habits and attitudes for the most part permanent, 163; ability to learn, 273f.

Adult education: new interest in, 21; a long-time growth, 21; new concepts of, 22; social orientation of, 23; new sense of public responsibility for, 23; expanding scope of, 24; wide variety of informal types of, 28; agencies of, 29ff.; under federal auspices, 30; aims of, 33f.; importance of, 34ff.; importance for religion, 35f.; involves development of power of reflective thought, 146; the setting for, 306; health education a primary element in, 339; use of handcrafts in, 348

Adult education movement: beginnings of the, 25

Adult religious education: See Religious education, adult

Adults: interests of, 33

Aesthetic enjoyment, 210

Agricultural extension, 29

American culture, 225

Americanization, 23

Amusements, 334, 342

Appreciation, 206f.

Attitudes, 130, 149, 206, 221

B

Bacon, Francis, 91

Belief: 102; compensatory, 152, 200, 205; function of, 256ff.; and faith, 260

Bennett, John C., 70, 207, 269

Bible: knowledge of, 60, 269f.; in the Protestant Reformation, 79; the center of Protestant education, 80f.; historical method in study of, 99; instruction in, as an aim, 102ff., 105; an element in worship, 202, 216; central place in church schools, 223; as sole and sufficient textbook of religious education, 279; in adult curriculum, 372f.

Body and mind, unity of, 338

Booth, William, 229

Brooks, Phillips, 51, 294

Brown, William Adams, 198

Brotherhood, 177, 190, 192

Bryce, James, 302

Burbank, Luther, 297

Burton, E. D., 302

Bushnell, Horace, 93, 167

C

Calvin, John, 79, 81, 86, 100

Capitalism, 77f., 83f.

Capitalistic ethic, 83f.

Change in the present age: nature and extent of, 1

Character: aggregate of habit systems, 158f.; contribution of religion to, 163ff.

Character, Christian, 104, 129, 148, 152, 154, 163

Character education, 128, 253f.

Chautauqua Literary and Scientific Circle, 21

Childhood education: conserving the values of, 35; importance of beginning with the child, 163

Christ: conception of, 59; as King, 100; vital union with, 87; sharing the spirit of, 235f.

Christian education: See Education, Christian

Christian experience, 41, 71, 76, 86f., 102f., 126f., 165, 197ff., 235, 247

Church: perspective on nature and function needed, 39; membership, attendance and growth, 40; distinction between the Church and the churches, 41; a basic institution of human society, 42, 140; social contribution of, 42; a conserving force, 45; its contribution to American life, 46; subject to institutional limitations, 47; distinction between the Church and the sect, 48; a

421